MW01289812

THE BETROTHED BRIDE OF MESSIAH:

Making

Herself

Ready

For

The

Bridegroom

Rick Deadmond

THE BETROTHED BRIDE OF MESSIAH:
Making Herself Ready For The Bridegroom
by Rick Deadmond

Printed in the United States of America

ISBN 978-1-60266-151-6

www.xulonpress.com

TABLE OF CONTENTS

THE BETROTHED BRIDE OF MESSIAH:
Making Herself Ready For The Bridegroom

Introduction To This Book:

In the pages that follow, the author will take the reader on a spiritual journey through the Scripture to show that God has a Divine Plan for the reconciliation of His creation. From the beginning God planned an Eternal Marriage with redeemed man. The spiritual concept of this Divine Marriage follows the natural in that planning and preparing for the wedding demands rehearsing.

God gave His Bride-to-be seven major festival appointments designed as rehearsals for the wedding. These are Holy Rehearsals that God has given for man to learn and experience His Plan in their lives. In the New Testament book of Revelation we read:

Revelation 19:7 *Let us be glad and rejoice, and give honour to him: for the marriage of the Lamb is come, and **his wife hath made herself ready**.* (KJV)

How is the bride of God to make herself ready for the Eternal Marriage? The wedding certainly will not surprise her. The bride has to be properly rehearsed and prepared for the marriage. This can only be accomplished through active participation and knowledge of God's Plan embedded in His Holy Rehearsal Festivals.

This book is written on a very deep level. New believers in Yeshua [The Hebrew name for Jesus], who have either a traditional Christian background or no Christian background at all, will find it very difficult to understand at first. New believers first need to learn the basics of the Torah and the history of Israel before moving onto a deeper level.

The material covered in these pages is based upon the Scripture coupled with ancient rabbinic commentaries and interpretation. The Christian 'church' has tried to sever itself from Judaism over the past two millennia, but the fact remains that 'she' was 'birthed' out of Judaism in the first century. The information provided in this book will correct errant teaching and help bridge the gap for Christians to cross back over time and regain possession of their Hebraic roots.

Those believing Gentiles, who have been 'digging' into their spiritual Hebraic roots, will be greatly benefited by this work. These people already understand their connection to Israel and the festivals, but might want to go much deeper in their faith. The magnitude of the information in this work will no doubt elevate their understanding of who they are and where they are going in their walk with God.

Even Messianic Jews, who believe that Yeshua is the Messiah, and who have been raised in the festivals, will be greatly encouraged by this writing. This book uses ancient liturgy from the Jewish festival prayer books in conjunction with the Scripture to teach its theme about the eschatological wedding. They will celebrate the festivals on an even deeper level after reading this book.

Jews who believe in the God of Abraham, Isaac, and Jacob, but do not believe that Yeshua is the Messiah, also might be interested in the concepts put forward in this work. The author is not trying to debate whether Yeshua is the Messiah, but bringing forward some of the ancient teachings and concepts of Judaism that may have been lost to the updated Judaism that Jews practice today. Using ancient texts, interpretations, and commentaries, along with their prayers to show the theme of the eschatological marriage may draw some Jews closer to their God. We should not lose sight of the fact that righteous Gentiles who believe that Yeshua is the Messiah also believe in the same God as the Jews. Although most orthodox Jews would disagree about this characterization of Yeshua, they too believe that the Scripture promises that God will send them 'The Messiah'.

No matter the person, this book is a challenge for God's people, Jew or Gentile, to get ready for His coming in whatever manner they perceive His arrival. The author upholds that believers in God are responsible for preparing themselves annually through the Divine Appointments of the Festivals. In the New Testament, Passover through Pentecost, was a very important time in Yeshua and His disciple's lives. According to the New Testament, the events of Yeshua's life centered on the Spring Festivals. If these Spring Festivals were so important then, how much more important will the Autumn Festivals of the Festival of Trumpets through Tabernacles be when the Messiah comes at the end of the age?

This book is well footnoted for the reader to research the material on his or her own. The author encourages the reader to challenge the thoughts and concepts laid out in this work and not to accept anything as truth until they are convinced of it by their own study. The author's prayer is that this writing may ignite the spark of God in others to even burn further up the path in comprehending God's festivals in relation to the Great Wedding.

Rick Deadmond

1

CROSSING OVER

There are Biblical terms used today which describe the ethnicity of the people in the Book we refer to as our Holy Bible, such as Hebrews, Israelites, and Jews. For most, all these terms would be considered as synonyms for the same group of people. But the fact remains, for example, that our forefather, Abraham, was neither Jew, nor an Israelite, but a Hebrew.

There are many throughout the world today that associate Israel with Judaism. Judaism is not so much a nationality but a religious expression. The term Jew today, however, represents all people, including biological Jews or other various nationalities, who practice the religion of Judaism. Nationality is determined by birth and does not change when one converts to a certain religion. Therefore, the terms Israel and Judaism are not synonymous.

How can Ethiopian Jews, Russian Jews, Spanish Jews, Hungarian Jews, American Jews, or any other Jew be a single nation? One is a Jew because they belong to the religion of Judaism. Here again, we see that Judaism and the nation of Israel are not identical. An Israelite is a descendant of the ancient nation of Israel. But not all who practice Judaism are biologically descended from national Israel.

The term 'Israel' is neither synonymous with 'Jew' as many believe. The term 'Jew' didn't exist among the ancient Israelites of the First Temple Period. Israelites are descendants of Jacob, whose name was changed to Israel by God [Genesis 32:28; 35:10]. Therefore, descendants of Jacob are not called Jews, but Israelites. The ten northern tribes of Israel that were taken into captivity by Assyria never came back to the Promised Land. However, a portion of the tribe of Judah that was taken into captivity by Babylon did come back to the Land. It was during their captivity and return that the term 'Jew' came into existence as a derivative for the tribe of Judah. However, Jews from the tribe of Judah are also Israelites.

What is a Hebrew?

Now that we have briefly attempted to define Judaism, Jew, and Israelite, let us move to the term 'Hebrew'. Abram, whose name God later changed to Abraham [Genesis 17:5], was the first to be called by the term 'Hebrew' in the Bible. Abram was the grandfather of Jacob [Israel], the progenitor of all Israelites. Therefore, Abram was neither a Jew nor an Israelite.

Genesis 14:13 *And there came one that had escaped, and told Abram the Hebrew...(KJV)*

In Genesis 14:13 a fugitive who had escaped the four kings who defeated Sodom and Gomorrah made haste and told Abram that his nephew Lot had been taken into captivity. Notice the wording 'Abram, the Hebrew,' (י ב ע ה ס ר ב א) - Avram ha Ivri.

The ancestors of Abram were Shemites [Genesis 11:10-27] from Mesopotamia [Aram], which was beyond the river Euphrates to the east. The word 'Hebrew' means 'across' as in 'across the river' from the perspective of the land of Canaan. Shem's great grandson, Eber, became the progenitor of the Hebrews according to Jewish tradition. In the Jewish midrash of Genesis Rabbah 42:13, we discover three possibilities to the meaning of Ivri [Hebrew]:

1. One possibility is that the word 'Hebrew' derives from Eber, the grandson of Noah.
2. A second possibility derives from the Hebrew word 'ever,' which means 'beyond' or 'across' as 'across the Euphrates'.
3. The third revolves around a spiritual allusion to Abraham's faith in God; hence on one side all the world served pagan gods, but he was on the other side [ever].[1]

Genesis 10:21-24 *Unto Shem also, <u>the father of all the children of Eber</u> (ע ב ר), the brother of Japheth the elder, even to him were children born. The children of Shem; Elam, and Asshur, and Arphaxad, and Lud, and Aram. And the children of Aram; Uz, and Hul, and Gether, and Mash. And Arphaxad begat Salah; and Salah begat <u>Eber</u>.* (KJV)

The Stone Edition Tanach renders Genesis 10:21 : *And to Shem, also to him were born; <u>he was the ancestor of all those who lived on the other side</u>...*[2]

The name 'Eber' in Hebrew is pronounced 'ever,' and can represent the man Eber or it just means 'across' or 'beyond'. The rabbis interpreted the KJV 'the children of Eber' in Genesis 10:21 as a preposition referring to all 'those who lived on the other side' of the Euphrates, and not the personal name 'Eber'. There are no distinctive markings in the Hebrew language to identify if 'ever' should be used as a personal name or preposition. Therefore, the rabbis deduced the interpretation from the context. Shem was the ancestor of those who dwelled across the river. The genealogy of Eber is in verse 24 and it really doesn't make much sense to translate the children of 'ever' in verse 21 as referring to the man 'Eber'.[3]

Joshua 24:2-3 *And Joshua said unto all the people, Thus saith the LORD God of Israel, Your fathers dwelt on<u> the other side of the flood [river]</u> (ב ע ב ר ה נ ה ר) in old time, even Terah, the father of Abraham, and the father of Nachor: and they served other gods. And I took your father Abraham from <u>the other side of the flood [river]</u> (ב ע ב ר ה נ ה ר), and led him throughout all the land of Canaan, and multiplied his seed, and gave him Isaac.* (KJV)

The word for 'flood' in Joshua 24 is referring to the Euphrates River. The Hebrew word 'ever' is translated as 'the other side'. Joshua was reminding the Israelites of God's kindness in redeeming their ancestors despite their involvement with paganism. Abram's ancestors dwelt on the other side [east] of the Euphrates, and God chose Abram from the other side of the Euphrates.[4]

Genesis 39:14 *That she called unto the men of her house, and spake unto them, saying, See, he hath brought in an Hebrew [referring to Joseph] unto us to mock us; he came in unto me to lie with me, and I cried with a loud voice:* (KJV)

Exodus 10:3 *And Moses and Aaron came in unto Pharaoh, and said unto him, Thus saith the LORD God of the Hebrews, How long wilt thou refuse to humble thyself before me? let my people go, that they may serve me.* (KJV)

To be a physical Ivri [Hebrew], according to the ancient Jewish sages, one had to be both from across the Euphrates and a descendant of Eber such as Abram. Abram's brother Nachor, although descended from Eber, was never called a Hebrew. Nachor remained with his father Terah never crossing over the Euphrates as did Abram. Although Ishmael and Abraham's second wife Keturah's children are his seed, the Bible never mentions them as Hebrews. Only the offspring of Abraham through Isaac and Jacob are considered Hebrews. For example, Jacob's son Joseph was called a Hebrew in Genesis 39:14.[5] In the book of Exodus when the Israelites were under Egyptian bondage, they were known as Hebrews.

Genesis 11:29 *And Abram and Nahor took them wives: the name of Abram's wife was Sarai; and the name of Nahor's wife, Milcah, the daughter of Haran, the father of Milcah, and the father of Iscah.* (KJV)

Genesis 24:4, 15, 29 *[Abraham said] But thou shalt go unto my country, and to my kindred, and take a wife unto my son Isaac... And it came to pass, before he had done speaking, that, behold, Rebekah came out, who was born to Bethuel, son of Milcah, the wife of Nahor, Abraham's brother, with her pitcher upon her shoulder... And Rebekah had a brother, and his name was Laban: and Laban ran out unto the man, unto the well.* (KJV)

Genesis 25:20 *And Isaac was forty years old when he took Rebekah to wife, the daughter of Bethuel the Syrian [Aramean] of Padan-aram, the sister to Laban the Syrian [Aramean].* (KJV)

Genesis 28:5 *And Isaac sent away Jacob: and he went to Padan-aram unto Laban, son of Bethuel the Syrian, the brother of Rebekah, Jacob's and Esau's mother.* (KJV)

According to Jewish tradition Abram and his brother Nahor married the sisters Sarai and Milcah respectively. The Scripture tells us that Abraham's brother, Nahor, and his wife Milcah had a son named Bethuel in Haran on the east side of the Euphrates River. Bethuel bore Rebekah, who became Abraham's son Isaac's wife. Rebekah's brother was named Laban, who bore Rachel and Leah, who eventually were married to Isaac's son Jacob [Israel]. The KJV calls Bethuel and Laban 'Syrians,' but it should be translated as Aramean [Strongs #761]. When Rebekah, Rachel, and Leah crossed over the Euphrates and came to Canaan, they according to definition were 'Hebrew'.

The same rabbis, well before the First Century, also mentioned that Abraham was called Ivrit [Hebrew] because he spoke the original language of those who lived across the Euphrates, specifically that of Shem and Eber. The Hebrews were loyal to the language of Eber which was Hebrew. Eber's other descendants spoke Aramaic, which is very similar to Hebrew, and therefore were called Aramean.[6]

DATES SINCE THE CREATION OF ADAM

NAME	BORN	DIED	AGE	SCRIPTURE
Adam	0	930	930	Genesis 5:3-5
Seth	130	1042	912	Genesis 5:6-8
Enos	235	1140	905	Genesis 5:9-11
Cainan	325	1235	910	Genesis 5:12-14
Mahalaleel	395	1290	895	Genesis 5:15-17
Jared	460	1422	962	Genesis 5:18-20
Enoch	622	987	365	Genesis 5:21-24
Methusaleh	687	1656 **FLOOD**	969	Genesis 5:25-27
Lamech	874	1651	777	Genesis 5:28-31
Noah	1056	2006	950	Genesis 5:28-29
Shem	1558	**2158**	600	Genesis 5:32; 11:10-11
Arphaxad	1658	2096	438	Genesis 11:12-13
Salah	1693	2126	433	Genesis 11:14-15
Eber	1723	2187	464	Genesis 11:16-17
Peleg	1757	**1996 BABEL**	239	Genesis 11:18-19
	DISPERSION			
Reu	1787	2026	239	Genesis 11:20-21
Serug	1819	2049	230	Genesis 11:22-23
Nahor	1849	1997	148	Genesis 11:24-25
Terah	1878	2083	205	Genesis 11:26-32
Abra[ha]m	1948	2123	175	Genesis 25:7
Isaac	2048	2228	180	Genesis 21:5 & 35:28
Jacob [Israel]	2108	2255	147	Genesis 25:26 & 47:28-31

Galatians 3:7 *Know ye therefore that they which are of faith, the same are the children of Abraham.* (KJV)

The rabbis also interpreted the word 'Hebrew' in a spiritual form: A Hebrew was one who had crossed over from serving the pagan gods to the worship of the One True God. Therefore it is quite possible when the New Testament calls Gentile believers in Yeshua, the children of Abraham through faith, that these believers are part of the all-inclusive understanding of being Hebrew. Therefore, Gentile believers, then, are not Israelites nor Jews, but could be represented as 'spiritual' Hebrews, who have crossed over from paganism to the worship of the one true God of Abraham, Isaac, and Jacob.

The preceding chart is 100% based upon Scripture and agrees totally with the chronology of the ancient Sages.[7] With the help of this chart, one other possible understanding of the term 'Hebrew' may be found. Abraham being called a Hebrew, which means 'from the other side,' might mean 'prior to the dispersion and confusion at the Tower of Babel.'

Where did Abraham learn the Hebrew language? What language did Noah and his sons speak before the Flood? Jewish tradition understands that before the Flood, Hebrew was the only spoken language. Even after the Flood until the Tower of Babel incident, Hebrew was still the only spoken language in the world. All other languages came as a result of God's judgment upon man at the Tower of Babel.

From the chart we learn that the Flood occurred 1656 years from Adam's creation by two witnesses. First, we are told in the Torah that Noah lived for 950 years; 350 years were lived after the Flood. The Bible confirms that he was 600 when the Flood came. By calculating his birth from the Scripture, Noah's 600th year was 1656 years after Adam was created.

Secondly, some say that loosely translated 'Methuselah' means, 'when he dies, [it] will come,' or the Flood will occur when he dies. Methuselah lived to be 969 years old and his death occurred in the year 1656 from Adam's creation [see chart].

Genesis 10:25 *And unto Eber were born two sons: the name of one was Peleg; for in his days was the earth divided; and his brother's name was Joktan.* (KJV)

Genesis 11:16 *And Eber lived four and thirty years, and begat Peleg:* (KJV)

The incident at the Tower of Babel [Genesis 11:1-9] is sandwiched between Shem's descendants ending Genesis 10 and Shem's descendants again afterward in Geneses 11. Shem's great-grandson, Eber, bore Peleg when he was thirty-four. The earth was 'divided' in Peleg's days. The Rabbi's interpret 'in his days' as his fullness of days or when he died.[8] There is absolute unity in Hebraic thought that the dispersion of the nations occurred in the year of Peleg's death, which we can see from the chart, was 1996 years after Adam's creation, or 340 years after the Flood occurred 1656 years from Adam's creation.

This opens up the door of ancient Hebraic thought to us today. Abraham was born when his father Terah was 70 [Genesis 11:26]. We are not told anything in the Torah about Abraham's first 75 years; only that he left Haran at the age of 75 for the land of Canaan. Two Christian assumptions are proven false based upon the Genesis account. First of all, Abraham did not receive his call to enter Canaan from Ur of the Chaldees. Very clearly in Genesis 12, Abraham was in Haran, which was still on the east side [other side of the river Euphrates], when God called him. When he crossed over into Canaan, Abraham was now considered a Hebrew [one who crossed over] to the inhabitants there.

Another error in Christian chronolgy is assuming that Abraham left Haran in Genesis 12 only after his father, Terah, had died [based on the end of Genesis 11]. However, Terah lived to be 205, and if Abraham was 75 when he left Haran, Terah would still live another 60 years. So what is the truth?

The commandment to Abraham was to leave his father's house. When they left Ur, Terah gathered the family together and migrated toward Haran [Genesis 11]. According to Joshua 24:2, mentioned earlier in this chapter, Abraham's father Terah and brother Nahor worshiped other gods. Abraham was called to leave Terah's house from Haran when he was 75, not because he had died, but to remove himself from the pagan worship, which he did not partake.

If the Dispersion at the Tower of Babel occurred in the year that Peleg died [1996], 340 years after the Flood, Abraham was 48 years old at the time. Also, Noah was still alive with his son Shem and his great-great grandson Eber, the father of the Hebrews. Now we can begin to understand the unaccountable 48 years of Abraham's life in Ur of the Chaldees. Jewish tradition has always held strongly that Abraham knew Noah, Shem and Eber very well.[9] As matter of fact, according to the chart, Noah died 10 years after the Dispersion from Babel, when Abraham was 58. Shem and Eber both outlived Abraham [according to the chart]. Shem and Eber were even alive when Isaac and Jacob lived. Shem died when Jacob was 50 and Eber died when Jacob was 79.

Here's something to think about! According to Biblical references from the chart, Abraham could have had direct contact with Noah, Shem, and Eber, who lived on both sides of the Flood. According to our time-line chart it is very possible that Adam had known Lamech for 56 years prior to the flood, and it would seem that Lamech had known Shem, his grandson, for 95 years. As a result of this historical data it would seem that Noah and Shem became the connection to the 'other side' before the Flood. In addition, there exists a good possibility that Abraham was given details about the pre-Flood days, about the Ark that floated upon the waters, Creation, etc.

This is exactly what ancient Jewish tradition teaches. Abraham spent 39 years in the house of Noah. Shem and Eber taught Abraham the ways of God. After Abraham had entered the land of Canaan, Shem and Eber had 'crossed over' and dwelled outside the ancient boundaries of Jerusalem. After Isaac was substituted with a ram burnt offering on Mount Moriah and his mother Sarah had died, Abraham sent him to sit under the teaching of Shem and Eber.[10]

According to the chart, in Jacob's 18th year, Salah, the father of Eber and grandson of Shem, died. At that time Isaac sent his younger son Jacob to the house of Shem and Eber, and he learned the instructions of the Lord, and Jacob remained in the house of Shem and Eber for thirty-two years.[11] But Esau his brother did not go, for he was not willing to go, and he remained in his father's house. When Isaac was 110 and Jacob 50, Shem died at the age of 600. Jacob returned to his father Isaac in Hebron after Shem had died.

Hebraic Roots and the Hebraic Language

Because Abram was already 48 years old at the time of the Tower of Babel and since according to the rabbis he did not participate in the sin of Babel, it is reasonable to conclude that Abraham's language was not confused. We find this conclusion by several rabbis as they described the Holy Tongue of Hebrew being passed from Noah, Shem, Eber, and eventually Abram.[12]

Therefore, the language before the Flood had now been passed to Abraham and his family on an exclusive basis. This explains how Hebrew could, seemingly, originate with Abraham. Hebrew, by definition, means 'beyond the river,' referring to Abraham who was beyond the Euphrates River. The point here is this: Adam, Lamech, Shem, and Abraham all spoke the same original language. Abraham had good opportunity to acquire much knowledge of Adam's time to Noah's time.

For several hundred years after the Flood mankind all spoke Hebrew until the Tower of Babel. God's covenant, of which we are partakers, was with Abraham. From this perspective, Abraham was called a Hebrew meaning 'from the other side' – prior to the dispersion and confusion, which connects to the time before the Flood. God had commanded the descendants of Noah to replenish the earth after the Flood. Instead, the 70 patriarchs that descended from Noah's three children after the Flood, stayed in the plain of Shinar and built a great city with a tower to make a name for themselves. God came, at Shavuot-Pentecost [according to Jewish tradition], and gave each of the 70 clans a different language, thus causing the dispersion that He formerly commanded. Since the people's attempted communications seemed as babbling or confusion, the place was called Babel. [We will discuss much more about these 70 nations in subsequent chapters].

Hebrew 11:8-10 *By faith Abraham, when he was called to go out into a place which he should after receive for an inheritance, obeyed; and he went out, not knowing whither he went. By faith he sojourned in the land of promise, as in a strange country, dwelling in tabernacles with Isaac and Jacob, the heirs with him of the same promise: For he looked for a city which hath foundations, whose builder and maker is God.* (KJV)

Hebrews 11:13 *These all died in faith, not having received the promises, but having seen them afar off, and were persuaded of them,* *and embraced them, and confessed that they were strangers and pilgrims on the earth.* (KJV)

The writer of Hebrews speaking of the pre-Flood patriarchs, Noah, Abraham and post-Flood patriarchs, calls them sojourners, pilgrims, and strangers on the earth. We like Abraham have received the Word of God's Promise for our physical and spiritual inheritance, but have not totally received them yet. The city we are all looking for is New Jerusalem. Until then we are ambassadors of the Most High God in a world that treats us like we don't belong. Could it be that 'faith' in God that Abraham accompanied with his sojourning in an otherwise occupied land be the definition of being Hebrew? How much more, on a spiritual level, are believers Hebrews, who are sojourning in occupied land!

In conclusion, if we understand that the word 'Hebrew' has a spiritual meaning of coming to know and worship God, then we can see how Noah, Shem, Eber, and Abraham played a role in bringing this term to our understanding.

BIBLIOGRAPHY

1. The JPS Torah Commentary - Genesis. Nahum M. Sarna. The Jewish Publication Society, Philadelphia, New York, Jerusalem, 1989. Page 107.

2. The Stone Edition Tanach. Edited by Rabbi Nosson Scherman. Mesorah Publications, Ltd., Brooklyn, New York, 1996. Page 21.

3. The Artscroll Tanach Series - Bereishis - Volume 1. Rabbi Meir Zlotowitz. Mesorah Publications, Ltd., Brooklyn, New York, 1986. Page 326.

4. Artscroll Tanach Series - Yeshoshua. Rabi Reuven Drucker. Mesorah Publications, Ltd. Brooklyn, New York,1982. Page 450.

5. The Artscroll Tanach Series - Bereishis - Volume 2. Rabbi Meir Zlotowitz. Mesorah Publications, Ltd., Brooklyn, New York, 1986. Page 1715.

6. The Artscroll Tanach Series - Bereishis - Volume 1. Rabbi Meir Zlotowitz. Mesorah Publications, Ltd., Brooklyn, New York, 1986. Page 485.

7. The Stone Edition Tanach. Edited by Rabbi Nosson Scherman. Mesorah Publications, Ltd., Brooklyn, New York, 1996. Page 2024.

8. The Artscroll Tanach Series - Bereishis - Volume 1. Rabbi Meir Zlotowitz. Mesorah Publications, Ltd., Brooklyn, New York, 1986. Page 329.

9. Book of Jasher. J. H. Parry & Company, Salt Lake City. 1887.

10. Ibid.

11. Ibid.

12. The Artscroll Tanach Series - Bereishis - Volume 1. Rabbi Meir Zlotowitz. Mesorah Publications, Ltd., Brooklyn, New York, 1986. Page 341.

2

INTRODUCTION TO GOD'S FESTIVALS

From the book of Genesis we learn that God created the sun and moon on the Fourth Day of Creation. From that moment the earth exhibited a physical day and night, as we still know today. The Light created on the First Day of Creation was obviously a different light than the sun. It was the Primeval Light or Spiritual Light [We will elaborate more upon Primeval Light in Chapter 11]. The Darkness it was separated from was Spiritual Darkness. This Primeval Light and Spiritual Darkness were called Day and Night respectively. However time was determined on the first Three Days of Creation [if time had already begun], it was certainly different from the time associated after the sun and moon were created on the Fourth Day. The Fourth Day marks the beginning semblance of a calendar.

Genesis 1:14-19 *And God said, Let there be lights in the firmament of the heaven to divide the day from the night; and let them be for <u>signs [OWOT]</u>, and for <u>seasons [MOEDIM]</u>, and for <u>days</u>, and <u>years</u>: And let them be for lights in the firmament of the heaven to give light upon the earth: and it was so. And God made two great lights; <u>the greater light [gadol]</u> to rule the day, and <u>the lesser [katan] light</u> to rule the night: he made the stars also. And God set them in the firmament of the heaven to give light upon the earth, And to rule over the day and over the night, and to divide the light from the darkness: and God saw that it was good. And the evening and the morning were the fourth day.* (KJV)

On the Fourth Day of Creation when God said, 'Let there be lights in the firmament of the heaven to divide the day from the night,' the lights specifically refer to the Sun and Moon. The Sun was the greater [gadol] Light, whereas the Moon was the lesser [katan] Light. We can clearly understand how the Sun and Moon were for 'Days and Years'. The Gadol [sun] determines the 'Days' and the 'Years' while the Katan [moon] determines the 'Months'. The Scripture states that the Sun and Moon were given for 'Signs' [OWOT] and 'Seasons' [MOEDIM]. What does this mean?

SIGNS = OWOT אות = STRONG'S #226 SIGNAL, MONUMENT, OMEN

SEASONS = MOEDIM מועדים = STRONG'S #4150
FESTIVALS, FIXED
APPOINTED
TIMES, REHEARSALS

Some of the Hebrew commentators treated the phrase 'signs and seasons [owot and moedim]' as a hendiadys, which is a single thought expressed by two words.[1] Therefore the 'Signs and Seasons' that became the result of the creation of the Sun and Moon are directly related to each other. We will see this as we continue our study on the Festivals.

Exodus 31:16-17 *Wherefore the children of Israel shall keep the* *sabbath, to observe the sabbath throughout their generations, for a* *perpetual covenant. It is a sign [OWOT] between me and the chil-* *dren of Israel for ever: for in six days the LORD made heaven and* *earth, and on the seventh day he rested, and was refreshed.* (KJV)

According to rabbinic history, some of the sages mentioned that the deeper understanding of the word 'owot' [signs] was directly related to the Sabbath.[2] In Exodus 31 the Sabbath itself is referred to as a Sign [owot]. Notice that in the seventh day Sabbath's context of being a 'Sign' [owot] in Exodus 31:16-17, the preceding six days of Creation are mentioned. We cannot have the Sabbath without the six days leading up to it.

Psalm 104:19 *He appointed the moon for seasons [moedim]: the sun knoweth his going down [sabbaths].* (KJV)

It is very clear from nature and Scripture that the Sabbath cannot occur without the cycle of the Sun and the Moedim [festivals] cannot occur without the Moon. According to Genesis 1, a Biblical day begins with the evening. Anciently in the cultures of the world, a new day began at sundown. According to Jewish practice [based upon Scripture] the Sabbath begins at sundown Friday evening, which is the beginning of the seventh day. The Moedim [festivals] have appointed dates at appointed times that are dependent on the timing of the New Moon [Rosh Chodesh]. Psalm 104:19 speaks of God appointing the Sun and Moon for these purposes.

Some rabbis link Psalm 104:19 to the Creation on the Fourth Day. It is very clear that the sages understood the term 'seasons' [moedim] in Genesis 1:14 as referring to the 'festivals'. Although the moon is obviously the smaller of the two lights, it is mentioned before the sun in Psalm 104:19 because night precedes day. The Tur [Orach Chaim 423] comments that Psalm 104 is recited as the Song of the Day for Rosh Chodesh, the festival of the New Moon, because verse 19 says that God made the moon for the festivals.[3]

Leviticus 23:2 *Speak unto the children of Israel, and say unto them, Concerning the feasts [moedim] of the LORD, which ye shall proclaim to be holy convocations [mikra kodesh - Holy rehearsals], even these are my feasts [moedim].* (KJV)

MIKRA KODESH שׁ ד ק א ר ק מ = STRONG'S #4744 HOLY
                                      CONVOCATIONS,
                                      REHEARSALS

Notice that Leviticus 23:2 says that these moedim-festivals are the 'feasts of the Lord' and 'My feasts'. The moedim-festivals do not belong to Israel or the Jewish people; they belong to God. They are God's festivals that were given to His redeemed people for a purpose. They were created and established by God on the Fourth Day of Creation before man was created. They are 'Appointed Times' for all of God's creation.

Also note in the same verse, that the term moedim-festivals are referred to in Hebrew as, 'Mikra Kodesh' [Strong's Concordance #4744], which literally means, 'Holy Rehearsals'. The Sabbath and festivals (moedim) were given as 'dress' rehearsals for a Great Heavenly Wedding that was planned by God from before the foundation of the earth. These festivals (moedim/rehearsals) were given to the bride from God so that she could make herself ready for the wedding. Christianity has tried and still is trying today to get prepared for the wedding without rehearsing. Even in natural weddings, rehearsals are considered an utmost necessity for proper preparedness.

Leviticus 23:3 *Six days shall work be done: but the seventh day is the sabbath of rest, an holy convocation [mikra kodesh - Holy rehearsal]; ye shall do no work therein: it is the sabbath of the LORD in all your dwellings.* (KJV)

Sabbath is listed as the first Mikra Kodesh [Holy Rehearsal] for the celestial wedding in Leviticus 23. While many today do not consider the Sabbath a festival because it occurs once a week, the Scripture lists it first before the seven yearly festivals are mentioned. Why? The weekly Sabbath is a macrocosm or big picture of Gods wedding rehearsal plan based upon the Greater Light [gadol], the Sun. The seven festivals that follow the Sabbath listed in Leviticus 23 are the microcosm, or a break down of God's wedding rehearsal plan, and are based upon the Lesser Light, [katan], the Moon.

There are seven High Sabbaths or Shabbaton within the seven festivals listed in Leviticus 23. They are the first [Nisan 15] and last day [Nisan 21] of the festival of Unleavened Bread, Shavuot [Sivan 6], Rosh Hashana [Tishri 1], Yom Kippur [Tishri 10], the first day [Tishri 15] of Succot [Tabernacles], and Shemini Atzeret [Tishri 22], which is the Eighth Day attached to Succot. These seven days or High Sabbaths correspond to the seventh day of the week, the Sabbath, which is directly connected to the preceding six days.[4]

Where is Rosh Chodesh, the festival of the New Moon, in these seven Festivals and Sabbath in Leviticus 23? Of course, since the seven festivals cannot be determined without the New Moon, Rosh Chodesh is embedded within them. In Solomon's Temple Rosh Chodesh [New Moon] had a higher status and sanctity then the Sabbath.[5] The New Moons were equated with the Sabbaths throughout Scripture?

Writing Before Babylonian Captivity:

2 Kings 4:23 *And he said, Wherefore wilt thou go to him to day? it is neither new moon, nor sabbath. And she said, It shall be well.* (KJV)

Isaiah 1:13 *Bring no more vain oblations; incense is an abomination unto me; the new moons and sabbaths, the calling of assemblies, I cannot away with; it is iniquity, even the solemn meeting.* (KJV)

Hosea 2:11 *I will also cause all her mirth to cease, her feast days [Chag - Sacrifices], her new moons, and her sabbaths, and all her solemn feasts [Moedim].* (KJV)

Isaiah 66:23 *And it shall come to pass, that from one new moon to another, and from one sabbath to another, shall all flesh come to worship before me, saith the LORD.* (KJV)

Writing During and After Babylonian Captivity:

Nehemiah 10:33 *For the shewbread, and for the continual meat offering, and for the continual burnt offering, of the sabbaths, of the new moons, for the set feasts, and for the holy things, and for the sin.* (KJV)

1 Chronicles 23:31 *And to offer all burnt sacrifices unto the LORD in the sabbaths, in the new moons, and on the set feasts, by number, according to the order commanded unto them, continually before the LORD:* (KJV)

2 Chronicles 2:4 *Behold, I build an house to the name of the LORD my God, to dedicate it to him, and to burn before him sweet incense, and for the continual shewbread, and for the burnt offerings morning and evening, on the sabbaths, and on the new moons, and on the solemn feasts of the LORD our God. This is an ordinance for ever to Israel.* (KJV)

2 Chronicles 8:13 *Even after a certain rate every day, offering according to the commandment of Moses, on the sabbaths, and on the new moons, and on the solemn feasts, three times in the year, even in the feast of unleavened bread, and in the feast of weeks, and in the feast of tabernacles.* (KJV)

Ezekiel 46:3 *Likewise the people of the land shall worship at the door of this gate before the LORD in the sabbaths and in the new moons.* (KJV)

The reason that the early perception of Rosh Chodesh [New Moon] was the major occasion of the two was because the Sabbath appeared to be a more restrictive day. Also compounded to this was the added element of atonement in the Temple ritual of Rosh Chodesh, which was clearly absent with the Sabbath. A goat was brought as a Sin-Offering as part of the Musaf [Additional Service and Sacrifices] associated with Rosh Chodesh in Temple times.[6]

If the Sabbath is a macrocosm of God's plan, then the Rosh Chodesh (New Moon) festival is of the grandest scale in symbolism of God's great plan. As a matter of fact, as we will see later in this work, the Sabbath (Sign/Owot) and the Seasons (festivals/moedim/rehearsals) all point to this rrandest theme of God's plan represented in Rosh Chodesh (New Moon) ceremony [in relationship to the Sun].

In ancient Israel the New Moon [Rosh Chodesh] occurred at the first visible crescent. The Israelites would have been watching the 'old moon' and notice it getting smaller and smaller in the morning sky. When the 'morning moon' disappeared, or as the rabbi's understood was 'concealed,' they would have waited for its reappearance one to three days later in the night sky. After its observation by Two Witnesses [credible] and the notification of the Sanhedrin, the news was relayed throughout Israel and the Diaspora by beacons or fires on the mountaintops, starting with the Mount of Olives in Jerusalem. The shofar [ram's horn] was sounded and Rosh Chodesh began!

After the Two Witnesses verified the New Moon to the Sanhedrin, the Nasi-President of the Sanhedrin would declare Rosh Chodesh by leading in a prayer called HaKadush HaChodesh (SANCTIFICATION OF THE NEW MOON). This prayer included the reciting of Psalm 19:4-5[7] and Song of Solomon 2:8.[8]

Psalm 19:4-5 *Their line is gone out through all the earth, and their words to the end of the world. In them hath he set a tabernacle for the _sun_, Which is as a _bridegroom_ coming out of his chamber, and rejoiceth as a strong man to run a race.* (KJV)

Song of Solomon 2:8 *The voice of my beloved! behold, he cometh leaping upon the mountains, skipping upon the hills.* (KJV)

Why would the Nasi sanctify the New Moon with a prayer about the Sun in Psalm 19? In Hebraic thought the Sun is in relationship with the Moon. The Sun was viewed as a picture of the Messiah, who in turn was a picture of the celestial Bridegroom. The Moon, therefore, symbolically represented Israel or the bride. This is why the festival of Rosh Chodesh (New Moon) is the only festival (moedim) that is solely dedicated to women. The Bridegroom [Messiah] sanctifies the New Moon [bride]. The light of the moon comes from the sun.

The sages also explained to us that the sanctification of the Moon should be recited with 'joy' and 'celebration' that should parallel that of a wedding.[9] The imagery of Song of Solomon 2:8 projects the Bridegroom (sun) coming for His bride (moon) 'leaping upon the mountains, skipping upon the hills' like that of the fires set on the hills to proclaim the New Moon [Rosh Chodesh]. The festival of Rosh

Chodesh (New Moon) is symbolic of marriage. In ancient times it was the Israelite custom to have weddings on Wednesday, the fourth day of the week, the day that the sun and moon were created.[10]

In Jewish literature Rosh Chodesh has a nickname associated with it as the festival of the Born-Again. Every month the Moon is born again at Rosh Chodesh. The new thin crescent is known in Hebrew as 'molad,' a word connoting 'birth'. Rosh Chodesh alludes to Israel's redemption as described by the renewal of her marriage bond with God.

Psalm 90:4 (KJV) *For a thousand years in thy sight are but as yesterday when it is past, and as a watch in the night.*

2 Peter 3:8 *But, beloved, be not ignorant of this one thing, that one day is with the Lord as a thousand years, and a thousand years as one day.* (KJV)

Before Rabbinic Judaism was formed as a defense to the Roman destruction of the Temple and the success of the Messianic Movement, it was a generally accepted fact by the rabbi's that a thousand years of man on earth was compared to one day with the Lord. This was an allusion to the Genesis Creation story: for six days God created or labored and on the seventh day He rested. Therefore, it was taught by the rabbi's that man would toil on the earth for six days (6,000 years) and eventually find his rest on the seventh day (the last 1,000 years known by Christians as the Millennium). They taught that the seventh millennium of rest was the Sabbath. The six thousand years was known as the Olam Hazeh (This Present Age), whereas the one thousand year Sabbath was known as the Athid Lavo [The Future Age or Coming], Malchut Shamayim [Kingdom of Heaven], or the Messianic Kingdom.

In ancient rabbinic literature the seventh day Sabbath was seen as symbolic of the Lord's bride. The Jews to this very day welcome the 'Queen of the Sabbath' as they sing the Kabbalat Shabbat every Friday evening welcoming the Sabbath.[11]

The Talmud makes the same connection:

Talmud - Mas. Shabbath 119a - *R. Hanina robed himself and stood at sunset of Sabbath eve [and] exclaimed, 'Come and let us go forth to welcome the queen Sabbath.' R. Jannai donned his robes, on Sabbath eve and exclaimed, 'Come, O bride, Come, O bride!'*

Talmud - Mas. Baba Kama 32b - *'Come, let us go forth to meet the bride, the queen!' Some [explicitly] read:'. . . to meet Sabbath, the bride, the queen.'*

The Sabbath is a Holy Rehearsal that gives an overall picture of the wedding of Messiah to His bride that is to be rehearsed on a weekly basis. It is a statute forever as long as the Sun continues to shine in the 'heavens'. If the believer wants to immediately begin rehearsing for their wedding with Messiah, the weekly Sabbath is the place to start. Next in line would be the observance of the monthly New Moon (Rosh Chodesh).

The seven major festivals (moedim/rehearsals) that follow the Sabbath in Leviticus 23 supply the details of the seven thousand year plan of God and show that there are two stages of marriage between the Bridegroom (sun) and bride (moon). In the next chapter we will look at the two stages of Hebraic (Biblical) Marriage. This is the foundation to understanding the meaning of Sabbath, New Moon, and the Festivals.

BIBLIOGRAPHY

1. The JPS Torah Commentary: Genesis. The Traditional Hebrew Text with the New JPS Translation Commentary by Nahum M. Sarna. The Jewish Publication Society, 1989. Page 9.

2. Yalkut Me'am Lo'ez - The Torah Anthology: Exodus. Volume VI. Translated by Rabbi Aryeh Kaplan. Moznaim Publishing Corporation, 1990. Page 352.

3. The Artscroll Tanach Series: Tehillim [Psalms]. Volume Two. Translation and Commentary by Rabbi Avrohom Chaim

Feuer. Mesorah Publications, Ltd., 1977, 1985, 1995. Page 1261.

4. The Artscroll Tanach Series: Vayikra [Leviticus]. Volume III (b). Translation and Commentary by Rabbis Nosson Scherman and Hersh Goldwurm. Mesorah Publications, Ltd., 1990. Page 395.

5. The Biblical and Historical Background of Jewish Customs and Ceremonies. Abraham P. Bloch. KTAV Publishing House, Inc., 1980. Pages 295-96.

6. Ibid. Page 295.

7. The Artscroll Tanach Series: Tehillim [Psalms]. Volume One. Translation and Commentary by Rabbi Avrohom Chaim Feuer. Mesorah Publications, Ltd., 1977, 1985, 1995. Page 243.

8. The Complete Artscroll Siddur. Rabbi Nosson Scherman. Mesorah Publications, Ltd., 1985. Page 651.

9.   Rama, Darchei Moshe 426, gloss to Shulchan Aruch, Orach Chayim 426:2.

10. A Jewish Wedding Guide: Made in Heaven. Rabbis Aryeh Kaplan. Moznaim Publishing Corporation, 1983. Page 77.

11. The Complete Artscroll Siddur. Rabbi Nosson Scherman. Mesorah Publications, Ltd., 1985. Page 350-53.

3

IT'S ALL ABOUT HEBRAIC MARRIAGE

The Two Stages of Biblical Marriage

The first step in ancient Biblical marriage was the proposal called 'shidukhin'. The father of the bridegroom usually chose the bride. The father would send his trusted servant, known as the agent of the father or shadkhan, to search out the bride.[1] An excellent example of this can be seen in Genesis 24. In this chapter, Abraham wishes to secure a bride for his son Isaac, and sends his servant Eliezer to accomplish the task. Rebecca consented to marry Isaac even before she ever met him. The concept that many arranged marriages were forced upon the children regardless of their desires just is not true. The woman had to consent to the marriage in order for a marriage to occur.[2]

After the young man [probably with his father] had secured the endorsement of the young woman's father, a price would have to be negotiated and paid for the bride. There appears to be two aspects of the purchasing price, the mohar that was required by the Torah [Scripture], and the nadan [dowry], which the bride brought into the marriage.[3]

Exodus 22:16 *And if a man entice a maid that is not betrothed, and lie with her, he shall surely endow [mohar] her to be his wife.* (KJV)

The mohar was a sum of money that the groom was bound by the Torah to pay to the bride's father. The amount varied based upon several factors and in some cases was considered a penalty. The mohar could be paid by the groom's service to the girl's father, for example, when Jacob worked for Laban, the father of both Leah and Rachel [Genesis 29:15-30]. In addition, an appointed task could substitute for the mohar, as Saul required of David for his daughter Michel [1 Samuel 18:25-27]. It appears that the mohar is not so much a price that was to be paid for the bride, but compensation to her father for losing a member of his household. There is also evidence that at the time of the father's inheritance to be administered that the mohar reverted to the daughter that was married. The evidence also suggests that if her husband died early that her father gave the original mohar to the daughter at the time of his death.[4]

The first stage of marriage is known as betrothal. Betrothal in Hebrew is known as erusin [Exodus 22:15; Deuteronomy 20:7; 22:23] or kiddushin. Betrothal [erusin] legally binds the bride and the groom together in a marriage contract, except they do not physically live together. During the betrothal, the bride remains at her father's house. During the betrothal [erusin] ceremony at the bride's father's home, the groom signifies his desire to make her his wife through a religious act known as kiddushin [Talmud - Kiddushin 2b]. The groom makes a verbal declaration that he is betrothing her as his wife.[5]

The Hebrew term kiddushin comes from the root kodesh, meaning 'holy' or 'sanctification'. An ancient Hebraic wedding was considered a religious ceremony and a holy occasion. After the kiddushin [betrothal] was performed, the bride is like 'holy' property to the groom. This act is similar to the sanctification of all Temple property as 'holy,' meaning that its use was forbidden to common men.[6]

The word betrothal [erusin] comes from the verb 'aras,' which is closely related to 'asar,' meaning 'to bind.' The erusin therefore has the power to bind a couple to each other although they are not 'fully' married. The Hebrew word aros also means 'to speak,' which may indicate that the erusin ceremony declares the woman to be already 'spoken for.' On an individual basis erusin has power to give the groom the status of a married man and the bride the status of a married woman. Erusin does not have the power to make the two married together as the second stage of Hebraic marriage does. During the betrothal [erusin] stage the pair is forbidden to each other physically.[7]

A written document is drawn up, known as a ketubah. This betrothal contract is called, in Hebrew, a shitre erusin. The ketubah is the marriage contract that states the bride price, the promises of the groom, and the rights of the bride. The word ketubah means, 'that which is written'. The groom promised to work for her, to honor, support, and maintain her, to provide food, clothing, and necessities, and to live together with her as husband and wife. The ketubah was the unalienable right of the bride and was directly related to the mohar or dowry. The ketubah must be executed and signed prior to the wedding ceremony.

Jeremiah 31:21-22 *Set thee up waymarks, make thee high heaps: set thine heart toward the highway, even the way which thou wentest: turn again, O virgin of Israel, turn again to these thy cities. How long wilt thou go about, O thou backsliding daughter? for the LORD hath created a new thing in the earth, A woman shall compass a man.* (KJV)

Hosea 2:19-20 *And I will betroth [asas] thee unto me for ever; yea, I will betroth [aras] thee unto me in righteousness, and in judgment, and in lovingkindness, and in mercies. I will even betroth [aras] thee unto me in faithfulness: and thou shalt know the LORD.* (KJV)

It was the ancient custom for the betrothed bride to circle the groom three times based upon Jeremiah 31 and Hosea 2.[8] In addition, both the bride and groom drink a cup of wine called the cup of the covenant that sealed the betrothal. The groom sips first from this cup, and then it is given to the bride. The very act of the bride drinking the wine seals the betrothal proposal.

The rite of betrothal (erusin) is completed when the groom gives something of value to the bride and she accepts it. The gift most often given today is the ring. When the groom places the ring on the bride's finger, the rite of betrothal is completed. This completed the rite known as kiddushin, which means 'sanctification'. In ancient times other gifts were given to the bride and her father when the marriage proposal was accepted. We see this clearly when Rebecca and her family accepted the marriage proposal for Abraham's son Isaac in Genesis 24.

The betrothed bride would then enter a mikvah, which is a ritual cleansing. Mikvah is a Hebrew word that means, 'pool' or 'body of water'. Mikvah is a ceremonial act of purification by the immersion in water. It indicates a separation from a former way to a new way. In the case of marriage, it indicates leaving an old life for a new life with your spouse. Immersing in the mikvah is considered a spiritual rebirth. The mikvah symbolically has the power to change a person completely.

At this point, the bridegroom leaves for his father's house to prepare the bridal chamber called the 'Chadar' for his bride. It was understood to be the man's duty to go away to be with his father, build a house, and prepare for the eventual final wedding. Before he goes, though, he will make a statement to the bride something to this effect: 'I am going to prepare a place for you to live; then I will return again to you and bring you there in full marriage'.

The bride was consecrated and set apart for a period of time while the bridegroom was away building the house. Before the bridegroom could go and get his betrothed bride, the groom's father had to be satisfied that his son had made every preparation. Only then would he give permission to his son to go and get his bride. In other words, while the bridegroom was working on the bridal chamber, it was his father who supervised the building of the bridal chamber. At the same time the father was observing his son to make sure he was mature enough and ready for this marriage. The groom did not know when his father would declare the bridal chamber fit and send him to fetch his bride. When the time came the father would ceremonially say to his son something like: 'The time has come, go and fetch your bride'.

During the interval, the betrothed bride was to wait eagerly for the return of the bridegroom. In the mind of the bride, the bridegroom could come at any time, even in the middle of the night or at midnight. Therefore, she had to be ready at all times. Even as the days and months lingered without the groom's return, she had to maintain a faith that he would return. During her wait the bride was engaged in learning the arts of cosmetics, perfume, and jewelry, etc. so that she could maintain an appealing presence to her husband.[9]

Traditionally, in ancient Israel, after about a year had elapsed, the father of the groom would send his son to fetch his betrothed bride.[10] The groom would appoint 'Two Witnesses' or 'Friends of the Bridegroom'; one would attend to the groom whereas the other would attend to the bride. The 'Friends of the Bridegroom' were known as 'Shoshvin'.[11] When the time came the bridegroom would return for the bride at her father's house by sending one of his 'Friends of the Bridegroom' to shout, 'Behold, the bridegroom comes' to the sound of the ram's horn (shofar). The time of the return of the bridegroom was usually at midnight.

The bride was stolen away from her father's house in a willful kidnaping scenario. A wedding procession would then lead her and the wedding party to the chuppah [wedding canopy], where the second stage of marriage would take place with the groom. The second stage of marriage is called nesuin. Nesuin is derived from the verb 'nasa,' which means 'to lift' or 'to take'. 'Nasa' is used in the Scripture for 'full marriage,' indicating that a man has taken the woman to be his wife.[12]

There was a sacred procession leading to the nesuin ceremony. The bride in Temple times was escorted atop a covered litter suspended on poles and borne on the shoulders of men. In this way the bride was viewed as a queen. Brides and grooms of antiquity wore diadems and crowns.[13] The bridegroom was led to the chuppah first. When the bridegroom approaches the chuppah, the cantor chants, 'Blessed is he who comes'. 'Blessed is he who comes' is an idiomatic expression in Hebrew meaning 'welcome,' where the groom is greeted like a king under the chuppah.[14]

After the ketubah-marriage contract is renewed to account for nesuin [second stage of marriage], the couple goes to the bridal chamber [chadar] where the marriage would be consummated. The couple would stay in that wedding chamber for seven days, or a week. The word 'week' in Hebrew is shavuah. It means a 'seven'. It can mean seven days or seven years, etc.

When the bride and the groom initially went into the wedding chamber, the 'friend of the bridegroom' stood outside the door. All the assembled guests of the wedding gathered outside, waiting for the 'friend of the bridegroom' to announce the consummation of the marriage, which was relayed to him by the groom. The marriage was consummated on the first night (Genesis 29:23). The blood-stained linen from this night was preserved. It was proof of the bride's virginity (Deuteronomy 22:13-21).[15]

After the shavuah, the ancient Biblical wedding feast was held at the bride's father's house [Genesis 29:22, Judges 14:10] where there would be great celebration and rejoicing for the new couple in Israel. The wedding feast normally lasted seven days, but could be extended if abundant sources of food and wine remained.[16] After the great wedding feast, the couple would return to the groom's new house and begin their new family together.

BIBLIOGRAPHY

1. A Jewish Wedding Guide: Made in Heaven. Rabbis Aryeh Kaplan. Moznaim Publishing Corporation, New York, Jerusalem, 1983. Pages 22-23.
2. Ibid. Pages 22-23.
3. Ibid. Page 117.
4. Ancient Israel: It's Life and Institutions. Roland De Vaux. William B. Eerdmans Publishing Company, Grand Rapids, Michigan, 1997. Pages 26-27.
5. The Biblical and Historical Background of Jewish Customs and Ceremonies. Abraham P. Bloch. KTAV Publishing House, Inc., New York, 1980. Pages 25-26.
6. Ibid. Page 26.
7. A Jewish Wedding Guide: Made in Heaven. Rabbis Aryeh Kaplan. Moznaim Publishing Corporation, New York, Jerusalem, 1983. Pages 134-35.

8.   The Biblical and Historical Background of Jewish Customs and Ceremonies. Abraham P. Bloch. KTAV Publishing House, Inc., New York, 1980. Page 33.
9.   Ibid. Page 26.
10. Ibid. Page 27.
11.   Jewish Wedding Guide: Made in Heaven. Rabbis Aryeh Kaplan. Moznaim Publishing Corporation, New York, Jerusalem, 1983. Page 63.
12. Ibid. Page 136.
13. The Biblical and Historical Background of Jewish Customs and Ceremonies. Abraham P. Bloch. KTAV Publishing House, Inc., New York, 1980. Pages 30.
14. Jewish Wedding Guide: Made in Heaven. Rabbis Aryeh Kaplan. Moznaim Publishing Corporation, New York, Jerusalem, 1983. Page 156.
15. Ancient Israel: It's Life and Institutions. Roland De Vaux. William B. Eerdmans Publishing Company, Grand Rapids, Michigan, 1997. Page 34.
16. Ibid. Page 34.

4

THE SPRING AND FALL FESTIVALS

In chapter 2 we discussed the relationship among the seven festivals [moedim] of God given in Leviticus 23 with the seventh-day Sabbath. These seven festivals can be further subdivided into the four spring festivals and the three autumn festivals. What does this mean?

In chapter 10 of this book we will address the understanding of two Messiahs' in ancient Judaism even dating back before the time of Yeshua. In this chapter we will introduce them to the reader. The spring festivals were fulfilled by Yeshua as the Messiah ben Joseph (the Suffering Messiah)[1] in that He was slain on Pesach [Passover], buried on Hag HaMatzah [Unleavened Bread], and raised in resurrection on Firstfruits of the Barley Harvest [Hag haBikkurim]. Fifty days later, after going to the Father in 'Heaven,' He sent the Ruwach HaKodesh (Holy Spirit) upon the believers in Messiah on Shavuot [Pentecost] to write the Torah upon their hearts and minds.

Ancient Judaism's second Messiah was known as Messiah ben David (Conquering Kingly Messiah).[2] His coming is laid out prophetically in the three autumn festivals - Rosh Hashana [Feast of Trumpets], Yom Kippur [Day of Atonement], and Succot [Tabernacles]. Rosh Hashana is a festival rich in symbolism about the coronation of the Messiah as King and also the second stage of marriage [nesuin] of the Messiah to the righteous believers [Rosh Hashana is also the New Moon (Rosh Chodesh) of the seventh month called Tishri]. This occurs on the seventh-day Sabbath [1,000-year millennial reign] after the preceding six days [6,000 years] have been accomplished. Yom Kippur has always been known in Jewish thought as the Day when the Messiah will come to Israel, redeem her, and set up the Messianic Kingdom. Succot [Tabernacles] has as one of its themes 'clouds of witnesses' as detailed in the New Testament book of Hebrews [12:1]. This speaks figuratively about the thousand-year reign of Messiah on the earth ruling as King out of Jerusalem when saints in resurrected bodies will dwell among those with flesh and blood bodies. The seven days of Succot are also symbolic of the wedding feast. There is an eighth day called Shemini Atzeret associated with the festival of Succot on Tishri 22, which hints to a return to the World to Come [Olam Haba/eternity] after the Millennium. This is when New Jerusalem, which is prepared as a bride, comes down from heaven upon the earthly Jerusalem [Revelation 21:2]. There is no sin in New Jerusalem and the Messiah is the temple and light of all the resurrected believers from all ages [Revelation 21:8; 22-23].

Clearly the spiring festivals are representative of first Messiah's coming as Mashiach ben Yosef, the Suffering Servant Messiah. The autumn festivals speak about the coming of Mashiach ben David, the Conquering King Messiah. We see that Rosh Hashana has marriage symbolism attached to it because it is also the Festival of Rosh Chodesh, the New Moon of the month of Tishri. It is the only festival on Rosh Chodesh, therefore, very clearly is symbolic of the second stage of marriage, nesuin. As a matter of fact, all three of the autumn festivals center upon the eschatological nesuin marriage between God and His people. The spring festivals teach about the betrothal [erusin] of God's people to Him. True to form, the festival of Shavuot [Pentecost] rabbinically pertains to marriage symbolism with Israel before God at Mt. Sinai.

The reader also needs to be aware of the different so-called 'seasons' that are built within the Jewish calendar. One 'season' is the first spring festival Pesach until the last spring festival Shavuot. Pesach through Shavuot was clearly known to the Jews as a specific season all linked together. The rabbis called Shavuot the 'atzeret' [conclusion] of Passover and also the eighth day of Passover [Unleavened Bread]. This was taught based upon Shavuot's connection to the Firstfruits of the Barley Harvest [during the festival of Unleavened Bread] offered for the forty-nine days preceding Shavuot. Shavuot itself was the fiftieth day since the Firstfruits of the Barley Harvest. The counting of the Omer was viewed as one long chol ha-moed [intermediate day of the festival]. This made Shavuot in a sense similar to Shemini Atzeret, which is the eighth and concluding day of Succot.[3]

Obviously a second established 'season' is from Rosh Hashana (Tishri 1) to the eighth and concluding day (Shemini Atzeret) of Succot on Tishri 22. Actually Shemini Atzeret was considered a separate Festival only attached to Festival of Succot based upon Numbers 29:35 which says, 'And on the eighth [shemini] day it shall be an assembly [atzeret] for you'.

The next day after Shemini Atzeret, Tishri 23, was known as Simhat Torah, where the new cycle in the annual Torah reading would begin. The Jewish New Year began on Tishri 1 called Rosh Hashana. However, in Jewish thought there is a phrase 'the turn of the year,' which means that the New Year wasn't viewed as beginning until the New Torah readings started on Simhat Torah (Tishri 23). From that perspective Shemini Atzeret (Tishri 22) was the conclusion of the festival of Rosh Hashanah (Tishri 1). Therefore on Rosh Hashana the New Year was 'Here Now But Not Yet' which is a very popular Jewish phrase. This can be applied to many things; for example, we have salvation now through Messiah, but our full salvation with resurrected bodies living in the Messianic Kingdom is not yet. We also have betrothal [erusin] marriage through Messiah now, but the full marriage [nesuin] is still yet to come.

Since Shavuot was considered the eighth (Atzeret) day of Pesach it was directly linked to Shemini Atzeret, the eighth day, on Tishri 22, at the conclusion of the festival of Succot. So the beginning of the wheat harvest at Shavuot (which was a continuation of harvest at the Firstfruits of the Barley Harvest during the seven days of the Festival of Unleavened Bread) wasn't over until the final harvest was over at Shemini Atzeret on Tishri 22. Similarly, the betrothal [erusin] that God offered on Shavuot wasn't over until the final marriage (wedding feast), which was associated with the festival of Succot and Shemini Atzeret.

Another well-established season was from Rosh Hashana, which actually encompassed two days, Tishri 1 and 2, until Yom Kippur on Tishri 10. Rosh Hashana is connected to Yom Kippur by what are known as the Days of Awe [Yamin Norim], which are the days in between. The seven days of Awe between the two days of Rosh Hashana and the one-day of Yom Kippur is a great picture of the seven years of the Birth Pangs of the Messiah [Tribulation]. The resurrection occurs on Rosh Hashana and the Messiah is crowned king and married to His Bride in 'Heaven'. Then the seven years of Birth Pangs occur on earth [while the bride and groom are in the wedding chamber for a shuvah] concluding with the return of Messiah with His Bride to Jerusalem on Yom Kippur when all of Israel will be delivered.

The New Moon [Rosh Chodesh] of the month Elul, the month preceding Tishri, marked the beginning of a forty-day period of Teshuvah [Return and Repentance]. Elul is always thirty days long and with the addition of the first ten days of Tishri ending on Tishri 10, Yom Kippur, the forty-day period was concluded. Rabbinically these forty days corresponded to Moses going up Mt. Sinai the second time to receive the commandments written on stones. He returned on Yom Kippur with the completed tablets. Therefore, Yom Kippur is understood to be the day when Messiah literally returns to Jerusalem to set up the Messianic Kingdom at the end of the Birth Pangs.

There are many more of these 'seasons' and many more aspects of the festivals to learn. But in this book we will only concern ourselves with what is relevant with respect to what we are studying. The major point of emphasis in this book will be the marriage symbolism as related to the festivals of God.

BIBLIOGRAPHY

1. The Messiah Texts. Raphael Patai. Wayne State University Press, Detroit. 1979. Pages 104-121.
2. Ibid. Pages 189-210.
3. The Book of Our Heritage. Eliyahu Kitov. Feldheim Publishers, New York and Jerusalem, 1997. Pages 772-73.

5

ISRAEL'S BETROTHAL TO GOD
OLD TESTAMENT - SPRING FESTIVALS

<u>Jeremiah 31:32</u> *Not according to the covenant that I made with their fathers in the day that I took them by the hand to bring them out of the land of Egypt; which my covenant they brake, although I was an husband unto them, saith the LORD:* (KJV)

<u>Jeremiah 2:2-3</u> (KJV) *Go and cry in the ears of Jerusalem, saying, Thus saith the LORD; I remember thee, the kindness of thy youth, the love of thine espousals (keluwlah), when thou wentest after me in the wilderness, in a land that was not sown. Israel was holiness unto the LORD, and the firstfruits of his increase (A term for Shavuot-Pentecost - Firstfruits of the Bikkurim): all that devour him shall offend; evil shall come upon them, saith the LORD.*

The prophet Jeremiah tells us that when Israel went after God in the Wilderness it was like they were betrothed to Him. He was Israel's husband. The Hebrew word for 'espousals' is 'keluwlah' [Strong's 3623] and means the 'condition of a bride before her [full] marriage'.[1] Israel was 'holiness unto the Lord' and 'the firstfruits of His increase' in a land that was not sown [the Wilderness]. At Mt. Sinai God called Israel to be His Holy nation [Exodus 19:6].

There are two festivals associated with 'firstfruits;' The Firstfruits of the Barley Harvest during the Festival of Unleavened Bread, and the Firstfruits of the Wheat Harvest at Shavuot [Pentecost]. Shavuot is the major of the two and is very clearly being referenced by Jeremiah. In other words, the prophet's poetic use of Israel's betrothal to God in the Wilderness is linked to the festival of Shavuot [Pentecost].

Exodus 19:17 *And Moses brought forth the people out of the camp to meet with God; and they stood at the nether part of the mount.* (KJV)

Exodus 19:10 *And the LORD said unto Moses, Go unto the people, and sanctify them to day and to morrow, and let them wash their clothes* (KJV)

The rabbis' midrashically spoke of Israel as a bride before God, her groom at Mt. Sinai. Acting as 'Friend of the Bridegroom,' Moses escorted Israel to Mt. Sinai [the Chuppah] where God as groom was already awaiting His bride. But before Moses brought 'her' before Sinai, Israel had to be immersed in a mikveh to be set aside for marriage to God. Since the metaphor of bride and groom apply to Israel and God, the Book of the Covenant [Torah] symbolically represents the ketubah, the betrothal marriage contract. The Covenant at Mt. Sinai spells out the obligations of God and Israel as a ketubah does for a husband and wife.[2]

Betrothal and Shavuot [Pentecost]

The tribe of Benjamin received betrothed wives on Shavuot according to the rabbis. Notice Shavuot's connection with 'marriage':

Judges 21:15-24 *And the people repented them for Benjamin, because that the LORD had made a breach in the tribes of Israel. Then the elders of the congregation said, How shall we do for wives for them that remain, seeing the women are destroyed out of Benjamin? And they said, There must be an inheritance for them that be escaped of Benjamin, that a tribe be not destroyed out of Israel. Howbeit we may not give them wives of our daughters: for the children of Israel have sworn, saying, Cursed be he that giveth a wife to Benjamin. Then they said, Behold, there is a feast of the LORD in Shiloh yearly in a place which is on the north side of Bethel, on the east side of* *the highway that goeth up from Bethel to Shechem, and on the south of Lebonah. Therefore they commanded the children of Benjamin, saying, Go and lie in wait in the vineyards; And see, and, behold, if the daughters of Shiloh come out to dance in dances, then come ye out of the vineyards, and catch you every man his wife of the daughters of Shiloh, and go to the land of Benjamin. And it shall be, when their fathers or their brethren come unto us to complain, that we will say unto them, Be favourable unto them for our sakes: because we reserved not to each man his wife in the war: for ye did not give unto them at this time, that ye should be guilty. And the children of Benjamin did so, and took them wives, according to their number, of them that danced, whom they caught: and they went and returned unto their inheritance, and repaired the cities, and dwelt in them. And the children of Israel departed thence at that time, every man to his tribe and to his family, and they went out from thence every man to his inheritance.* (KJV)

Jewish tradition holds that King David was born and died on Shavuot [Talmud - Shabbat 30b]. Likewise Solomon was crowned king on the same day of his father's death; Shavuot. But the Scripture says that Solomon was 'married' on the same day, Shavuot, he was crowned the new King of Israel. The wedding of King Solomon allegorically refers to Messiah and Israel:

Song of Songs 3:11 *Go forth, O ye daughters of Zion, and behold king Solomon with the crown wherewith his mother crowned him in the day of his espousals, and in the day of the gladness of his heart.* (KJV)

King Asa renewed the covenant [renewal of betrothal] on Shavuot. Notice the role of the Spirit and the unity of heart and soul. We will come back to these characteristics and Shavuot later:

2 Chronicles 15:1-12 *And the Spirit of God came upon Azariah the son of Oded: And he went out to meet Asa, and said unto him, Hear ye me, Asa, and all Judah and Benjamin; The LORD is with you, while ye be with him; and if ye seek him, he will be found of you; but* *if ye forsake him, he will forsake you. Now for a long season Israel hath been without the true God, and without a teaching priest, and without law. But when they in their trouble did turn unto the LORD God of Israel, and sought him, he was found of them. And in those times there was no peace to him that went out, nor to him that came in, but great vexations were upon all the inhabitants of the countries. And nation was destroyed of nation, and city of city: for God did vex them with all adversity. Be ye strong therefore, and let not your hands be weak: for your work shall be rewarded. And when Asa heard these words, and the prophecy of Oded the prophet, he took courage, and put away the abominable idols out of all the land of Judah and Benjamin, and out of the cities which he had taken from mount Ephraim, and renewed the altar of the LORD, that was before the porch of the LORD. And he gathered all Judah and Benjamin, and the strangers with them out of Ephraim and Manasseh, and out of Simeon: for they fell to him out of Israel in abundance, when they saw that the LORD his God was with him. So they gathered themselves together at Jerusalem in the third month [Sivan], in the fifteenth year of the reign of Asa. And they offered unto the LORD the same time, of the spoil which they had brought, seven hundred oxen and seven thousand sheep. And they entered into a covenant to seek the LORD God of their fathers* with all their heart and with all their soul; (KJV)

The First Calendar

Any seeking believer in God who endeavors to study the Tanach [Old Testament] quickly realizes they must think Hebraically to comprehend it. The full riches of the Scripture cannot be realized in any other mind-set. The western world's way of thinking must be suppressed.

For one thing the Hebrew calendar is quite different from any of the Gentile calendars. But as one reads the Bible and understands history, they will recognize that the calendar was an important fabric woven into Israeli life. The festivals of God are intermingled with the Hebrew calendar so much so that to eliminate one of them also eliminates the other.

Genesis 7:11, 24 *In the six hundredth year of Noah's life, in the second month, the seventeenth day of the month, the same day were all the fountains of the great deep broken up, and the windows of heaven were opened...And the waters prevailed upon the earth an hundred and fifty days.* (KJV)

Genesis 8:3, 4 *And the waters returned from off the earth continually: and after the end of the hundred and fifty days the waters were abated...And the ark rested in the seventh month, on the seventeenth day of the month, upon the mountains of Ararat.* (KJV)

Clearly in the account of the Flood in the days of Noah we find a calendar in use. The waters continued upon the earth for one hundred and fifty days. The Flood began on the seventeenth day of the second month and the Ark came to rest on Mt. Ararat on the seventeenth day of the seventh month. This means that the one hundred and fifty days occupied exactly five months making a month exactly thirty days long. So here in the first book of the Bible we see that a calendar was already in use and there were thirty days for a month.

Genesis 8:5-14 *And the waters decreased continually until the tenth month: in the tenth month, on the first day of the month, were the tops of the mountains seen. And it came to pass at the end of forty days, that Noah opened the window of the ark which he had made: And he sent forth a raven, which went forth to and fro, until the waters were dried up from off the earth. Also he sent forth a dove from him, to see if the waters were abated from off the face of the ground; But the dove found no rest for the sole of her foot, and she returned unto him into the ark, for the waters were on the face of the whole earth: then he put forth his hand, and took her, and pulled her in unto him into the ark. And he stayed yet other seven days; and again he sent forth the dove out of the ark; And the dove came in to him in the evening; and, lo, in her mouth was an olive leaf plucked off: so Noah knew that the waters were abated from off the earth. And he stayed yet other seven days; and sent forth the dove; which returned not again unto him any more. And it came to pass in the six hundredth and first year, in the first month, the first day of the month,* *the waters were dried up from off the earth: and Noah removed the covering of the ark, and looked, and, behold, the face of the ground was dry. And in the second month, on the seven and twentieth day of the month, was the earth dried.* (KJV)

The account of the Flood in Genesis tells us about the waters continuing to subside between the seventh and tenth months. The Bible actually focuses in on the first day of the tenth month when Noah could see the tops of the mountains. He then lets forty days go by before he opens the window of the Ark. We have already established that each month consisted of thirty days; therefore, Noah would have opened the window on the tenth day of the eleventh month.

From the opening of the window Noah released a raven and a dove to see if they could find land. The waters still covered the surface of the earth and he waited for another seven days, which would have been the seventeenth day of the eleventh month. Noah sent forth the dove again which came back with an olive leaf. Another seven days transpired before the dove was sent out for the last time. This occurred on the twenty-fourth day of the eleventh month. The dove never returned indicating that the waters had subsided. However, Noah knew that the ground was yet soft and muddy and waited inside the Ark. If we assume that there were twelve months in a year at that time, then thirty-six (thirty days for the twelfth month plus six days left in the eleventh month) days remained in that year.

The Bible tells us that on the first day of the first month that the ground was dry. This easily establishes that there were twelve months in a year and thirty days in each month. The total number of days in a year would have been three hundred and sixty.

We will find that the Jews used two primary calendars with the Old Testament. One was based upon the religious practices and the other upon Civil Law or Creation. The Religious Calendar did not take shape until Israel made its exodus into the wilderness from Egypt. The following is the ancient traditional Jewish Civil calendar:

	Month	Days	Gentile/Equivalent
1.	Tishri or Ethanim	30	September/October
2.	Marchesvan or Bul	30	October/November
3.	Chislev	30	November/December
4.	Tebeth	30	December/January
5.	Shebat	30	January/February
6.	Adar	30	February/March
7.	Nisan or Abib	30	March/April
8.	Iyyar or Ziv	30	April/May
9.	Sivan	30	May/June
10.	Tammuz	30	June/July
11.	Av or Ab	30	July/August
12.	Elul	30	August/September

One may notice right away that the three hundred and sixty days in the year are short of the current 365.25 days that it takes for the earth to orbit the sun. There are events in the Bible such as the day when the sun stood still [Joshua 10:12-13] and when the sundial moved back ten degrees [2 Kings 20:11] that suggest some supernatural phenomena in the heavens. These could possibly account for the differences in the calendar today.

The Religious Calendar

When God delivered Israel from Egyptian bondage He changed their calendar from the Civil Calendar to the Religious Calendar. But the evidence suggests that both calendars were in use when Israel came into the Promised Land. God didn't abolish the Civil Calendar.

It is almost like the earth had a physical birthday when it was created and Israel had her birthday when she became a nation. The earth went by the Civil Calendar whereas the nation of Israel went by the Religious Calendar to mark this event. This parallels the concept of two births. First we all have a physical birthday when we we are born. Secondly, when believers in God become born-again of the spirit, they have a spiritual birth. However, the believer still acknowledges his physical birthday as well as their spiritual birthday.

The religious calendar was based upon the principles of seven. The seventh day of the week was a Sabbath Day. The seventh month represents the Sabbath Month. Every seventh year was to be a Sabbath Year. After seven cycles of seven years (forty nine years) there was a special Sabbath Year. This fiftieth year was called the Year of Jubilee [Yovel].

By the First Century several calendars were in use by the Jews, but all were established with the lunar cycle based upon the new moon. When members of the Sanhedrin became convinced that the new moon was present they declared the beginning of the new month. There was no set pattern for the months. When the new moon was seen the next month was declared. Some months were only twenty-nine days while others remained at thirty days. About every third year (seven times every nineteen years) the leap month, Ve-Adar, was added at the end of the religious calendar so that the lunar cycle would balance with the solar cycle. If they didn't do this the calendar season of winter would eventually rotate to the summer and vice versa. For the twelve months of the religious (lunar) calendar there is either 353, 354, or 355 days depending upon the start of the new moons for that year.

Exodus 12:1-2 *And the LORD spake unto Moses and Aaron in the land of Egypt, saying, This month shall be unto you the beginning of months: it shall be the first month of the year to you.*

Moses led the children of Israel out of Egypt during the month of Nisan, which was the seventh month according to the Civil Calendar. But God told Moses to make Nisan the first month in the beginning of Israel as a nation to form the Religious Calendar. The calendar rotated exactly six months as the first month of the Civil Calendar became the seventh month of the Religious Calendar. The Religious Calendar is as follows:

	Month	**Gentile/Equivalent**
1.	Nisan or Abib	March/April
2.	Iyyar or Ziv	April/May
3.	Sivan	May/June
4.	Tammuz	June/July
5.	Av or Ab	July/August
6.	Elul	August/September
7.	Tishri or Ethanim	September/October
8.	Marchesvan or Bul	October/November
9.	Chislev	November/December
10.	Tebeth	December/January
11.	Shebat	January/February
12.	Adar	February/March
13.	Ve-Adar	Leap Year of 29 or 30 Days
		7 times every 19 Years to balance
		lunar and solar cycles

The first commandment that God gave Israel through Moses was not to keep the Passover, but to keep the New Moon [Rosh Chodesh] of the month of Nisan.[3] That particular Rosh Chodesh was the 'rebirth' of the moon, which corresponded to Israel's birth as a nation who gained its freedom from God Himself. Once Rosh Chodesh Nisan was sanctified, then all the events related to Passover would fall into order.

The First Passover and Exodus

Exodus 12:3-6 *Speak ye unto all the congregation of Israel, saying, In the tenth day of this month they shall take to them every man a lamb, according to the house of their fathers, a lamb for an house: And if the household be too little for the lamb, let him and his neighbour next unto his house take it according to the number of the souls; every man according to his eating shall make your count for the lamb. Your lamb shall be without blemish, a male of the first year: ye shall take it out from the sheep, or from the goats: And ye shall keep it up until the fourteenth day of the same month: and* *the whole assembly of the congregation of Israel shall kill it in the evening*. (KJV)

Before the first Passover Lambs were sacrificed, the Israelites were instructed by Moses to set aside an unblemished lamb on the tenth day of Nisan. The lamb was to be kept 'up until' Nisan 14. Each household was to tie their lamb up for this time as they continued to inspect it for imperfections.[4] The family cared for the lamb and they probably grew fond of it.

Exodus 5:3 *And they said, The God of the Hebrews hath met with us: let us go, we pray thee, three days' journey into the desert, and sacrifice unto the LORD our God; lest he fall upon us with pestilence, or with the sword.* (KJV)

Before Moses instructed the Israelites to choose their lamb, he demanded to Pharaoh to let them go on a three-day journey into the wilderness to hold a feast and make sacrifice to God. Pharaoh refused and God commanded Moses to send nine different plagues upon Egypt. But Pharaoh would not give into the demand during these nine plagues. The reader should keep this reference of 'a three-day journey' in mind. All Moses was asking Pharaoh was for this three-day excursion into the wilderness, and then they would return to Pharaoh and Egypt because Pharaoh owned them as slaves.

It was after the ninth plague that Moses instructed all the people of Israel in Egypt to select an unblemished lamb and watch it 'up until' the fourteenth day of Nisan. Each household chose their lamb on the tenth of Nisan as already mentioned.

Exodus 12:7-11 *And they shall take of the blood, and strike it on the two side posts and on the upper door post of the houses, wherein they shall eat it. And they shall eat the flesh in that night, roast with fire, and unleavened bread; and with bitter herbs they shall eat it. Eat not of it raw, nor sodden at all with water, but roast with fire; his head with his legs, and with the purtenance thereof. And ye shall let nothing of it remain until the morning; and that which remaineth of it until the morning ye shall burn with fire. And thus shall ye eat* *it; with your loins girded, your shoes on your feet, and your staff in your hand; and ye shall eat it in haste: it is the LORD'S passover.* (KJV)

The father, male head, or male firstborn of household would lay his hand on the lamb and declare the sacrifice to God. He would cut the throat of the lamb and apply blood to the lintel and on each side post around the door. Inside this 'marked' house they would later eat the Passover meal.

The entire assembly of Israel was to kill the lambs at exactly the same time: 'In the evening' [the Hebrew literally says 'between the evenings']. To understand the expression, 'between the evenings' ['bain harbayim' in Hebrew] when the Passover lambs were to be killed, one needs to understand the Biblical day. The Biblical day, as recorded in Genesis 1, begins in the evening at sunset. From sunset to sunrise, approximately 6:00 P.M. to 6:00 A.M., is considered the 'night' part of the day. From sunrise to sunset, roughly 6:00 A.M. to 6:00 P.M. is the 'day' part of the day.

The morning part of the day was divided into three 'unequal' portions. From about 6:00 A.M. unto 10:00 A.M., when the sun was obviously to the east was called 'boker,' or morning. From 10:00 A.M. until noon was called 'tzohoraim,' or noon. Finally, from 12:00 noon until sunset [approximately 6:00 P.M.] was called 'erev,' or afternoon.[5]

The Pesach lamb was to be sacrificed 'between the evenings'. As just stated from 12:00 noon too about 6:00 P.M. was considered the 'evening' part of the day. The period of 12:00-3:00 P.M. was called the 'minor evening oblation,' which was considered the first setting of the sun when the shadows begin to lengthen. The period of 3:00-6:00 P.M. was called the 'major evening oblation,' which was actually the time when the sunset.[6]

Rabbi Hertz relates that the Talmud teaches that the 'first evening' is when the heat of the sun begins to decrease at about 3:00 P.M., whereas the 'second evening' commences with the sunset.[7] Josephus, the first century historian, mentions that the Passover sacrifice was slaughtered between the ninth and eleventh hours of the day, which corresponds between 3:00 and 5:00 P.M.[8]

Exodus 12:9 *Eat not of it raw, nor sodden at all with water, but roast with fire; his head with his legs, and with the purtenance [innards] thereof.* (KJV)

The Israelites prepared and roasted the Passover lambs after they were slaughtered. The tractate Pesachim details Jewish tradition on how the Passover lamb was prepared for roasting in Egypt. In preparing the lamb, the intestines were removed and wrapped around the lamb's head. The lamb was called the crowned sacrifice. In order to evenly cook the lamb from the inside out, a pomegranate stick was thrust through it from the buttock to the mouth in a vertical position. The lamb's carcass was held open by placing a cross piece in a horizontal position and tying a leg on each end. [Talmud, Pesachim 74a]

Which Day was the Egyptian Passover?

In the time of Yeshua, as well as today, Passover was combined with the seven days of the festival of Unleavened Bread. The first night of Unleavened Bread, Nisan 15, was the time of the Passover Seder. In the Temple, the Passover lambs were sacrificed 'between the evenings' on the 14th day of Nisan. The lambs were prepared and were eaten at the Passover Seder after sundown, which was Nisan 15, the first day of Unleavened Bread.

The Pharisees had combined the two festivals of Passover and Unleavened Bread into one. But was it always that way? According to the following Scriptures the Passover was a separate festival from the seven days of Unleavened Bread:[9]

Leviticus 23:5-6 *In the fourteenth day of the first month at even is the LORD's passover. And on the fifteenth day of the same month is the feast of unleavened bread unto the LORD: seven days ye must eat unleavened bread.* (KJV)

Numbers 9:2-5 *Let the children of Israel also keep the passover at his appointed season. In the fourteenth day of this month, at even, ye shall keep it in his appointed season: according to all the rites* *of it, and according to all the ceremonies thereof, shall ye keep it. And Moses spake unto the children of Israel, that they should keep the passover. And they kept the passover on the fourteenth day of the first month at even in the wilderness of Sinai: according to all that the LORD commanded Moses, so did the children of Israel.* (KJV)

Numbers 28:16-17 *And in the fourteenth day of the first month is the passover of the LORD. And in the fifteenth day of this month is the feast: seven days shall unleavened bread be eaten.* (KJV)

In Egypt all Israel sacrificed their lambs 'between the evenings' on Nisan 13, and they were eaten after sunset on Nisan 14. More than twenty-four hours later, the Israelites began their journey out from Egypt on Nisan 15. This is easily seen from the book of Numbers:

Numbers 33:3 *And they departed from Rameses in the first month, on the fifteenth day of the first month; on the morrow after [the day after] the passover the children of Israel went out with an high hand in the sight of all the Egyptians.* (KJV)

Also, consider the following verses:

Exodus 12:22 *And ye shall take a bunch of hyssop, and dip it in the blood that is in the bason, and strike the lintel and the two side posts with the blood that is in the bason; and none of you shall go out at the door of his house until the morning.* (KJV)

Exodus 12:30-31 *And Pharaoh rose up in the night, he, and all his servants, and all the Egyptians; and there was a great cry in Egypt; for there was not a house where there was not one dead. And he called for Moses and Aaron by <u>night</u>, and said, Rise up, and get you forth from among my people, both ye and the children of Israel; and go, serve the LORD, as ye have said.* (KJV)

God instructed Moses and the Israelites that after the blood of the Passover lamb had been applied to the door of their homes, they were to stay within their dwellings until morning. It was forbidden for any Israelite to go outside their home on the evening of Nisan 14 at the Passover in Egypt. However, after Pharaoh's firstborn son was killed, he summoned Moses and Aaron by night. We have already read in the Scripture that the Israelites left Egypt after midnight on Nisan 15. The obvious conclusion is that a full twenty-four hours had passed after Pharaoh's firstborn son had died at night on Nisan 14 when the Passover was eaten. On the next night, Nisan 15, he summoned Moses and Aaron.

Joshua 5:10 *And the children of Israel encamped in Gilgal, and kept the passover on the fourteenth day of the month at even in the plains of Jericho.* (KJV)

2 Chronicles 30:13, 15 *And there assembled at Jerusalem much people to keep the feast of unleavened bread in the second month, a very great congregation...Then they killed the passover on the fourteenth day of the second month: and the priests and the Levites were ashamed, and sanctified themselves, and brought in the burnt offerings into the house of the LORD.* (KJV)

2 Chronicles 35:1, 17 *Moreover Josiah kept a passover unto the LORD in Jerusalem: and they killed the passover on the fourteenth day of the first month...And the children of Israel that were present kept the passover at that time, and the feast of unleavened bread seven days.* (KJV)

Ezra 6:19, 22 *And the children of the captivity kept the passover upon the fourteenth day of the first month...And kept the feast of unleavened bread seven days with joy: for the LORD had made them joyful, and turned the heart of the king of Assyria unto them, to strengthen their hands in the work of the house of God, the God of Israel.* (KJV)

After forty years in the Wilderness, Israel kept the Passover on the 14th day of Nisan under Joshua. Nisan 14 was the day that the Passover was held on throughout the entire First Temple period [when Israel was in obedience to God]. This is evidenced by the two spiritual revivals under king Hezekiah and king Josiah of Judah sparked first by holding the Passover on Nisan 14. In Hezekiah's case, the people and the priests were not ritually clean on Nisan 14, so it was postponed until exactly one month later on the 14th of the month. This was permissible under the Torah [see Numbers 9:10-12].

According to the book of Ezra, even after the First Temple's destruction and Israel's captivity, those who came back to the Promised Land and rebuilt the Temple, kept the Passover on Nisan 14. So, when exactly did the Jews start keeping the Passover on Nisan 15, the first day of the festival of Unleavened Bread? We really don't know for sure, but sometime before the first century, probably between 300-100 B.C.E., the Pharisees were successful in combining the Passover on Nisan 14 into the first day of the festival of Unleavened Bread on Nissan 15.

Even in the first century, there were splinter groups that continued to offer their Passover Lambs 'between the evenings' on Nisan 13, and had their Seder in the evening of Nisan 14, a full day earlier than the Pharisees and the people. Both the Sadducees and the Samaritans observed Passover in this manner.[1]

Luke 22:1 *Now the feast of unleavened bread drew nigh, which is called the Passover.* (KJV)

During the days of Yeshua, the entire seven days of Unleavened Bread had come to be known as Passover. Basically, the Pharisees had eliminated the need for Nisan 14, and placed the Passover elements into the first day of Unleavened Bread on Nisan 15. But this practice appears to be in opposition to the clear instructions given through the Torah of Moses.

According to Exodus 12 the Passover lambs were sacrificed at the end of Nisan 13 just before sunset. The Passover meal was actually eaten after sundown, which was on 14th day of Nisan. The Israelites ate the lamb with bitter herbs and unleavened bread called 'matzah'. They ate standing up with their sandals on their feet and staffs in their hand. They could not go outside once they settled in the house for the meal and the blood of the lamb was applied to the door.

Exodus 12:14-16,18 *And this day shall be unto you for a memorial; and ye shall keep it a feast to the LORD throughout your generations; ye shall keep it a feast by an ordinance for ever. Seven days shall ye eat unleavened bread; even the first day ye shall put away leaven out of your houses: for whosoever eateth leavened bread from the first day until the seventh day, that soul shall be cut off from Israel. And in the first day there shall be an holy convocation, and in the seventh day there shall be an holy convocation to you; no manner of work shall be done in them, save that which every man must eat, that only may be done of you...In the first month, on the fourteenth day of the month at even, ye shall eat unleavened bread, until the one and twentieth day of the month at even.* (KJV)

During the festival of Unleavened Bread God instituted two 'holy convocations', which are called 'High Sabbath Days' by the Jews. The Hebrew word for 'convocation' simply means 'an assembly or public gathering' and also relates to the connotation of 'rehearsal'. To have these public gatherings all other 'things' must be stopped or closed, thus making it almost equivalent to a Sabbath Day but definitely of less sanctity. The weekly Sabbath was always on Friday evening (6:00 P.M.) until Saturday evening (6:00 P.M.). But the first day of the feast of Unleavened Bread, Nisan 15, was also to be celebrated as a High Sabbath.

For seven days Israel was to eat unleavened bread. They were not to put leaven in their bread because they didn't have time to wait for the dough to rise. They had to be ready to depart Egypt at any time. The seventh day of Unleavened Bread (Nisan 21) was also to be celebrated as a High Sabbath (convocation) day. From the beginning of the 14th of Nisan with the Passover meal until the end of the 21st of Nisan the Israelites were to eat unleavened bread.

Exodus 12:12-13 *For I will pass through the land of Egypt this night, and will smite all the firstborn in the land of Egypt, both man and beast; and against all the gods of Egypt I will execute judgment: I am the LORD. And the blood shall be to you for a token upon the houses where ye are: and when I see the blood, I will pass over you,* *and the plague shall not be upon you to destroy you, when I smite the land of Egypt.* (KJV)

The children of Israel had to stay in their houses after they ate the Passover meal early on the 14th day of Nisan because of the tenth plague God was about to send against Egypt. The firstborn of every house and beast was to be killed by the death angel if there was no Passover lambs' blood on the lintels and the doorposts. The houses of the Israelites with the blood upon them were protected.

Exodus 12:22,23 *And ye shall take a bunch of hyssop, and dip it in the blood that is in the basin, and strike the lintel and the two side posts with the blood that is in the basin; and none of you shall go out at the door of his house until the morning. For the LORD will pass through to smite the Egyptians; and when he seeth the blood upon the lintel, and on the two side posts, the LORD will pass over the door, and will not suffer the destroyer to come in unto your houses to smite you.* (KJV)

The Hebrew word for 'Passover' has a far deeper meaning then just the death angel 'passing over' the Israelite houses with blood upon them. The Hebrew word 'pasah' (Passover) is not connected to any other Hebrew word, but it is related to the Egyptian word 'pesh' from which the children of Israel probably understood living in Egypt all those years. 'Pesh' means to 'spread wings over' such as an eagle spreading her wings over her young to protect them.[11] The Lord Himself probably stood guard at the houses where the blood was applied protecting the inhabitants inside from the death angel. The Lord's 'wings' passed over the inhabitants protected by the blood of the lamb. Exodus 12:23 literally states that 'the Lord will pass over the door' and will prevent the destroyer from entering.

The 'basin' was not a container like we would normally think. The word is an Egyptian word meaning a ditch that was dug just in front of the doorways of the houses to prevent flooding inside. The people placed a container in the ditch to prevent seepage. The 'basin' is actually the 'threshold,' which we will talk about in chapter nine of this book. The Israelites killed their Passover lambs right by the doors, where they were about to smear the blood, and the blood from the animal ran into the ditch or basin. They painted the blood on the doorposts and lintel with a hyssop brush. The blood in the basin at the bottom of the door was already there before they painted the blood upon the lintel, which was the top of the door. Then they painted the two sides of the door. The door was sealed with the blood of the lamb on all four sides.

Exodus 12:29,31 *And it came to pass, that at midnight the LORD smote all the firstborn in the land of Egypt, from the firstborn of Pharaoh that sat on his throne unto the firstborn of the captive that was in the dungeon; and all the firstborn of cattle...And he called for Moses and Aaron by night, and said, Rise up, and get you forth from among my people, both ye and the children of Israel; and go, serve the LORD, as ye have said.* (KJV)

At midnight on the night of the 14th of Nisan, the death angel killed Egypt's firstborn sons. Finally, Pharaoh had enough because his own lineage was cut off. He called for Moses and Aaron 'by night,' which we have already demonstrated had to be the next night of Nisan 15. Pharaoh told them to gather the children of Israel together and go on their three-day journey into the wilderness and serve their God. Pharaoh understood that they would return to Egypt after three days.

Exodus12:33-39 *And the Egyptians were urgent upon the people, that they might send them out of the land in haste; for they said, We be all dead men. And the people took their dough before it was leavened, their kneadingtroughs being bound up in their clothes upon their shoulders. And the children of Israel did according to the word of Moses; and they borrowed of the Egyptians jewels of silver, and jewels of gold, and raiment: And the LORD gave the people favour in the sight of the Egyptians, so that they lent unto them such things as they required. And they spoiled the Egyptians. And the children of Israel journeyed from Rameses to Succoth, about six hundred thousand on foot that were men, beside children. And a mixed multitude went up also with them; and flocks, and herds, even very much cattle.*

And they baked unleavened cakes of the dough which they brought forth out of Egypt, for it was not leavened; because they were thrust out of Egypt, and could not tarry, neither had they prepared for themselves any victual. (KJV)

Exodus 3:21-22 *And I will give this people favour in the sight of the Egyptians: and it shall come to pass, that, when ye go, ye shall not go empty: But every woman shall borrow of her neighbour, and of her that sojourneth in her house, jewels of silver, and jewels of gold, and raiment: and ye shall put them upon your sons, and upon your daughters; and ye shall spoil the Egyptians.* (KJV)

Genesis 15:14 *And also that nation, whom they shall serve, will I judge: and afterward shall they come out with great substance.* (KJV)

Before Israel left Egypt, the Egyptians gave many gifts to the Israelites for their journey. It appears that the Egyptians favored the Israelites in contrast to their master Pharaoh and his army. This was in fulfillment of the prophecy given to Abraham and his seed earlier (Genesis 15:10). The rabbi's interpreted the Hebrew construction of these verses to mean that the Egyptian's were 'saved' or 'delivered' through their gift-giving to the Israelites. In other words, the Israelites would not hold a grudge upon the Egyptian people for their mistreatment at the hands of Pharaoh. The Egyptians didn't lend the gifts to the Israelites, but gave to them favorably according to the Hebrew text. Rabbi Hertz very clearly demonstrates that the Hebrew word for 'spoil' (ל צ נ - natzal) in Exodus 3:22 and 12:36 should be rendered 'saved' as in 'saving the Egyptians'.[12]

Exodus 15:16 *Fear and dread shall fall upon them; by the greatness of thine arm they shall be as still as a stone; till thy people pass over, O LORD, till the people pass over, which thou hast purchased.* (KJV)

The ancient rabbis and Biblical prophets compared God's taking of Israel as His nation to a marriage. Israel was God's bride. The wealth of the Egyptians that was freely given to the Israelites before they left Egypt was considered the gift [such as a ring today] to 'seal' the betrothal between God and Israel. God purchased the Israelites as His bride.[13]

Exodus 13:18-20 *But God led the people about, through the way of the wilderness of the Red sea: and the children of Israel went up harnessed out of the land of Egypt. And Moses took the bones of Joseph with him: for he had straitly sworn the children of Israel, saying,_ God will surely visit you; and ye shall carry up my bones away hence with you. And they took their journey from Succoth, and encamped in Etham, in the edge of the wilderness.* (KJV)

Numbers 33:6 *And they departed from Succoth, and pitched in Etham, which is in the edge of the wilderness.* (KJV)

Moses led the Hebrew people out of Egypt during the morning hours of Nisan 15 in haste. They were on their way before the break of dawn. The Israelites left Rameses toward the city of Succoth. Succoth was the place where Joseph's bones were buried. Joseph had prophesied before he died that Israel was to carry his bones from Egypt when they left. After securing Joseph's bones Israel departed for Etham, which was located on the edge of the wilderness near the Red Sea [Hebrew Yam Suf - Reed Sea]. The Bible states that they pitched their tents in Etham.

Genesis 50:24-26 *And Joseph said unto his brethren, I die: and God will surely visit you, and bring you out of this land unto the land which he sware to Abraham, to Isaac, and to Jacob. And Joseph took an oath of the children of Israel, saying, God will surely visit you, and ye shall carry up my bones from hence. So Joseph died, being an hundred and ten years old: and they embalmed him, and he was put in a coffin in Egypt.* (KJV)

What was the importance of Moses and Israel taking Joseph's bones with them? This act in itself was in defiance to Pharaoh. The prophecies that Israel would one day occupy Canaan were tied to

Joseph's bones. The very fact that Israel took them indicated to Pharaoh that they were not returning after three days. When Joseph states in Genesis 50, 'God will surely remember you,' the verb is repeated twice 'pa<u>kod</u> yif<u>kod</u>,' literally translating as 'remember He will remember you'.

In the ancient rabbinical writings, this phraseology in the Hebrew implied a 'double' remembrance. God would first remember the Israelites in the days of Moses during the month of Nisan as we are studying regarding the Exodus from Egypt. The final remembrance will come at the hands of the Messiah in the month of Tishri, which will be the material of a later chapter in this book.[14]

Numbers 33:7 *And they removed from Etham, and turned again unto Pihahiroth, which is before Baalzephon: and they pitched before Migdol.* (KJV)

After encamping at Etham, Moses led the people to the region of Pihahiroth. The Israelites made camp again before Migdol. According to the Torah this was Israel's second encampment after coming out of Egypt.

Exodus 14:5, 8-9,19,20 *And it was told the king of Egypt that the people fled: and the heart of Pharaoh and of his servants was turned against the people, and they said, Why have we done this, that we have let Israel go from serving us?... And the LORD hardened the heart of Pharaoh king of Egypt, and he pursued after the children of Israel: and the children of Israel went out with an high hand. But the Egyptians pursued after them, all the horses and chariots of Pharaoh, and his horsemen, and his army, and overtook them encamping by the sea, beside Pihahiroth, before Baalzephon...And the angel of God, which went before the camp of Israel, removed and went behind them; and the pillar of the cloud went from before their face, and stood behind them: And it came between the camp of the Egyptians and the camp of Israel; and it was a cloud and dark-ness to them, but it gave light by night to these: so that the one came not near the other <u>all the night</u>.* (KJV)

Because of Pharaoh's wickedness, God allowed his heart to be hardened toward the Israelites. He was under the impression that they would return after three days when he let them depart. When Moses went to Succoth to gather Joseph's bones, Pharaoh must have realized the prophecy of Joseph's bones being returned to Canaan. Pharaoh knew that Moses had no intention of bringing the people back to Egypt and organized his army in pursuit of them. Therefore, sometime after the 15th of Nisan, when it was realized that Joseph's bones had been taken, Pharaoh began his pursuit of the Israelites. He engaged his entire army after the Israelites and pursued them until finally catching up to them near Pihahiroth. The Hebrew text implies that both camps had come in sight of one another at Pihahiroth. The angel of the Lord made a pillar-like cloud between Pharaoh's army and the children of Israel. The cloud brought darkness to Pharaoh's army so that they could not find the Hebrews. But the cloud brought light to the children of Israel who were beside the Reed Sea.

Exodus 14:21-22 *And Moses stretched out his hand over the sea; and the LORD caused the sea to go back by a strong east wind all that night, and made the sea dry land, and the* waters *were divided. And the children of Israel went into the midst of the sea upon the dry ground: and the* waters *were a wall unto them on their right hand, and on their left.* (KJV)

During this night, which rabbinic tradition associates to the seventh day of the Festival Unleavened Bread, Nisan 21, Moses divided the waters of the Reed Sea and caused dry ground to appear.[15] Nisan 21 is the other 'High Sabbath' [Holy Convocation] associated with the seven days of Unleavened Bread. While the cloud of darkness held the Egyptians back, Israel journeyed across the Reed Sea to the other side safely. God instructed Moses to lift up his rod and stretch out his hand over the sea and the sea parted and the 'waters' were divided.

Psalm 136:13 *To him which divided the Red sea into* parts*: for his mercy endureth for ever*: (KJV)

The plural 'waters' used in Exodus 14 is very significant when one considers 'parts' in Psalm 136:13. Christianity has the concept that all Israel crossed the Reed Sea through one dry pathway, but Jewish tradition believes otherwise. Jewish tradition has always understood that the Reed Sea was divided into twelve 'parts,' one for each of the tribes to make their crossing.[16]

Accounting for the wives, children, and the mixed multitude, there were probably over two to three million people that left Egypt under Moses direction. When you take into account the livestock brought with them, it was literally a 'nation' on the move. Rough calculations demonstrate that they needed a campground area of several hundred square miles.

The Bible says they crossed the Yam Suf [Reed Sea] in one night. If they went on a narrow path, double file, the line would be several hundred miles long and would require 'weeks' of days and nights to get through. If the Israelites had crossed the Sea five thousand abreast, it would have been necessary for an opening of around three miles to be made. This event was truly a miracle from God and leaves open more possibilities than what has been portrayed in the movies, etc.

Notice the redundancy in Psalm 136 of 'divided the Red sea into parts'. If there was only one path the Hebrew would say 'divided the Red Sea'. The Hebrew word for 'parts' is Gezerim ג ז ר י ם, which is only used one other time in the Tanakh [Old Testament]. When Abram divided the animals, Genesis 15:17 calls them Gezerim 'pieces'. There were definitely more than two animal pieces divided up in Genesis 15. This leaves the 'door' open that there could have been twelve separate pathways in the Reed Sea for Israel to cross over.

Exodus 14:16, 21 *But lift thou up thy rod, and stretch out thine hand over the sea, and divide [baka] it: and the children of Israel shall go on dry ground through the midst of [center] the sea... And Moses stretched out his hand over the sea; and the LORD caused the sea to go back by a strong east wind all that night, and made the sea dry land, and the waters were divided [baka]. (KJV)*

Even the account in Exodus leaves ambiguity as to how the waters of the Reed Sea [Yam Suf] were divided. God caused a 'strong east wind' to make the 'sea to go back'. The word 'back' is not even in the Hebrew text. The Hebrew actually says that the strong east wind made 'the sea follow it' or 'behave to its power'.

The Hebrew word for 'divided' in Exodus 14:21 is 'baka'. 'Baka' can be used to divide something in half, or many parts or pieces. One cannot make a claim by the usage of 'baka' alone. The Hebrew word for 'through the midst of' is 'tavek'. 'Tavek' literally means 'in the middle [center] of a thing'. 'Tavek' implies that all the children of Israel would pass through the middle of the Yam Suf on dry ground in order to get to the other side. If there were twelve paths, the Israelites would still have passed through the center of the Sea. Therefore the Hebrew words used in the crossing of the Reed Sea don't specifically indicate that there was only one path created. This in combination with Psalm 136:13 leaves open the possibility that the rabbi's account of twelve paths may be correct.

Exodus 14:23-25, 27-28 *And the Egyptians pursued, and went in after them to the midst of the sea, even all Pharaoh's horses, his chariots, and his horsemen. And it came to pass, that in the morning watch the LORD looked unto the host of the Egyptians through the pillar of fire and of the cloud, and troubled the host of the Egyptians, And took off their chariot wheels, that they drave them heavily: so that the Egyptians said, Let us flee from the face of Israel; for the LORD fighteth for them against the Egyptians...And Moses stretched forth his hand over the sea, and the sea returned to his strength when the morning appeared; and the Egyptians fled against it; and the LORD overthrew the Egyptians in the midst of the sea. And the waters returned, and covered the chariots, and the horsemen, and all the host of Pharaoh that came into the sea after them; there remained not so much as one of them.*

When the darkness subsided at the break of dawn, the Egyptians saw the Reed Sea parted and Israel across the other side. According to Jewish tradition, in the early morning hours of the 21st day of Nisan, Pharaoh and his army pursued them across the divided waters. But the Lord caused the wheels of their chariots to fall off thus stranding them between the 'walls' of waters that divided the sea.

Psalm 136:15 *But overthrew <u>Pharaoh</u> and his host in the Red sea: for his mercy endureth for ever.* (KJV)

Exodus 15:19 *For <u>the horse of Pharaoh</u> went in with his chariots and with his horsemen into the sea, and the LORD brought again the waters of the sea upon them; but the children of Israel went on dry land in the midst of the sea.* (KJV)

Moses released the waters to fall upon the Egyptians after Israel had successfully crossed over to the other side. All were drowned including Pharaoh as the scripture states that not one of them remained. Now that Pharaoh, his firstborn to the throne, and all his leading military captains were dead, the ownership of the Hebrew people was broken. They were free completely on the other side of the Reed Sea. Israel emerged alive and free from the depths of the Reed Sea that morning.

We are given the approximate time in Scripture that Israel crossed the Reed Sea and Pharaoh and his armies were destroyed. Exodus 14:24 states that these events occurred 'in the morning watch'. By the time of the first century, the Romans had divided the night into four watches; 6-9 P.M., 9-12 midnight, 12-3 A.M., and 3-6 A.M.[17] But before this time Jews had divided the watches into three time periods.[18] According to the rabbis, the 'morning watch' in which the Israelites crossed the Reed Sea, was between the hours of 2-6 A.M. The other two watches were 6-10 P.M. and 10 P.M.-2 A.M. respectively.[19]

The Festival of Unleavened Bread - Hag HaMatzah

We have discussed that the sacrificed Passover lamb on the late afternoon of the 13th of Nisan was eaten after dusk when the night turned to the 14th of Nisan. The Passover lamb was eaten with bitter herbs and unleavened bread. The obvious purpose of the unleavened bread associated with the seven days of the Festival, was to make sure the children of Israel had bread to take on their exodus. They didn't have time to put leaven in the bread and wait for it to rise.

The 15th of Nisan was the beginning of seven days of eating unleavened bread called Hag HaMatzah [Festival of Unleavened Bread]. The 15th and the 21st (the first and last days of the Feast) of Nisan were to be celebrated as holy convocations [rehearsal assemblies] and Sabbaths as we have already mentioned. These were not the weekly Sabbaths but called 'High' Sabbaths or Shabbaton.

Oftentimes in the Scripture sin is symbolized by 'leaven'. The putting away of all leaven is a perfect picture of God's people being sanctified; set apart for God. The blood of the Passover lamb was upon the doors of the Israelite homes for protection but they had removed all the leaven beforehand. This picture demonstrates that redemption follows after all leaven (sin) of the old life is put away. Leaven was something that every housewife and cook used in everyday life in ancient times. Leaven causes dough to become puffed up so that the end product is more in volume but not in weight. The sin of pride causes people to be puffed up, elevating the perception of theimselves as higher than reality.

The ancient Hebrews used the sourdough method of leavening their bread. Before the dough was formed into loaves ready for baking, a chunk of the raw dough was broken off and set aside in a cool and moist place. The next day when it was time to bake another batch of bread, the reserved lump of dough was then mixed into the fresh batch of flour and water to leaven the next loaves. Again a chunk was set aside from the newly mixed dough and the process continued.[20] The common yeast spores to the previous loaves of bread organically linked each 'new generation' of bread. The human race bears this same kind of link to the sin nature of our first father, Adam. Thus, for Israel, the putting away of all leaven symbolized breaking the old cycle of sin and starting out afresh from Egypt to walk as a new nation before the Lord.

The bitter herbs they ate with the Passover meal reminded them of their hardships under Pharaoh's taskmasters. Bitterness often speaks of death. The bitter herbs are also a reminder that the first-born of Israel lived because the Passover lambs died.

Exodus 12:8 *And they shall eat the flesh in that night, roast with fire, and unleavened bread; and with bitter herbs they shall eat it.* (KJV)

Rabbinical exegesis of all the Scriptures regarding the festivals of Passover and Unleavened Bread reveal that it was only a command-ment on the first night of Nisan 15 to eat unleavened bread. There is no requirement that unleavened bread be eaten on the six remaining days of the seven-day festival of Unleavened Bread. The require-ment on those days is not to eat anything with Chametz (or leaven) in it. Of course, their conclusions are based upon the Passover Seder being moved to the evening of Nisan 15, because originally it was held on the evening of Nisan 14. The Scripture is clear that unleav-ened bread must be eaten with the Passover on Nisan 14 just prior to the start of the festival of Unleavened Bread.

Exodus 12:39 *And they baked unleavened cakes of the dough which they brought forth out of Egypt, for it was not leavened; because they were thrust out of Egypt, and could not tarry, neither had they prepared for themselves any victual.* (KJV)

The Matzah [Unleavened Bread] that was eaten with the Passover was called 'lechem oni,' bread of affliction. This again symbolizes the embittered Israelite lives while in Egypt. When they cried out in faith to God, He released them from their bondage. Unleavened bread that was eaten during the seven days of the festival of Unleavened Bread was symbolic of redemption, since the Israelites departed Egypt with much gold and silver. These matzot [unleavened bread] remind us of the speed and swiftness with which the Israelites had to leave Egypt, witnessing to the direct intervention of God, which compelled Pharaoh to suddenly release them despite his relentless opposition. The Passover reminds us of the events of Nisan 14, the pre-exodus period, whereas Unleavened Bread depicts the actual departure from Egypt.[21] Unleavened Bread is considered the 'food of poverty,' or 'the food of faith'. The unleavened bread symbolizes the faith of the Israelites who departed Egypt for the Wilderness without preparing proper provisions.

During their forty-year sojourn in the Wilderness, the Israelites nourishment came from the manna, the miraculous sustenance that fell from Heaven each day. Their dependence on the manna was an exercise in faith and trust in God. This lesson was meant for future generations as well. In Hebrew manna is מ נ, pronounced 'mawn'. When the people first saw the manna, they asked מ נ ה ו א, 'What is it?' [Exodus 16:15] It is significant that the letters מ נ ה ו א also form the word for faith, emunah א מ ו נ ה.[22]

Psalm 78:24-25 *And had rained down manna upon them to eat, and had given them of the corn [Hebrew – Grain] of heaven. Man did eat angels' food: he sent them meat to the full.* (KJV)

Although the manna came ready to eat, probably like bread, it could also be ground and used like unprocessed grain to make many delicacies. The man who ate manna became infused with intense faith in God. Malbim mentions that manna had a duel identity. In its external appearance it was bread, but according to the psalm it was angel food in its inner essence. Those who were wise recognized the true blessing of the manna and appreciated their privileged opportunity for spiritual growth. The manna also came in a sanitary package of fresh dew, which fell conveniently wherever they camped. The manna supplied energy, which was completely absorbed by all the limbs of the body. There was no waste eliminated from the Israelites when they entirely ate a manna diet.[23]

Exodus 16:35 *And the children of Israel did eat manna forty years, until they came to a land inhabited; they did eat manna, until they came unto the borders of the land of Canaan.* (KJV)

Exodus 16:1, 4 *And they took their journey from Elim, and all the congregation of the children of Israel came unto the wilderness of Sin, which is between Elim and Sinai, on the fifteenth day of the second month after their departing [30 days after Nisan 15] out of the land of Egypt...Then said the LORD unto Moses, Behold, I will rain bread from heaven for you; and the people shall go out and* *gather a certain rate every day, that I may prove them, whether they will walk in my law, or no.* (KJV)

According to the Scripture and tradition, the Israelites survived on the unleavened bread they had brought out of Egypt in haste for thirty days. On the 15th day of the second month, the manna from God began to rain down from heaven. The manna continued to appear in the morning dew into the 40th year of Israel's sojourn in the Wilderness. When they came to the borders of the land of Canaan, the manna ceased to appear.[24]

A liturgical name for the festival of Unleavened Bread is Zeman Herutenu, 'Season of Our Freedom,' which marks the establishment of the children of Israel as a free and independent people. Philo called the Festival of Unleavened Bread the 'Crossing-Feast' as he traced the name not to the passing over of the Israelites by the destroying angel, but to the crossing of Israel itself from Egypt.

Passover in the Land of Canaan

Numbers 9:1-3 *And the LORD spake unto Moses in the wilderness of Sinai, in the first month of the second year after they were come out of the land of Egypt, saying, Let the children of Israel also keep the passover at his appointed season. In the fourteenth day of this month, at even, ye shall keep it in his appointed season: according to all the rites of it, and according to all the ceremonies thereof, shall ye keep it.* (KJV)

Joshua 5:10 *And the children of Israel encamped in Gilgal, and kept the passover on the fourteenth day of the month at even in the plains of Jericho.* (KJV)

Exactly one year after leaving Egypt on Nisan 14, God commanded Israel to hold the Passover rite in the Wilderness. The Passover was not kept during the next thirty-nine years in the Wilderness until after Israel had crossed the Jordan and entered the land of Canaan and was stationed at Gilgal. It is noteworthy that the crossing of the Jordan was timed for the Passover season and that the first two official rites ordered by Joshua were the rites of circumcision and the Paschal lamb. Thereafter the covenant was complete and irrevocable. The annual paschal lamb, brought on the thirteenth of Nisan, was to be a visible reminder to the Israelites of their historic declaration of faith and their obligation under the covenant concluded on that day.

Joshua 5:11-12 *And they did eat of the old corn of the land on the morrow after the Passover [Nisan 15], unleavened cakes, and parched corn in the selfsame day. And the manna ceased on the morrow [Nisan 16] after they had eaten of the old corn of the land; neither had the children of Israel manna any more; but they did eat of the fruit of the land of Canaan that year.* (KJV)

Before Joshua brought Israel into the Promised Land, they celebrated the Passover. The Passover lambs were killed at the appointed time 'between the evenings' of Nisan 13 and eaten with unleavened bread after sundown on Nisan 14. But what bread did Israel eat? The Scripture says, 'they did eat of the old corn of the land on the morrow after the Passover...' 'The morrow after' in Hebrew is 'mochorath,' and literally translates as 'the next day'.[25] The day after the Passover on Nisan 14 is the first day of the festival of Unleavened Bread, which is Nisan 15. After they had crossed the Jordan, the Israelites ate of the old corn of the land on Nisan 15.

The manna that God gave from 'Heaven' during the years in the Wilderness ceased on 'the next day,' which was Nisan 16 after the people ate of the stored grain of the land on Nisan 15. This date of Nisan 16, when the manna ceased, will become very significant later. The very fact that God would have sent manna down during the Passover indicates that it was unleavened. Therefore, manna is connected to unleavened bread, as the unleavened bread brought from Egypt lasted for thirty days and was replaced with the manna for 40 years until Passover again after the Israelites entered Canaan. After the manna ceased on Nisan 16, the Israelites were eligible to eat the fruit of the land [the new grain] of Canaan.

Numbers 11:9 *And when the dew fell upon the camp in the night, the manna fell upon it.* (KJV)

Exodus 16:4-5 *Then said the LORD unto Moses, Behold, I will rain bread from heaven for you. And when the children of Israel saw it, they said one to another, It is manna: for they wist not what it was. And Moses said unto them, This is the bread which the LORD hath given you to eat.* (KJV)

The 'dew' that fell in the early spring was considered the beginning of the 'early rain' to the Jews. The 'dew' became the first sign that life was being restored to the Land after the long winter as plant life would begin to sprout over night. The Hebrew word for 'dew' is 'tal' ל ט. The 'Dew' (Former Rain) became associated within the teachings of Judaism as a symbol for 'Teaching [Torah], Resurrection, Life, and the Messiah'.

Deuteronomy 32:2 *My doctrine shall drop as the rain, my speech shall distil as the dew, as the small rain upon the tender herb, and as the showers upon the grass:* (KJV)

Jews know Deuteronomy 32 as Ha'azinu, which was recited every morning by the Sanhedrin in the Chamber of Hewn Stone in the Temple where they held court. Verse 2 relates God's Teaching to the 'Rain' and the 'Dew'. The manna that was sent from Heaven to feed Israel in the Wilderness fell with the 'dew'. Moses called the manna that rained 'the Bread from Heaven'. When the dew evaporated, the manna became visible.[26]

The manna that came from Heaven with the dew was a 'Teaching' from God. The manna pointed to the 'Bread of Heaven', which sustained eternal life. The dew was the 'teaching' that accompanied the Bread. When all the dew (teaching) was removed all that remained was the Bread. In other word's God was teaching that the Torah and Commandments given by Him were all pointing to the Messiah that was to come. Yeshua said that He was the true Bread from Heaven. His teaching (dew) supported the life-giving sustenance that only He could give as the Bread (Living) from Heaven.

If Messiah is the Bread that will sustain us forever, then we have to connect the Resurrection with the Bread and the Dew as Yeshua did by saying, 'this is the will of him that sent me, that everyone which seeth the Son, and believeth on him, may have everlasting life: and I will raise him up at the last day' (John 6:40 KJV).

Isaiah 26:19 *Thy dead men shall live, together with my dead body shall they arise. Awake and sing, ye that dwell in dust: for thy dew is as the dew of herbs, and the earth shall cast out the dead.* (KJV)

The prophet Isaiah in no uncertain terms links the Resurrection of the Dead with 'dew...as the dew of herbs'. After the long winter it is the dew (beginning of the early rain) that awakens life from the earth. Spiritually, it is the Teaching of God in His Messiah that will bring life to the dead. Yeshua the Messiah is 'the Resurrection and the Life' (John 11:25).

Deeper Insights into the Passover Sacrifice

Exodus 3:18 *And they shall hearken to thy voice: and thou shalt come, thou and the elders of Israel, unto the king of Egypt, and ye shall say unto him, The LORD God of the Hebrews hath met with us: and now let us go, we beseech thee, three days' journey into the wilderness, that we may sacrifice to the LORD our God.* (KJV)

Exodus 5:3 *And they said, The God of the Hebrews hath met with us: let us go, we pray thee, three days' journey into the desert, and sacrifice unto the LORD our God; lest he fall upon us with pestilence, or with the sword.* (KJV)

Exodus 8:27 *We will go three days' journey into the wilderness, and sacrifice to the LORD our God, as he shall command us.* (KJV)

The importance of the Passover lamb is probably demonstrated through Moses' initial request that Pharaoh permit the Israelites to go into the Wilderness to sacrifice to the Lord. This act in itself would have constituted an act of defiance toward Pharaoh for

Israel's freedom to practice their religion. The Egyptians worshiped the lambs and would have considered it an abomination for Israel to slaughter their Passover lambs in Egypt. Because of Pharaoh's unwillingness to submit to God's decree, a drawn-out contest forced him to comply, when Moses commanded Israel to slaughter their Passover lambs in Egypt.[27]

The Feast of the Firstfruits of the Barley Harvest

Leviticus 23:5-14 *In the fourteenth day of the first month at even is the LORD's passover. And on the fifteenth day of the same month is the feast of unleavened bread unto the LORD: seven days ye must eat unleavened bread. In the first day ye shall have an holy convocation: ye shall do no servile work therein. But ye shall offer an offering made by fire unto the LORD seven days: in the seventh day is an holy convocation: ye shall do no servile work therein. And the LORD spake unto Moses, saying, Speak unto the children of Israel, and say unto them, When ye be come into the land which I give unto you, and shall reap the harvest thereof, then ye shall bring a sheaf of the firstfruits of your harvest unto the priest: And he shall wave the sheaf before the LORD, to be accepted for you: <u>on the morrow after the sabbath</u> the priest shall wave it. And ye shall offer that day when ye wave the sheaf an he lamb without blemish of the first year for a burnt offering unto the LORD. And the meat offering thereof shall be two tenth deals of fine flour mingled with oil, an offering made by fire unto the LORD for a sweet savour: and the drink offering thereof shall be of wine, the fourth part of an hin. And ye shall eat neither bread, nor parched corn, nor green ears, until the selfsame day that ye have brought an offering unto your God: it shall be a statute for ever throughout your generations in all your dwellings.* (KJV)

The Feast of Firstfruits was the day that the priest would wave the firstfruits of the grain harvest before the Lord after Israel was in the Land. Israel could not perform this commandment in the Wilderness; it could only be performed when they entered the Land of Canaan. It was called the omer (sheaf) of the firstfruits of the barley harvest. The priest was to wave the omer 'on the morrow' following the Sabbath. The Hebrew word for 'on the morrow' is again 'mochorath,' which means 'the next day'.

Many of the religious leaders hotly debated which day this should occur because of the High Sabbath associated with the feast of Unleavened Bread. But the Sadducees [priests] believed that this Scripture was referring to the weekly Sabbath. Since the weekly Sabbath was always from sundown on Friday until sundown on Saturday, the feast of Firstfruits according to them always occurred on the next day, which was Sunday. When the feast of Firstfruits was observed after this manner, it had a fixed day of the week, but not a fixed day of the month of Nisan.

The Pharisees interpreted that the 'morrow after the Sabbath,' when the feast of Firstfruits was to be observed, was referring to the day after the High Sabbath or convocation of the 15th of Nisan, the first day of the feast of Unleavened Bread.[28] Therefore it didn't matter which day of the week the 15th of Nisan came. The feast of Firstfruits according to the Pharisees should always occur on the day after, the 16th of Nisan. Whereas the Sadducees had a fixed day of the week (Sunday) and not day of the month, the Pharisees had a fixed day of the month (Nisan 16) and not day of the week.

The Pharisees did their own ritual in collecting the firstfruits outside the Temple. The Talmud tells of the Pharisees' ceremony that had incorporated some rituals that were directly aimed toward the Sadducees to show publicly that they were wrong in their interpretation of the Firstfruits always being on Sunday after the weekly Sabbath.[29]

Who was right - the Sadducees or the Pharisees? This writer believes that in this particular instance the Pharisees were right and the Firstfruits of the Barley Harvest was to be observed always on Nisan 16th, the day after Nisan 15th, the High Sabbath of Unleavened Bread. We have the evidence of the manna being ceased by God on Nisan 16 when Israel crossed the Jordan and entered the Promised Land. The connection is the waving of the barley firstfruits, so that the new grain of the Land can be consumed. On Nisan 15, they could only eat of the old grain of the Land.

The Firstfruits ceremony was called Yom Bikkurim [Day of Firstfruits] or Sfirat Haomer. Since it comes on the heels of the major festival of Passover, both Jews and Christians often over-look it. Sfirat Haomer literally means 'the Counting of the Sheaf'. The barley is the earliest harvest that occurs in Israel. It was the perfect time to offer the grain offering to the Lord in the Temple. The message was loud and clear: If God has been faithful to bless us with this early harvest, he will most certainly provide the harvest of later summer.

The sheaf of the barley Firstfruits was brought to the Azarah of the Temple. The barley was threshed out with reeds so that none of the grains were crushed. Then the barley was winnowed. The barley grains were then placed into a special container, a perforated pan. The pan was passed over a fire where each of the kernels was to be touched by the fire. After the grains had been roasted, they were laid out on the floor for the wind to cool them. Then they were ground into meal. The barley meal was then sifted. There was a series of thirteen sieves each succeeding one finer than the other. The grains passed through the sieves until the Temple Treasurer could put his hands in the flour and none of it would adhere to his fingers. The barley flour is refined to the greatest degree to be presented to the Lord.

After adding oil and frankincense, the barley flour was baked into a loaf of bread. Remember that no leaven is used because this first-fruits offering is during the Festival of Unleavened Bread. Leaven is symbolic of sin, so the refined barley flour is symbolic of perfection without sin. A handful of the dough was taken and burned on the altar. The dough was also waved before the Lord. The priest would wave it forward and backwards, and then up and down called tenufah. The bread was finally made with four corners projecting upward.[30]

The firstfruits of the Barley Harvest represent the crudest of grains being changed into flour to become food for the people. It represents growth and life coming from the death of the seed in the ground. The grain being sifted into purity represents perfection.

The Counting of the Omer

We have previously studied the sacrifice of the Passover lamb in Egypt as occurring at approximately 3:00 P.M. on Nisan 13. The Egyptian Passover meal was held in the evening of Nisan 14. Israel left Egypt more than twenty-four hours later on Nisan 15th, the first day of the festival of Unleavened Bread. The firstfruits of the barley could only be waved when Israel came into the Land. Therefore, the Firstfruits ceremony was not held when they came out of Egypt until they entered the Land during the time of Joshua. In the Land Israel was to count forty-nine days of the Omer of barley:

Leviticus 23:15-17 *And ye shall count unto you from the morrow after the sabbath [Sunday], from the day that ye brought the sheaf of the wave offering [The firstfruits of the barley harvest]; seven sabbaths shall be complete [49 days]: Even unto the morrow after the seventh sabbath shall ye number fifty days [Pentecost]; and ye shall offer a new meat offering unto the LORD. Ye shall bring out of your habitations two wave loaves of two tenth deals: they shall be of fine flour; they shall be baken with leaven; they are the firstfruits unto the LORD.* (KJV)

The offering brought to the priest at the start of the Omer was meal ground from the barley grain, a raw material representing the base food for animals. After the forty-nine days of the counting of the Barley Omer [when Israel was in the Land], leavened wheat was offered on Shavuot [Pentecost, the fiftieth day]. Shavuot commemorates Israel receiving the Torah at Mt. Sinai in the Wilderness.

Israel was to evaluate their behavior and work to improve themselves, particularly by being more faithful to God and dedicated to His ways, more humble, and unified with all other believers. The counting of the Omer period was the time when Israel's soul was cleansed and provided with its spiritual sustenance.[31] The counting of the Omer was also a time to cleanse Israel from all encrustations of evil and contamination.[32] The rabbis wrote much about these forty-nine days of the Omer as symbolic to Israel's repentance, sanctification and purification.[33]

Individually, the forty-nine days of the counting of the Omer symbolically represent the purification of one's soul. It is a time that the flesh should come under subjection to the spiritual. When other believers enter into the same level of purity, unmatched unity in each other and God is the result. The sages devised a construct to help the people in this matter. It is based on seven Divine qualities.

These seven Divine qualities were personified in seven Shepherds and each shepherd was emphasized for one full week [seven days] of the total forty-nine days of the counting of the Omer. The first week was personified with Abraham and loving-kindness. The second week was personified with Isaac and strength. The third week was personified with Jacob and glory. The fourth week was personified with Moses and eternity. The fifth week was personified with Aaron and holiness. The sixth week was personified with Joseph and moral virtue. And, finally the seventh week was personified with David and sovereignty.[34]

The sages of old taught when Israel came out of Egypt that a forty-nine day period was needed before they stood before Mt. Sinai to receive the Torah. Through this period Israel gradually improved adding each of the seven virtues until finally they achieved complete sovereignty as a kingdom of priests and a holy nation to the rest of the world. It was on the fiftieth day, Shavuot, when the eternal Torah sanctified them.[35]

The counting of the Omer is to be a stairway ascending to the festival of Shavuot, exactly fifty days after the Firstfruits of the Barley Harvest, which occurred at the festival of Unleavened Bread. Coming to Shavuot should be looked at as coming to the Mountain of God [Mt. Sinai] to receive His Torah and the power to live Holy before a Holy God while awaiting bodily resurrection. The forty-nine days of the counting of the Omer is listed in the Torah with the festivals because they connect Passover with Shavuot. The sages called Shavuot the Atzeret [conclusion] of Passover. Passover initiated the seven days of the festival of Unleavened Bread and the forty-nine days of the counting of the Omer connected them to Shavuot. These forty-nine days were understood to be a prolonged chol ha-mo'ed [intermediate day] of one long festival season. Shavuot, therefore, was viewed as the eighth and concluding day of Passover [Unleavened Bread].[36]

In Hebraic mystical thought the forty-nine days of the counting of the Omer were viewed as the courting days of a bridegroom with his bride. The picture in symbols is very clear. God chose His Bride

Israel at the Passover in Egypt, which He bought with a price. The forty-nine day period in the wilderness was Israel's courting relationship with God before He married her on the fiftieth day, Shavuot.

Preparation for Shavuot [Pentecost] at Mt. Sinai

The release from physical bondage alone at Passover was not spiritual freedom. True spiritual freedom involves the discipline to achieve it, which means being able to control the natural desire for immediate gratification that can distract. Passover offers physical freedom, but Shavuot offers spiritual freedom. The purpose of Israel's physical freedom at Passover was to achieve her spiritual freedom at Shavuot.

Exodus 19:1-3 *In the third month, when the children of Israel were gone forth out of the land of Egypt, the same day came they into the wilderness of Sinai. For they were departed from Rephidim, and were come to the desert of Sinai, and had pitched in the wilderness; and there Israel camped before the mount. And Moses went up unto God, and the LORD called unto him out of the mountain, saying, Thus shalt thou say to the house of Jacob, and tell the children of Israel...(KJV)*

The Sages taught that Israel arrived at Sinai as a united people, 'like one man with one heart,' and this unity was a precondition for their receiving the Torah. Their introspection and self-improvement, which the Omer counting represents, brought harmony and peace.[37] Exodus 19:2 says, 'Israel camped before the Mount,' using the Hebrew singular verb for 'camped' with the plural noun Israel. Grammatically the plural form of 'camped' should have been used. God was teaching through His Torah that Israel had become 'a single heart [soul]' through the process of the counting of the Omer.[38]

Up until this point Israel had experienced strife and division in the Wilderness. Unity was a prerequisite for the receiving of the Torah, however. Israel finally overcame the strife and embraced harmony just prior to the fiftieth day, Shavuot. The rabbis understood that the Israelites were interrelating and sharpening one another. Israel had truly become like-minded [like one person] and thus was now fit to receive the Torah.[39]

The Betrothal of Israel at Mt. Sinai on Shavuot

Although the Torah is clearly a legal covenant and constitution, there are hints that it also represents another document. Many of the sages recognized the Torah symbolically as a 'ketubah'. A ketubah is the formal written document for a marriage contract. At Mt. Sinai God represents the bridegroom and Israel His bride. Therefore, the ketubah [marriage contract] and Torah covenant are one in the same.[40]

Deuteronomy 33:4 *Moses commanded us a law [Torah], even the inheritance [heritage] of the congregation of Jacob.* (KJV)

The sages believed that the Torah was the instrument of betrothal between God and Israel. In Deuteronomy 33:4 the Torah is referred to as a 'heritage'. The rabbis taught not to read the word for 'heritage,' morashah, but as me'orasah, which means betrothal.[41]

Exodus 19:4 *Ye have seen what I did unto the Egyptians, and how I bare you on eagles' wings, and brought you unto myself.* (KJV)

Exodus 6:6-7 *Wherefore say unto the children of Israel, I am the LORD, and I will bring you out from under the burdens of the Egyptians, and I will rid you out of their bondage, and I will redeem you with a stretched out arm, and with great judgments: And I <u>will take</u> you to me for a people, and I will be to you a God: and ye shall know that I am the LORD your God, which bringeth you out from under the burdens of the Egyptians.* (KJV)

The first hint of marriage is found in Exodus 6:6-7. In this passage, God tells Moses what He intends to do for Israel through him. The verb, 'will take,' is used elsewhere in the Tanach [Old Testament] among other uses, to describe what happens when a man 'takes' a woman to be his wife. In the context of Exodus 6, then, it appears that God is betrothing Israel to be His wife. Also in Exodus 19:4 God said He had 'brought' Israel unto Himself at Mt. Sinai. Once again this is an allusion to God taking Israel for His bride.

According to traditional Jewish thinking, the wedding between God and Israel took place at Mt. Sinai. Although the Biblical text does not specify that a wedding was taking place, the similarities between the events that occurred at Mt. Sinai and a traditional Jewish wedding are striking. A deeper look at the Hebrew Scriptures does imply that a marriage ceremony took place on Mt. Sinai between God and Israel.

Exodus 19:5-6 *Now therefore, if ye will obey my voice indeed, and keep my covenant, then ye shall be a <u>peculiar treasure</u> unto me above all people: for all the earth is mine: And ye shall be unto me a kingdom of priests, and an holy nation. These are the words which thou shalt speak unto the children of Israel.* (KJV)

Exodus 19:5-6 occurs during the period that would become the counting of the Omer. Every groom has an endearing name for his bride, which reminds him of how much she means to him. God gave Israel such a name. In Exodus 19:5-7, God tells Israel that she is His 'peculiar treasure'. The Hebrew word, 'segulah,' is also found in secular texts from the same period. The ancient kings would describe how important they considered certain objects from a conquered nation by claiming it as 'segulot'. While the king valued all of his possessions, only a certain few of the treasures were especially honored as such. These especially honored objects were the king's 'segulot'. Thus, when God calls Israel His 'segulah,' it is a special term of honor. God cares for all His creation, but Israel is His special bride.[42]

Exodus 19:10, 14 *And the LORD said unto Moses, Go unto the people, and sanctify them to day and to morrow, and let them wash their clothes...And Moses went down from the mount unto the people, and sanctified the people; and they washed their clothes.* (KJV)

God commanded Moses to sanctify the people by washing their clothes. This was an act of sanctification which made them

Holy before the Lord and capable of coming into His presence. The Israelites didn't 'wash their clothes' as in doing the laundry. It was a ceremonial immersion to prepare them for their encounter with the Holy One of Israel. They immersed themselves and then individually immersed their clothes so that they would be sanctified before the Lord. Immersion was the means through which Israel originally entered into the betrothal marriage covenant with God.[43] We must also remember that a bride would immerse herself before the ceremony in the ancient Hebraic marriage.

Jeremiah 2:2-3 (KJV) *Go and cry in the ears of Jerusalem, saying, Thus saith the LORD; I remember thee, the kindness of thy youth, the love of thine espousals (Hebrew word means Betrothal), when thou wentest after me in the wilderness, in a land that was not sown. Israel was holiness unto the LORD, and the firstfruits of his increase (A term for Shavuot-Pentecost - Firstfruits of the Bikkurim): all that devour him shall offend; evil shall come upon them, saith the LORD.*

Jeremiah tells us that when Israel was betrothed to God in the Wilderness that they were the 'firstfruits of His increase,' which is a direct reference to the betrothal ceremony at Mt. Sinai on Shavuot [Firstfruits of the Wheat Harvest]. We also learned in Exodus 19 that Israel was to be a 'holy nation'. The prophet parallels Israel as 'Firstfruits of His increase' with 'Holiness unto the LORD'.

The ancient rabbis wrote that Israel as God's 'Holy Nation' meant that they were to be separate from the other nations [Gentiles]. Israel was to be like a chaste virgin set-aside for the Lord. They were to be separate, according to their writings, by not pursuing after the false gods/goddesses and idolatry of all other religions. They were to be separate by not seeking after any other groom except the Holy One of Israel. This, too, is what it means for the believers in Yeshua to be a 'Chosen Generation,' 'Peculiar People,' 'Royal Priesthood,' and a 'Holy Nation' [1 Peter 2:9]. To be separate [Holy] means to abstain from idolatry and the mixing of false religion with the worship of the One Holy God.

2 Corinthians 11:2 *For I am jealous over you with godly jealousy: for I have espoused you to one husband, that I may present you as a chaste virgin to Christ.* (KJV)

In referring to the Corinthian Ekklesia (congregation), Paul uses the same terminology. 'Espoused' here should be understood as 'Betrothed'. She is to be a 'chaste virgin to Messiah'. From this we can conclude that the Ekklesia-Church is betrothed to Yeshua as Israel was betrothed to God. In the wilderness, Moses, the First Redeemer, immersed Israel. According to the New Tesament, the Ekklesia (congregation) is immersed into God through Yeshua.

Exodus 19:16-17 *And it came to pass on the third day in the morning, that there were thunders and lightnings, and a thick cloud upon the mount, and the voice of the trumpet exceeding loud; so that all the people that was in the camp trembled. And Moses brought forth the people out of the camp to meet with God; and they stood at the nether part (Hebrew - Tachat) of the mount.* (KJV)

Moses brought Israel to Mt. Sinai 'on the third day'. This was after they had immersed themselves and it was the third day from Sivan 3, making it Sivan 6. This was Shavuot, the fiftieth day after Israel would count the Omer when they came into the Land.

Now we turn our attention to Exodus 19:17 where the KJV states that Moses brought the people to the 'nether part' of Mt. Sinai. Other versions say that he brought Israel to the 'foot' of the mountain. But the Hebrew word for 'nether part' or 'foot' is 'tachat,' which literally means 'underneath' the mountain. The KJV of Deuteronomy 4:11 gets it right when it states, 'And ye came near and stood under (Hebrew tachat) the mountain; and the mountain burned with fire unto the midst of heaven, with darkness, clouds, and thick darkness'. Mt. Sinai then was the real Chuppah or covering for the Betrothal ceremony between God and Israel. The Torah or the Betrothal Contract [Ketubah] was given from God to Israel to make her his Bride and Nation.

Exodus 19:18-19 *And mount Sinai was altogether on a smoke, because the LORD descended upon it in fire: and the smoke thereof ascended as the smoke of a furnace, and the whole mount quaked greatly. And when the voice of the trumpet sounded long, and waxed louder and louder, Moses spake, and God answered him by a voice.* (KJV)

There were tremendous signs associated with the giving of the Torah/Covenant/Betrothal Contract (ketubah) at Mt. Sinai. Of course this day took place on Shavuot, which God commanded all of Israel to celebrate as a feast every year as the Firstfruits of the Wheat Harvest, fifty days after the Firstfruits of the Barley Harvest (which occurred during the Festival of Unleavened Bread). There was smoke and fire and trembling at Mt. Sinai with a trumpet (Shofar - ram's horn) sounding louder and louder.

Deuteronomy 4:11-15 *And ye came near and stood under the moun-tain; and the mountain burned with fire unto the midst of heaven, with darkness, clouds, and thick darkness. And the LORD spake unto you out of the midst of the fire: ye heard the voice of the words, but saw no similitude; only ye heard a voice. And he declared unto you his covenant, which he commanded you to perform, even ten commandments; and he wrote them upon two tables of stone. And the LORD commanded me at that time to teach you statutes and judgments, that ye might do them in the land whither ye go over to possess it. Take ye therefore good heed unto yourselves; for ye saw no manner of similitude on the day that the LORD spake unto you in Horeb [another name for Sinai] out of the midst of the fire:* (KJV)

After God gave Israel the Betrothal Covenant there were more signs of thundering, lightning, the mountain smoking and the noise of the shofar. It is interesting to recount some Jewish Midrashim that discuss the giving of the Torah at Mount Sinai on that Shavuot (Pentecost).

According to Exodus Rabbah 5.9:

When God gave the Torah on Sinai, He displayed untold marvels to Israel with His voice. What happened? God spoke and the Voice reverberated throughout the world...It says, And all the people witnessed the thunderings (Exodus 20:15). Note that it does not say 'the thunder,' but 'the thunderings;' wherefore Rabbi Johanan said that God's voice, as it was uttered, split up into 70 voices, in 70 languages, so that all the nations should understand. When each nation heard the Voice in their own vanacular their souls departed [i.e., they were in fear], save Israel who heard but who were not hurt...[44]

In the book The Midrash Says, by Rabbi Moshe Weissman, the author wrote:

In the occasion of Matan Torah [the giving of the Torah], the Bnai Yisrael [children of Israel] not only heard Hashem's [the Lord's] Voice but actually saw the sound waves as they emerged from Hashem's [the Lord's] mouth. They visualized them as a fiery substance. Each commandment that left Hashem's [the Lord's] mouth traveled around the entire Camp and then to each Jew individually, asking him, 'Do you accept upon yourself this Commandment with all the halochot [Jewish law] pertaining to it?' Every Jew answered 'Yes' after each commandment. Finally, the fiery substance which they saw engraved itself on the luchot [tablets].[45]

Hebrews 12:18-19 *For ye are not come unto the mount (Sinai) that might be touched, and that burned with fire, nor unto blackness, and darkness, and tempest, And the sound of a trumpet, and the voice of words (plural - Greek Rhema); which voice they that heard entreated that the word should not be spoken to them any more:* (KJV)

Most Christians would outright reject these Midrashim quoted above as religious fiction. But the New Testament book of Hebrews confirms these Midrashim. In speaking of the signs associated with the giving of the Torah at Mt. Sinai, the writer of Hebrews mentions 'the voice of words,' a quote from Deuteronomy 4:12. The Greek word interpreted as 'words' is 'Rhema'. In this instance it is in the plural - Rhemas. Rhema is defined as the 'individual voice of God spoken to an individual'. In other words, Israel heard 'the voice of words (tongues or languages)' at Mt. Sinai at the giving of the Torah on Shavuot (Pentecost). One singular voice of God was being heard as many voices.

Deuteronomy 32:8 *When the Most High divided to the nations their inheritance, when he separated the sons of Adam, he set the bounds of the people according to the number of the children of Israel [Jacob].* (KJV)

Genesis 46:26-27 *All the souls that came with Jacob into Egypt, which came out of his loins, besides Jacob's sons' wives, all the souls were threescore and six; And the sons of Joseph, which were born him in Egypt, were two souls: all the souls of the house of Jacob, which came into Egypt, were threescore and ten [70].* (KJV)

Exodus 1:5 *And all the souls that came out of the loins of Jacob were seventy souls: for Joseph was in Egypt already.* (KJV)

Deuteronomy 10:22 *Thy fathers went down into Egypt with three-score and ten persons [70]; and now the LORD thy God hath made thee as the stars of heaven for multitude.* (KJV)

The concept of seventy nations speaking seventy languages is biblically based upon the number of 'souls' that came from the loins of Jacob [Israel] when they sojourned to Egypt. Exactly sixty-six came down from the land of Canaan and we are told to add Joseph and his two sons, who were already in Egypt, to make a grand total of sixty nine. But the Torah says there were seventy souls?

The majority of the sages stated that Levi's wife conceived a daughter named Yochebed on the way to Egypt accounting for the one missing in Genesis 46. However, this is never actually mentioned in the written Torah. Other rabbinic sources claim that God went down with them into Egypt and He is the seventieth.[46] Since the Messiah is the Promised Seed of Abraham, Isaac and Jacob, the seventieth person could be a reference to Him being in the loins of Jacob [through Judah], when they came down to Egypt.

In Deuteronomy 32:8 the Scripture tells us that God divided the boundaries of nations 'according to the number of the children of Israel [Jacob]'. Seventy nations were created that would later mimic the number of Jacob's offspring who went into Egypt.[47] But the origin of the seventy nations with seventy basic languages goes back to the Tower of Babel in Genesis 11, according to rabbinic tradition. God divided the people into seventy different nations with their appropriate languages after the incident at Babel. Up until this time all the people had originally spoke Hebrew, which was also the language before the Flood.[48] Jewish tradition states that God came down to the Tower of Babel on Shavuot to confuse the language. Also, the Scripture makes it clear that the people were trying to accomplish a 'false' unity against the purposes of God.

BIBLIOGRAPHY

1. Gesenius' Hebrew-Chaldee Lexicon to the Old Testament. H.W.F. Gesenius. Baker Books, Grand Rapids, MI, 1979. Page 399.

2. Jewish Wedding Guide: Made in Heaven. Rabbis Aryeh Kaplan. Moznaim Publishing Corporation, New York, Jerusalem, 1983. Pages 78,79,99,150.

3. Yalkut Me'am Lo'ez - The Torah Anthology: Exodus Volume 2 [book 5 in the series]. Translated by Rabbi Aryeh Kaplan. Moznaim Publishing Corporation, New York, Jerusalem, 1979. Page 38.

4. Artscroll Judaica Series - Tz'enah Ur'enah - The Weekly Midrash - Volume 1 Genesis-Exodus. Edited by Rabbi Nosson Scherman & Rabbi Neir Zlotowitz. Mesorah Publications, Ltd., Brooklyn, New York, 1983. Page 349.

5. Yalkut Me'am Lo'ez - The Torah Anthology: Exodus Volume 2 [book 5 in the series]. Translated by Rabbi Aryeh Kaplan. Moznaim Publishing Corporation, New York, Jerusalem, 1979. Page 52.

6. The JPS Torah Commentary: Exodus. Commentary by Nahum M. Sarna. The Jewish Publication Society, Philadelphia, New York, Jerusalem, 1991. Page 55.

7. Pentateuch and Haftorahs. Dr. J H Hertz. Soncino Press, 1997. Page 254

8. The Works of Josephus - The Wars of the Jews Book 6, Chapter 9, Section 3. Translated by William Whiston, A.M. Hendrickson Publishers, Peabody, Massachusetts, 1987. Page 749.

9. The JPS Torah Commentary - Exodus. Nahum M. Sarna. The Jewish Publication Society, Philadelphia, New York, Jerusalem, 1991. Page 57.

10. Which Day is the Passover? Phinehas Ben Zadok. Page 27.

11. Christ in the Passover: Why is this night different? Ceil and Moishe Rosen. Moody Press, Chicago, 1978. Page 22.

12. Pentateuch and Haftorahs. Dr. J H Hertz. Soncino Press, 1997. Page 217

13. Jewish Wedding Guide: Made in Heaven. Rabbis Aryeh Kaplan. Moznaim Publishing Corporation, New York, Jerusalem, 1983. Page 46.

14. The Artscroll Tanach Series - Bereishis [Genesis] Volume 1b. Translation and Commentary by Rabbi Meir Zlotowitz. Mesorah Publications, Ltd., Brooklyn, New York, 1977. Pages 2226-2228.

15. The Book of Our Heritage - Volume 2. Eliyahu Kitov. Feldheim Publishers, New York, Jerusalem, 1968. Page 701.

16. The Artscroll Tanach Series -Tehillim [Psalms 73-150]. Commentary by Rabbi Avrohom Chaim Feuer. Mesorah Publications, Ltd., Brooklyn, New York, 1977. Page 1613.

17. The Complete WordStudy New Testament. Spiros Zodhiates, Th. D. World Bible Publishers, Inc., Iowa Falls, Iowa 1992. Page 945.

18. Vine's Amplified Expository Dictionary of New Testament Words. W.E. Vine. World Bible Publishers, Inc., Iowa Falls, Iowa, 1991. Page 856.

19.   The JPS Torah Commentary: Exodus. Commentary by Nahum M. Sarna. The Jewish Publication Society, Philadelphia, New York, Jerusalem, 1991. Page 74.

20.   The New Manners and Customs of Bible Times. Ralph Gower. Moody Press, Chicago, 1987. Page 46.

21.   The Biblical and Historical Background of the Jewish Holy Days. Abraham P. Bloch. KTAV Publishing House, Inc., New York, 1978. Pages 112-113.

22.   The Artscroll Tanach Series -Tehillim [Psalms 73-150]. Commentary by Rabbi Avrohom Chaim Feuer. Mesorah Publications, Ltd., Brooklyn, New York, 1977. Page 980.

23.   Ibid. Pages 980-81.

24.   The Biblical and Historical Background of the Jewish Holy Days. Abraham P. Bloch. KTAV Publishing House, Inc., New York, 1978. Pages 112.

25.   Gesenius' Hebrew-Chaldee Lexicon to the Old Testament. H.W.F.Gesenius. Baker Books, Grand Rapids, Michigan, 1979. Page 4280.

26.   Yalkut Me'am Lo'ez - The Torah Anthology: Exodus Volume 2 [book 5 in the series]. Translated by Rabbi Aryeh Kaplan. Moznaim Publishing Corporation, New York, Jerusalem, 1979. Page 276.

27.   The Biblical and Historical Background of the Jewish Holy Days. Abraham P. Bloch. KTAV Publishing House, Inc., New York, 1978. Pages 103.

28.   Pentateuch and Haftorahs. Dr. J H Hertz. Soncino Press, 1997. Page 520

29.   Yalkut Me'am Lo'ez - The Torah Anthology: Leviticus Volume 2 [book 12 in the series]. Translated by Rabbi Aryeh Kaplan. Moznaim Publishing Corporation, New York, Jerusalem, 1990. Page 159.

30.   Ibid. Pages 159-160.

31.   The Book Of Our Heritage: The Jewish Year And Its Days Of Significance - Volume 2. Eliyahu Kitov. Feldheim Publishers, Jerusalem, New York, 1997. Page 687.

32. Pesach: Its Observance, Laws And Significance - Artscroll Mesorah Series. Mesorah Publications, Ltd. Brooklyn, New York, 1994. Page 86.

33. Shavuos: Its Observance, Laws And Significance - Artscroll Mesorah Series. Mesorah Publications, Ltd. Brooklyn, New York, 1995. Page 34.

34. The Book Of Our Heritage: The Jewish Year And Its Days Of Significance - Volume 2. Eliyahu Kitov. Feldheim Publishers, Jerusalem, New York, 1997. Page 683-685.

35. Ibid. Page 686.

36. The Book Of Our Heritage: The Jewish Year And Its Days Of Significance - Volume 3. Eliyahu Kitov. Feldheim Publishers, Jerusalem, New York, 1997. Page 772-773.

37. Shavuos: Its Observance, Laws And Significance - Artscroll Mesorah Series. Mesorah Publications, Ltd. Brooklyn, New York, 1995. Page 35.

38. The Book Of Our Heritage: The Jewish Year And Its Days Of Significance - Volume 3. Eliyahu Kitov. Feldheim Publishers, Jerusalem, New York, 1997. Page 761.

39. Shavuos: Its Observance, Laws And Significance - Artscroll Mesorah Series. Mesorah Publications, Ltd. Brooklyn, New York, 1995. Page 85.

40. Seasons Of Our Joy. Arthur Waskow. Beacon Press, Boston, Massachusetts, 1982. Page 187.

41. The Book Of Our Heritage: The Jewish Year And Its Days Of Significance - Volume 3. Eliyahu Kitov. Feldheim Publishers, Jerusalem, New York, 1997. Page 761.

42. Torah Rediscovered. Ariel and D'vorah Berkowitz. First Fruits of Zion, Littleton, Colorado, 1996. Page 12.

43. The Aryeh Kaplan Anthology II. Mesorah Publications, Ltd., Brooklyn, New York, 1997. Page 331-332.

44. The Shavuot Anthology. Philip Goodman. The Jewish Publication Society, Philadelphia, Jerusalem, 1974. Pages 46-47.

45. The Midrash Says on Shemot. Rabbi Moshe Weissman. Benei Yakov Publications, New York, 1980. Page 182.

46. Yalkut Me'am Lo'ez - The Torah Anthology: Genesis Volume 4 [book 3b in the series]. Translated by Rabbi Aryeh Kaplan. Moznaim Publishing Corporation, New York, Jerusalem, 1991. Page 471-472.

47. Yalkut Me'am Lo'ez - The Torah Anthology: Deuteronomy Volume 5 [book 19 in the series]. Translated by Rabbi Eliyahu Touger. Moznaim Publishing Corporation, New York, Jerusalem, 1991. Page 101.

48. Yalkut Me'am Lo'ez - The Torah Anthology: Deuteronomy Volume 5 [book 19 in the series]. Translated by Rabbi Eliyahu Touger. Moznaim Publishing Corporation, New York, Jerusalem, 1991. Page 101.

6

ISRAEL'S DIVORCE & BETROTHAL RENEWAL

Israel's Divorce

Galatians 3:7-9 *Know ye therefore that they which are of faith, the same are the children of Abraham. And the scripture, foreseeing that God would justify the heathen through faith, <u>preached before the gospel</u> unto Abraham, saying, <u>In thee shall all nations be blessed</u>. So then they which be of faith are blessed with faithful Abraham.* (KJV)

Genesis 12:2-3 *And I will make of thee a great nation, and I will bless thee, and make thy name great; and thou shalt be a blessing: And I will bless them that bless thee, and curse him that curseth thee: and <u>in thee shall all families of the earth be blessed</u>.* (KJV)

What is the Gospel defined by Scripture? The answer to this question is of major importance to correctly understand the plan of God. Most Christians believe that the Gospel did not exist until 'Jesus' showed up on the scene. This does not line up with the whole of Scripture. Another definition of the Christian Gospel is that it represents only the Good News that Yeshua has died for our sins and resurrected for believers to gain eternal life. However, this statement is not the explicit definition of the Gospel. The Gospel or 'Good News/Glad Tidings' began with Abraham as Paul clearly states that the Gospel message was preached to Abraham. The message of the Gospel is that 'in Abraham all the nations shall be blessed [through faith in God]'.

It is the 'seed' [singular seed] of Abraham, which is Messiah Yeshua, according to Paul that brings this blessing to the nations.

To understand Israel's divorce and marriage renewal, we must then understand the term 'Gospel' as used in the New Testament. These two are inseparably linked together. First we will go back to the Tanach [Old Testament] regarding the marriage relationship between God and Israel.

Exodus 19:3-6 *And Moses went up unto God, and the LORD called unto him out of the mountain, saying, Thus shalt thou say to the house of Jacob, and tell the children of Israel; Ye have seen what I did unto the Egyptians, and how I bare you on eagles' wings, and brought you unto myself. Now therefore, if ye will obey my voice indeed, and keep my covenant [Written Torah], then ye shall be a peculiar treasure unto me above all people: for all the earth is mine: And ye shall be unto me a kingdom of priests, and an holy nation. These are the words which thou shalt speak unto the children of Israel. (KJV)*

Exodus 24:3-8 *And Moses came and told the people all the words of the LORD, and all the judgments: and all the people answered with one voice, and said, All the words which the LORD hath said will we do. And Moses wrote all the words of the LORD, and rose up early in the morning, and builded an altar under the hill, and twelve pillars, according to the twelve tribes of Israel. And he sent young men of the children of Israel, which offered burnt offerings, and sacrificed peace offerings of oxen unto the LORD. And Moses took half of the blood, and put it in basons; and half of the blood he sprinkled on the altar. And he took the book of the covenant [Written Torah], and read in the audience of the people: and they said, All that the LORD hath said will we do, and be obedient. And Moses took the blood, and sprinkled it on the people, and said, Behold the blood of the covenant, which the LORD hath made with you concerning all these words. (KJV)*

We know from history that Israel did not remain faithful to their marriage contract [Torah] with God. First, there was the Golden Calf

[Exodus 32] and the Twelve Spies [Numbers 13 & 14] incidents. So God killed them off in the wilderness and brought up another generation in place of their rebellious forbears. About forty years later when this new generation was ready to possess the land of Canaan under Joshua's leadership, the original marriage covenant of Torah was once again renewed and ratified. This marriage contract applied to their particular generation and all the Israelites of future generations:

Deuteronomy 29:10-15 *Ye stand this day all of you before the LORD your God; your captains of your tribes, your elders, and your officers, with all the men of Israel, Your little ones, your wives, and thy stranger that is in thy camp, from the hewer of thy wood unto the drawer of thy water: That thou shouldest enter into covenant with the LORD thy God, and into his oath, which the LORD thy God maketh with thee this day: That he may establish thee to day for a people unto himself, and that he may be unto thee a God, as he hath said unto thee, and as he hath sworn unto thy fathers, to Abraham, to Isaac, and to Jacob. Neither with you only do I make this cove-nant and this oath; But with him that standeth here with us this day before the LORD our God, and also with him that is not here with us this day:* (KJV)

All through the book of Deuteronomy Moses attempted to convince Israel of their obligation to walk according to the Law, the marriage contract called the Torah that their fathers rejected:

Deuteronomy 5:28-33 *And the LORD heard the voice of your words, when ye spake unto me; and the LORD said unto me, I have heard the voice of the words of this people, which they have spoken unto thee: they have well said all that they have spoken. O that there were such an heart in them, that they would fear me, and keep all my commandments [Written Torah] always, that it might be well with them, and with their children for ever! Go say to them, Get you into your tents again. But as for thee, stand thou here by me, and I will speak unto thee all the commandments, and the statutes, and the judgments, which thou shalt teach them, that they may do* *them in the land which I give them to possess it. Ye shall observe to do therefore as the LORD your God hath commanded you: ye shall not turn aside to the right hand or to the left. Ye shall walk in all the ways which the LORD your God hath commanded you, that ye may live, and that it may be well with you, and that ye may prolong your days in the land which ye shall possess.* (KJV)

Moses spoke one last time to the Twelve Tribes of Israel:

Deuteronomy 30:1-5 *And it shall come to pass, when all these things are come upon thee, the blessing and the curse, which I have set before thee, and thou shalt call them to mind among all the nations, whither the LORD thy God hath driven thee, And shalt return unto the LORD thy God, and shalt obey his voice according to all that I command thee this day, thou and thy children, with all thine heart, and with all thy soul; That then the LORD thy God will turn thy captivity, and have compassion upon thee, and will return and gather thee from all the nations, whither the LORD thy God hath scattered thee. If any of thine be driven out unto the outmost parts of heaven, from thence will the LORD thy God gather thee, and from thence will he fetch thee: And the LORD thy God will bring thee into the land which thy fathers possessed, and thou shalt possess it; and he will do thee good, and multiply thee above thy fathers.* (KJV)

Although Moses tried to communicate the importance of Israel keeping the marriage contract, his prophetic side knew that she would fall short and fall out of favor with God. This led to these words as a witness to all of us forever:

Deuteronomy 31:24-30 *And it came to pass, when Moses had made an end of writing the words of this law in a book [Written Torah], until they were finished, That Moses commanded the Levites, which bare the ark of the covenant of the LORD, saying, Take this book of the law [Written Torah], and put it in the side of the ark of the covenant of the LORD your God, that it may be there for a witness against thee. For I know thy rebellion, and thy stiff neck: behold, while I am yet alive with you this day, ye have been rebellious against* *the LORD; and how much more after my death? Gather unto me all the elders of your tribes, and your officers, that I may speak these words in their ears, and call heaven and earth to record against them. For I know that after my death ye will utterly corrupt your-selves, and turn aside from the way which I have commanded you; and evil will befall you in the latter days; because ye will do evil in the sight of the LORD, to provoke him to anger through the work of your hands. And Moses spake in the ears of all the congregation of Israel the words of this song, until they were ended.* (KJV)

Exactly as Moses had spoken, Israel rebelled against God, His Law (Torah), and marriage contract. The writings of the prophets point this out. Why didn't Israel just pass away into oblivion because of their breaking of the vows? If it were not for the sanctification of the Name of the Lord and the eternal promises given to Abraham, Isaac, and Jacob, this would have happened as a natural occurrence of God's judgment as has happened to many cultures before and after Israel's existence. Despite their rebellion, Israel still remained foremost in God's heart and this will help bring us to the Biblical definition of the 'Gospel'.

Jeremiah 31:31-32 *Behold, the days come, saith the LORD, that I will make a new covenant with the house of Israel, and with the house of Judah: Not according to the covenant that I made with their fathers in the day that I took them by the hand to bring them out of the land of Egypt; which my covenant they brake, <u>although I was an husband unto them</u>, saith the LORD:* (KJV)

God was a faithful husband to both houses of Israel, even after their separation into two kingdoms after Solomon's reign. Israel was like a married woman that God uniquely had chosen for Himself.

Ezekiel 16:6-8 *And when I passed by thee, and saw thee polluted in thine own blood, I said unto thee when thou wast in thy blood, Live; yea, I said unto thee when thou wast in thy blood, Live. I have caused thee to multiply as the bud of the field, and thou hast increased and waxen great, and thou art come to excellent ornaments: thy breasts* *are fashioned, and thine hair is grown, whereas thou wast naked and bare. Now when I passed by thee, and looked upon thee, behold, thy time was the time of love; and I spread my skirt over thee, and covered thy nakedness: yea, I sware unto thee, and entered into a covenant with thee, saith the Lord GOD, and thou becamest mine.* (KJV)

Ezekiel 16 details the love God had for His special consecrated bride. But Israel was never seemingly content with receiving God's love just as Moses had prophesied. For several centuries God gave repeated warnings of love to Israel, whom He had chosen out of the midst of the nations, to cease from her spiritual adulteries and fornication. God pleaded through the prophets for Israel to return to her marriage contract, the Torah, which they had rebelled against. Of course, Israel did not heed the warnings of the Faithful Husband, so God divided the spiritual and physical unity of Israel into two camps - the northern kingdom of the ten tribes of Israel and the southern kingdom of Judah [with Benjamin]. This may have in some symbolic way followed the pattern of Jacob's two brides, Leah and Rachel, who were the Matriarchs of all Israel.

God finally divorced the ten tribes of the Northern Kingdom of Israel for their unwavering adultery and collectively gave them a divorce decree called a 'Get'. God put Israel out of His House, which was the land of Canaan. Because the southern kingdom of Judah also went and played the harlot, God had every right according to His Word to put her away also. God did send Judah into Babylonian Captivity, but because of His promise to David saying, 'your house and your kingdom shall endure before Me forever; your throne shall be established forever' [2 Samuel 7:12-17; 1 Kings 8:25; 9:5; 1 Kings 15:4-5], He kept her from assimilation into the nations. God even allowed a remnant of Judah to return to the Land and rebuild the Temple.

Hosea 2:2 *Plead with your mother, plead: for she is not my wife, neither am I her husband: let her therefore put away her whore-doms out of her sight, and her adulteries from between her breasts;* (KJV)

Jeremiah 3:8 *And I saw, when for all the causes whereby back-sliding Israel committed adultery I had put her away, and given her a bill of divorce; yet her treacherous sister Judah feared not, but went and played the harlot also.* (KJV)

God gave the Northern Kingdom of Israel a valid divorce decree. Israel was no longer considered God's bride for she had no husband. Israel, being divorced, was free to attach herself [marry] to another religious ideology although she remained in judgment from God. However, the Southern Kingdom of Judah, although a harlot, remained married to God as a bride only because of God's favor and the merit of Abraham, Isaac, Jacob, and no less David.

It is at this point many could get confused in trying to unravel the Biblical record. The promise to the patriarchs was also given to all the Twelve Tribes through Moses. The prophets prophesied that all Israel [including Judah] would be God's beloved bride by being called by His Name. Also, God even swore an oath by His Name that these things would occur, thus making His promises irrevocable as the writer of Hebrews pointed out from Genesis 22:17, and recorded in Hebrews 6:13-14:

Hebrews 6:13-14 *For when God made promise to Abraham, because he could swear by no greater, he sware by himself, Saying, Surely blessing I will bless thee, and multiplying I will multiply thee.* (KJV)

This raises a fair question as to how the irrevocable promises of God can be fulfilled when more than half of 'the Bride' had been given a certificate of divorce and thrown out for her adultery? We have a picture of God's plan through the life and words of the prophet Hosea who prophesied to the Northern Kingdom of Israel. God chose Hosea to be a symbolic picture of steadfast love, eternal promise, and complete redemption for the Northern Kingdom who are called the 'lost sheep' of the House of Israel.

Hosea 1:2-10 *The beginning of the word of the LORD by Hosea. And the LORD said to Hosea, Go, take unto thee a wife of whoredoms* *and children of whoredoms: for the land hath committed great whoredom, departing from the LORD. So he went and took Gomer the daughter of Diblaim; which conceived, and bare him a son. And the LORD said unto him, Call his name Jezreel; for yet a little while, and I will avenge the blood of Jezreel upon the house of Jehu, and will cause to cease the kingdom of the house of Israel. And it shall come to pass at that day, that I will break the bow of Israel in the valley of Jezreel. And she conceived again, and bare a daughter. And God said unto him, Call her name Loruhamah: for I will no more have mercy upon the house of Israel; but I will utterly take them away. But I will have mercy upon the house of Judah, and will save them by the LORD their God, and will not save them by bow, nor by sword, nor by battle, by horses, nor by horsemen. Now when she had weaned Loruhamah, she conceived, and bare a son. Then said God, Call his name Loammi: for ye are not my people, and I will not be your God. Yet the number of the children of Israel shall be as the sand of the sea, which cannot be measured nor numbered; and it shall come to pass, that in the place where it was said unto them, Ye are not my people, there it shall be said unto them, Ye are the sons of the living God.* (KJV)

God commanded Hosea to take a whore to be his wife. This prophecy definitely has a two-edged aspect to it with one clearly being judgment and the other mercy. We must remember that it is not because Israel deserves God's mercy, but because of irreversible promises of God to Abraham, Isaac, and Jacob. God's purpose for this great display of mercy on His part was to draw all Israel unto repentance. From the Scriptures, we are able to see the results of such an unending love:

Hosea 2:7 *And she shall follow after her lovers, but she shall not overtake them; and she shall seek them, but shall not find them: then shall she say, I will go and return to my first husband; for then was it better with me than now.* (KJV)

Hosea 2:16-20 *And it shall be at that day [Hebraism for Messianic times], saith the LORD, that thou shalt call me Ishi; and shalt call* *me no more Baali. For I will take away the names of Baalim out of her mouth, and they shall no more be remembered by their name. And in that day will I make a covenant for them with the beasts of the field, and with the fowls of heaven, and with the creeping things of the ground: and I will break the bow and the sword and the battle out of the earth, and will make them to lie down safely. And I will betroth [aras] thee unto me for ever; yea, I will betroth [aras] thee unto me in righteousness, and in judgment, and in lovingkindness, and in mercies. I will even betroth [aras] thee unto me in faithfulness: and thou shalt know [intimately in marriage] the LORD.* (KJV)

It is interesting that God speaks about a betrothal in Hosea 2, represented by the Hebrew word 'aras.' Why would God betroth Israel in the future when He already betrothed her in the wilderness? The Northern Kingdom of Israel is not married to God in this prophecy because she is already divorced. This is why the point of a future betrothal is mentioned. Once rejected, Israel would return in the future and be accepted as a people to God.

Jeremiah 31:31-32 *Behold, the days come, saith the LORD, that I will make a new covenant with the house of Israel, and with the house of Judah: Not according to the covenant that I made with their fathers in the day that I took them by the hand to bring them out of the land of Egypt; which my covenant they brake, although I was an husband unto them, saith the LORD:* (KJV)

The prophecy of the New Covenant given by Jeremiah is to be fulfilled ultimately with the house of Israel and the house of Judah. The two will be united as one again, being the holy bride of God. But how is all this possible according to the Scripture?

Understanding the New Covenant as Betrothal

Deuteronomy 24:1-4 *When a man hath taken a wife, and married her, and it come to pass that she find no favour in his eyes, because he hath found some uncleanness in her: then let him write her a bill of divorcement, and give it in her hand, and send her out of his* *house. And when she is departed out of his house, she may go and be another man's wife. And if the latter husband hate her, and write her a bill of divorcement, and giveth it in her hand, and sendeth her out of his house; or if the latter husband die, which took her to be his wife; Her former husband, which sent her away, may not take her again to be his wife, after that she is defiled; for that is abomination before the LORD: and thou shalt not cause the land to sin, which the LORD thy God giveth thee for an inheritance.* (KJV)

A 'Get' (Bill of Divorce) that occurred only after the Betrothal marriage had different legalities than a 'Get' occurring after Nesuin marriage. Those Hebrew couples that had reached the second stage of Nesuin marriage and then divorced were not allowed by the Scriptures to marry each other again. The reason was that they had already engaged in marital relations [Deuteronomy 24:1-4]. The Scripture says, 'When a man hath taken a wife, and marries her'. A husband is marrying his wife twice. He has already taken a wife in betrothal and now he is marrying her in full Nesuin marriage. So this prohibition only applies where the marriage has reached Nesuin and not Erusin [betrothal].

It was an ancient part of Jewish law based upon these Torah verses that a couple only betrothed (meaning they haven't had marital relations nor lived together) could get divorced and eventually come back together again. In other words, Israel as a divorced betrothed bride, could be betrothed to God again, if she repented and changed her ways and desired to be faithful to the marriage contract, the Torah and God.

Yeshua came to Judah [still married to God, but unfaithful] in the first century pleading with the Jews to repent [to return to the Torah/Marriage Contract] and enter the Kingdom of God. God had sent Yeshua to persuade the betrothed bride to return to Him. Collectively the Jewish nation had drifted far away from God and did not heed the call.

Matthew 23:37-39 *O Jerusalem, Jerusalem, thou that killest the prophets, and stonest them which are sent unto thee, how often would I have gathered thy children together, even as a hen gathereth* *her chickens under her wings, and ye would not! Behold, your house is left unto you desolate. For I say unto you, Ye shall not see me henceforth, till ye shall say, Blessed is he that cometh in the name of the Lord.* (KJV)

Jeremiah 22:5 *But if ye will not hear these words, I swear by myself, saith the LORD, that this house shall become a desolation.* (KJV)

Psalm 118:26 *Blessed be he that cometh in the name of the LORD: we have blessed you out of the house of the LORD.* (KJV)

After three and a half years of ministry, Yeshua realized that Judah collectively had rejected Him. It was the day before His death that Yeshua gave His last words spoken in public for all ears to hear: the lament of Matthew 23:37-39. Here we see His heart of compassion for the people of Jerusalem. He alludes to the passage in Jeremiah 22:5 which says, 'If you do not hear these words...this House shall become a desolation'. It was a sad allusion toward the coming destruction of Jerusalem and desolation of the Temple.

As Yeshua makes His final exit from the Temple, He announces that He will not return until that day when Israel proclaims Baruch Haba b'Shem Adonai (Blessed is He who comes in the Name of the LORD)! These words are the same Messianic acclamation that accompanied His triumphal entry a few short days earlier. He alludes, then, to another triumphal entry at the time of Mashiach ben David's [Kingly Messiah] coming. The words, 'Blessed is He Who Comes in the Name of the LORD' is a formula from Jewish wedding custom, spoken when the groom enters the chuppah (Marriage canopy) to be wed to His bride.[1] When the bride and groom meet under the chuppah for the nesuin-marriage, Psalm 118 is read. The message was clear! Judah would not see their Messiah until the nesuin marriage when Israel as a whole had repented and entered the Kingdom of God.

The New Covenant is Really The Renewed Covenant [Torah/Law]

Now we need to continue with the study of the Torah in relationship to the New Covenant. Most Christians don't realize that the Greek translated as 'New Testament' actually means 'New Covenant'. How does the Torah relate to the New Covenant? Is it true as most Christian scholars interpret, that the New Covenant has replaced the Old Covenant (just as some believe that the Church has replaced Israel)? Or is there a relationship between the Torah and the New Covenant that many believers have failed to recognize? There are many examples from history that show how covenants and national constitutions have been modified or amended. For example, consider the Bill of Rights, which are amendments to the United States Constitution. Lawmakers don't replace the entire Constitution they only update it. The New Covenant does not do away with the Torah Covenant from Mt. Sinai, but amends it.

The Hebrew verb 'new,' 'chadash' ש ד ח is the same word that is used for the 'renewal' of the moon every thirty days. Of course, this is called a month. But in Hebrew, 'month' and 'new' contain the same root, 'chadash'. But do we get a brand-new moon every month that replaces the former? Absolutely not! The appearance of the new moon is only 'renewed'. Likewise, the New Covenant is not a brand-new, never before existing covenant. Rather, it is an amended and renewed covenant to account for the completed work of Messiah.[2]

We have already seen that Moses renewed the Torah Covenant with the generation that entered into the Promised Land. When a covenant was renewed, the stipulations were sometimes altered to fit the needs of the generation that was renewing the covenant. However, a renewal does not set aside the original covenant, it expands, adapts, and updates it for the current reality. Jeremiah intended the New Covenant to be understood as a 'Renewed Covenant'. In retrospect the New Covenant promises in Jeremiah 31 are actually the same promises that God had previously made to Israel:

Jeremiah 31:31-33 *Behold, the days come, saith the LORD, that I will make a <u>new covenant </u>with the house of Israel, and with the house of Judah: Not according to the covenant that I made with their fathers in the day that I took them by the hand to bring them out of the land of Egypt; which my covenant they brake, although I was an husband unto them, saith the LORD: But this shall be the covenant that I will make with the house of Israel; After those days, saith the LORD, I will put my <u>law [Hebrew Torah] </u>in their inward parts, and write it in their hearts; and will be their God, and they shall be my people.* (KJV)

1. God's Torah - Jeremiah 31:33
2. 'I will be their God and they will be My people' Jeremiah 31:33 (Exodus 6:7)
3. 'They will know the Lord' - Jeremiah 31:34 (Exodus 6:7)
4. Forgiveness of sin - Jeremiah 31:34 (Exodus 34:6-7)
5. Creation of a new heart - Jeremiah 31:33 (Deuteronomy 30:6)

So how can we call the New Covenant brand new? The book of Hebrews mentions that it was necessary to make some adjustments because of the new situation that the believers in Yeshua found themselves:

Hebrews 8:7-9 *For if that first covenant had been faultless, then should no place have been sought for the second. For finding fault with them, he saith, Behold, the days come, saith the Lord, when I will make a new covenant with the house of Israel and with the house of Judah: Not according to the covenant that I made with their fathers in the day when I took them by the hand to lead them out of the land of Egypt; because they continued not in my covenant, and I regarded them not, saith the Lord.* (KJV)

Many teachers understand Hebrews 8:7 as stating that there was a fault with the first covenant [Torah-Law-Marriage Contract] and a new covenant was needed to replace it. This is like saying that God messed up with the Torah-Law and had to figure out how to make His plan work a different way. Other New Testament Scriptures refer to the Law-Torah as Holy and Righteous. How could something that was determined as Holy and Righteous from God be flawed? The problem, or fault, was not found in the contents or terms of the covenant. But as Hebrews 8:8 says, God 'found fault with them'. These 'people' were those of Jeremiah's day (and before), when the revelation of the Renewed Covenant was given.

Hebrews 4:2 *For unto us was the gospel preached, as well as unto them: but the word preached did not profit them, not being mixed with faith in them that heard it.* (KJV)

The 'Gospel' had been available through the Abrahamic and Mosaic covenants, but because of their lack of faith Israel did not realize or embrace those truths. There was nothing wrong with the marriage covenant that God offered all of Israel. The people who failed the covenant were stubborn and hardhearted toward God.

Luke 22:20 *Likewise also the cup after supper, (Yeshua) saying, This cup is the new testament [Greek - Covenant] in my blood, which is shed for you.* (KJV)

Yeshua announced the New Covenant to His disciples, who were all Jewish, at His last Passover. This covenant was the fulfillment of the New Covenant prophesied by Jeremiah, but in Yeshua's day only a remnant believed in their 'hearts' that Yeshua was the Messiah of the New Covenant.[3]

The Mishnah states that the third cup of the four during the Passover Seder was the most significant. This third cup had two names: 'the cup of blessing,' named after the blessing after the meal, and 'the cup of redemption,' representing the blood of the Passover lamb.[4]

John 14:1-6 *Let not your heart be troubled: ye believe in God, believe also in me. In my Father's house are many mansions: if it were not so, I would have told you. I go to prepare a place for you. And if I go and prepare a place for you, I will come again, and receive you unto myself; that where I am, there ye may be also. And* *whither I go ye know, and the way ye know. Thomas saith unto him, Lord, we know not whither thou goest; and how can we know the way? Jesus saith unto him, I am the way, the truth, and the life: no man cometh unto the Father, but by me.* (KJV)

Although the 'cup of redemption' is not mentioned in John 13, it is very clear from the context that it is the same account of the other Gospel's 'last Passover' of Yeshua with His disciples, but from a different perspective. When we come to John 14, we are still at the Passover Seder with Yeshua speaking words to His students. When Yeshua says, 'I go to prepare a place for you. And if I go and prepare a place for you, I will come again, and receive you unto myself,' it is clearly a picture of the Jewish Betrothal marriage ceremony. When He says, 'I am the way, the truth, and the life,' He was talking about the Torah. The ancient Jewish writings speak of the Torah as 'the Way,' 'the Truth,' and 'the Life'. Yeshua was claiming that He was the Living Renewed Torah.

In the Betrothal ceremony it was customary for the parties to share a cup of wine after agreeing on the Shitre Ureshin (The Betrothal Contract). It appears that Yeshua is associating the third cup of wine at the Passover Seder (The cup of redemption) to a Shitre Ureshin. If this is the case then Yeshua was fulfilling the making of the Renewed Covenant that was prophesied by Jeremiah to Israel.

Revelation 19:7-9 *Let us be glad and rejoice, and give honour to him: for the marriage of the Lamb is come, and his wife hath made herself ready. And to her was granted that she should be arrayed in fine linen, clean and white: for the fine linen is the righteousness of saints. And he saith unto me, Write, Blessed are they which are called unto the marriage supper of the Lamb. And he saith unto me, These are the true sayings of God.* (KJV)

Yeshua stated that He would return for His Bride in John 14, which is exactly what the husband would say to his betrothed bride upon leaving her father's house. During the wait, which was an unknown time, except to the fathers' of the couple, the bridegroom would prepare a place for her while she made preparations to be ready for his return. At the bridegroom's return a procession would lead both of them to the second stage of marriage, nesuin. After the Ketubah (second-stage marriage contract) is given, then both enter the wedding chamber to consummate the marriage. After the consummation of the marriage the couple then joins in the wedding feast. This appears to be what is implied in Revelation 19. If all this is correct then it appears that the Covenant or Torah will be renewed one more time with the ketubah at the nesuin marriage.

In Ezekiel 40-48, we read about the final Millennial Temple after Messiah sets up His Kingdom on earth. There is no High Priest in this Temple. However, the leader, who leads in the sacrifices, is called the Nasi, or Prince. The Messiah ben David is a kingly prince. Very clearly the sacrificial system will be re-instituted during the Messianic Kingdom, but how can this be? In God's purpose of things, he has designed for another renewing of His Covenant/Torah to account for this change. It is God's final attempt to redeem as much of mankind who will submit to relationship with Him.

This 'Supernal [Renewed] Torah' of the Messiah is a concept found throughout Jewish literature. For example:

Genesis Rabbah 98:9 - *When he, about whom it is written, 'Lowly and riding upon an ass' (Zechariah 9:9) will come...he will elucidate for them the words of the Tora...and elucidate for them their errors.*[5]

Ecclesiastes Rabbah 11:1 - *The whole Tora which you learn in this world is vanity against the Torah of the World to Come. For in this world a man learns Tora and forgets, but in the Future to Come (he will not forget), as it is written, 'I will put My Tora in their inward parts and in their heart I will write it'. (Jeremiah 31:33).*[6]

Midrash Alpha Beta diR. Akiba, BhM 3:27-29 - *In the future the Holy One, blessed be He, will sit in the Garden of Eden and expound (the Torah) ... the Holy One, blessed be He, will expound to them the meanings of a new Tora which he will give them through the Messiah.*[7]

Chesed l'Avraham (Abraham Azulai) 13c-14a - *This is the secret of the Tora which the Holy One, blessed be He, will renew for Israel ... The Torah will remain in her place. But at present her words are combined in physical combinations, as they were needed for this physical world. But in the future, when the children of Adam will divest themselves of this physical body and will ascend and attain to the mystery of the body which Adam the first man had before he sinned, then they will become adepts in the mystery of the Torah, when that which is hidden will be revealed.*[8]

Yemenite Midrash, pp. 349-350 - *In the future, the Holy One, blessed be He, will seat the Messiah in the supernal Yeshiva (House of Study), and they will call him 'the Lord,' just as they call the creator ... And the Messiah will sit in the Yeshiva, and all those who walk on the earth will come and sit before him to hear a new Torah and new commandments and the deep wisdom which he teaches Israel.*[9]

The New Torah or New Covenant was not considered a brand new covenant. The Hebraic writers consider the New Torah/Covenant as the same Eternal Torah given to Israel by God at Mt. Sinai. The New Torah/Covenant is the teaching of the deeper insights of the Eternal Torah that have yet to be revealed to man. It was left for the Messiah to teach this New Torah/Covenant to Israel.[10]

Hebrews 9:15 *And for this cause he (Yeshua) is the mediator of the new testament, that by means of death, for the redemption of the transgressions that were under the first testament, they which are called might receive the promise of eternal inheritance.* (KJV)

The central element of the Renewed Torah/Betrothal Covenant is Messiah's completed atonement through His shed blood. Thus, Messiah is appropriately called 'the mediator of a Renewed Covenant' in Hebrews 9:15 with His blood being the sign of the Renewed Covenant (Luke 22:20). Messiah's blood, which cleanses us from our sin, enables the deep spiritual promises of the Renewed Covenant to become a reality for the one who trusts in Him.

We must understand that the New Covenant experienced in the first century up until our day through believing in Yeshua is the first fruits [Here Now But Not Yet] of the ultimate fulfillment of the New Covenant spoken of by Jeremiah. In the days of the fulfillment of the New Covenant, Israel and Judah will return to God and His Torah together as one people. This only will happen during the Messianic Kingdom. So the New Covenant available today through Yeshua's atoning work is the first fruits of the final harvest.

Where do the believers in Messiah from the nations fit into this plan of God? Once again, it is during the Messianic Kingdom when the New Covenant offered to Gentiles also will be ultimately fulfilled. God's call to Israel will never change. She is to be a 'Light' to the nations. When all Israel accepts their Messiah, she will then be able to fulfill her God-given mandate. No other nation, except Israel has this call to be the 'light' to the world by 'reflecting' the 'Light' of Messiah.

But at the first fruits of the New Covenant stage when Messiah offered Himself as the atoning offering, it was necessary for a renewing of the covenant to reflect the change of multitudes from the nations being grafted into Israel. Previously, the numbers of the gentiles who were grafted in had been minimal to what occurred after Yeshua's death and resurrection. Paul stated that before Messiah came, the Gentiles were 'excluded from the Commonwealth of Israel, and strangers to the covenants of promise' (Ephesians 2:12). Through Yeshua, however, 'the Gentiles are fellow heirs and fellow members of the body, and fellow partakers of the promise in Messiah Yeshua through the gospel' (Ephesians 3:6). Again we see Messiah as the central element in the renewing of the covenant.

Romans 4:11 *And he (Abraham) received the sign of circumcision, a seal of the righteousness of the faith which he had yet being uncircumcised: that he might be the father of all them that believe, though they be not circumcised; that righteousness might be imputed unto them also: (KJV)*

Colossians 2:11 *In whom also ye are circumcised with the circumcision made without hands, in putting off the body of the sins of the flesh by the circumcision of Christ:* (KJV)

A search of all Scripture reveals, with the exception of Noah, that God never made a covenant specifically with the Gentiles or any other nation except Israel. The Gentile believers today teach that the New Covenant was made for the 'Church'. But this is a great error and is centered on the devilish 'Replacement Theology' where the Church has replaced Israel. The Renewed Covenant is explicitly made with the house of Israel and Judah according to Jeremiah 31 and Hebrews 8. The new Gentile believers in Yeshua are 'grafted' into the 'Commonwealth of Israel'. The so-called Church new covenant is not a new and separate covenant from Israel's covenant.

The Bible tells us in Genesis 12:3 that Abraham is to be a blessing for all nations. Referring to this verse, Paul says in Romans 4:11, that in addition to being the father of the Jewish people, Abraham is also 'the father of all who believe without being circumcised' [Gentiles]. It is through Abraham that those who follow God in faith, whether Jew or Gentile, are part of the 'family' of God.

Romans 7:1-4 *Know ye not, brethren, (for I speak to them that know the law,) how that the law hath dominion over a man as long as he liveth? For the woman which hath an husband is bound by the law to her husband so long as he liveth; but if the husband be dead, she is loosed from the law of her husband. So then if, while her husband liveth, she be married to another man, she shall be called an adulteress: but if her husband be dead, she is free from that law; so that she is no adulteress, though she be married to another man. Wherefore, my brethren, ye also are become dead to the law [Pharisaical oral torah] by the body of Christ; that ye should be married to another, even to him who is raised from the dead, that we should bring forth fruit [Firstfruits of the Barley Harvest] unto God.* (KJV)

On Passover Yeshua became the Lamb that was sacrificed for those who believe in Him. His blood is the purchase price, mohar, for their salvation. He delivered them from Satan and sin through His blood. Judah's failure with its betrothal to God had been dissolved with the groom's [Yeshua] death. She is now free to become betrothed to God again through the New Torah/Covenant. But this New Covenant paves the way for Gentiles who believe to also become betrothed to God in the same manner. Paul's writing in Romans 7 states that believers are now free to betroth 'him [Yeshua] who is raised from the dead'.

Ephesians 2:12-16 *That at that time ye were without Christ, being aliens [Gentiles] from the commonwealth of Israel, and strangers [Gentiles] from the covenants of promise, having no hope, and without God in the world: But now in Christ Jesus ye who sometimes were far off are made nigh by the blood of Christ. For he is our peace, who hath made both [Jew and Gentile] one, and hath broken down the middle wall of partition between us; Having abolished in his flesh the enmity, even the law of commandments contained in ordinances; for to make in himself of twain [Jew and Gentile] one new man, so making peace; And that he might reconcile both [Jew and Gentile] unto God in one body by the cross, having slain the enmity thereby:* (KJV)

Hebrews 9:16-17 *For where a testament is, there must also of necessity be the death of the testator. For a testament is of force after men are dead: otherwise it is of no strength at all while the testator liveth.* (KJV)

With Yeshua's death and resurrection the renewed covenant [Torah] went into effect. The renewed covenant is basically the betrothal ketubah for those who believe in Him. Through Yeshua's death, the promises of the covenant are also given to the Gentiles who believe in Him through faith. Yeshua's death brings both believing Jews [and Israelites] and Gentiles into One Body. Although a person's Will only went into effect after they had died, the Torah has nothing to say about someone who had died and was resurrected. Even though Yeshua lives, His death brings the promises of the covenant/marriage to all those who believe.

Once a believer has been bought with Yeshua's blood and freed from sin to be betrothed to Him, they can come into the chuppah [at Mt. Sinai and Acts 2] and receive the immersion of the Holy Spirit. The Holy Spirit hovers over the believer like a betrothal chuppah and the New Covenant Torah is written upon their mind and heart. This is the believer's spiritual circumcision, the sign of the Renewed Covenant. We will discuss these aspects as how they relate to the Festival of Shavuot [Pentecost] in a later chapter.

Immersion and Grafting into Abraham

Genesis 12:2 *And I will make of thee a great nation, and I will bless thee, and make thy name great; and thou shalt be a blessing:* (KJV)

In Genesis 12:2 God speaks directly to Abram: 'I will make of thee great nation'. From this one word 'make' Jewish writers gave plenty of interpretations called Midrash. One in particular was Reb Berekiah who believed that God was trying to communicate something by using the verb 'make' instead of something like 'establish'. He suggests that God was saying that from Abram would come a great nation only after he was 'remade' by Him. Reb Berekiah taught that it is as if God said to Abram, 'I will make you a great nation, that is after I have created you as a new creation you will be fruitful and multiply' (Genesis Rabbah 39:11).[11]

Romans 4:16-17 *Therefore it is of faith, that it might be by grace; to the end the promise might be sure to all the seed; not to that only which is of the law, but to that also which is of the faith of Abraham; who is the father of us all, (As it is written, I have made thee a father of many nations,) before him whom he believed, even God, who quickeneth the dead, and calleth those things which be not as though they were.* (KJV)

Galatians 6:15 *For in Christ Jesus neither circumcision availeth any thing, nor uncircumcision, but a new creature.* (KJV)

2 Corinthians 5:17 *Therefore if any man be in Christ, he is a new creature: old things are passed away; behold, all things are become new.* (KJV)

Galatians 3:6-7 *Even as Abraham believed God, and it was accounted to him for righteousness. Know ye therefore that they which are of faith, the same are the children of Abraham.* (KJV)

At least this one rabbi believed that Abram's transformation into a great nation wasn't based upon procreation and a physical seed. In his opinion it was God remaking Abram into a 'new creation' that would fulfill the promise. This is very similar to Paul's teaching in the New Testament that Abraham received the promises of God through his faith, which was accounted for righteousness. Abram was 'recreated,' if you will, into Abraham, who is the father of many nations. Paul uses this recreation of Abraham as the model of salvation by faith.

Paul tells us that by the attribute of this same faith that Abraham had, the Gentiles also are new creations through Yeshua. Paul even goes further and states that Gentile believers in Messiah Yeshua are spiritual recreated children of Abraham. He is stating that through the droves of Gentile believers in Yeshua, Abraham has become a great nation.

Genesis 12:2 *And I will make of thee a great nation, and I will bless thee, and make thy name great; and thou shalt be a blessing:* (KJV)

Other sages in the Midrash Rabbah take note of the word blessing in the phrase 'thou shalt be a blessing'. The word for blessing in Hebrew sounds similar for the word 'pool'. Similar sounding Hebrew words were a device used by the sages to bring further understanding to a subject. Using this similar sounding word for 'blessing,' the midrash of these sages says, 'You will be an <u>immersion pool</u> (berekah): Just as a pool purifies the unclean, in the same way you <u>bring near to Me those who are far away</u>' [Genesis Rabbah 29:11]'.[12]

Ephesians 2:12-13 *That at that time ye were without Christ, being aliens from the commonwealth of Israel, and strangers from the covenants of promise, having no hope, and without God in the world: But now in Christ Jesus ye who sometimes were far off are made nigh by the blood of Christ.* (KJV)

This 'immersion pool' interpretation is directly linked to the issue of conversion in a mikveh [baptismal pool]. Look at Paul's words in Ephesians 2:13 and how they relate to Gentiles coming to faith in Messiah and then being added [converted] to the Commonwealth of Israel. In Judaism of the first century and today, the final stage of a Gentile conversion, is the immersion in a Mikveh. According to these rabbis, Abraham is like a mikvah, in which Gentile converts, are immersed in as part of the ritual to become Abraham's seed. According to Paul, Gentile believers who are immersed into Yeshua are symbolically recreated as children of Abraham.

Genesis 12:4-5 *So Abram departed, as the LORD had spoken unto him; and Lot went with him: and Abram was seventy and five years old when he departed out of Haran. And Abram took Sarai his wife, and Lot his brother's son, and all their substance that they had gathered, and the souls that they had gotten in Haran; and they went forth to go into the land of Canaan; and into the land of Canaan they came.* (KJV)

According to extra-Biblical Jewish sources, Abraham was busily making proselytes from the Gentiles. His mission was to bring the knowledge of God to people who were embedded with paganism. Who were 'the souls that they [Abram and Sarai] had gotten?' This was well before Isaac was born when Sarai was barren. The souls they made in Haran were proselytes. Rav Leazar said: 'It refers rather to the proselytes they had made. The verse, as it is written is to teach you that he who brings a Gentile near to God and converts him is as though he had created him' (Torah Temimah).[13]

How was it that Abraham was to be a blessing and that all the nations were blessed through him? It was his conversion of the Gentiles to faith in his God. As a mikveh is the avenue by which

Gentiles convert to Judaism, Abraham is the source by which Gentiles are brought into relationship with God. As a mikveh brings those Gentiles who were once far from God near to Him, so also is Abraham the medium, which brings the pagan Gentiles into the knowledge of God. In comparing Abraham to a mikveh, the sages of old believed that he was to be a blessing to all nations by converting Gentiles to faith in God.

Genesis 12:3 *And I will bless them that bless thee, and curse him that curseth thee: and in thee shall all families of the earth be blessed.* (KJV)

There is another concept of the rabbis related to Genesis 12 that directly coincides with the teaching of Paul in the New Testament on the relationship between converted Gentiles and Abraham. The Artscroll Bereishis [Genesis] commentary cites an opinion regarding the words, 'and in thee shall all families of the earth be blessed'. Several rabbis are of the opinion that the verb <u>v'nivracu</u> ו נ ב ר כ ו, which literally means, '<u>will be blessed</u>,' is related to the Mishnaic Hebrew term <u>mavrik</u> מ ב ר י ך, which means '<u>to intermingle, to graft</u>,' through their common root barak ב ר ך. The rabbis point out that nowhere else but in this verse do we find 'barak,' in the sense of 'blessing,' in the niphal conjugation. The same verbal root, however, is commonly found in this form in regard to 'grafting' of plants. Thus, one might translate the verse as 'in thee shall all families of the earth be <u>grafted</u>'.[14]

Rabbi Eleazar expounded, What is meant by the verse, 'And all peoples on earth will be blessed through you?' The Holy One, blessed be He, said to Abraham, 'I have two goodly shoots to engraft on you: Ruth the Moabitess and Naamah the Ammonitess'. All the families of the earth, even the other families who live on the earth are blessed only for Israel's sake. All the nations of the earth, even the ships that go from Gaul to Spain are blessed only for Israel's sake (Yavamoth 63a).

Deuteronomy 23:3 *An Ammonite or Moabite shall not enter into the congregation of the LORD; even to their tenth generation shall they not enter into the congregation of the LORD for ever:* (KJV)

The peshat [literal] meaning of Genesis 12:3 is about blessing and has nothing to do with the grafting of plants. However, in the Talmud, Rabbi Eleazar explains how two Gentile women, Ruth the Moabite and Naamah the Ammonite, came to be regarded as part of Israel and became mothers of the Davidic line of kings. Deuteronomy 23:3 states that no Ammonite or Moabite or any of their descendants may enter the congregation of the LORD. Then how was it possible that both Ruth and Naamah are mothers of the Kings of Israel? Obviously, they were no longer to be considered Moabite and Ammonite according to the Scripture. They had to be engrafted into Israel through Abraham.

This midrashic interpretation of grafting into Abraham aligns itself to Jewish tradition portraying him as evangelizing the nations. With the grafting symbolism Abraham's faith could be compared to a tree of some sort. When Gentiles leave their pagan religions and convert to Abraham's God, they are like branches cut off from the tree of their pagan faith. These Gentile branches are then grafted into Abraham as being grafted into a tree of faith in the One True God. How are all the nations of the earth blessed through Abraham? They are blessed because they have been grafted into him.

Romans 11:17-26 *And if some of the branches be broken off, and thou, being a wild olive tree, wert graffed in among them, and with them partakest of the root and fatness of the olive tree; Boast not against the branches. But if thou boast, thou bearest not the root, but the root thee. Thou wilt say then, The branches were broken off, that I might be graffed in. Well; because of unbelief they were broken off, and thou standest by faith. Be not highminded, but fear: For if God spared not the natural branches, take heed lest he also spare not thee. Behold therefore the goodness and severity of God: on them which fell, severity; but toward thee, goodness, if thou continue in his goodness: otherwise thou also shalt be cut off. And they also, if they abide not still in unbelief, shall be graffed in: for God is able to* *graff them in again. For if thou wert cut out of the olive tree which is wild by nature, and wert graffed contrary to nature into a good olive tree: how much more shall these, which be the natural branches, be graffed into their own olive tree? For I would not, brethren, that ye should be ignorant of this mystery, lest ye should be wise in your own conceits; that blindness in part is happened to Israel, until the fulness of the Gentiles be come in. And so all Israel shall be saved: as it is written, There shall come out of Sion the Deliverer, and shall turn away ungodliness from Jacob:* (KJV)

The Apostle Paul must have been aware of this interpretation of Abraham being a blessing to the nations. It is fascinating that both Paul and Rabbi Eleazar lived about the same time. Paul turns the teaching of Gentiles being grafted in Abraham as related to being grafted into an Olive Tree.

In Romans 11 the Gentile believers are regarded as wild olive branches grafted into an olive tree. In the Old Testament Israel is called a thriving olive tree (Jeremiah 11:16. Hosea 14:6). David speaks of himself as an olive tree flourishing in the house of God (Psalm 52:8). Paul uses this metaphor of the olive tree to demonstrate how Jewish and Gentile believers are bound together. The 'Church' cannot be separated from Israel. With all that we have studied thus far, the root of the olive tree is symbolic of Abraham, Isaac, and Jacob. Through faith in God as these patriarchs possessed, so too would the Gentiles come into salvation in Him. Any Gentile congregation that seeks to separate from the olive tree of Israel ceases to be a Biblical 'congregation' as laid out in the New Testament Scriptures.[15]

Galatians 3:8 *And the scripture, foreseeing that God would justify the heathen through faith, preached before the gospel unto Abraham, saying, In thee shall all nations be blessed.* (KJV)

Christianity has tried to put a spin on the 'Gospel' that separates it from its Hebraic perspective. Without Abraham, Isaac, and Jacob there is no 'Gospel' according to Scripture. Paul associates Genesis 12:3: In thee [Abraham] shall all nations be blessed [grafted] as the full message and mystery of the 'Gospel'.

Genesis 12:7 *And the LORD appeared unto Abram, and said, Unto thy seed will I give this land...(KJV)*

Although God promised that through Abraham the Gentiles would be blessed/grafted, later in Genesis 12:7 there is a further development to the blessing. God promises Abram a seed. He says to Abram, 'To your seed I will give this land'.

Genesis 22:17-18 *That in blessing I will bless thee, and in multiplying I will multiply thy seed as the stars of the heaven, and as the sand which is upon the sea shore; and thy seed shall possess the gate of his enemies; And in thy seed shall all the nations of the earth be blessed; because thou hast obeyed my voice.* (KJV)

The birth of Isaac was the literal seed of Abraham that was promised. God said to Abraham, 'in thy seed shall all the nations of the earth be blessed'. The promise has expanded in this verse to 'in your seed'. So the promise that all nations shall be blessed through Abraham is transferred to his seed Isaac.

Genesis 26:4 *And I will make thy seed to multiply as the stars of heaven, and will give unto thy seed all these countries; and in thy seed shall all the nations of the earth be blessed;* (KJV)

Genesis 28:14 *And thy seed shall be as the dust of the earth, and thou shalt spread abroad to the west, and to the east, and to the north, and to the south: and in thee and in thy seed shall all the families of the earth be blessed.* (KJV)

We then see the promise of this blessing to the nations being passed to Isaac's seed Jacob. In Genesis 28:14 Jacob's seed inherits the promised blessing to the Gentiles. How do we make sense of all this?

Galatians 3:16 *Now to Abraham and his seed were the promises made. He saith not, And to seeds, as of many; but as of one, And to thy seed, which is Christ.* (KJV)

Because Messiah Yeshua was the promised seed [singular] of Abraham, the blessing/grafting comes through Him. Every time we have encountered the blessing being passed to 'seed,' it is always in the singular form of the noun. The promised 'seed' of Abraham, and therefore Isaac and Jacob as well, according to Paul, is not a multitude of nations. The 'seed' is one person, namely the Messiah Yeshua, by whom many nations are blessed and recreated as the 'seed' of Abraham.

Galatians 3:26-29 *For ye are all the children of God by faith in Christ Jesus. For as many of you as have been baptized into Christ have put on Christ. There is neither Jew nor Greek, there is neither bond nor free, there is neither male nor female: for ye are all one in Christ Jesus. And if ye be Christ's, then are ye Abraham's seed, and heirs according to the promise.* (KJV)

Whether one is a Jew or a Gentile, those that belong to Messiah, are accounted as 'seed' of Abraham by their faith. Of course, this has nothing to do with genetics, but is totally a spiritual thing. And yet we realize that there is a physical seed of Abraham. God's call is for the physical seed of Abraham to also be spiritual seed. This is a true Jew. However, a Gentile who is grafted into Israel is not Jewish.

Paul's comparison of Israel to an olive tree in Romans 11 shows forth the principle of adoption. Gentiles who are grafted into the tree of Israel are adopted from the nations. This engrafting process makes these Gentiles a full-fledged part of Israel connected to the same root. Therefore, both the natural offspring [bloodline Jews] and spiritual offspring [believing Jews and Gentiles] of Abraham comprise what Paul called the 'Commonwealth of Israel'.

The Sons of Joseph

Genesis 48:5 *And now thy two sons, Ephraim and Manasseh, which were born unto thee in the land of Egypt before I came unto thee into Egypt, are mine; as Reuben and Simeon, they shall be mine.* (KJV)

When reading the story of Jacob giving blessings to Joseph's sons in Genesis 48, there is an apparent hidden ritual within the text of middle-eastern adoption. The ancient custom for adoption involved those being adopted to sit on the lap of the one adopting. Through this act Ephraim and Manasseh belongs to Jacob just as Reuben and Simeon. They were full-fledged brothers now with the other tribes. This act of adoption made Ephraim and Manasseh brothers to their own father Joseph.

Also, we discover that Ephraim and Manasseh actually received Jacob's first-born blessing because he intended to make Joseph his first-born son. When Jacob was at the house of Laban, his real love was for his daughter Rachel and not Leah. Joseph was Rachel's first-born and in respect for her he passed on the firstborn right to Joseph's two sons in a double blessing where both of them were raised to the status of patriarchs of Israel.

Genesis 48:19 *And his father refused, and said, I know it, my son, I know it: he also shall become a people, and he also shall be great: but truly his younger brother shall be greater than he, and his seed shall become a multitude of nations.* (KJV)

Romans 11:25 *For I would not, brethren, that ye should be igno-rant of this mystery, lest ye should be wise in your own conceits; that blindness in part is happened to Israel, until the fulness of the Gentiles be come in.* (KJV)

Instead of putting his right hand on Manasseh, Jacob puts it on Ephraim the younger of the two. Joseph attempts to tell his father of the mistake he is making, but Jacob makes it clear that what he was doing was from God. Manasseh, the older brother, was blessed to become a great people. But Ephraim, the younger brother, was blessed to be even greater. Jacob said that Ephraim's 'seed' would become a 'multitude of nations'. In Hebrew it is better translated as a 'fullness of Gentiles'.

Ephraim and Manasseh were raised in Egypt and for all practical purposes would be considered Gentile Egyptians. Their mother was an Egyptian daughter of a pagan priest [Genesis 41:45]. But here they are adopted into Israel as Jacob's 'seed'. They were now sons of Israel in their ancestry. Could this be a picture of the spiritual adoption of Gentiles into Israel [Abraham]?

The Gentiles who believe in Messiah Yeshua are reckoned as the 'seed' of Abraham. They are adopted into Israel based upon the 'first born of God' status of Yeshua. Gentiles grafted into Paul's olive tree have become heirs with Israel. Paul then states that a partial blindness has happened to Israel until the 'fullness of the Gentiles' comes in. This is the same phrase that Jacob used in blessing Ephraim. It could be that Paul was inferring that the Gentile believers adopted into Israel are to be viewed as the 'seed' of Ephraim, the 'fullness of the Gentiles' and possibly an extension of the Abrahamic seed blessings.

BIBLIOGRAPHY

1. A Jewish Wedding Guide: Made in Heaven. Rabbi Aryeh Kaplan. Moznaim Publishing Corporation, New York, Jerusalem, 1983. Page 156.
2. Torah Rediscovered. Ariel and D'vorah Berkowitz. First Fruits of Zion, Inc., Littleton, Colorado, 1996. Pages 63-64.
3. The Church and the Jews. Dan Gruber. Serenity Books, Hagerstown, Maryland, 1997. Pages 80-82.
4. Christ in the Passover. Ceil and Moishe Rosen. Moody Press, Chicago, Illinois, 1978. Page 59.
5. The Messiah Texts. Raphael Patai. Wayne State University Press, Detroit, Michigan, 1979, Page 250.
6. Ibid. Page 250.
7. Ibid. Pages 252-253.
8. Ibid. Page 255.
9. Ibid. Pages 256- 257.
10. Ibid. Page 256.
11. The Mystery of the Gospel. D. Thomas Lancaster. First Fruits of Zion, Littleton, Colorado, 2003, Page 28.
12. Ibid. Page 30.
13. The Artscroll Tanach Series - Bereishis [Genesis]. Mesorah Publications, Ltd., Brooklyn, New York, 1995, Page 435.

14.   Ibid. Page 432.

15.   Our Father Abraham. Marvin R. Wilson. William B. Eerdmans Publishing Company - Grand Rapids, Michigan & Center for Judaic-Christian Studies - Dayton, Ohio, 1989, Pages 12-15.

7

ISRAEL'S BETROTHAL TO GOD
NEW TESTAMENT - SPRING FESTIVALS

In this chapter the author will attempt to show how the events associated with Yeshua and His Congregation were centered upon the Spring Festivals just as Israel came out of Egypt and came to Mt. Sinai. As Israel's relationship with God in the wilderness was described by marriage terminology, so also we will see the New Testament people of God in relationship with Him through matrimony. Most Christians understand that everything in the New Testament was totally brand new as compared to the Old Testament, but the same exact themes were reenacted.

John 16:7-8 *Nevertheless I tell you the truth; It is expedient for you that I go away: for if I go not away, the Comforter will not come unto you; but if I depart, I will send him unto you. And when he is come, he will reprove the world of sin, and of righteousness, and of judgment:* (KJV)

John 15:16 *Ye have not chosen me, but I have chosen you, and ordained you, that ye should go and bring forth fruit, and that your fruit should remain: that whatsoever ye shall ask of the Father in my name, he may give it you.* (KJV)

It is the purpose of the Holy Spirit to reprove men of sin and lead them to God. Just as the father of the bridegroom usually chose a Hebrew bride, so does the Father choose the believers in the Yeshua. A bridegroom chose his bride to pour his love into her that she might love him also in return. This can be seen in Ephesians:

Ephesians 5:25 Husbands, love your wives, even as Christ also loved the church, and gave himself for it. (KJV)

Exodus 19:8 *And all the people answered together, and said, All that the LORD hath spoken we will do. And Moses returned the words of the people unto the LORD.* (KJV)

1 Peter 1:8 *Whom having not seen, ye love; in whom, though now ye see him not, yet believing, ye rejoice with joy unspeakable and full of glory:* (KJV)

Today, the believers in the Messiah consent to become His bride even though they have never seen Him. The Israelites at Mt. Sinai never saw God face to face, only through signs and wonders. They too accepted Him and promised to keep His Word. This is similar to a wedding ceremony where the bride says, 'I do'.

Matthew 26:39 *And he went a little further, and fell on his face, and prayed, saying, O my Father, if it be possible, let this cup pass from me: nevertheless not as I will, but as thou wilt.* (KJV)

1 Peter 1:18-19 *Forasmuch as ye know that ye were not redeemed with corruptible things, as silver and gold, from your vain conversation received by tradition from your fathers; But with the precious blood of Christ, as of a lamb without blemish and without spot:* (KJV)

Yeshua, the Bridegroom, paid a very great price for His bride. The price He paid was His life. Yeshua had this weight on His soul as He sought the Father in the Garden of Gethsemane before His crucifixion. The bride's mohar price was His life.

Historically, God betrothed Himself to Israel at Mount Sinai (Jeremiah 2:2; Hosea 2:19-20). Whenever one accepts the Messiah into their heart and life, they become betrothed to Him while living on the earth. The Bridegroom gave gifts to His beloved bride to show His love for her. When He left His betrothed bride to go build a home for her, He gave her the gift of the Holy Spirit expressed as 'gifts of the Spirit' in the New Testament. These gifts are to identify who is His bride and that she is spoken for and no other will have her.

Luke 22:20 *Likewise also the cup after supper, saying, This cup is the new testament in my blood, which is shed for you.* (KJV)

1 Corinthians 11:25-26 *After the same manner also he took the cup, when he had supped, saying, This cup is the new testament in my blood: this do ye, as oft as ye drink it, in remembrance of me. For as often as ye eat this bread, and drink this cup, ye do shew the Lord's death till he come.* (KJV)

Jeremiah 31:31 *Behold, the days come, saith the LORD, that I will make a new covenant with the house of Israel, and with the house of Judah:* (KJV)

What Christianity calls 'Communion' is really based upon what Yeshua did with the Passover elements at His last Passover Seder with His disciples. His blood was not yet shed and His body not yet offered when He made His remarks over them. He said this is the 'new covenant' in my blood in fulfillment of what Jeremiah prophesied. The new covenant was offered to both houses of Israel, and of course, those Gentiles who attached themselves to her and her God. As we mentioned previously in this book, the new covenant today is just a first fruits of the new covenant that will be fully manifested during the Messianic Kingdom.

The Communion cup was actually the Passover cup anciently known as the 'cup of redemption'.[1] Those same disciples and subsequent believers after Yeshua's last Passover celebrated the unleavened bread and wine in remembrance to the mohar price [His Life] He paid, but also in expectation of His return for His Betrothed Bride. So from this aspect the 'cup of redemption' also commemorated Yeshua offering a marriage proposal to His chosen. Subsequently, when the believer takes this cup again, they are actually remembering the betrothal proposal that they accepted from their Bridegroom. Believers continue to remember this betrothal proposal until the Bridegroom comes and takes them to the final stage of Biblical marriage. The communion service was instituted by the Bridegroom to remember our vows every year at Passover. This understanding of the proposal cup also fits with what Yeshua said during His Last Passover Seder:

John 14:1-3 *Let not your heart be troubled: ye believe in God, believe also in me. In my Father's house are many mansions: if it were not so, I would have told you. I go to prepare a place for you. And if I go and prepare a place for you, I will come again, and receive you unto myself; that where I am, there ye may be also.* (KJV)

This statement by Yeshua clearly demonstrates His intention of betrothing His disciples as His bride. This terminology that the bridegroom would go and return for his betrothed bride would encourage her to keep faith that he would return and take her to his place of dwelling. Therefore, the New Testament [Covenant] Passover aligns itself with the purposes of the Egyptian Passover, to offer a betrothal marriage to Israel.

The Crucifixion of Yeshua on Passover

Mark 15:25 *And it was the third hour, and they crucified him.* (KJV)

Luke 23:44-46 *And it was about the sixth hour, and there was a darkness over all the earth until the ninth hour. And the sun was darkened, and the veil of the temple was rent in the midst. And when Jesus had cried with a loud voice, he said, Father, into thy hands I commend my spirit: and having said thus, he gave up the ghost.* (KJV)

The Scripture recounts that Yeshua hung on the cross from the third hour until the ninth, six hours before He died. The third hour was approximately 9:00 A.M. and the ninth hour 3:00 P.M. Therefore, sometime around 3:00 P.M. on Nisan 13 Yeshua died. This author does not believe that Yeshua was crucified at the same time when the Pharisees and the common people of Israel sacrificed their Passover lambs 'between the evenings' on Nisan 14. The Pharisees combined the Passover into the first day of the Festival of Unleavened Bread. For Yeshua to fulfill the 'Mosaic' Passover, He must be killed 'between the evenings' on Nisan 13. There is evidence as presented in an earlier chapter that the Sadducean priests as well as the Samaritans sacrificed their Passover lambs 'between the evenings' on Nisan 13 according to the Mosaic Law in the first century. At this time, the author believes, but not dogmatically, that Yeshua's crucifixion on the afternoon of Nisan 13 was probably on a Wednesday.

What is the significance of Yeshua being crucified at the third hour? It would make sense that if Yeshua's crucifixion were to be identified with certain of the Mosaic sacrifices, that the timing is very significant. The Torah requires two daily worship services in the Temple (Leviticus 6:9-13; Numbers 28:3-8). These daily services are called the ה מ י ד Tamid (Continual Burnt Offering). Every day on the Temple Altar, a male lamb was sacrificed as a burnt offering for the morning Continual Burnt Offering. Each subsequent sacrifice that day, whether communal, personal, or musaf [for festivals, etc.] was placed on top of it. It remained on the fire of the Altar all day.

After the day's Temple services had been completed and all the sacrifices and offerings had been brought, the second male lamb was slaughtered as a Continual Burnt Offering and placed on top of the remains of that day's offerings on the Altar. This second lamb burned on the Altar throughout the night. When the next morning arrived, the ashes from the previous day's sacrifices were removed. A new male lamb for the morning Continual Burnt Offering was slaughtered and placed upon the Altar at the third hour. This process was to continue indefinitely, hence the name, Continual Burnt Offering. The morning Tamid service began at dawn and reached its conclusion at the third hour, which was about 9:00 A.M.[2]

Numbers 28:4 *The one lamb shalt thou offer in the morning, and the other lamb [evening continual burnt offering] shalt thou offer at even [bein ha-arbayim];* (KJV)

In Numbers 28:4 we learn that the evening Tamid could have a linguistic association with the Passover sacrifice because of the Hebrew words translated 'at even' are 'bein ha-arbayim,' which is the same Hebrew phrase used when the Passover lambs are sacrificed 'between the evenings' on Nisan 13.

The JPS Torah Commentary says:

'Hebrew bein ha-arbayim, a term that clearly means between sunset and dark. This would imply that the Tamid was the very last sacrifice of the day before the Temple doors were closed. The rabbis, however, interpret the term to mean the waning day or afternoon, which they specify as the ninth hour or about 3:00 P.M.'[3]

<u>**Exodus 12:6**</u> *And ye shall keep it up until the fourteenth day of the same month: and the whole assembly of the congregation of Israel shall kill it <u>in the evening</u> [bein ha-arbayim]. (KJV)*

On the 13th of Nisan the entire assembly of Israel was to kill the Passover lambs in Egypt at exactly the same time: bein ha-arbayim. The lambs were actually eaten after sunset on Nisan 14 with unleavened bread and bitter herbs. We have discussed the time of the Passover lambs being slaughtered in a previous chapter. We have a problem of both the Passover lambs and the afternoon Continual Burnt Offering needing to be offered at the same time of the day. What was the procedure?

To accommodate the tens of thousands of Passover lambs that were sacrificed in the afternoon of Nisan 14 [the Pharisee practice in the first century] in the Temple, the evening Continual Burnt Offering was sacrificed an hour earlier. Every other day of the year the evening Tamid was offered at the ninth hour. The Passover lamb takes precedence over the evening Tamid.

'...The [afternoon] Tamid is slaughtered at eight and a half hours and is offered at nine and a half hours. On the eve of the Passover it [the evening Tamid] is slaughtered at seven and a half hours and offered at eight and a half hours...[But] on the eve of Passover, when

there is the Passover offering after it, we advance it one hour and sacrifice it at seven and a half hours...' (Talmud Pesachim 58a)[4]

The Talmud explains that the Tamid offerings were sacrificed an hour before they were burnt on the altar. It would take this long for the body to be properly cut in pieces and prepared for the altar. On a normal day the morning Tamid would be sacrificed at about 8:30 A.M. and offered on the Altar at 9:30AM, while the afternoon Tamid was slaughtered at 2:30 P.M. and offered at 3:30 P.M.

As mentioned earlier, the evening Tamid was to be the last sacrifice of each day. However, there is one exception; the Passover lambs. The Passover lambs were always sacrificed after the evening Tamid. Because of the quantity of Passover lambs being slaughtered in the Temple Courtyard, the evening Tamid was moved up one hour earlier sacrificed at about 1:30 P.M. and offered on the Altar at 2:30 P.M. According to the Talmud the Passover lambs were sacrificed and offered between 2:30 - 3:30 P.M. on Nisan 14 [the Pharisees practice in the first century], the ninth hour.

The same Talmudic reference of Pesachim states if Nisan 14 occurred on the eve of a Sabbath, hence Friday afternoon, the Tamid and Passover sacrifices were moved up an additional hour earlier.[5] In this case the Tamid was sacrificed at 12:30 P.M. and offered at 1:30 P.M. The Passover lambs would then be slaughtered and offered between 1:30-2:30 P.M., which would be considered the eighth hour. The reason for this was that the Passover lambs had to be roasted by Torah law and they could not be cooked when the Sabbath began at sundown on Friday night at approximately 6:00 P.M. These facts alone demonstrate that Yeshua could not have been crucified on a Friday known in Christianity as Good Friday; otherwise His relationship to the Passover sacrifice has no meaning. If the Passover lambs were sacrificed on a Friday they must be offered during the 8th hour instead of the 9th hour as compared to it occurring on any other day of the week. Therefore, we conclude that Yeshua could not be crucified at the ninth hour on a Friday afternoon prior to the onset of the weekly Sabbath, and be the Passover Lamb. The concept of Good Friday is just a man-made myth!

The busiest day of the year in the Temple during the first century was Nisan 14, when the worshipers flocked to the Temple like 'sheep' to offer their Passover lambs. According to the Talmud, once the High Priest was instructed by Herod Agrippa II to count the kidneys taken from Passover lambs before they were burned on the Altar to determine the number of lambs that were sacrificed. Tens if not hundreds of thousands of lambs were sacrificed according to the account.[6]

Matthew 27:45 *Now from the sixth hour there was darkness over all the land unto the ninth hour.* (KJV)

The Gospels tell us, that from the sixth to ninth hours that Yeshua was on the cross, there was darkness over all the land. So from around noon until 3:00 P.M. this darkness prevailed. The Talmud and other Jewish sources that are pharisaically based are silent about any darkness occurring at any particular Passover on the afternoon of Nisan 14. As this author already stated, the evidence suggests that this darkness occurred in the afternoon of Nisan 13 [Wednesday], the Mosaic Passover.

This darkness could not have been a solar eclipse because it was the middle of the lunar month [full moon would be Nisan 15] and it would be impossible for one to occur when the moon was located on the opposite side of the earth from the sun. It had to be a supernatural darkness that came upon the land as Yeshua fulfilled the Mosaic Passover Lamb requirements. Maybe symbolically as Yeshua became sin for us, the Father in 'Heaven' turned His face away from His Son. This darkness persisted from about noon until 3:00 P.M. until Yeshua breathed His last breath.

An exciting parallel to this darkness associated with Yeshua's crucifixion are the Jewish traditions surrounding the death of the First Redeemer Moses. One tradition mentions the darkening of the sun at noon (the sixth hour) on the day Moses died. Another tradition has Moses death occurring at the time of Minchah or afternoon Tamid [Continual Burnt Offering] sacrifice, which was performed in the Temple during the ninth hour (Chasidah).[7]

Mark 15:37-39 *And Jesus cried with a loud voice, and gave up the ghost. And the veil of the temple was rent in twain from the top to the bottom.*

It is an ancient Jewish custom to rend one's garments as a mourning rite. As a matter of fact, if a Jew witnesses another's last breath, they were obligated to rend their garments. As Yeshua breathed His last breath about 3:00 P.M., Wednesday, Nisan 13, the curtain of the Temple was rent from top to bottom as a garment rent in two.

In the ancient Aramaic Targum the word used for the curtain in the Temple is פ ר ג ו ד, pargodh, a word that can also be used to denote a tunic. As such, the Temple veil is like the tunic of God.[8] The Father rent His garments over the death of His Son, Yeshua the Messiah.

1 Corinthians 5:7 *Purge out therefore the old leaven, that ye may be a new lump, as ye are unleavened. For even Christ our passover is sacrificed for us:* (KJV)

Truly, Messiah Yeshua is our Passover Who was sacrificed for us!

Wednesday Evening Nisan 13 Turning To Nisan 14 - The Day of Preparation

Mark 15:42-47 *And now when the even was come, because it was the preparation, that is, the day before the sabbath, Joseph of Arimathaea, an honourable counsellor, which also waited for the kingdom of God, came, and went in boldly unto Pilate, and craved the body of Jesus. And Pilate marvelled if he were already dead: and calling unto him the centurion, he asked him whether he had been any while dead. And when he knew it of the centurion, he gave the body to Joseph. And he bought fine linen, and took him down, and wrapped him in the linen, and laid him in a sepulchre which was hewn out of a rock, and rolled a stone unto the door of the sepulchre. And Mary Magdalene and Mary the mother of Joses beheld where he was laid.* (KJV)

In the first century, the Jews had a preparation day before every festival and weekly Sabbath. Passover was the only festival that did not begin at a sundown beginning a new day. Passover officially started at the sixth hour [noon] of the day. In the first century, the Pharisees led the people to observe the afternoon of Nisan 14 as the beginning of Passover, which they linked to the seven days of Unleavened Bread that immediately commenced at sundown.

The preparation 'before the Sabbath' referred to in Mark 15 is not Friday before the weekly Sabbath. The Sabbath, in context here, is the High Sabbath [Shabbaton] of Nisan 15, the first day of the festival of Unleavened Bread. If Yeshua died at 3:00 P.M. [the ninth hour] 'between the evenings' on Nisan 13, then exactly twenty-four hours later, on Nisan 14 would be the time that the Pharisees and the people would sacrifice their Passover lambs. It was on the 'preparation' that Yeshua was crucified.

Mark says that after Yeshua had died and 'when the even[ing] was come' that Joseph of Arimathaea sought His body for proper burial. It was still Nisan 13, but very late in the day and nearly sunset when the day would turn to Nisan 14. It was 'the day before the [High] Sabbath' of Nisan 15, the first day of the feast of Unleavened Bread.

John 19:31 *The Jews therefore, because it was the preparation, that the bodies should not remain upon the cross on the sabbath day, (for that sabbath day was an high day,) besought Pilate that their legs might be broken, and that they might be taken away.* (KJV)

Some concerned Jews who probably believed in Yeshua sought to have His and the two thieves' legs broken so they would die faster. Roman crucifixions could last for a few days before the victim died. But every breath demanded that they push up from their legs to release the diaphragm to breathe. When the legs were broken, the crucified person could no longer push up to breathe and died relatively quick at that point.

The implication from John 19:31 is that Yeshua and the two criminals were still alive. So in context, this verse is stating something before His death at 3:00 P.M. on Nisan 13. Again, we are told it was the 'Preparation' day. Later we learn in John 19:32-33 that the Roman soldiers came and broke the legs of the two criminals who were still alive, but found Yeshua already dead. Therefore, they did not break Yeshua's legs. The Scripture tells us that the Jew's were concerned about the crucified bodies remaining upon the execution stake on the 'Sabbath day'. Once again, this is not the weekly Sabbath, but we are told explicitly that it was the 'High Day' of Nisan 15, the beginning of the festival of Unleavened Bread.

Deuteronomy 21:22-23 *And if a man have committed a sin worthy of death, and he be to be put to death, and thou hang him on a tree: His body shall not remain all night upon the tree, but thou shalt in any wise bury him that day; (for he that is hanged is accursed of God;) that thy land be not defiled, which the LORD thy God giveth thee for an inheritance.* (KJV)

It was against Jewish law for a criminal to be executed on a Sabbath, which includes the High Sabbath of Nisan 15, the first day of the feast of Unleavened Bread. The Jews were concerned that the Romans would not deal with these executed Jews according to their laws. The Torah explicitly states in Deuteronomy 21 that a person cannot be executed and allowed to hang upon the 'tree' over night. This was an abomination to God and disrespectful toward the Promised Land.

Luke 23:50-56 *And, behold, there was a man named Joseph, a counsellor; and he was a good man, and a just: (The same had not consented to the counsel and deed of them;) he was of Arimathaea, a city of the Jews: who also himself waited for the kingdom of God. This man went unto Pilate, and begged the body of Jesus. And he took it down, and wrapped it in linen, and laid it in a sepulchre that was hewn in stone, wherein never man before was laid. And that day was the preparation, and the sabbath drew on. And the women also, which came with him from Galilee, followed after, and beheld the sepulchre, and how his body was laid. And they returned, and* *prepared spices and ointments; and rested the sabbath day according to the commandment.* (KJV)

At this point we have learned that Yeshua was buried in the sepulcher right about sunset when Nisan 13 was turning to Nisan 14. As we look at our scenario thus far, the author has brought out his belief that Yeshua's crucifixion took place 'between the evenings' on Nisan 13, a full 24 hours before the Pharisees and all Israel offered their Passover lambs in the Temple. Thursday Nisan 14 gave way to Nisan 15, the High Sabbath, at sundown. During the day on Friday was still the High Sabbath of Nisan 15 until sundown. This means that Friday evening at sundown, which was the beginning of the weekly Sabbath, was Nisan 16. We will pick up with this shortly.

Interestingly, according to calculations done by the Rabbanan, the Exodus from Egypt began on a Friday.[9] What day did the Exodus start? It started on Nisan 15 and after midnight, which was Friday morning according to Rabbanan. According to this view, the Mosaic Law required that the Passover lambs in Egypt be sacrificed 'between the evenings' on Nisan 13, which would have been a Wednesday. It is quite possible that not only does the crucifixion of Yeshua at Passover coincide with the Egyptian Passover sacrifices, but also they may have occurred on the same day of the week.

Exodus 13:18-20 *But God led the people about, through the way of the wilderness of the Red sea: and the children of Israel went up harnessed out of the land of Egypt. And Moses took the bones of Joseph with him: for he had straitly sworn the children of Israel, saying, God will surely visit you; and ye shall carry up my bones away hence with you. And they took their journey from Succoth, and encamped in Etham, in the edge of the wilderness.* (KJV)

Another fascinating element is that the Israelites visited the tomb of Joseph to retrieve his bones after they began their exodus, which started on Nisan 15. Joseph's bones were taken from Egypt, 'the seat of idolatry'. Yeshua was buried in another Joseph's tomb, that of 'Arimathaea'. Arimathaea represents the Greek form of the city called Ramah, which in Hebrew means, 'seat of idolatry'.[10]

The Third Day - Three Days and Three Nights

The traditional teaching that Yeshua was crucified on Good Friday in the afternoon and was resurrected the following 'Easter' Sunday is unbiblical. First of all, it was not the time of Easter, but Passover, when Yeshua was crucified and resurrected. There just is not a count of 'three days and nights' between His death and resurrection to fulfill Scripture. Do the Scripture references to 'three days and three nights' mean exactly three twenty-four hour periods [seventy two hours]?

All the references to Yeshua's resurrection on the third day in the New Testament are as follows:

Matthew 16:21 *From that time forth began Jesus to shew unto his disciples, how that he must go unto Jerusalem, and suffer many things of the elders and chief priests and scribes, and be killed, and be raised again the third day.* (KJV)

Matthew 17:23 *And they shall kill him, and the third day he shall be raised again. And they were exceeding sorry.* (KJV)

Matthew 20:19 *And shall deliver him to the Gentiles to mock, and to scourge, and to crucify him: and the third day he shall rise again.* (KJV)

Matthew 27:64 *Command therefore that the sepulchre be made sure until the third day, lest his disciples come by night, and steal him away, and say unto the people, He is risen from the dead: so the last error shall be worse than the first.* (KJV)

Mark 9:31 *For he taught his disciples, and said unto them, The Son of man is delivered into the hands of men, and they shall kill him; and after that he is killed, he shall rise the third day.* (KJV)

Mark 10:34 *And they shall mock him, and shall scourge him, and shall spit upon him, and shall kill him: and the third day he shall rise again.* (KJV)

Luke 9:22 *Saying, The Son of man must suffer many things, and be rejected of the elders and chief priests and scribes, and be slain, and be raised the third day.* (KJV)

Luke 18:33 *And they shall scourge him, and put him to death: and the third day he shall rise again.* (KJV)

Luke 24:7 *Saying, The Son of man must be delivered into the hands of sinful men, and be crucified, and the third day rise again.* (KJV)

Luke 24:46 *And said unto them, Thus it is written, and thus it behoved Christ to suffer, and to rise from the dead the third day:* (KJV)

Acts 10:39-40 *And we are witnesses of all things which he did both in the land of the Jews, and in Jerusalem; whom they slew and hanged on a tree: Him God raised up the third day, and shewed him openly;* (KJV)

John 2:19-22 *Jesus answered and said unto them, Destroy this temple, and in three days I will raise it up. Then said the Jews, Forty and six years was this temple in building, and wilt thou rear it up in three days? But he spake of the temple of his body. When therefore he was risen from the dead, his disciples remembered that he had said this unto them; and they believed the scripture, and the word which Jesus had said.* (KJV)

All of the preceding verses very clearly mention Yeshua's resurrection as coinciding with the Third Day. From the Hebraic understanding 'on the third day' means after two days have passed. It could be immediately at the outset of the third day or by the end of the third day, that Yeshua's resurrection would have fulfilled these verses.

Matthew 27:63 *Saying, Sir, we remember that that deceiver said, while he was yet alive, After three days I will rise again.* (KJV)

Mark 8:31 *And he began to teach them, that the Son of man must suffer many things, and be rejected of the elders, and of the chief priests, and scribes, and be killed, and after three days rise again.* (KJV)

The preceding two verses say that Yeshua's resurrection will occur 'after' three days. These two verses seemingly contradict the other verses just listed. If this were true then Yeshua cannot be the Messiah because He resurrected before the three full days had passed from His death. This is kind of a silly argument, because if Yeshua is resurrected, He must be the Messiah. The Greek probably states 'after three days' literally, but we have to interpret Scripture by Scripture. Hebraically saying 'after three days' here is idiomatic of 'on the third day'.

Matthew 12:40 *For as Jonas was three days and three nights in the whale's belly; so shall the Son of man be three days and three nights in the heart of the earth.* (KJV)

The main argument for a mandatory seventy-two hour period in the grave comes from this verse in Matthew that compares Yeshua's burial to 'the three days and three nights' that Jonah spent in the belly of the whale. Once again to take this as referring literally to a full seventy-two hour period falls far short of Hebraic thinking. 'The three days and three nights' of Jonah over the centuries also became idiomatic of 'on the third day,' which we can establish.

1 Corinthians 15:4 *And that he was buried, and that he rose again the third day according to the scriptures:* (KJV)

Paul says in 1 Corinthians that Yeshua 'rose again the third day' very clearly short of a seventy-two hour period. But he also states that it was 'according to the Scriptures [plural]'. But there are no Scriptures in the Old Testament that speak directly about the future

Messiah's resurrection on the third day. But there is an ancient Midrash concerning the third day, which a man of Paul's stature would have obviously been taught by the leading Pharisees. Clearly, the three days and three nights of the prophet Jonah being in the belly of a 'whale' was related to the third day:

ON THE THIRD DAY etc. (Genesis 22:4). It is written, After two days He will revive us, on the third day He will raise us up, that we may live in His presence (Hosea 6:2). E.g. on the third day of the tribal ancestors: And Joseph said unto them the third day: This do, and live (Gen. XLII, 18); on the third day of Revelation: And it came to pass on the third day, when it was morning (Ex. XIX, 16); on the third day of the spies: And hide yourselves there three days (Josh. II, 16); on the third day of Jonah: And Jonah was in the belly of the fish three days and three nights (Jonah II. 1); on the third day of those returning from the Exile: And we abode there three days (Ezra VIII, 32); on the third day of resurrection: 'After two days He will revive us, on the third day He will raise us up'; on the third day of Esther: Now it came to pass on the third day, that Esther put on her royal apparel (Est. V, 1)-i.e. she put on the royal apparel of her ancestor. For whose sake? The Rabbis say: For the sake of the third day, when Revelation took place. R. Levi maintained: In the merit of what Abraham did on the third day, as it says, ON THE THIRD DAY, etc. AND SAW THE PLACE AFAR OFF (ib.). What did he see? He saw a cloud enveloping the mountain, and said: 'It appears that that is the place where the Holy One, blessed be He, told me to sacrifice my son.' [Genesis Rabbah 56:1]

'On the third day' has its preeminent interpretation from Abraham's sacrifice of his son, Isaac in Genesis 22:4. Jewish sources relate the Akeidah [the binding of Isaac] story to the resurrection and the Messiah. When Yeshua said He would be raised 'on the third day,' midrashically one was to think back to Abraham and Isaac in the land of Moriah.

Genesis 22:2, 4, 6-14 *And he said, Take now thy son, thine only son Isaac, whom thou lovest, and get thee into the land of Moriah; and* *offer him there for a burnt offering upon one of the mountains which I will tell thee of...Then <u>on the third day</u> Abraham lifted up his eyes, and saw the place afar off...And Abraham took the wood of the burnt offering, and laid it upon Isaac his son; and he took the fire in his hand, and a knife; and they went both of them together. And Isaac spake unto Abraham his father, and said, My father: and he said, Here am I, my son. And he said, Behold the fire and the wood: but where is the lamb for a burnt offering? And Abraham said, My son, God will provide himself a lamb for a burnt offering: so they went both of them together. And they came to the place which God had told him of; and Abraham built an altar there, and laid the wood in order, and bound Isaac his son, and laid him on the altar upon the wood. And Abraham stretched forth his hand, and took the knife to slay his son. And the angel of the LORD called unto him out of heaven, and said, Abraham, Abraham: and he said, Here am I. And he said, Lay not thine hand upon the lad, neither do thou any thing unto him: for now I know that thou fearest God, seeing thou hast not withheld thy son, thine only son from me. And Abraham lifted up his eyes, and looked, and behold behind him a ram caught in a thicket by his horns: and Abraham went and took the ram, and offered him up for a burnt offering in the stead of his son. And Abraham called the name of that place Jehovah-jireh: as it is said to this day, In the mount of the LORD it shall be seen.* (KJV)

There are tremendous parallels with Isaac to Yeshua. First of all Isaac was miraculously conceived of his barren mother Sarah just as Yeshua was miraculously conceived of a virgin woman. Both Isaac and Yeshua were considered the only begotten of their father. Isaac was bound for certain death on Mount Moriah where Yeshua was later bound to the cross. Both Isaac and Yeshua lived, however.

Abraham laid the wood on Isaac to carry that he was to be sacrificed upon, just as Yeshua carried His cross before He was crucified on it. This is a vivid connection to the Messiah. The Midrash Rabbah puts it like this: 'Like one who carries on his own shoulder the stake upon which he is to be executed, Isaac carried the wood'. [Genesis Rabbah 56:3].

Many Jews and Christians alike have reservations as to why God would command Abraham to offer his son as a human sacrifice. Human sacrifices are forbidden in the Law. The Sages of old interpreted God's command to Abraham as meaning that he was to offer Isaac up upon the altar for a burnt sacrifice, but was not to kill him. God never told Abraham to kill his son. This is why the angel stopped the knife. Abraham had been faithful to the commandment.[11]

When they came to the spot on Mount Moriah where Isaac was to be sacrificed, he asked his father, 'Where is the lamb'? Abraham replied to Isaac, 'God will provide Himself a lamb'. The Hebrew word for 'provide' literally implies that God will see or seek out for Himself a lamb. As we will see in more detail in a later chapter, Isaac is connected to the Passover and God accounted his faithfulness to be a willing sacrifice as the merit of an actual sacrifice. One ancient writer said:

Why does it say, 'God will see...?' The LORD answers: 'I see the blood of the Akeidah of Isaac: as it is said, 'And Abraham called the name of that place Adonai-Yireh (The LORD sees)." And elsewhere it says, 'And as he was about to destroy, the LORD saw and changed His mind'. (1 Chronicles 21:15) What did He see? He saw the blood of the Akeidah: as it is said, 'God will see for Himself the lamb' (Genesis 22:8).[12]

Most commentators put the story of the Akeidah of Isaac on Rosh Hashana or Yom Kippur. However, Exodus Rabbah quite plainly puts the Akeidah on Passover.[13] The rabbis understood the merit of Isaac's willing sacrifice as an atonement that prevents God's wrath. It would not be a leap to say that the blood of the lamb on the doors in Egypt on Passover symbolized the 'blood' of Isaac. When God saw the blood on the doors, he was reminded of the Akeidah of Isaac and did not kill the firstborn of the house. The Egyptian Passover therefore looks both to the past merit of Isaac and to the future merit of Messiah. After all both Isaac and Messiah are both classified as Abraham's seed in Scripture [Galatians 3:16].

As already stated the Hebrew Akeidah means 'binding'. It comes from the verb akod ד ק ע translated as 'bound' in Genesis 22:9. It literally translates as marked with 'stripes' or 'striations'.[14] This verb is used for the 'markings' left by ropes on the wrists and ankles that are bound hand and foot. It would appear that the story of the Akeidah of Isaac has to do with the 'markings' left on his body. Even with Yeshua's resurrected body, the doubting Thomas could feel the scars in His hands and side. Yeshua was the Ultimate Akeidah sacrifice, bound to the wood with nails to his wrists and ankles forever scarred for all eternity as a reminder of redemption's cost.

John 8:56 *[Yeshua said] Your father Abraham rejoiced to see <u>my day</u>: and <u>he saw it</u>, and was glad.* (KJV)

Abraham lifted up his eyes and saw a 'ram caught in the thicket by its horns'. The KJV says 'behind him a ram caught in a thicket'. In Hebrew the word for 'behind' is 'achar' א ח ר and literally means 'afterward' or 'in the future'. This grammatical form of 'achar' grabbed the attention of many rabbis because how could Abraham lift up his eyes and see a ram literally 'behind' him. This alludes to the future Akeidah of Messiah in the 'achareit yamim,' which means 'the last days'.

Hebrews 11:17-19 *By faith Abraham, when he was tried, offered up Isaac: and he that had received the promises offered up his only begotten son, Of whom it was said, That in Isaac shall thy seed be called: Accounting that God was able to raise him up, even from the dead; from whence also he received him in a figure.* (KJV)

The writer of Hebrews proves that Abraham had faith in God to send His Messiah in the future by the very fact of his willingness to obey God by sacrificing his promised son Isaac. The Scripture says of Abraham's belief: 'Accounting that God was able to raise him up'. Even if he was allowed to offer Isaac, Abraham believed that God would raise him from the dead.

By 'faith' Abraham 'received him (Isaac) in a figure'. Abraham saw Isaac's resurrection from the dead as a 'figure'. The Greek word for 'figure' is 'parabole,' from which we get the word 'parable'. In this instance it should be rendered 'figuratively speaking'. It is very clear that the offering of Isaac had Messianic significance and was foreshadowing things to come, namely, the death and resurrection of Messiah Yeshua. Abraham believed in the Messiah that God had promised man from the beginning. Because he trusted that God would some day send His Messiah, it was imputed to him for righteousness.

The rabbis of old taught the story of the Akeidah as if Isaac had been sacrificed and his ashes lay on the altar.[15] How did Isaac live? He lived as if he was resurrected from the dead. More than likely this 'parable' of Isaac symbolically dying and being resurrected was based upon ancient Midrashim such as:

When the sword touched Isaac's throat his soul flew clean out of him. And when He let His voice be heard from between the cherubim, 'Lay not thy hand upon the lad,' the lad's soul was returned to his body. Then his father unbound him and Isaac rose, knowing that in this way the dead would come back to life in the future; whereupon he began to recite, 'Blessed are You, LORD, who resurrects the dead' (Pirkei de R. Eliezer, 31).[16]

The rabbis also mentioned that the ram caught in the thicket was predestined for this sacrifice from the six days of creation, or since the foundation of the world (Avot 5:6).[17] This ram prefigured the Messiah who was slain from the foundation of the world [Revelation 13:8; Hebrews 9:26; 1 Peter 1:19-20].

In Jewish mysticism the left horn [shofar] of this ram was blown at Mt. Sinai when Israel received the Torah. The right horn, which was said to be larger, will be blown at the coming of Messiah. But Rabbi Bechaye raises the question of how could these horns of the ram be used when it was burnt as an offering to the Lord [the horns are burnt also]. His answer is astounding! God created a new ram out of the ashes.[18]

Hebrews 11:10, 16 *For he [Abraham] looked for a city which hath foundations, whose builder and maker is God...But now they desire a better country, that is, an heavenly: wherefore God is not ashamed to be called their God: for he hath prepared for them a city.* (KJV)

The KJV states that Abraham called the name of that place [Moriah - the future location of the Temple] 'Jehovah-jireh: as it is said to this day, In the mount of the LORD it shall be seen'. In

Hebrew, Abraham named the place Adonai-Yireh that translates, as 'The LORD will see'. God will see for Himself a lamb on this very same mountain in the future.

Traditionally this ancient place of Moriah was located at the city called Shalem ש ל ם [Genesis 14:18; Psalm 76:2; Hebrews 7:1-2]. But in Genesis 22 Abraham named the place Yireh י ר א ה. When David purchased the threshing floor at this same location God synthesized these two names, Yireh plus Shalem, into Yerushalayim [Jerusalem] י ר ו ש ל ם, which means 'Peace will be seen'.[19] This speaks to the future when Messiah will rule His Kingdom of peace from this place.

To count days Hebraically is quite different from counting them in western thought. For example, in the western world, a child turns one year old on their first birthday. Although they are starting their second year of life, they remain one year old until they have completed two full years. This same child in ancient Biblical thought would be considered a year old upon birth. After exactly a full year has gone by, the child is recognized as two years old because he is beginning his second year of life. Therefore, the Hebraic way of counting is inclusive.

Now let's return to a proper understanding of the 'third day'. In Hebraic and rabbinical thought any part of a day is recognized as that whole day.[20] If we take this inclusive counting method and apply it to the events of Yeshua's death and resurrection, we conclude the following:

Day 1 - Nisan 13 Death 'between the evenings' about 3:00 P.M.   Wednesday
Night 1 - Nisan 14   Wednesday
                                                              night

Day 2 - Nisan 14   Thursday
Night 2 - Nisan 15 - High Sabbath   Thursday
                                                              night

Day 3 - Nisan 15 - High Sabbath   Friday
Night 3 - Nisan 16   Friday Night

According to Hebraic thought the resurrection of Yeshua could have occurred anytime after Friday night fulfilling the prophecy of Him being dead 'three days and three nights'. We will return to the day of His resurrection shortly. But first we will bring in some other verses that shed light to the counting of the days after Yeshua's death.

Matthew 27:62-66 *Now the next day, that followed the day of the preparation, the chief priests and Pharisees came together unto Pilate, Saying, Sir, we remember that that deceiver said, while he was yet alive, After three days I will rise again. Command therefore that the sepulchre be made sure until the third day, lest his disciples come by night, and steal him away, and say unto the people, He is risen from the dead: so the last error shall be worse than the first. Pilate said unto them, Ye have a watch: go your way, make it as sure as ye can. So they went, and made the sepulchre sure, sealing the stone, and setting a watch.* (KJV)

Matthew 28:11-15 *Now when they were going, behold, some of the watch came into the city, and shewed unto the chief priests all the things that were done. And when they were assembled with the elders, and had taken counsel, they gave large money unto the soldiers, Saying, Say ye, His disciples came by night, and stole him away while we slept. And if this come to the governor's ears, we will persuade him, and secure you. So they took the money, and did as they were taught: and this saying is commonly reported among the Jews until this day.* (Kev)

The chief Priests [Sadducees] and Pharisees knew full well of Yeshua's prophecy that He would arise after His death on the third day. They didn't believe this, but were concerned that Yeshua's disciples would steal His body away from the tomb at night and claim He fulfilled His prophecy of resurrection. They were afraid of the 'false' Messianic fervor this would result in among the Jews. For that reason they went to Pilate asking for a sealed stone and a guard to be placed at His tomb. How long did they plan to have the guard watch His tomb?

Notice that these leaders came to Pilate on 'the next day that followed the day of preparation'. The Pharisee's Passover lambs were sacrificed about 3:00 P.M. on Nisan 14 and they ate them at the Seder after sunset when it turned to Nisan 15, the first day of the feast of Unleavened Bread. 'The next day,' which was Friday Nisan 15, was the third day that Yeshua was in the tomb according to our Hebraic count. These chief Priests and Pharisees knew that it was 'high time' to put a guard at the tomb to prevent Yeshua's body from being stolen to fulfill His third day resurrection prophecy. This is why they asked Pilate for the guard on Friday Nisan 15, instead of Thursday, Nisan 14. The third day was upon them.

Contrary to depictions in movies, etc., it was not a Roman guard that camped before Yeshua's tomb. When they asked Pilate for help, he told them, 'Ye have a watch'. He was referring to the Levitical guards of the Temple. Some of the Levitical guards stood watch over Yeshua's tomb. After Yeshua's resurrection, Matthew 28 informs us that some of these guards came to the chief priests. It is highly unlikely that a Roman guard would report to the chief priests. It is also very unlikely that the chief priests could bribe a Roman guard with money to lie that they fell asleep while the disciples of Yeshua came at night and stole His body. This is very important because the guards and the chief priests are admitting that Yeshua's resurrection occurred at night. What night? It was Friday night, the evening of the weekly Sabbath. But 'night' from Hebraic perspective, is from approximately 6:00 P.M. unto 6:00 A.M. It is highly unlikely that the Jews would believe their story if they fell asleep early in the night. Sometime after midnight would be more believable, because this is when people normally sleep. In western thinking however, after midnight is Saturday morning and is still the weekly Sabbath. From this evidence, it would appear that Yeshua arose from the dead sometime in the early hours of Saturday morning, which was the weekly Sabbath.

Luke 24:20-21 *And how the chief priests and our rulers delivered him to be condemned to death, and have crucified him. But we trusted that it had been he which should have redeemed Israel: and beside all this, to day is the third day since these things were done.* (KJV)

After Yeshua was raised from the dead, Luke says, 'To day is the third day since these things were done [Yeshua's death]'. Very clearly the writer is saying that the resurrection happened 'on the third day,' not after three full days.

Friday Evening Nisan 15 Turning to Nisan 16, The Weekly Sabbath

Most Bible scholars would agree that if we have fifty texts saying one thing doctrinally, and a couple of texts that appear to disagree with the other fifty, it is paramount to examine those couple of texts thoroughly to see if their original interpretation is faulty. It would not be acceptable to cast aside the fifty agreeing texts and just accept the two opposing texts. One must look to the preponderance of the evidence.

By this same reasoning, if the Greek word 'Sabbaton' [Strong's #4521] is translated Sabbath, or Sabbaths, fifty nine out of sixty eight times that it is used in the New Testament and is arbitrarily translated 'first day of the week' only eight times, it would seem thorough to fully examine why this translation is given in these instances. Of these eight times that 'Sabbaton' is translated as 'first day of the week [Sunday],' six refer to Yeshua's resurrection:

1. **Matthew 28:1** *In the end of the sabbath, as it began to dawn toward the first day of the week, came Mary Magdalene and the other Mary to see the sepulchre.* (KJV)

2. **Mark 16:2** *And very early in the morning the first day of the week, they came unto the sepulchre at the rising of the sun.* (KJV)

3. **Mark 16:9** *Now when Jesus was risen early the first day of the week, he appeared first to Mary Magdalene, out of whom he had cast seven devils.* (KJV)

4. **Luke 24:1** *Now upon the first day of the week, very early in the morning, they came unto the sepulchre, bringing the spices which they had prepared, and certain others with them.* (KJV)

5. **John 20:1** *The first day of the week cometh Mary Magdalene early, when it was yet dark, unto the sepulchre, and seeth the stone taken away from the sepulchre.* (KJV)

6.   <u>John 20:19</u> *Then the same day at evening, being the first day of the week, when the doors were shut where the disciples were assembled for fear of the Jews, came Jesus and stood in the midst, and saith unto them, Peace be unto you.* (KJV)

The English translations of the New Testament all agree that Yeshua rose from the dead early in the morning on Sunday, which is the 'first day of the week'. But is this what the Greek actually states, or has someone 'changed' the meaning to promote an agenda? We will go through each one of these verses and the reader can determine the truth from them by the evidence presented.

The first thing to address here is that the verse and chapter numbers are not in the original text and was not added until the Middle Ages. Even punctuation has to be translated. Although, there are obvious errors, no one doubts the sincerity of those who numbered the Bible to help us read it more efficiently. The oldest Greek texts of the New Testament were written all in capital letters without any spacing between words. There were no punctuation marks such as periods and commas. The translators placed all these into the text along with the chapter and verse numbers. These can never be thought of as divinely inspired.[21]

<u>Matthew 27:66</u> *So they [the chief priests and Pharisees] went, and made the sepulchre sure, sealing the stone, and setting a watch.* (KJV)

We can see how a chapter break at Matthew 28:1 might cause the flow of the text to be interrupted. The two Marys' came to Yeshua's sepulcher 'in the end of the Sabbath, as it began to dawn toward the first day of the week'. In context, the last verse in Matthew 27 that discusses the chief priests and Pharisees posting a Levitical guard outside Yeshua's tomb, is directly connected to Matthew 28:1. But first we need to look at the translation of Matthew 28:1 to continue.

The phrase 'in the end of the Sabbath,' is 'opse de Sabbaton' in Greek. The impression from the translation of the entire verse is that the Sabbath is over. However, the Greek word 'opse' means 'late,' not that something is totally ended or over. Also, the word

151

'Sabbaton,' is Sabbath, but it is definitely in the plural form. The corrected translation of the first part of the verse should be rendered like: 'Late on the Sabbaths'.

Obviously, the translator automatically thought weekly Sabbath when they saw 'Sabbaton'. But our study of the Hebraic festivals reveals that a High Sabbath was celebrated on Nisan 15, the first day of the festival of Unleavened Bread. This was the Friday before Yeshua's resurrection. Yeshua was resurrected on the next day, Nisan 16, the weekly Sabbath. Therefore, two Sabbaths were celebrated back-to-back. 'Late on the Sabbaths' represents that the High Sabbath of Nisan 15 had concluded and that the midway point of the weekly Sabbath had passed, which was approximately 6:00 A.M. Saturday morning on Nisan 16.

The next phrase 'as it began to dawn' is translated from the Greek 'epiphosko,' which means 'drawing toward light'. Other verses clearly state that the women came to the grave in the early morning at the rising of the sun. Therefore, the context is Saturday morning, Nisan 16, on the weekly Sabbath. The text reads thus far: 'Late on the Sabbaths, as it began drawing toward light'.

'The first day of the week' comes from the Greek 'mian Sabbaton'. Well, this is Sunday, according to the translators. But is this a valid translation? The Greek word 'mia' [Strong's # 3391] does not mean 'first,' it means 'one'. A form of 'mia' is used sixty-two times in the New Testament and in all but nine cases the word is translated 'one' in the KJV. In seven of these nine instances 'mia' is translated 'first' in the phrase 'first day of the week. The remaining two verses are:

Titus 3:10 *A man that is an heretic after the first and second admonition reject*;

Revelation 17:17 *For God hath put in their hearts to fulfil his will, and to agree, and give their kingdom unto the beast, until the words of God shall be fulfilled.*

The word 'first' [mia] in Titus 3:10 should be translated 'one' and the verse would thus be rendered: A man that remains a heretic after one or two admonitions is rejected. In Revelation 17:17 'mia' is translated as 'agree' in the KJV, but should be rendered 'and to be one'.

Next, the word 'day' in 'first day of the week' is never in the text. It should not be there! The word for 'week' is the same word Sabbaton used earlier in Matthew 28:1 and means 'Sabbath,' or in this case it is plural again: 'Sabbaths'. Therefore, the word for word translation is as follows:

'Late on the Sabbaths, as it began drawing toward light on one of the Sabbaths,' Mary Magdalene and the other Mary came to see the sepulcher.

Without understanding the Hebraic festivals, the translators could not decipher what this verse was really saying. 'One of the Sabbaths' is the way the Hebrew writers expressed the weekly Sabbaths that occurred during the count of the omer toward Shavuot [Pentecost]: [22]

Leviticus 23:15-16 *And ye shall <u>count</u> unto you from the morrow after the sabbath, from the day that ye brought the sheaf of the wave offering; <u>seven sabbaths</u> shall be complete: Even unto the morrow after the seventh sabbath shall ye number fifty days; and ye shall offer a new meat offering unto the LORD.* (KJV)

In a previous chapter we studied the counting of the omer of barley. Leviticus 23 commands Israel to 'count' from the 'next day' after the Sabbath. The Sabbath listed here is Nisan 15, the first day of the Feast of Unleavened Bread. The day after Nisan 15 is always Nisan 16, which the barley sheaf was waved before the Lord in the Temple. Nisan 16 was always day one of the count of the omer. Israel was to count forty-nine days of the omer and then the fiftieth day was Shavuot [Pentecost], the waving of the wheat sheaf.

But notice the phraseology that Israel was to 'count' until 'seven Sabbaths' were complete. These were not seven literal Sabbaths, but seven 'weeks' of Sabbaths [forty-nine days]. When Nisan 16 fell on a weekly Sabbath, Shavuot [Pentecost] also fell on a weekly Sabbath after seven full weeks had been completed. There were always exactly seven weekly Sabbaths during the forty-nine day omer count. Apparently, the tradition developed among the Jews by the first century to call any of these 'Sabbaths' during the count of the omer 'one of the Sabbaths'. The author believes that the evidence will bear this out as we continue to look at the Scriptures.

The next verse to be studied regarding the timing of Yeshua's resurrection is Mark 16:2 where it is stated that the two Marys along with Salome came to His sepulcher 'very early in the morning the first day of the week'. 'Early in the morning' comes from the Greek 'proi,' and it is used to denote the very early morning hours before sunrise [see Mark 1:35]. The women set out for Yeshua's sepulcher in the morning when it was still dark and by the time they had arrived the sun was rising.

In Mark 16:2 we are told that this morning was 'the first day of the week'. The Greek for 'first day of the week' is 'mia ton Sabbaton'. Literally, this means exactly 'one of the Sabbaths'. Mark is telling the reader that Yeshua was raised in the morning of the weekly Sabbath, which happened to be 'one of the Sabbaths' during the count of the omer toward Shavuot [Pentecost].

Luke [24:1] records the next verse where he informs us that the women came to Yeshua's sepulcher 'very early in the morning,' 'upon the first day of the week'. 'Early in the morning' in this verse comes from the Greek 'orthros,' which means 'daybreak' or 'dawn' when the sun is rising. 'The first day of week' is the same Greek expression 'mia ton Sabbaton,' meaning 'one of the Sabbaths' of the counting of the omer.

We now turn to the Gospel according to John [20:1] where it is stated 'early, when it was yet dark,' Mary Magdalene came to Yeshua's sepulcher on 'the first day of the week'. 'Early' is the same Greek word 'proi' as used in Mark 16:2. The Greek word used for 'dark' is 'skotia,' which means 'dimness'. Once again the impression is given that the women went to the grave when it was dark at the outset of the sunrise. 'The first day of the week,' comes from the same 'mia ton Sabbaton,' 'one of the [weekly] Sabbaths' of the counting of the omer.

Mark 16:9 *Now when Jesus was risen early the first day of the week, he appeared first to Mary Magdalene, out of whom he had cast seven devils.* (KJV)

Now let's look at our final resurrection verse regarding the usage of the English translation 'the first day of the week'. It comes from Mark 16:9 where we are told explicitly that Yeshua arose early on 'the first day of the week,' and appeared to Mary Magdalene.

Before we go any further, we must highlight this verse with a reader's caution. Codex S, the oldest Semitic version of Mark ends with Mark 16:8. The two oldest Greek manuscripts also end with verse 8.[23] More than likely Mark did not write the verses 9-20 in chapter 16. They were definitely added later and are not original. This will be detected in the Greek.

The Greek for 'the first day of the week' is not the standard 'mia ton Sabbaton' [even used by Mark in 16:2], but 'proti Sabbatou'. 'Proti' definitely means 'first' and not 'one'. 'Also 'Sabbatou' is singular for 'Sabbath' instead of the standard 'Sabbaton [Sabbaths]. Literally 'proti Sabbatou' means, 'first [of the] Sabbath'.

This author believes that Mark 16:9-20 is not divinely inspired and needs to be looked at very carefully because of its later addition. The scribe who penned this knew the Hebrew way of interpreting 'mia ton Sabbaton' as 'one of the Sabbaths' of the count of the omer. After the first century, the trend of the 'Gentile' church was to move Yeshua's resurrection from the weekly Sabbath to the 'first day of the week,' Sunday. This is all connected to Easter replacing Passover and Sunday worship replacing the Saturday Sabbath. The author who penned 'proti Sabbatou' knew he needed to change two things: (1) 'one' to 'first' to make it grammatically fit Sunday, 'the first day of the week,' and (2) Sabbaths [plural] to Sabbath and make it represent a 'week'. Since the Greek of Mark 16:9 does not align itself with the other Gospel accounts of 'one of the Sabbaths,' this author rejects it as evidence that Yeshua rose from the dead on Sunday. In addition Mark himself in 16:2 clearly states with the other Gospels that Yeshua had risen on 'mia ton Sabbaton,' 'one of the Sabbaths' of the counting of the omer.

John 20:19 *Then the same day at evening, being the first day of the week, when the doors were shut where the disciples were assembled for fear of the Jews, came Jesus and stood in the midst, and saith unto them, Peace be unto you.* (KJV)

In John 20:19 we are told it was 'the first day of the week' that Yeshua appeared to His disciples in resurrected form behind locked doors. It was the 'same day at evening'. What day was it? It was the weekly Sabbath that Yeshua had resurrected on earlier in the chapter. But it was now Saturday evening, before the sun had set. The Greek for 'the first day of the week' is 'mia Sabbaton,' 'one of the Sabbaths' of the counting of the omer.

Acts 20:6-7, 13-22 *And we sailed away from Philippi after the days of unleavened bread, and came unto them to Troas in five days; where we abode seven days. And upon the first day of the week, when the disciples came together to break bread, Paul preached unto them, ready to depart on the morrow...And we went before to ship, and sailed unto Assos, there intending to take in Paul: for so had he appointed, minding himself to go afoot. And when he met with us at Assos, we took him in, and came to Mitylene. And we sailed thence, and came the next day over against Chios; and the next day we arrived at Samos, and tarried at Trogyllium; and the next day we came to Miletus. For Paul had determined to sail by Ephesus, because he would not spend the time in Asia: for he hasted, if it were possible for him, to be at Jerusalem the day of Pentecost. And from Miletus he sent to Ephesus, and called the elders of the church. And when they were come to him, he said unto them, Ye know, from the first day that I came into Asia, after what manner I have been with you at all seasons, Serving the Lord with all humility of mind, and with many tears, and temptations, which befell me by the lying in wait of the Jews: And how I kept back nothing that was profitable unto you, but have shewed you, and have taught you publickly, and from house to house, Testifying both to the Jews, and also to the Greeks, repentance toward God, and faith toward our Lord Jesus Christ. And now, behold, I go bound in the spirit unto Jerusalem, not knowing the things that shall befall me there:* (KJV)

On Paul's third missionary trip he was in Philippi during the seven days of the feast of Unleavened Bread. The counting of the omer began on Nisan 16, the day after the High Sabbath of Nisan 15. The weekly Sabbath during those seven days of the festival of Unleavened Bread was the first of 'one of the Sabbaths' of the counting of the omer. Paul, then, sailed to Troas in five days and stayed there another seven. Depending if Paul left exactly after the seven days of Unleavened Bread, it was either the second or third of 'one of the Sabbaths' of the counting of the omer. It was somewhere around the twentieth day of the counting of the Omer when Paul gathered the disciples in Troas together to break bread [to eat the Sabbath meal]. Acts 20:7 states that Paul and these disciples were gathered together upon 'the first day of the week'. Again, the Greek is 'mia ton Sabbaton,' which literally means 'one of the Sabbaths' of the counting of the omer.

Another four or five days are attested to in these verses in Acts 20 before Ephesus is mentioned. We can conclude that probably somewhere about halfway through the forty-nine day count of the omer had transpired. Paul did not have time to sail to Ephesus because he desired to be in Jerusalem for the feast of Shavuot [Pentecost], thus proving that this all takes place during the forty-nine days of the counting of the omer. From Miletus Paul summoned the elders of Ephesus together and affirmed to them that he was ready to meet his destiny in Jerusalem at Pentecost.

1 Corinthians 16:1-8 *Now concerning the collection for the saints, as I have given order to the churches of Gillette, even so do ye.* <u>*Upon the first day of the week*</u> *let every one of you lay by him in a store, as God hath prospered him, that there are no gatherings when I come. And when I come, whomsoever ye will approve by your letters, they will I send to bring your liberality unto Jerusalem. And if I go meets also, they shall go with me. Now I will come unto you, when I shall pass through Macedonia: for I do pass through Macedonia. And it may be that I will abide, yea, and winter with you, that ye may bring me on my journey whithersoever I go. For I will not see you now by the way; but I trust to tarry a while with you, if the Lord permit. But I will tarry at Ephesus until* <u>*Pentecost*</u>. (KJV)

On Paul's third missionary trip while in Ephesus during the days of the counting of the omer, he became aware of reports of contentions among the Corinthian believers [1 Corinthians 1:11]. A delegation of at least three men was sent from the Corinthian church to meet Paul in Ephesus to address these issues [1 Corinthians 16:17]. Therefore, 1 Corinthians 16 is written from the perspective that it was sometime between Passover and Pentecost.

Paul could not visit all the churches in his proximity at that time because he strongly desired to be in Jerusalem at Pentecost for the Temple celebration. He was to stay in Ephesus until he made that journey to Jerusalem. It was Paul's custom to raise a collection for the impoverished saints in Jerusalem through the churches spread abroad [Romans 15:25-26]. When he knew that he was journeying to Jerusalem, he gave the opportunity to the churches to send with him their generosity.

Scholars have taken 1 Corinthians 16 totally out of its context, and mandated Sunday as a day that all saints are to give offerings [collections] to the church. Paul was giving instructions to the Corinthians, as he did to the churches in Galatia, on how they could give to the poor saints in Jerusalem. The poor saints were to receive the collections, not a church to pay for its functions. Paul told them he would not be able to be there at this time because of his journey to Jerusalem, but Paul was willing for them to send their charity through their selected representatives with him when he journeyed to Jerusalem for Pentecost.

Paul told the Corinthians to 'lay up' for the Jerusalem saints as God had prospered them. This was to be set-aside in their homes upon 'the first day of the week'. 'The first day of the week,' comes from the Greek 'mian Sabbatou,' which literally translates as 'one of the Sabbath [singular]'. Why Sabbath is in the singular form here, the author does not know. But 'mian' does not mean 'first [day],' it means 'one'. In context, the Corinthians were being instructed to 'lay up' these goods either on a particular Sabbath, or just one of Sabbaths during the counting of the omer. The context is that these goods would be shortly going to Jerusalem with Paul.

The saints in Jerusalem were impoverished because of the recent famine that swept Judea [Acts 11:27-30]. Their need was not money because money could buy very little food in Judea. They needed famine relief, which included nonperishable food and other items such as clothing, water, etc. In 1 Corinthians 16, Paul is talking about laying aside these extra items to be taken to Jerusalem quickly when he makes his pilgrimage for Pentecost.

Also, the Jews did not handle money on the Sabbath. Paul, being a Torah-observant Jew, would never have taught his Gentile converts to disregard the Sabbath in this manner, but there would be no problem in setting aside 'food' in the home for such purposes on the Sabbath. Since Paul would have to leave Ephesus during the forty-nine day counting of the omer period in order to reach Jerusalem by Pentecost, the context of 'one of the Sabbath' almost assuredly refers to one of the seven Sabbaths during this count. Paul may have been referring to a certain Sabbath which after he intended to leave Ephesus for Jerusalem.

1 Corinthians 15:20-23 *But now is Christ risen from the dead, and become the firstfruits of them that slept. For since by man came death, by man came also the resurrection of the dead. For as in Adam all die, even so in Christ shall all be made alive. But every man in his own order: Christ the firstfruits; afterward they that are Christ's at his coming.* (KJV)

In the chapter before [1 Corinthians 15], Paul clearly relates Yeshua's resurrection to the Firstfruits of the Barley Harvest and the counting of the omer. 1 Corinthians may have been written during the counting of the omer, which was fresh upon his mind. This gives a clear link between these two chapters.

Luke 6:1 *And it came to pass on the second sabbath after the first, that he went through the corn fields [sporimos: G4702 - fields of grain]; and his disciples plucked the ears of corn [stachus: G4719 - ear of grain], and did eat, rubbing them in their hands.* (KJV)

We have one more instance of 'one of the Sabbaths' during the count of the omer being referred to in the New Testament. Luke 6:1 says it was 'the second Sabbath after the first'. The Greek is 'Sabbaton dueterproton'. Most experts believe that this refers to the second Sabbath of the seven during the count of the omer. However, some feel that it refers to the first weekly Sabbath after the High

Sabbath of Nisan 15. Either way, this Sabbath is during the count of the omer.

Notice that Luke 6:1 states that Yeshua and His disciples were in the 'corn fields' on this Sabbath. The Greek word for 'corn fields' is 'sporimos,' which specifically means 'fields of grain'. It can be any grain - wheat or barley. During the feast of Unleavened Bread wheat is not ripe. Only barley is beginning to ripe at that time. Yeshua's disciples plucked the 'ears of corn'. 'Ears of corn' comes from the Greek word 'stachus,' meaning an 'ear of grain'. Once again, this could be any grain. Since the context is early in the counting of the omer, the disciples were plucking barley grain.

Yeshua, the Resurrected Heavenly High Priest

John 20:16-20 *Jesus saith unto her, Mary. She turned herself, and saith unto him, Rabboni; which is to say, Master. Jesus saith unto her, Touch me not; for I am not yet ascended to my Father: but go to my brethren, and say unto them, I ascend unto my Father, and your Father; and to my God, and your God. Mary Magdalene came and told the disciples that she had seen the Lord, and that he had spoken these things unto her. Then the same day at evening, being the first day of the week [one of the Sabbaths], when the doors were shut where the disciples were assembled for fear of the Jews, came Jesus and stood in the midst, and saith unto them, Peace be unto you. And when he had so said, he shewed unto them his hands and his side. Then were the disciples glad, when they saw the Lord.* (KJV)

In human flesh Yeshua was The Prophet and Suffering Servant Messiah, the sacrifice of Israel. It must be emphasized that Yeshua was not a human sacrifice, but was a Heavenly Sacrifice. In His resurrection Yeshua becomes priestly, as we will further develop.

When Mary hears the Master's voice and recognizes Him, she probably fell to the ground in adoration and attempted to grasp His feet. But Yeshua tells her, 'Touch me not; for I am not yet ascended to My Father'. What did He mean? It is obvious that He wasn't against Mary touching Him because He lets the disciples later that day inspect His scarred hands and side. The Scripture explicitly states that Thomas touched Him [Matthew 20:26-27]. The reason that Mary was instructed not to touch Him is because He had not yet ascended to the Heavenly Father. This is not the ascension to the Right Hand of the Throne of the Father, which comes forty days later.

In the Temple, the priests carried the blood of the sacrificial animals to the Altar in special sanctified vessels. In the process if any priest that had been rendered unclean ritually touched them, the blood and the sacrifice were invalidated [Mishnah Zevachin 2:1]. With a little conjecture it would be reasonable to think that a priest turning to carry the vessel of blood to the Altar would say to his brethren, 'Touch me not, for I have not yet ascended to the Altar'.

Hebrews 9:14 *How much more shall the blood of Christ, who through the eternal Spirit offered himself without spot to God, purge your conscience from dead works to serve the living God?* (KJV)

In His suffering state Yeshua was the heavenly sacrificial offering for atonement. In actuality He fulfilled all the purposes of the Temple sacrifices and more. But Yeshua can never be compared to an animal sacrifice. He was offered from an eternal perspective from the foundation of the world. He was the only begotten of the Father and as such was an Eternal Sacrifice. How Yeshua fulfilled all symbolism related to the Temple and Biblical sacrifices is beyond the scope of this book.

Hebrews 8:5 *Who serve unto the example and shadow of heavenly things, as Moses was admonished of God when he was about to make the tabernacle: for, See, saith he, that thou make all things according to the pattern shewed to thee in the mount.* (KJV)

Hebrews 11:1 *Now faith is the substance of things hoped for, the evidence of things not seen.* (KJV)

At Mt. Sinai Moses was given a vision of the heavenly 'tavnit' [pattern] for the Tabernacle/Temple. Moses was instructed to construct the Tabernacle and all its furnishings based upon the heavenly pattern that he saw. We must keep in mind that there is a Heavenly Jerusalem, Temple, or Gan Edan [Garden of Eden] in Eternity or the Olam Haba [World To Come].[24] The Earthy Jerusalem and Temple are only a 'shadow' of the real. Since we are bound to this world we often see what 'exists' as the real substance. But it is truly what we don't see that is reality and true substance.

Hebrews 5:6 *As he saith also in another place, Thou art a priest for ever after the order of Melchisedec.* (KJV)

Psalm 110:4 *The LORD hath sworn, and will not repent, Thou art a priest for ever after the order of Melchizedek.* (KJV)

In His resurrected state Yeshua is the Heavenly High Priest after the order of Melchizedek who offered His blood in the Heavenly Sanctuary. The book of Hebrews clearly contrasts Yeshua's priesthood with the Aaronic priesthood. It must be emphasized that there was nothing wrong with the Aaronic priesthood because it was ordained of God. It was the priesthood of the 'shadow' Temple, but the priesthood of the Heavenly Temple is of a higher order, the order of Melchizedek. It is an order that is greater than the Aaronic order. It is an order that the Aaronic order was fashioned after.

Hebrews 9:24 *For Christ is <u>not</u> entered into the holy places made with hands, which are the figures of the true; but into heaven itself, now to appear in the presence of God for us:* (KJV)

Hebrews 9:11-12 *But Christ being come an high priest of good things to come, by a greater and more perfect tabernacle, not made with hands, that is to say, not of this building; Neither by the blood of goats and calves, but by his own blood he entered in once into the holy place, having obtained eternal redemption for us.* (KJV)

Hebrews 10:19-21 *Having therefore, brethren, boldness to enter into the holiest by the blood of Jesus, By a new and living way, which he hath consecrated for us, through the veil, that is to say, his flesh; And having an high priest over the house of God.* (KJV)

The Scripture makes it very clear that Yeshua did not enter the earthly Temple as its High Priest. He entered the Heavenly Temple as The High Priest. The blood of animals is required in the earthly Temple, but Yeshua offered His own blood in the Heavenly Temple. Every year and on a continual basis the Aaronic priesthood had to offer the blood of animals in the Earthly Temple. Yeshua offered His blood once, and for all, in the Heavenly Temple.

So when did Yeshua offer His blood as the High Priest of the heavenly Temple? It strongly appears that when He told Mary not to touch Him for He had yet ascended to the Father, that He was speaking of Himself as the High Priest delivering the blood to the Altar. Because He allowed the disciples to touch Him later that same day, it seems clear that Yeshua ascended into the Heavenly Temple the same day of His resurrection, Saturday [Sabbath], Nisan 16. After applying His blood, He immediately returned to the earth and walked among His disciples for forty days [Acts 1:3].

The Resurrection Firstfruits

Matthew 27:52-53 *And the graves were opened; and many bodies of the saints which slept arose, And came out of the graves after his resurrection, and went into the holy city, and appeared unto many.* (KJV)

These two verses in Matthew 27 have been glossed over by Christian theologians and purposely avoided because of its difficulty to explain. Immediately after Yeshua's resurrection, Matthew tells a unique story not mentioned by the other Gospel writers. 'Graves were opened' and 'many bodies of the saints which slept arose' and 'came out of the graves after His resurrection' and 'went into the holy city [Jerusalem], and appeared to many'. We must take this as fact that many saints were resurrected with Yeshua as firstfruits of the Barley Harvest, which occurred on the Sabbath of Nisan 16 that year. What happened to these resurrected saints? Were their resurrected bodies only after the manner of Lazarus' resurrection? Or were they glorified bodies after Yeshua's resurrection? Did they also ascend to heaven to be with the Father as Yeshua did later? Or did they live and die physically again as Lazarus? We may never know the truth of all this on this side of Eternity, but taken as truth at least some dead saints came out of their graves that day and people saw them again.

The Feast of the Firstfruits of the Barley Harvest

The grain from the new crop could not be harvested until the first omer was harvested and brought to the Temple for a ceremonial waving to the Lord. Since barley ripened first in Israel, the omer offering was always barley. The priest was to wave the omer on the day following the High Sabbath of Nisan 15, the first day of the festival of Unleavened Bread, which, of course, is Nisan 16. After it was offered, the Israelites could then eat of the land they had sowed that year.

The Talmud records that the Pharisees 'mocked' the Sadducees' interpretation of the Firstfruits always being waved on a Sunday, by a public ceremony that overemphasized that the Firstfruits of the Barley Harvest was to be celebrated on Nisan 16. On the Pharisee's Day of Preparation, which was the Passover on Nisan 14, Pharisaic officials would go out into the barley fields of Gaggoth Zerifin and bind standing barley together in the open field so that it could be reaped with much fanfare among the people.

At sundown, the start of Nisan 15 and the Pharisee's Passover Seder, the Jews kept the High Sabbath [Shabbaton]. On the next day as the sun was setting and about to turn to Nisan 16, the bound barley was reaped and collected in three containers. At the time of Yeshua's death and resurrection this occurred on Friday evening just before the weekly Sabbath began. The Pharisees brought the baskets of barley to the priests in the Temple that night. During the night the priests prepared the barley for the Festival of the Firstfruits ceremony the next morning [Saturday], which was still Nisan 16.

The barley was threshed out so that none of the grains were crushed. The barley grains were then placed into a special container, which was a perforated pan. The pan was passed over a fire where each of the kernels was to be touched by the fire. The grains were then exposed to wind to blow away chaff. The grain was then taken to the sieves of the Temple for sifting. There were a series of thirteen sieves each succeeding one finer than the other. The grains were passed through the sieves until the Temple Treasurer could put his hands in the flour and none would adhere to his fingers. The barley flour was refined to the greatest degree to be presented to the Lord.

After adding oil and frankincense, the barley flour mixture was brought near to the altar and a portion of it was offered upon it. The remainder of the dough was then waved in the four directions and up and down called tenufah. Bread was then made with four corners projecting upward. This Unleavened Barley bread was then shared among the priests. [Talmud - Mas. Menachoth 64a, 65a, 66a]

The Firstfruits of the Barley Harvest represents the crudest of grains being changed into flour to become food for the people. It represents growth and life coming from the death of the seed in the ground. The grains being sifted into purity represents perfection. What a picture of Yeshua's death and resurrection!

Hebrews 9:23-24 *It was therefore necessary that the patterns of things in the heavens should be* <u>*purified*</u> *with these; but the heavenly things themselves with better sacrifices than these. For Christ is not entered into the holy places made with hands, which are the figures of the true; but into heaven itself, now to appear in the presence of God for us:* (KJV)

While the waving of the barley omer was taking place in the Temple on the weekly Sabbath [Saturday] of Nisan 16, a wave offering of a much higher scale was taking place in the Heavenly Temple. Sometime that morning after telling Mary not to touch Him, Yeshua ascended into the Heavenlies as the ultimate wave offering to God.

This Firstfruits ceremony was called Yom Bikkurim or Sfirat, which literally means 'the counting of the sheaf'. It speaks of the earliest harvest that takes place in Israel, the barley harvest. On an agricultural level the people understood that if God was faithful to bless them with the early harvest, that He would definitely bless them with the harvest of later summer. Yeshua's resurrection on the Biblical Firstfruits of the Barley Harvest represents the early harvest with

God's promise to bless His people with resurrection at the end of the final harvest.

1 Corinthians 15:20-23 *But now is Christ risen from the dead, and become the firstfruits of them that slept. For since by man came death, by man came also the resurrection of the dead. For as in Adam all die, even so in Christ shall all be made alive. But every man in his own order: Christ the firstfruits; afterward they that are Christ's at his coming.* (KJV)

1 Corinthians 15 shows a vital link between Sfirat Haomer and the doctrine of resurrection. Paul is actually making a technical reference to the Holy Day of the Sfirat Haomer. It is not merely that Yeshua was the first to rise bodily from the grave, but that by so doing, He is the direct fulfillment of the feast of Firstfruits. The bringing of the Sfirat Haomer was definitely linked to the season of spring, which was when vegetation began to grow everywhere from the ground. It is a harvest festival and the barley dough was waved before the Lord. Think of it: the grain that came from the earth was now lifted up high for all to see! Yeshua's resurrection fulfilled the Firstfruits of the Barley Harvest!

Leviticus 23:15-17 *And ye shall count unto you from the morrow after the sabbath [Sunday], from the day that ye brought the sheaf of the wave offering [The firstfruits of the barley harvest]; seven sabbaths shall be complete [49 days]: Even unto the morrow after the seventh sabbath shall ye number fifty days; and ye shall offer a new meat offering unto the LORD. Ye shall bring out of your habitations two wave loaves of two tenth deals: they shall be of fine flour; they shall be baken with leaven; they are the firstfruits unto the LORD.* (KJV)

The Biblical counting of the omer began at the Messiah's resurrection on Saturday, Nisan 16. Israel was to count seven full weeks of Sabbaths [forty-nine total days]. Following these forty-nine days on another Saturday Sabbath, the festival of Pentecost [Shavuot] was to be celebrated. Two sheaves of wheat were to be offered to the

Lord. Shavuot is also known as the Firstfruits of the Wheat Harvest. So through the counting of the omer, Shavuot is connected to the Passover. We have already mentioned in an earlier chapter that Shavuot was viewed as the Atzeret [conclusion] of Passover.

1 Corinthians 15:50-53 *Now this I say, brethren, that flesh and blood cannot inherit the kingdom of God; neither doth corruption inherit incorruption. Behold, I shew you a mystery; We shall not all sleep, but we shall all be changed, In a moment, in the twinkling of an eye, at the last trump: for the trumpet shall sound, and the dead shall be raised incorruptible, and we shall be changed. For this corruptible must put on incorruption, and this mortal must put on immortality.* (KJV)

Paul continues his theme about Messiah being the Firstfruits of the Barley Harvest in 1 Corinthians 15 by mentioning that all believers in Yeshua will one day receive an incorruptible body at His Coming as He and the resurrected firstfruits received. Obviously, Yeshua in a resurrected body had achieved incorruption and immortality. But the believers in Yeshua who still have flesh and blood bodies are mortal and corrupt. These bodies cannot inherit the Kingdom of God and therefore must be resurrected at a future time.

We had mentioned how the sheaf of the barley was purified to its purest form through the Temple sieves at the Firstfruits of the Barley Harvest. Barley, as our human flesh, is the crudest of all grains. It is changed into pure flour, a representation of the believer's purified body. The resurrected have no need of further purification. But you and me who are believers in Yeshua with flesh and blood bodies require ongoing purification until ultimately we will be permanently changed through resurrection. The counting of the omer teaches about this ongoing purification. The counting of the omer is to be a stepladder ascending to the festival of Shavuot, exactly fifty days after the Firstfruits of the Barley Harvest. Coming to Shavuot should be looked at as coming to the Mountain of God [Mt. Sinai] to receive His Torah and the power to live Holy before a Holy God while we await our bodily resurrection.

The forty-nine days of the counting of the omer after Yeshua's resurrection was a time of reflection and seeking for His disciples. It was a time for them to purify themselves and have the encrustation of the world fall off of them. It was a time of preparation to receive God's Torah from Mt. Sinai. What the disciples of Yeshua went through during these forty-nine days was directly related to what the Israelites went through in the wilderness, but on a higher level. After the crossing of the Reed Sea, the Israelites were staring directly at God at Mt. Sinai to become His betrothed bride. Likewise, the disciples were facing the reality of this marriage covenant as they awaited the Promise of the Father.

Luke 24:49-51 *And, behold, I send the promise of my Father upon you: but tarry ye in the city of Jerusalem, until ye be endued with power from on high. And he led them out as far as to Bethany, and he lifted up his hands, and blessed them. And it came to pass, while he blessed them, he was parted from them, and carried up into heaven.* (KJV)

Acts 1:1-5, 8-14 *Until the day in which he was taken up, after that he through the Holy Ghost had given commandments unto the apostles whom he had chosen: To whom also he shewed himself alive after his passion by many infallible proofs, being seen of them forty days, and speaking of the things pertaining to the kingdom of God: And, being assembled together with them, commanded them that they should not depart from Jerusalem, but wait for the promise of the Father, which, saith he, ye have heard of me. For John truly baptized with water; but ye shall be baptized with the Holy Ghost not many days hence... But ye shall receive power, after that the Holy Ghost is come upon you: and ye shall be witnesses unto me both in Jerusalem, and in all Judaea, and in Samaria, and unto the uttermost part of the earth. And when he had spoken these things, while they beheld, he was taken up; and a cloud received him out of their sight. And while they looked stedfastly toward heaven as he went up, behold, two men stood by them in white apparel; Which also said, Ye men of Galilee, why stand ye gazing up into heaven? this same Jesus, which is taken up from you into heaven, shall so* *come in like manner as ye have seen him go into heaven. Then returned they unto Jerusalem from the mount called Olivet, which is from Jerusalem a sabbath day's journey. And when they were come in, they went up into an upper room, where abode both Peter, and James, and John, and Andrew, Philip, and Thomas, Bartholomew, and Matthew, James the son of Alphaeus, and Simon Zelotes, and Judas the brother of James. These all continued with one accord in prayer and supplication, with the women, and Mary the mother of Jesus, and with his brethren.* (KJV)

According to Acts 1:3, during the first forty days of the omer, Yeshua showed Himself to the disciples as well as others and gave many convincing proofs that He was alive. He appeared to them over a period of forty days and spoke about the Kingdom of God. All His post- resurrection appearances fell within the days of the omer count. Yeshua commanded the disciples [including the women] to stay in Jerusalem and await the coming of the Promise of the Father. They were all in one accord and in one place just as Israel was before Mt. Sinai when they received the Torah. They had been counting the omer and were being cleansed to a purified state.

1 Corinthians 15:5-7 *And that he was seen of Cephas, then of the twelve: After that, he was seen of above five hundred brethren at once; of whom the greater part remain unto this present, but some are fallen asleep. After that, he was seen of James; then of all the apostles.* (KJV)

Just after His resurrection, Yeshua appeared to Mary, Peter and two other disciples while they traveled to Emmaus. He also appeared in the midst the apostles. On the eighth day of the counting of the omer He appeared to Thomas. He also appeared to five hundred people all at once, and then appeared to James. He also appeared to seven of the disciples as they fished out at sea. On the fortieth day after His resurrection, He led the disciples out to a hill near Bethany, and He was seen ascending to heaven.

Yeshua took His disciples one last time to the Mount of Olives, which on the opposite side of Jerusalem was located near the village of Bethany. His last act after He had talked with them was to lift up His scarred hands with palms open toward the disciples. The index finger and the thumb of each hand touched its counterpart as they were spread apart. He would split his fingers so as to have a gap between the third and fourth fingers of each hand forming the Hebrew letter shin שׁ, the symbol for God's Name [Shaddai]. This was the sign of the priesthood. Yeshua then blessed His disciples singing the priestly benediction:

The LORD bless thee, and keep thee:
The LORD make his face shine upon thee, and be gracious unto thee:
The LORD lift up his countenance upon thee, and give thee peace.
((Numbers 6:23-26- KJV)

In Judaism the phrase 'He lifted up His hands and blessed them,' is an idiomatic expression for giving the priestly blessing.[25] By doing this, Yeshua was reaffirming His priesthood to the disciples. While He blessed His disciples He was 'parted' from them as He ascended to the right hand of the Father. In other words they saw His feet as He was blessing them while ascending.

When the priests would bless the people in Temple times with the Aaronic blessing [Numbers 6:23-26], the people would look at the priest's feet in respect for God's Name being represented through the priest's hands. The priest was also usually on a raised platform when blessing the people making it easier for them to look upon his bare feet.

The Seven Weeks of the Counting of the Omer is Concluded

We have seen that Acts 1:3 reveals that Yeshua had shown Himself to many for forty days after His resurrection. On that fortieth day of the counting of the omer, Yeshua ascended up into the Heavens from the Mount of Olives. The process of the disciples being refined and ready for the blessing that was to come ten days later at Shavuot was almost complete. The Firstfruits of the Barley Harvest at Yeshua's resurrection had produced many resurrected saints that came out from the graves. The Scripture indicates that these resurrected saints appeared to many throughout Jerusalem, and probably Judea and Galilee for the same forty days that Yeshua was around after His resurrection. The Scripture gives us no indication what happened to these resurrected believers. One would have to assume that if they had resurrected bodies, they probably supernaturally ascended to Heaven with Yeshua as Firstfruits of the Heavenly Kingdom.

But the disciples and other believers were left behind in physical bodies. The days of the counting of the omer with Yeshua teaching them had purified them until the 'day of Pentecost was fully come'. This means that the forty-nine days of the counting of the omer were complete and the next day, the fiftieth day, was Shavuot, which again fell on the weekly Sabbath that year. This was the Firstfruits of the Wheat Harvest.

To understand what was about to transpire with the disciples at Shavuot we need to remember Israel's Exodus from Egypt. On the fiftieth day from Nisan 16 in Egypt they were standing before Mt. Sinai on Shavuot ready to receive the Torah of God in betrothal marriage symbolism.

Acts 2:1-11 *And when the day of Pentecost was fully come, they were all with one accord in one place. And suddenly there came a sound from heaven as of a rushing mighty wind, and it filled all the house where they were sitting. And there appeared unto them cloven tongues like as of fire, and it sat upon each of them. And they were all filled with the Holy Ghost, and began to speak with other tongues, as the Spirit gave them utterance. And there were dwelling at Jerusalem Jews, devout men, out of every nation under heaven. Now when this was noised abroad, the multitude came together, and were confounded, because that every man heard them speak in his own language. And they were all amazed and marvelled, saying one to another, Behold, are not all these which speak Galilaeans? And how hear we every man in our own tongue, wherein we were born? Parthians, and Medes, and Elamites, and the dwellers in Mesopotamia, and in Judaea, and Cappadocia, in Pontus, and Asia, Phrygia, and Pamphylia, in Egypt, and in the parts of Libya about Cyrene, and strangers of Rome, Jews and proselytes, Cretes* *and Arabians, we do hear them speak in our tongues the wonderful works of God.* (KJV)

On the fiftieth day after the beginning of the counting of the omer, the same marvels that occurred at Mt. Sinai also happened with God's voice at Pentecost in Acts 2. The disciple's unity and refinement caused them to receive the Promise of the Father: That they would be immersed with the Ruwach haKodesh [Holy Spirit] (Acts 1:5). The Scripture says 'there came a sound from heaven as of a rushing mighty wind'. The same display that came from Heaven at Mt. Sinai was now coming down into the Temple. Shavuot was a pilgrimage festival and the people would gather in the Temple for the services. The idea of the disciples still being in 'an upper room' just doesn't fit the sequence of events. The Hebrew word 'Ruwach' [Spirit] also means 'wind,' so there is a play in the wording here.

The Greek word for 'house' in Acts 2:2 is 'oikos'. 'Oikos' is number 3624 according to the Strong's Concordance and means 'of uncertain affinity; a dwelling (more or less extensive, literal or figurative); by implication a family (more or less related, literal or figuratively): KJV— home, house (-hold), temple'.

Matthew 12:4 *How he entered into the house (Oikos) of God, and did eat the shewbread, which was not lawful for him to eat, neither for them which were with him, but only for the priests?* (KJV)

Matthew 21:13 *And said unto them, It is written, My house (Oikos) shall be called the house (Oikos) of prayer; but ye have made it a den of thieves.* (KJV)

Luke 11:51 *From the blood of Abel unto the blood of Zacharias, which perished between the altar and the temple (Oikos): verily I say unto you, It shall be required of this generation.* (KJV)

John 2:16 *And said unto them that sold doves, Take these things hence; make not my Father's house (Oikos) an house of merchandise.* (KJV)

Acts 7:47 *But Solomon built him an house (Oikos).* (KJV)

Oikos is a general Greek word that means a dwelling place. As one can see sometimes it is used to designate the Temple. In rabbinic literature the term 'The House' is often substituted for the Temple. Acts 2:6 says that the disciple's immersion into the Ruwach hakodesh was 'noised abroad' to the Jewish pilgrims from all the nations. It is hard to imagine that all these people would have noticed this event if it had taken place in an upper room of a house. The text appears to indicate that as soon as the disciples were immersed in the Ruwach that they began to speak 'as the Spirit gave them utterance'. Jews could sit in the large Court of the Women, which was not just for women. When Shavuot was 'fully come' a large percentage of the Jewish worshipers would have been in the Courtyard of the Women. Another possible place they could have gathered was at Solomon's Colonnade, which was located at the eastern part of the walkway surrounding the outer court of Herod's Temple mentioned in the writings of Josephus.

Acts 2:41 *Then they that gladly received his word were baptized: and the same day there were added unto them about three thousand souls.* (KJV)

Where did the disciples immerse three thousand new believers into water? There were immense mikvot [immersion complex] at the southern step for the worshipers to immerse themselves before entering the Temple proper. It was rabbinical halachah that all had to immerse to change their 'status' before entering the Jewish court-yards. This complex was designed to hold the large numbers of pilgrims that came to the feasts. It seems in all likelihood that these new converts were immersed into Yeshua there.

Acts 2:1 *And when the day of Pentecost was fully come, they were all with one accord in one place.* (KJV)

Acts 2:46 *And they, continuing daily with one accord in the temple, and breaking bread from house (Oikos) to house (Oikos), did eat their meat with gladness and singleness of heart,* (KJV)

We learn at the end of Acts 2 that the new believers continued 'daily with one accord in the temple'. This indicates that the disciples were 'all with one accord in one place' in the Temple. Why Luke chose a different Greek word for 'temple' here and used (Oikos) for 'house to house' is probably to distinguish the Temple from a literal house within the same sentence structure.

The upper room was significant only to the narrative of Acts 1. There was a ten-day intermission between the end of Acts 1 and Acts 2. There is no indication that they are still in that upper room in Acts 2.

All Jewish men were required to present themselves before the Lord at the Temple in Jerusalem on Shavuot. For the disciples to be at Jerusalem on Shavuot and not be in the Temple was a violation of the Torah and would have removed any credibility from them. The people would not have gathered around them if they thought they were breaking the Torah.

Luke 24:52-53 *And they worshipped him, and returned to Jerusalem with great joy: And were continually in the temple, praising and blessing God. Amen.* (KJV)

Luke has already made it clear that the disciples met every day in the Temple where they worshiped God continuously. If they were in the Temple on normal days, how much more so would they have been in the Temple on a festival day.

Acts 2:15 *For these are not drunken, as ye suppose, seeing it is but the third hour of the day.* (KJV)

It appears that the outpouring of the Holy Spirit in Acts 2 occurred at the time of Morning Prayer [9:00 A.M., the third hour]. We know in Acts 3:1 that Peter and John kept the times of prayer in the Temple courts.

Acts 3:11 *And as the lame man which was healed held Peter and John, all the people ran together unto them in the porch that is called Solomon's, greatly wondering.* (KJV)

Acts 5:12 *And by the hands of the apostles were many signs and wonders wrought among the people; (and they were all with one accord in Solomon's porch.* (KJV)

Solomon's Colonnade is a possible place where the outpouring of the Ruwach haKodesh occurred. There in the outer Temple courts, men and women could freely assemble together. Subsequent to Acts 2, Solomon's Colonnade became the established place of assembly for the Jerusalem believers. Notice that in Acts 5:12 we are told that the apostles themselves performed signs and wonders at Solomon's Porch. They were also in one accord. Could this be an allusion to where they were in one accord in Acts 2?

'There appeared unto them cloven tongues like as of fire, and it sat upon each of them'. The same thing that happened at Mt. Sinai with the 'fire and tongues' occurred in Acts 2 with the disciples as mentioned previously in this book. These divided tongues of fire 'sat' upon each one of them. The Greek word for 'sat' here is 'kathizo,' and means figuratively 'to settle or hover over'. Whereas all Israel was under the chuppah of Mt. Sinai and the voice-fire of God went around to each individual and hovered over them, so did something similar occur with the disciples at Shavuot. 'A mighty rushing wind [Spirit]' hovered over all of them like a chuppah and then separated on each one individually, lingering over them like a tongue-fire. The disciples were betrothed to God through Yeshua the Messiah.

Jews from all over the Diaspora were in Jerusalem for the pilgrimage festival of Shavuot. This Jewish counterpart represented all the nations of the known world. The phenomena that was happening spread throughout the Temple and the entire multitude came together to see for themselves what was happening. When the disciples were speaking the wonderful works of God including the message of Messiah Yeshua every one of these Diaspora Jews understood what they were saying in their own native language.

Acts 2:21-24, 32-33, 38-39 *And it shall come to pass, that whosoever shall call on the name of the Lord shall be saved. Ye men of Israel, hear these words; Jesus of Nazareth, a man approved of God among you by miracles and wonders and signs, which God did by him in the midst of you, as ye yourselves also know: Him, being delivered by the determinate counsel and foreknowledge of God, ye have taken, and by wicked hands have crucified and slain...Whom God hath raised up, having loosed the pains of death: because it was not possible that he should be holden of it. This Jesus hath God raised up, whereof we all are witnesses. Therefore being by the right hand of God exalted, and having received of the Father the promise of the Holy Ghost, he hath shed forth this, which ye now see and hear...Then Peter said unto them, Repent, and be baptized every one of you in the name of Jesus Christ for the remission of sins, and ye shall receive the gift of the Holy Ghost. For the promise is unto you, and to your children, and to all that are afar off, even as many as the Lord our God shall call.* (KJV)

These Jews who repented and were immersed into Yeshua received the Promise of the Father, the Immersion of the Ruach haKodesh [Holy Spirit] just as the disciples. They would go back to their homes in their nations after Shavuot. It was through these Jews that the Gospel message was first spread to all the nations.

Notice that these Jews had to repent, meaning to turn toward Messiah and Torah, and then be immersed into Yeshua. Afterwards they would receive the Ruach [Spirit]. Repentance brought them into the unity of the faith [disciples] symbolized by the counting of the omer. Immersion into Yeshua was their sanctification or setting apart to be made holy for marriage to Yeshua just as Moses immersed Israel to sanctify them prior to receiving Torah at Mt. Sinai. The Ruach hovered over them like a wedding canopy just like Mt. Sinai hovered over Israel as a chuppah in the wilderness.

But how does the Torah given to Israel in the wilderness as a ketubah (betrothal contract) relate to the Promise of the Father [Immersion of the Ruach haKodesh] given to the believers in Acts 2?

Jeremiah 31:21-22, 31-33 *Set thee up waymarks, make thee high heaps: set thine heart toward the highway, even the way which thou wentest: turn again, O virgin of Israel, turn again to these thy cities. How long wilt thou go about, O thou backsliding daughter? for the LORD hath created a new thing in the earth, A woman shall compass a man...Behold, the days come, saith the LORD, that I will make a new covenant with the house of Israel, and with the house of Judah: Not according to the covenant that I made with their fathers in the day that I took them by the hand to bring them out of the land of Egypt; which my covenant they brake, although I was an husband unto them, saith the LORD: But this shall be the covenant that I will make with the house of Israel; After those days, saith the LORD, I will put my law in their inward parts, and write it in their hearts; and will be their God, and they shall be my people.* (KJV)

Hebrews 8:8-10 *For finding fault with them, he saith, Behold, the days come, saith the Lord, when I will make a new covenant with the house of Israel and with the house of Judah: Not according to the covenant that I made with their fathers in the day when I took them by the hand to lead them out of the land of Egypt; because they continued not in my covenant, and I regarded them not, saith the Lord. For this is the covenant that I will make with the house of Israel after those days, saith the Lord; I will put my laws into their mind, and write them in their hearts: and I will be to them a God, and they shall be to me a people:* (KJV)

The writer of Hebrews quotes from Jeremiah 31 in proclaiming that the New Covenant in Messiah's blood would be made with the houses of Judah and Israel. The law [Torah] would be written 'in their inward parts [mind]' and 'in their hearts'. The Jewish sages had much to say about this New Covenant. They said that when Messiah came that He would give Israel a New Torah. It wasn't 'new' in the sense of not being related to the previous covenant, but renewed to account for the changes for to the Messiah's presence in the Kingdom.

2 Corinthians 3:2-3 *Ye are our epistle written in our hearts, known and read of all men: Forasmuch as ye are manifestly declared to be the epistle of Christ ministered by us, written not with ink, but with the Spirit of the living God; not in tables of stone, but in fleshy tables of the heart.* (KJV)

Therefore, the Torah was given out again at Shavuot in Acts 2. But instead of the Torah just being written 'in tables of stone' like at Mt. Sinai, the Ruwach [Spirit of the Living God] placed the Torah in 'fleshy tables of the heart' in Acts 2. The immersion of the believers with the Ruach haKodesh was the Promise of the Father to 'circumcise' the heart where the Torah became a part of their being. The obedience of the Torah was now an inward act, and not just an outward one. Paul says that a real Jew is one who is circumcised in the heart, inwardly, meaning that they are partakers of the New Covenant immersed in the Ruwach.

Was there a concept in ancient Judaism of 'circumcision of the heart' before Jeremiah prophesied about the Torah being 'in their inward parts' and written 'in their hearts?' Moses was the first to discuss it in Deuteronomy 30:6: And the LORD thy God will <u>circumcise</u> thine <u>heart</u>, and the heart of thy seed, to love the LORD thy God with all thine heart, and with all thy soul, that thou mayest live.

The Pentateuch & Haftorahs says of Deuteronomy 30:6, 'So that it [their hearts] be no longer closed up, impenetrable, and unreceptive of spiritual teaching. God would help Israel to fulfill His ideal of duty. The words of Jeremiah 31:32, 'I will put my law in their inward parts, and in their heart will I write it,' are taken by Nachmanides to express this particular teaching in Deuteronomy'.[26]

BIBLIOGRAPHY

1.   The Church and the Jews. Dan Gruber. Serenity Books, Hagerstown, Maryland, 1997. Page 80.
2.   The Temple - It's Ministry and Services. Alfred Edersheim. WM. B. Eerdmans Publishing Company, Grand Rapids, Michigan, 1990. Page 143.

3. The JPS Torah Commentary - Numbers. The Jewish Publication Society, Philadelphia - New York, 1990. Page 239.
4. Talmud - Seder Moed Mas. Pesachim. Soncino CD-Rom Edition.
5. Ibid.
6. Talmud -Pesachim 64b
7. Torah Club Volume Four - Vayechi. First Fruits of Zion, Littleton, Colorado. Page 238.
8. The New Testament and Rabbinic Judaism. David Daube. Hendrickson Publishers, Peabody, Massachusetts, 1956. Pages 24-25.
9. The Biblical and Historical Background of the Jewish Holy Days. Abraham P. Block. KTAV Publishing House, Inc., New York, 1978. Page 186.
10. Rosh Hashana and the Messianic Kingdom to Come. Joseph Good. Hatikva Ministries, Port Arthur, Texas, 1989. Pages 23-24.
11. Artscroll Tanach Series - Bereishis - Volume 1. Translated by Rabbi Meir Zlotowitz. Mesorah Publications, Ltd., Brooklyn, New York, 1986. Page 802.
12. Early Rabbinic Writings. Hyam Macoby. Cambridge University Press, Great Britain, 1988.
13. Exodus Rabbah 15:11
14. Gesenius' Hebrew-Chaldee Lexicon to the Old Testament. H.W.F. Gesenius. Baker Books, Grand Rapids, Michigan, 1979. Page 649.
15. Tz'enah Ur'enah - Volume 1. Translated by Miriam Stark Zakon. Mesorah Publications, Ltd., Brooklyn, New York, 1994. Page 111.
16. The Last Trial: on the Legends and Lore of the Command to Abraham to Offer Isaac as a Sacrifice: The Akeidah. Spiegel, Shalom. Jewish Lights Publishing, Wood Stock, Vermont, 1993.
17. Artscroll Tanach Series - Bereishis - Volume 1. Translated by Rabbi Meir Zlotowitz. Mesorah Publications, Ltd., Brooklyn, New York, 1986. Page 805.

18. Tz'enah Ur'enah - Volume 1. Translated by Miriam Stark Zakon. Mesorah Publications, Ltd., Brooklyn, New York, 1994. Page 383.

19. Artscroll Tanach Series - Bereishis - Volume 1. Translated by Rabbi Meir Zlotowitz. Mesorah Publications, Ltd., Brooklyn, New York, 1986. Page 807.

20. Talmud - Pesachim 4a

21. The Rod of an Almond Tree in God's Master Plan. Peter A. Michas. WinePress Publishing, Mukilteo, Washington, 1997. Page 211-212.

22. Messiah: Understanding His Life and Teachings in Hebraic Context - Volume 2. Avi ben Mordecai. A Millennium 7000 Communications Int'l, 1997. Pages 93-94.

23. Hebraic-Roots Version New Testament. Translated by James S. Trimm. Society for the Advancement of Nazarene Judaism, Hurst, Texas, 2001. Page 125.

24. Artscroll Tanach Series - Tehillim - Volume 2. Translated by Rabbi Avrohom Chaim Feuer. Mesorah Publications, Ltd., Brooklyn, New York, 1977. Pages 1517-1518.

25. Talmud - Taanit 26a-b and Megillah 23b-24b.

26. Pentateuch & Haftorahs. Dr. J.H. Hertz, C. H. Soncino Press. London, 1997. Page 881.

8

THE SIGNIFICANCE OF PASSOVER

Everything starts with the Passover

This chapter requires some background about Abraham and the chronology of Scripture. To begin we must understand that all the chapters that we read in the Torah, including the book of Genesis, are not always written in chronological order. For instance, many of the events recorded in the book of Exodus regarding the wilderness wandering of the Israelites are easily proven not to be in chronological order.

Abraham emerges from the pages of Genesis as the first patriarch whom we are allowed to know well after the Flood. Enoch, Shem, Eber, and Noah great as they were, are allotted only a few verses, whereas the story of Abraham requires 14 chapters to tell (Gen. 12-25). Abraham was promised that he would be the father of many nations (Gen. 17:4) and that through him all the families of the earth would be blessed (Gen. 12:3). So Abraham is a key figure indeed!

Genesis 11:26 *And Terah lived seventy years, and begat Abram, Nahor, and Haran.* (KJV)

Genesis 11:32 *And the days of Terah were two hundred and five years: and Terah died in Haran.* (KJV)

Genesis 12:4 *So Abram departed, as the LORD had spoken unto him; and Lot went with him: and Abram was seventy and five years old when he departed out of Haran.* (KJV)

The first promises from God to Abram are recorded in Genesis 12. Christian theology has assumed that Abram departed Haran at the age of 75 when his father Terah died at the age of 205. Genesis 12 therefore occurs after Terah dies at the end of Genesis 11 in chronological order. But this is not accurate according to the Torah.

Up until Abraham, the book of Genesis records the ages of the fathers at the births of their sons. For all of the preceding patriarchs, the year of the principal son's birth was listed, followed by the statement that the father also begat other sons and daughters. This appears to be the same pattern, except that the other two sons are named. The clear intent seems to be that Terah was age seventy at Abraham's birth, and that he had two other sons named Nahor and Haran. Rabbinic sources mention that Terah was seventy years old when Abram was born.[1]

If one assumes that Abram left immediately after Terah died, then Terah was 130 (205-75) at Abram's birth, which is contrary to the Torah. Terah clearly lived to 205 meaning that Abram was 135 (205-70) when Terah died in Haran. This means that Terah lived another sixty years after Abram departed Haran at the age of seventy-five. Rabbinic sources attest to this fact in the Torah.[2] Therefore Genesis 12 occurs before Genesis 11:32 and is not chronological. This is the precedent to understand the meanings put forth in this chapter.

Genesis 15:1 *After these things the word of the LORD came unto Abram in a vision...*(KJV)

A literal reading of the opening verse of Genesis 15 would suggest that Abram received his vision and made the covenant between the cut pieces of animals immediately after he defeated the four kings in Genesis 14. However, 'After these things,' cannot automatically be assumed to represent chronology. In this case, 'After these things,' only means a transition to discuss other events in Abram's life. Genesis 12, 13, and 14 are written in chronological order. 'After these things' in Hebrew is referring to a new line of thought beginning in Genesis 15. As a matter of fact, the testimony of the Scripture dictates that the covenant represented in Genesis 15 actually took place prior to the events in Genesis 12-14.[3] This is very important and the reader needs to hear this out before jumping off the bandwagon.

In Christian theology, which is not always congruent with how the Hebrew mind thinks, Abram was marching up and down the land of Canaan in Genesis 12-14, went to Egypt during a famine, and then returned to Canaan only to defeat the four kings. God made several appearances to Abram during this time and promised him a seed that would inherit the Land. Abram built several altars and dedicated them to the Lord. Then, all of sudden, in Genesis 15, God makes this blood covenant with Abram promising all the same things that He had already spoken to him. This sounds good, but can be proved to not be entirely accurate.

Genesis 11:31 *And Terah took Abram his son, and Lot the son of Haran his son's son, and Sarai his daughter in law, his son Abram's wife; and they went forth with them from Ur of the Chaldees, to go into the land of Canaan; and they came unto Haran, and dwelt there.* (KJV)

Genesis 15:7 *And he said unto him, I am the LORD that brought thee out of Ur of the Chaldees, to give thee this land to inherit it.* (KJV)

One clue that Genesis 15 occurred before Genesis 12-14 is the announcement from God that He had brought Abram out of Ur of the Chaldees into the land of Canaan for an inheritance. In Genesis 11, Terah had brought his family including Abram out of Ur to head toward the land of Canaan. But they never made it; they stopped in Haran and dwelt there many years.

Nowhere in Genesis 12-14 does God mention that He had brought Abram out of Ur unto the Land of Canaan. But in Genesis 15:7 God does make this reference, which indicates that this was the beginning of the covenant that God made with Abram. Genesis 12-

14 is a record of events that occurred after the covenant was already in effect. This is very important! If Abram was seventy-five years old when he left his father Terah for good in Haran to live in Canaan in Genesis 12-14, then it was before he was seventy-five when the covenant in Genesis 15 occurred. This also suggests that Abram had come down from Haran into Canaan before he left his father's house for good in Genesis 12. Clearly the covenant of Genesis 15 took place in the Land of Canaan because God said that He would give Abram 'this land to inherit'.

Joshua 10:13 *And the sun stood still, and the moon stayed, until the people had avenged themselves upon their enemies. Is not this written in the book of Jasher? So the sun stood still in the midst of heaven, and hasted not to go down about a whole day.* (KJV)

2 Samuel 1:17-18 *And David lamented with this lamentation over Saul and over Jonathan his son: (Also he bade them teach the children of Judah the use of the bow: behold, it is written in the book of Jasher.)* (KJV)

Both Joshua and Samuel make references to the book of Jasher [Sefer HaYashar]. Now the author is not suggesting that the book of Jasher should be equated to the canon of Scripture, but when two prophetic witnesses from the Scripture testify to the validity of what is recorded in Jasher, we would be foolish not to consider its content. To reject that the book of Jasher has nothing to offer the reader would be like slapping Joshua and Samuel, two men of God, in the face for even mentioning it.

The book of Jasher has survived from antiquity and has been translated into English today. These prophets referred to the book of Jasher because it is considered the most accurate book about the chronology of events of the Scriptures along with another source entitled Seder Olam. Regarding the timing of Abram's covenant of 'Between the Halves' in Genesis 15, the book of Jasher has this to say:

Jasher 13:17-28 *And it was in the fifteenth year of Abram's dwelling in the land of Canaan, which is the seventieth year of the life of*

Abram, and the Lord appeared to Abram in that year and he said to him, I am the Lord who brought thee out from Ur Casdim to give thee this land for an inheritance. Now therefore walk before me and be perfect and keep my commands, for to thee and to thy seed I will give this land for an inheritance, from the river Mitzraim [Egypt] unto the great river Euphrates. And thou shalt come to thy fathers in peace and in good age, and the fourth generation shall return here in this land and shall inherit it forever; and Abram built an altar, and he called upon the name of the Lord who appeared to him, and he brought up sacrifices upon the altar to the Lord. At that time Abram returned and went to Haran to see his father and mother, and his father's household, and Abram and his wife and all belonging to him returned to Haran, and Abram dwelt in Haran five years. And many of the people of Haran, about seventy-two men, followed Abram and Abram taught them the instruction of the Lord and his ways, and he taught them to know the Lord. In those days the Lord appeared to Abram in Haran, and he said to him, Behold, I spoke unto thee these twenty years back saying, Go forth from thy land, from thy birth-place and from thy father's house, to the land which I have shown thee to give it to thee and to thy children, for there in that land will I bless thee, and make thee a great nation, and make thy name great, and in thee shall the families of the earth be blessed. Now therefore arise, go forth from this place, thou, thy wife, and all belonging to thee, also every one born in thy house and all the souls thou hast made in Haran, and bring them out with thee from here, and rise to return to the land of Canaan. And Abram arose and took his wife Sarai and all belonging to him and all that were born to him in his house and the souls which they had made in Haran, and they came out to go to the land of Canaan. And Abram went and returned to the land of Canaan, according to the word of the Lord. And Lot the son of his brother Haran went with him, and Abram was seventy-five years old when he went forth from Haran to return to the land of Canaan. And he came to the land of Canaan according to the word of the Lord to Abram, and he pitched his tent and he dwelt in the plain of Mamre, and with him was Lot his brother's son, and all belonging to him. And the Lord again appeared to Abram and said, To thy seed will I give this land; and he there built an altar to the Lord who appeared to him, which is still to this day in the plains of Mamre.[4]

According to the book of Jasher Abram was seventy years old when the 'Covenant of Between the Halves' recorded in Genesis 15 took place. This will be very important as this chapter unfolds. Abram was in the land of Canaan during this time, but had yet to make a total break from his father's house in Haran. At seventy Abram returned to Haran for the next five years and was busy making Gentile converts to the Lord God. The book of Jasher records the conversion of seventy-two men and their families who came to Canaan with Abram when he was seventy-five. Abram then left his father's house for good at the age of seventy-five and 'returned' to the land of Canaan. This is where Genesis 12 picks up the story.

The Seder Olam also confirms that Abram's trip to Canaan in Genesis 12 was his second, five years after he first traveled there as recorded in Genesis 15. This source also states that Abram's war with the kings in Genesis 14 occurred after his second trip.[5]

Galatians 3:6-9 *Even as Abraham believed God, and it was accounted to him for righteousness. Know ye therefore that they which are of faith, the same are the children of Abraham. And the scripture, fore-seeing that God would justify the heathen through faith, preached before the gospel unto Abraham, saying, In thee shall all nations be blessed. So then they which be of faith are blessed with faithful Abraham. (KJV)*

Galatians 3:17-18 *And this I say, that the covenant [with Abraham], that was confirmed before of God in Christ, the law, which was four hundred and thirty years after, cannot disannul, that it should make the promise of none effect. For if the inheritance be of the law, it is no more of promise: but God gave it to Abraham by promise. (KJV)*

Genesis 15:6 *And he believed in the LORD; and he counted it to him for righteousness. (KJV)*

Genesis 12:3 *And I will bless them that bless thee, and curse him that curseth thee: and in thee shall all families of the earth be blessed.* (KJV)

Paul clearly establishes the true meaning of the Gospel message: 'In Abraham shall all nations be blessed'. The message of the Gospel preceded the New Testament. Notice that Paul first quotes Genesis 15:6 regarding how God accounted Abraham's faith in Him for righteousness. Those who have faith in God through believing in Yeshua as the Messiah have faith equated to that of Abraham. As Abraham before them, believers' faith in Yeshua is accounted to them for righteousness. Paul first links the believer's covenant with Messiah to Abraham's covenant recorded in Genesis 15.

Then Paul makes mention of the true Gospel message, 'In thee all nations shall be blessed,' by quoting Genesis 12:3. Paul clearly links Genesis 12 in chronology after Genesis 15. Also Paul clearly establishes that the Covenant offered by Yeshua the Messiah is the reaffirming of the covenant with Abraham. To not make this connection is to miss the importance of the believer's New Covenant in Messiah. This directly relates the New Covenant to Abraham and his 'seed,' which Paul clearly establishes as the 'single seed' of Messiah. As we will see, this will also clearly establish the link of the New Covenant with Yeshua and Abraham's covenant in Genesis 15 exclusively with the Passover. After all, Yeshua ratified the covenant with His disciples at His Last Passover Seder.

Notice that Paul was well aware of the 430 years that occurred between the Exodus from Egypt (and giving of the Torah at Mt. Sinai), and Abraham's 'Covenant of Between the Halves' recorded in Genesis 15. As a rabbi, sitting under Rabbi Gamaliel, the Nasi [President] of the Sanhedrin, Paul would have been very knowledgeable about the Hebraic understanding of the chronologies. Now we will try to sort all this out and understand what Paul and the other learned rabbis understood.

Genesis 15:18 *In the same day the LORD made a covenant with Abram, saying, Unto thy seed have I given this land, from the river of Egypt [Nile River] unto the great river, the river Euphrates:* (KJV)

It should first be pointed out what is usually missed by the Christian theologians. The 'Covenant of Between the Parts' in Genesis 15 was a promise of inheritance for Abram's seed. It did not only include where the Canaanites lived, but also included the territory west to the Nile River and east unto the Euphrates River. This will ultimately be realized during the Messianic Kingdom. Therefore, Goshen, where the Israelites dwelt in Egypt was on the east of the Nile and was included in the inheritance.

Genesis 15:13-16 *And he said unto Abram, Know of a surety that thy seed shall be a stranger in a land that is not theirs, and shall serve them; and they shall afflict them four hundred years; And also that nation, whom they shall serve, will I judge: and afterward shall they come out with great substance. And thou shalt go to thy fathers in peace; thou shalt be buried in a good old age. But in the fourth generation they shall come hither again: for the iniquity of the Amorites is not yet full.*(KJV)

God tells Abram that 'his seed' will be a stranger [a sojourner, or a Hebrew] in a land that is not theirs for four hundred years. The key to the four hundred years is in reference to Abram's 'seed'. Abraham's seed will serve those in the Land and be afflicted by them four hundred years. God says also 'that nation' which is obviously a connection to the Egyptian bondage. There is a transition here from being a stranger in the Land [from the Nile to the Euphrates] for four hundred years and being under a specific nation [Egypt] whom they will serve before being freed to enter the land of Canaan. It should not be taken from the text that they will serve the nation [Egypt] for the four hundred years, but that the Egyptian experience will be a part of and will conclude the four hundred years. The 'fourth generation' in which Abram's seed will come out of this nation [Egypt] is not the same as the four hundred years of sojourning in the Land that is not theirs and the four hundred and thirty years given in Exodus 12:40.[6]

Passover and the Abrahamic Covenant

Genesis 15:12-21 *And when the sun was going down, a deep sleep fell upon Abram; and, lo, an horror of great darkness fell upon him. And he said unto Abram, Know of a surety that thy seed shall be a stranger in a land that is not theirs, and shall serve them; and they shall afflict them four hundred years; And also that nation, whom they shall serve, will I judge: and afterward shall they come out with great substance. And thou shalt go to thy fathers in peace; thou shalt be buried in a good old age. But in the fourth generation they shall come hither again: for the iniquity of the Amorites is not yet full. And it came to pass, that, when the sun went down, and it was dark, behold a smoking furnace, and a burning lamp that passed between those pieces. In the same day the LORD made a covenant with Abram, saying, Unto thy seed have I given this land, from the river of Egypt unto the great river, the river Euphrates: The Kenites, and the Kenizzites, and the Kadmonites, And the Hittites, and the Perizzites, and the Rephaims, And the Amorites, and the Canaanites, and the Girgashites, and the Jebusites.* (KJV)

Exodus 12:40-42, 51 *Now the sojourning of the children of Israel, who dwelt in Egypt, was four hundred and thirty years. And it came to pass at the end of the four hundred and thirty years, <u>even the selfsame day</u> it came to pass, that all the hosts of the LORD went out from the land of Egypt. It is a night to be much observed unto the LORD for bringing them out from the land of Egypt: this is that night of the LORD to be observed of all the children of Israel in their generations...And it came to pass <u>the selfsame day</u>, that the LORD did bring the children of Israel out of the land of Egypt by their armies.* (KJV)

Exodus 13:3-5 *And Moses said unto the people, Remember this day, in which ye came out from Egypt, out of the house of bondage; for by strength of hand the LORD brought you out from this place: there shall no leavened bread be eaten. This day came ye out in the month Abib [another name for Nisan]. And it shall be when the LORD shall bring thee into the land of the Canaanites, and the Hittites,* *and the Amorites, and the Hivites, and the Jebusites, which he sware unto thy fathers to give thee, a land flowing with milk and honey, that thou shalt keep this service in this month.* (KJV)

It was exactly on this night, the 15ᵗʰ of Nisan [the first day of Unleavened Bread] after Abraham had taken the animals as instructed by God, that God made a covenant with him. How do we know it was Nisan 15? Moses tells Israel that they came out of Egypt 'the selfsame day'. Notice the covenant was made after the sun went down making it the next day. On that day, the 15ᵗʰ of Nisan, God made this covenant with Abraham that Moses reminded the children of Israel of as they were leaving Egypt.

The Torah Anthology says,

'Once the time had come, God did not wait even an instant. The decree given to Abraham at the pact Between halves was given on 15 Nisan. Now, 430 years later, on the exact same day, and at the exact same time of the day, the last of the Israelites left Egypt...The Torah thus says that all the Israelites left Egypt 'on that very day' - the same day as the Pact Between Halves'.[7]

Obviously, there is a thirty-year gap between the four hundred years mentioned in Exodus 12:40 and by Paul in Galatians 3:17, with the four hundred years of sojourning of Abram's seed in Genesis 15:13. We know from Jewish tradition from Seder Olam, Sefer HaYashar [book of Jasher], and other writings that Abram was seventy years old when the Covenant was 'cut' in Genesis 15. Thirty years later when Abram was one hundred years old would then be the start of the four hundred years of sojourning in the Land according to Genesis 15:13. What happened when Abram was one hundred years old? Isaac, 'his seed' was born. If God's word is perfect and the Covenant Between the Halves was cut at Passover [which became synonymous with the festival of Unleavened Bread] exactly four hundred and thirty years before the Exodus on Nisan 15, then we should expect an exact date for the four hundred years to have been accomplished at the same time. In other words, Isaac should have been born at Passover also.

It was the birth of Isaac, Abraham's 'seed,' that initiated the four hundred years described to us in Genesis 15. From that time the family of Abraham were sojourners in the land that was not yet theirs. After Isaac's birth Abraham sojourned in the land of the Philistines [Genesis 21:34]. Isaac also sojourned in the land of the Philistines [Genesis 26:3]. Jacob sojourned in the Canaanite lands, while his sons sojourned in Egypt [Genesis 47:4]. But it was only after the death of Joseph that the Israelites became slaves to Pharaoh in Egypt.[8]

Genesis 25:26 *And after that came his brother out, and his hand took hold on Esau's heel; and his name was called Jacob: and Isaac was threescore years old when she bare them.* (KJV)

Genesis 47:9 *And Jacob said unto Pharaoh, The days of the years of my pilgrimage are an hundred and thirty years: few and evil have the days of the years of my life been, and have not attained unto the days of the years of the life of my fathers in the days of their pilgrimage.* (KJV)

The Scripture tells us that Isaac was sixty years old when Jacob was born. The Scripture also tells us that Jacob was one hundred and thrity years old when he and his entire family entered Egypt. This means that the first one hundred and ninty years of the sojourning of the seed of Abram after Isaac's birth was outside of Egypt. This also tells us that the Israelites only spent two hundred and ten years in Egypt [400 - 190 = 210]. Of course, the great Egyptian affliction and bondage upon the Israelites only occurred at the end of those two hundred and ten years.[9]

Exodus 6:18 *And the sons of Kohath; Amram, and Izhar, and Hebron, and Uzziel: and the years of the life of Kohath were an hundred thirty and three years.* (KJV)

Exodus 6:20 *And Amram took him Jochebed his father's sister to wife; and she bare him Aaron and Moses: and the years of the life of Amram were an hundred and thirty and seven years.* (KJV)

Exodus 7:7 *And Moses was fourscore years old, and Aaron fourscore and three years old, when they spake unto Pharaoh.* (KJV)

Adding the life spans of Kohath, Amram, and Moses together and then subtracting the amount of years that their lives overlapped can also account for the two hundred and ten years in Egypt. The Torah informs us that Israel left Egypt when Moses was eighty years old. Kohath was a son of Levi. Amram was a son of Kohath, and Moses was a son of Amram.

Jewish tradition also accounts for the two hundred and ten years total of Israel being in Egypt in another manner. Moses' father Amram married Jochebed, Amram's father's [Kohath] sister. Moses' mother Jochebed was born as Jacob and his sons entered Egypt. She was one hundred and thirty years old when she gave birth to Moses. If we add Moses being eighty years old when he brought Israel out of Egypt, we arrive at a total of two hundred and ten years in Egypt.[10]

The actual oppression or affliction by the Egyptians is said to have begun with the birth of Moses' sister Miriam מ ר י ם, which in Hebrew means 'bitterness'. The Egyptians embittered the lives of the Israelites. The slavery started at her birth and lasted for the last eighty-six years they were in Egypt before Moses brought them out. The servitude of the Israelites did not begin until all of the original sons of Jacob had died.[11]

The four generations mentioned in the covenant of Genesis 15 are from Kohath, the son of Levi. They include Kohath, Amram, and Moses. The fourth generation, which included the children of Moses, returned to Canaan as God had foretold Abraham.[12]

Isaac born at Passover

It is a well-established Jewish tradition that Isaac was born at the season of Passover. The author would like to study this out and see the clues that the Scripture gives to show that Isaac was indeed born at Passover [Nisan 15, the first day of the festival of Unleavened Bread], exactly four hundred years before Moses brought Israel out of Egypt. Remember that the rabbi's are interpreting backwards after they had combined the two festivals of Passover and Unleavened Bread. Technically, Isaac would have been born of the first day of the festival of Unleavened Bread.

The Torah Anthology says,

'On the first day of Pesach in the afternoon, she [Sarah] gave birth to Isaac'.[13]

Genesis 17:1 *And when Abram was ninety years old and nine, the LORD appeared to Abram, and said unto him, I am the Almighty God; walk before me, and be thou perfect.* (KJV)

Genesis 17:4-5 *As for me, behold, my covenant is with thee, and thou shalt be a father of many nations. Neither shall thy name any more be called Abram, but thy name shall be Abraham; for a father of many nations have I made thee.* (KJV)

Genesis 17:15-16 *And God said unto Abraham, As for Sarai thy wife, thou shalt not call her name Sarai, but Sarah shall her name be. And I will bless her, and give thee a son also of her: yea, I will bless her, and she shall be a mother of nations; kings of people shall be of her.* (KJV)

Genesis 17:21 *But my covenant will I establish with Isaac, which Sarah shall bear unto thee at this <u>set time</u> [Moed] in the next year.* (KJV)

Genesis 17:24-27 *And Abraham was ninety years old and nine, when he was circumcised in the flesh of his foreskin. And Ishmael his son was thirteen years old, when he was circumcised in the flesh of his foreskin. In the selfsame day was Abraham circumcised, and Ishmael his son. And all the men of his house, born in the house,*

and bought with money of the stranger, were circumcised with him.
(KJV)

Abram receives an appearance from the Lord when he was ninety-nine years old, one year before the birth of Isaac as recorded in Genesis 17. God changes Abram's name to Abraham and Sarai to Sarah. God declares that Abraham will 'be a father of many nations' and that Sarah will 'be a mother of nations'.

In Genesis 17:21 God tells Abraham that his biological seed will be named Isaac a year before he is born. Notice that God specifically says, 'Sarah shall bear unto thee at this set time [Moed] in the next year'. The Hebrew word for 'set time' is 'moed' and means 'appointed time, festival'. It is used to describe the festivals of God and no less so for the Moed [Festival] of Passover [Unleavened Bread] as recorded in Exodus 13:10, 23:15 and Leviticus 23:4-5. The Hebrew says that at the festival of next year Isaac will be born. More specifically the text says that at the festival exactly in one year Isaac will be born. In other words the appearance of God to Abram in Genesis 17 at this 'moed' is exactly a year before Isaac is to be born. Remember that Abram was ninety-nine years old in Genesis 17, but in a year he would be one hundred.

After Abram's encounter with God, he circumcises Ishmael, himself, and the men of his entire household on the exact same Moed, festival day. Although, the men in Abram's household were Gentiles, they were considered as proselytes and therefore should be circumcised. However, Acts 15 makes it abundantly clear that when Gentiles come into the Covenant of Abraham through Messiah that they are not required to be circumcised. The only exception would be if a male Gentile marries a Jewish woman or a male Gentile is a permanent part of a Jewish household.

Exodus 12:48 *And when a stranger shall sojourn with thee, and will keep the passover to the LORD, let all his males be circumcised, and then let him come near and keep it; and he shall be as one that is born in the land: for no uncircumcised person shall eat thereof.*
(KJV)

If this Moed was Passover [Unleavened Bread], then we have the first required circumcision for Abraham and his 'physical' seed associated with the Passover. How significant is this? Today the Jews do not sacrifice Passover lambs because there is no Temple. If there were a Temple in Jerusalem, Jews would sacrifice Passover lambs and eat them inside the walls of Jerusalem. God's word demands that only the circumcised can eat the Passover lamb. However, outside the walls of Jerusalem a Gentile is permitted to participate in the Passover, because a Passover Lamb would never be sacrificed for the Seder outside the walls of Jerusalem. But clearly God put an emphasis on circumcision of Abraham's physical seed in relation to the Passover.

Were the Israelites in Egypt circumcised? They would have to be in order to have the Passover before they left Egypt. The Bible itself does not tell us that Moses circumcised all the Hebrew males before the Passover, but one would believe that they were circumcised.

So very clearly rabbinical thought understands that circumcision was part of the Passover of the Exodus. Genesis 17 gives us a hint of this. Also notice that Abram was given a new name [and Sarai too] in association with circumcision and Passover. A Hebrew infant was to be circumcised from this day forward on the eighth day from birth. It was at this time that the infant was officially given his name.

This may be the significance of the Shabbaton on the seventh day of the festival of Unleavened Bread, Nisan 21. Remember that any part of a day to the Jewish mind is considered one day. If Isaac were born as Nisan 14 was turning into Nisan 15, then the eighth day would be Nisan 21, the other Shabbaton [High Holy Day] of the festival of Unleavened Bread.

Genesis 18:1-6 *And the LORD appeared unto him in the plains of Mamre: and he sat in the tent door in the heat of the day; And he lift up his eyes and looked, and, lo, three men stood by him: and when he saw them, he ran to meet them from the tent door, and bowed himself toward the ground, And said, My Lord, if now I have found favour in thy sight, pass not away, I pray thee, from thy servant: Let a little water, I pray you, be fetched, and wash your feet, and rest yourselves under the tree: And I will fetch a morsel of bread, and* *comfort ye your hearts; after that ye shall pass on: for therefore are ye come to your servant. And they said, So do, as thou hast said. And Abraham hastened into the tent unto Sarah, and said, Make ready quickly three measures of fine meal, knead it, and make cakes upon the hearth.* (KJV)

Jewish commentators recognize that Genesis 18 occurs at the same time of Abraham's circumcision or when he was still recovering.[14] It takes about three days for an adult male to recover from the pain associated with circumcision. So if Genesis 17 occurred at Passover, then at the most Genesis 18 occurs two or three days into the seven days of Unleavened Bread.

The account in the book of Jasher reads:

Jasher 18:3-4 *And <u>in the third day</u> Abraham went out of his tent and sat at the door to enjoy the heat of the sun, during the pain of his flesh. And the Lord appeared to him in the plain of Mamre, and sent three of his ministering angels to visit him, and he was sitting at the door of the tent, and he lifted his eyes and saw, and lo three men were coming from a distance, and he rose up and ran to meet them, and he bowed down to them and brought them into his house.*[15]

Abraham served unleavened bread to these angels because it was the precursor to the season of the festival of Unleavened Bread. Abraham 'hastened' into Sarah's tent and told her to make the bread quickly. There wasn't time to bake with leaven. This was an allusion to Abraham's seed in the future baking unleavened bread to be ready to leave Egypt in haste.[16]

Genesis 18:13-14 *And the LORD said unto Abraham, Wherefore did Sarah laugh, saying, Shall I of a surety bear a child, which am old? Is any thing too hard for the LORD? At the time appointed I will return unto thee, according to the time of life, and Sarah shall have a son.* (KJV)

God says, 'at the time appointed' [Moed-festival] Sarah will have a son. Again, this is a reference to Isaac being born at Passover. Traditional Jewish translations of 'I will return unto thee according to the time of life' is rendered 'I will return to you at this time next year'.[17]

Genesis 19:1-3 *And there came two angels to Sodom at even; and Lot sat in the gate of Sodom: and Lot seeing them rose up to meet them; and he bowed himself with his face toward the ground; And he said, Behold now, my lords, turn in, I pray you, into your servant's house, and tarry all night, and wash your feet, and ye shall rise up early, and go on your ways. And they said, Nay; but we will abide in the street all night. And he pressed upon them greatly; and they turned in unto him, and entered into his house; and he made them a feast, and did bake unleavened bread, and they did eat.* (KJV)

Apparently two of these three angels that appeared unto Abraham had been commissioned by God to destroy Sodom and Gomorrah. So apparently as the next day is ready to begin [at sundown] the angels arrive in Sodom. It was still during the festival of Passover [Unleavened Bread]. Notice that Lot baked the angels 'unleavened' bread. Jewish tradition teaches that Sodom and Gomorrah were destroyed on the precursor of the days of the festival of Unleavened Bread.[18]

Genesis 21:1-5 *And the LORD visited Sarah as he had said, and the LORD did unto Sarah as he had spoken. For Sarah conceived, and bare Abraham a son in his old age, at the set time [Moed] of which God had spoken to him. And Abraham called the name of his son that was born unto him, whom Sarah bare to him, Isaac. And Abraham circumcised his son Isaac being eight days old, as God had commanded him. And Abraham was an hundred years old, when his son Isaac was born unto him.* (KJV)

After Sodom and Gomorrah were destroyed, Abraham moved his tent into the land of the Philistines on the eastern shore of the Land of Canaan, still within the territory promised by God to his offspring. After his encounter with King Abimelech, Abraham is given more riches and allowed to settle in Gerar in the land of the Philistines. It is here that Isaac was born as recorded in Genesis 21.

Isaac was born at the 'set time,' which God had earlier spoken to Abraham. 'Set time' is the Hebrew 'Moed,' which of course is translated as festival and feast elsewhere in the Scriptures. This 'Moed,' of course, was the first day of Passover [Unleavened Bread]. Some rabbis even say that Isaac was born on the night of Passover.[19]

Isaac was the Promised Seed of Abraham and was the first infant to be circumcised on the eighth day from his birth. It is probable that Abraham named him at his circumcision. Believers in Yeshua, who are circumcised in their hearts by the Spirit of Promise, are all considered by God the children of the Promise:

Romans 9:7-9 *Neither, because they are the seed of Abraham, are they all children: but, In Isaac shall thy seed be called. That is, They which are the children of the flesh, these are not the children of God: but the children of the promise are counted for the seed. For this is the word of promise, At this time will I come [Passover], and Sarah shall have a son.* (KJV)

Galatians 3:14 *That the blessing of Abraham might come on the Gentiles through Jesus Christ; that we might receive the promise of the Spirit through faith.* (KJV)

Galatians 4:28 *Now we, brethren, as Isaac was, are the children of promise.* (KJV)

Paul says in Romans 9:9 that the Word of Promise is this: 'At this time will I come, and Sarah shall have a son'. This is a paraphrase of Genesis 18:14 and as we have pointed out is referring to the appointed time of Passover. Israel did not become a nation, practice God's Torah, and serve God until they were first 'redeemed' by God from their Egyptian bondage. Pharaoh owned them as slaves and they continued in bondage until Passover. Likewise, all people are owned by Satan and are in bondage to him, unless God 'redeems' them from him.

Before we can enter into a betrothal relationship [Shavuot-Pentecost] with God, we must first be 'redeemed'. The Israelites were redeemed with the Passover in Egypt. Likewise, anyone seeking to be redeemed spiritually today must return to the Passover of Yeshua's Death and Resurrection. There is no other way to bypass redemption. We become the spiritual Children of Promise as Isaac, when Yeshua becomes our Pesach Offering.

If we have drifted away from the LORD after we have accepted His Passover redemption, there is a need for renewal. Many times we embrace God's Passover redemption for our lives, but through circumstances allow the enemy to regain ownership over our lives. One must go back to the Passover of Yeshua and renew their redemption and not desire to stay in Egypt. Everything starts with Passover!

Exodus 6:6-7 *Wherefore say unto the children of Israel, I am the LORD, and I will bring you out from under the burdens of the Egyptians, and I will rid you out of their bondage, and I will redeem you [go'el] with a stretched out arm, and with great judgments: And I will take you to me for a people, and I will be to you a God: and ye shall know that I am the LORD your God, which bringeth you out from under the burdens of the Egyptians. (KJV)*

More than likely God's 'redemption' and 'purchase' of Israel is descriptively mentioned in Scripture as 'pictures' of salvation instead of being doctrines that perfectly reflect these terms. The Scripture calls God the 'Redeemer' [Hebrew Go'el] of Israel. The 'Go'el' being near kin was responsible for guarding and repossessing persons and/or property for the extended family.

The two phrases 'I will take you' and 'I will be to you' are biblically and rabbinically connected to marriage and in this case is referring to Israel's betrothal at Mt. Sinai.[20] The marriage at Sinai occurred at Shavuot [Pentecost]. Shavuot is the Atzeret [conclusion] of Passover. Before the betrothal is ratified there must first be the redemption of Passover. Israel was redeemed from under the burdens of the Egyptians. Everything begins with Passover!

Deuteronomy 7:8 *But because the LORD loved you, and because he would keep the oath which he had sworn unto your fathers, hath the LORD brought you out with a mighty hand, and redeemed [padah] you out of the house of bondmen, from the hand of Pharaoh king of Egypt.* (KJV)

In other Scriptures the Hebrew word 'padah' is used to describe the redemption of Israel. Padah has the meaning of buying something that was not originally the new owner's property, whereas go'el implies a buying back what was his originally.[21] So how does one rectify the use of 'padah' and 'go'el' for 'Redemption?' They appear to be opposed to one another. The author believes that both words are applicable to God's redemption of Israel at Passover, depending upon the angle of the Scripture. On one hand God 'owned' Israel through His Covenant with Abraham, Isaac and Jacob before Egypt even came into the picture. In this case God is the 'Go'el' (Redeemer). On the other hand, at the time of the Exodus Pharaoh owned Israel. From this perspective God 'Redeemed' [Hebrew padah] Israel from him.

Several times padah and go'el are used in Hebrew parallelism, meaning the same thing is said twice but in a different way. Here is an example:

Jeremiah 31:11 *For the LORD hath <u>redeemed [padah]</u> Jacob, and <u>ransomed [go'el]</u> him from the hand of him that was stronger than he.* (KJV)

Exodus 15:13, 16 *Thou in thy mercy hast led forth the people which thou hast redeemed [go'el]: thou hast guided them in thy strength unto thy holy habitation...Fear and dread shall fall upon them; by the greatness of thine arm they shall be as still as a stone; till thy people pass over, O LORD, till the people pass over, which thou hast purchased [qanah].* (KJV)

In Exodus 15:16 we are told that God 'purchased' Israel. The Hebrew word for 'purchased' is 'qanah'. 'Qanah' appears to be the means such as money to do the redeeming, whereas 'padah' and 'go'el' appear to be the position of the one doing the redeeming. God as the 'go'el' and 'padah,' purchased [qanah] Israel by the blood of the Passover Lamb. For example:

Ruth 4:8, 10 *Therefore the kinsman [go'el] said unto Boaz, Buy [qanah] it for thee. So he drew off his shoe...Moreover Ruth the Moabitess, the wife of Mahlon, have I purchased [qanah] to be my wife, to raise up the name of the dead upon his inheritance, that the name of the dead be not cut off from among his brethren, and from the gate of his place: ye are witnesses this day.* (KJV)

In order for Boaz as the 'go'el' to take Ruth for his wife, he had to first buy or purchase her. The Megillah of Ruth is one of the texts that are read on Shavuot [Pentecost]. Ruth's redemption process began during the season of Passover, specifically the Firstfruits of the Barley Harvest as Ruth 1:22 states, 'they [Ruth and Naomi] came to Bethlehem in the beginning of barley harvest'.

Galatians 4:5 *To redeem [exagorazo] them that were under the law, that we might receive the adoption of sons.* (KJV)

Galatians 3:13-14 *Christ hath redeemed [exagorazo] us from the curse of the law, being made a curse for us: for it is written, Cursed is every one that hangeth on a tree: That the blessing of Abraham might come on the Gentiles through Jesus Christ; that we might receive the promise of the Spirit through faith.* (KJV)

1 Peter 1:18-19 *Forasmuch as ye know that ye were not redeemed [lutroo] with corruptible things, as silver and gold, from your vain conversation received by tradition from your fathers; But with the precious blood of Christ, as of a lamb without blemish and without spot:* (KJV)

Titus 2:13-14 *Looking for that blessed hope, and the glorious appearing of the great God and our Saviour Jesus Christ; Who gave himself for us, that he might redeem [lutroo] us from all iniquity, and purify unto himself a peculiar people, zealous of good works.* (KJV)

Colossians 1:14 *In whom we have redemption [apolutosis] through his blood, even the forgiveness of sins:* (KJV)

Acts 20:28 *Take heed therefore unto yourselves, and to all the flock, over the which the Holy Ghost hath made you overseers, to feed the church of God, which he hath purchased [peripoieomai] with his own blood.* (KJV)

We also see a wide variety of Greek words used in the New Testament for 'redeem, redeemed, redemption, and purchased'. But the same Hebraic concept is clearly seen. Believers in Yeshua are redeemed as 'adopted' firstborn sons from the slavery of Satan and sin [Pharaoh and slavery]. But God knew us before the foundation of the world and has also reclaimed us as the children of Abraham. The price that was paid for our redemption is Yeshua's blood, which is our Passover.

Passover Implications

We have learned in this chapter that the Covenant God cut with Abraham in Genesis 15 occurred at Passover [the first day of Unleavened Bread, Nisan 15], exactly four hundred and thirty years before the Exodus Passover. We also highlighted that the Promise of God in Abraham's Covenant, that he would have a 'seed' to inherit the Promised Land, was fulfilled in Isaac's birth exactly thirty years later at Passover. The four hundred years of sojourning promised by God in Abraham's Covenant began with Isaac's birth.

After the incident of the Golden Calf in the first few months in the wilderness, God commanded Moses to hold the Passover in the second year of the wilderness wandering as a starting over point (Numbers 9). The Passover was not kept again in the wilderness as the children of Israel that left Egypt were disobedient and God ordained that they die in the wilderness. Then the new generation of Israelites born in the wilderness kept the Passover before conquering the Land as a symbol of renewal (Joshua 5). At this point God had commanded Israel to keep the Passover every year at its appointed time while they inherited the Land.

Over the centuries, Israel would decline spiritually and turn away from their covenant that God made with Abraham and confirmed through Isaac and Jacob. When a new righteous king would come to power that desired to return to the Torah and the Covenant of their forefathers, the first celebration to be observed was the Passover. Passover is a symbol of renewal, revival, repentance, and return to God. This occurred during the days of Hezekiah (2 Chronicles 30) and Josiah (2 Kings 23; 2 Chronicles 35). After Ezra returned from Babylonian captivity and restored Jerusalem, the Passover was kept (Ezra 6:19).

Yeshua, the ultimate 'Promised Seed,' is also tied to the Passover. The Passover Seder that Yeshua had with His disciples where He announced that the Unleavened Bread represented His afflicted body, and the cup of wine represented His shed blood, was a renewal of the Covenant that God had made with Abraham at Passover. In that Covenant God had promised that Abraham would be a father of many nations and this was understood to be spiritual seed that included Gentile believers. For this reason alone Gentile believers should keep the Passover 'in remembrance' of what Yeshua accomplished for us 'as often as we keep it'. The Passover also points to our future 'full' redemption with resurrected bodies as Yeshua stated that He would not partake of the Passover again until He sits down with us in His Kingdom.

Passover represents the beginning of renewal as the springtime begins to burst forth on the earth. The festivals, including the Passover, are Holy Convocations or rehearsals for what God is planning. In other words, they are rehearsals for a grand wedding. If we don't rehearse, we won't be ready for the wedding of the Lamb.

2 Chronicles 28:2-4 *For he [Ahaz] walked in the ways of the kings of Israel, and made also molten images for Baalim. Moreover he burnt incense in the valley of the son of Hinnom, and burnt his children in the fire, after the abominations of the heathen whom the LORD had cast out before the children of Israel. He sacrificed also and burnt incense in the high places, and on the hills, and under every green tree.* (KJV)

When the nation of Judah went into spiritual decline, drifting away from God, a renewal or revival was in order, or else God would just punish their wickedness. King Hezekiah inherited the throne of Judah from his father Ahaz. King Ahaz was one of the worse kings that Judah ever had bringing idolatry and abominations to the forefront of public life.

2 Chronicles 30:1 *And Hezekiah sent to all Israel and Judah, and wrote letters also to Ephraim and Manasseh, that they should come to the house of the LORD at Jerusalem, to keep the passover unto the LORD God of Israel.* (KJV)

King Hezekiah initiated a major Pesach celebration in Jerusalem before attempting to do anything else. He reestablished the Temple service and purified it from contamination. Passover is one of the pilgrimage festivals and Hezekiah implored all who could to attend this national Passover event. It worked because the latter half of Hezekiah's reign was marked with God blessing Judah with great economic success rivaling Solomon's day.

2 Chronicles 35:18-19 *And there was no passover like to that kept in Israel from the days of Samuel the prophet; neither did all the kings of Israel keep such a passover as Josiah kept, and the priests, and the Levites, and all Judah and Israel that were present, and the inhabitants of Jerusalem. In the eighteenth year of the reign of Josiah was this passover kept.* (KJV)

Under the reigns of Manasseh and Amon, Judah returned to their spiritual depravity. When King Josiah came to power, he learned of a Torah scroll being found in the Temple that had been closed up. Whatever Josiah read caused him to go through the land breaking down all of the images of Baal and Asherah, etc. Then Josiah held a national Passover renewal for the entire kingdom. Many in Judah returned to the Torah of God in his generation. Everything spiritually begins with Passover!

BIBLIOGRAPHY

1. The JPS Torah Commentary - Genesis, Nahum M. Sarna. The Jewish Publication Society, Philadelphia, New York, Jerusalem, 1989. Page 88.
2. The Artscroll Tanach Series - Bereishis - Volume 1. Rabbi Meir Zlotowitz. Mesorah Publications, Ltd., Brooklyn, New York, 1986. Page 353.
3. Ibid. Page 589.
4. Book of Jasher. J. H. Parry & Company, Salt Lake City. 1887.
5. The Artscroll Tanach Series - Bereishis - Volume 1. Rabbi Meir Zlotowitz. Mesorah Publications, Ltd., Brooklyn, New York, 1986. Page 589.
6. The JPS Torah Commentary - Genesis, Nahum M. Sarna. The Jewish Publication Society, Philadelphia, New York, Jerusalem, 1989. Page 116.
7. Yalkut Me'am Lo'ez - The Torah Anthology - Exodus II - Book 5 in the series. Translated by Rabbi Aryeh Kaplan. Moznaim Publishing Corporaton, New York , Jerusalem, 1979. Page 113.
8. The Artscroll Tanach Series - Bereishis - Volume 1. Rabbi Meir Zlotowitz. Mesorah Publications, Ltd., Brooklyn, New York, 1986. Pages 525-526.
9. The JPS Torah Commentary - Genesis, Nahum M. Sarna. The Jewish Publication Society, Philadelphia, New York, Jerusalem, 1989. Page 116.
10. The Artscroll Tanach Series - Shir haShirim. Rabbi Meir Zlotowitz. Mesorah Publications, Ltd., Brooklyn, New York, 1977. Page 105.
11. The Artscroll Tanach Series - Bereishis - Volume 1. Rabbi Meir Zlotowitz. Mesorah Publications, Ltd., Brooklyn, New York, 1986. Page 526.
12. Ibid. Pages 531 - 532].
13. Yalkut Me'am Lo'ez - The Torah Anthology - Genesis II - Book 2 in the series. Translated by Rabbi Aryeh Kaplan.

Moznaim Publishing Corporaton, New York , Jerusalem, 1989. Page 277.

14. The Artscroll Tanach Series - Bereishis - Volume 1. Rabbi Meir Zlotowitz. Mesorah Publications, Ltd., Brooklyn, New York, 1986. Pages 625.

15. Book of Jasher. J. H. Parry & Company, Salt Lake City. 1887.

16. The Artscroll Tanach Series - Bereishis - Volume 1. Rabbi Meir Zlotowitz. Mesorah Publications, Ltd., Brooklyn, New York, 1986. Pages 632-636.

17. Ibid. Page 647.

18. Ibid. Page 680.

19. Yalkut Me'am Lo'ez - The Torah Anthology - Genesis II - Book 2 in the series. Translated by Rabbi Aryeh Kaplan. Moznaim Publishing Corporaton, New York , Jerusalem, 1989. Page 278.

20. The JPS Torah Commentary - Exodus, Nahum M. Sarna. The Jewish Publication Society, Philadelphia, New York, Jerusalem, 1991. Page 32.

21. The JPS Torah Commentary - Numbers, Jacob Milgrom. The Jewish Publication Society, Philadelphia, New York, Jerusalem, 1990. Page 152.

9

THE PASSOVER-THRESHOLD COVENANT
CROSSING OVER REVISITED

In Christianity the Old Testament is primarily viewed as a history book of creation and the nation of Israel. It is much more than that; the Bible is a Middle Eastern Book of Covenants and cannot be interpreted with a Western mind-set. In the ancient Orient or Middle East, one would never break a blood covenant; they would rather die than become cursed. A blood covenant was taken extremely seriously.

The Primitive Altar

The threshold or doorsill of a family dwelling was the earliest form of an altar.[1] In some ancient rabbinic writings the use of 'gate' or 'door' had application for making a covenant. When a guest crossed the threshold of one's home, they were bound by the covenant of hospitality to honor, serve and protect that guest. Failure to do so would bring a curse upon their household. By the same token, a guest enters into the same covenant and returns the favor. He would never do his host harm.

Much of this ancient practice is still done today in primitive cultures with some variations. In each of these instances of a threshold covenant, an animal was sacrificed and its blood flowed into a basin at the threshold of the door. If a guest stepped 'on' one's threshold when the blood was there, it was considered like 'spitting' in the host's face. However, if one 'crossed-over' [stepped-over] one's threshold filled with blood, it was the establishing of a covenant between the host and the guest.

John 10:1, 2, 7-10 *Verily, verily, I say unto you, He that entereth not by the door into the sheepfold, but climbeth up some other way, the same is a thief and a robber. But he that entereth in by the door is the shepherd of the sheep...Then said Jesus unto them again, Verily, verily, I say unto you, I am the door of the sheep. All that ever came before me are thieves and robbers: but the sheep did not hear them. I am the door: by me if any man enter in, he shall be saved, and shall go in and out, and find pasture. The thief cometh not, but for to steal, and to kill, and to destroy: I am come that they might have life, and that they might have it more abundantly.* (KJV)

In the Gospel of John, Yeshua uses terminology of the threshold on the highest order. Yeshua says He is the 'Door' to abundant life. To cross this threshold of life we must go through Him. Anyone who does not enter through the door of the sheepfold, but gets in some other way, is a thief or robber whose intention is to steal, kill, and destroy. This is interesting because one who never crossed over the threshold of a dwelling was not bound by the covenant code of hospitality to the host. In other words, those who enter the home through some other means could rob or harm the host and not break any laws of threshold covenant hospitality. In this scenario, the thief and host have become enemies.

The family threshold altar is also seen in ancient Middle-Eastern marriage customs. In some places a lamb or goat was sacrificed at the threshold of the groom's home. When he brought his new bride home, she was obliged to step across the spilled blood. By doing this she was considered as adopted into that family.[2] The well-known universal custom of the groom carrying his bride over the threshold of her new home is directly related to this subject. There is a Jewish legend recorded in chapter 30 of Pirqe de R. Eliezer of Abraham's son Ishmael marrying an Amalekite wife. Abraham sends notice to Ishmael that he needs to 'change his threshold,' which is understood to mean he needs to put away [divorce] the Amalekite and marry a proper woman.

The Egyptian 'Crossing Over' of Passover

When Moses instructed the Israelites to hold the Passover, they were not surprised as to its meaning. To welcome a guest by blood covenant through the threshold of the door was common knowledge and practice in Egypt. Through this crossing-over covenant the guest would become as one of the family through 'adoption'. Through Moses God had announced His arrival in advance as a guest in Egypt. He told them what night to sacrifice the lamb and apply the blood at the threshold of the Israelite doors to welcome Him as their guest. God also instructed them that if a welcome threshold covenant was not prepared, He would consider that home His enemy and the firstborn's life would be required.

Exodus 12:22 *And ye shall take a bunch of hyssop, and dip it in the blood that is in the <u>bason [Hebrew - saph]</u>, and strike the lintel and the two side posts with the blood that is in the bason; and none of you shall go out at the door of his house until the morning.* (KJV)

The lamb was clearly killed over the basin [saph] and the blood drained from the lamb's neck into it. But should the Hebrew word 'saph' be translated as 'basin' in the KJV or other English translations of the Bible?

Judges 19:27 *And her lord rose up in the morning, and opened the doors of the house, and went out to go his way: and, behold, the woman his concubine was fallen down at the door of the house, and her hands were upon the threshold [saph].* (KJV)

I Kings 14:17 *And Jeroboam's wife arose, and departed, and came to Tirzah: and when she came to the threshold [saph] of the door, the child died;* (KJV)

Zephaniah 2:14 *And flocks shall lie down in the midst of her, all the beasts of the nations: both the cormorant and the bittern shall lodge in the upper lintels of it; their voice shall sing in the windows;*

desolation shall be in the thresholds [saph]; for he shall uncover the cedar work. (KJV)

Clearly 'basin' in Exodus should be translated as 'threshold' to give the correct understanding of the making of this threshold covenant between God and Israel. In that welcome with blood there was covenant protection from God as He came into Egypt to execute judgment upon His enemies. Through the acts of Pharaoh, the Egyptians refused to submit to God's authority. The time of their judgment had come. The Threshold Covenant of blood on the Israelite doors distinguished them from the Egyptians. God went into the home where a welcome was prepared and brought them life. He also went into the houses that did not prepare a welcome and brought them death.

Exodus 12:23 *For the LORD will pass through to smite the Egyptians; and when he seeth the blood upon the lintel, and on the two side posts, the LORD will pass over the door, and will not suffer the destroyer to come in unto your houses to smite you.* (KJV)

The Septuagint [Greek translation of the Old Testament] renders the Hebrew word 'saph' as 'thyra,' meaning 'doorway,' in the story of the Exodus. One of the early Church Fathers, Jerome, gives 'limen,' which means 'threshold,' for the Hebrew word 'saph'. In the Talmud, Rabbi Ishmael called the Passover 'basin' a threshold.[3]

The common understanding of the term 'Passover,' in connection with the Israelite Exodus, is that the Lord passed by those homes where the doorways were bloodstained and did not enter them. A true reading of the Exodus account and the knowledge of the Threshold crossing-over rite do not justify this interpretation. The Hebrew word for 'Passover' has a far deeper meaning then just the death angel 'passing over' the Israelite houses with blood upon them.

Exodus 12:13, 23 *And the blood shall be to you for a token upon the houses where ye are: and when I see the blood, I will pass over you, and the plague shall not be upon you to destroy you, when I smite the land of Egypt. For the LORD will pass through to smite the*

Egyptians; and when he seeth the blood upon the lintel, and on the two side posts, the LORD will pass over the door, and will not suffer the destroyer to come in unto your houses to smite you. (KJV)

The Hebrew verb 'pesakh' [pass over] is derived from the root 'pasakh,' which means, 'to cross over'. This concept is still preserved in the Hebrew word Tiphsakh, which is the name of the city Thapsacus on the banks of the Euphrates. Tiphsakh means 'crossing,' apparently so called from the ford of the Euphrates at that place.[4]

Exodus 12 says that the Lord only will 'cross over' the 'door' of the homes that He sees the 'blood' covenant of welcoming. The homes where the Lord has crossed over into a threshold covenant, the destroyer will not enter and smite the firstborn. The Lord must physically [spiritually] see the blood of the Passover lamb 'applied' to the threshold in order to enter into a covenant.

'Pesakh' (pass over) is not connected to any other Hebrew word. But it may be related to the Egyptian word 'pesh' from which the children of Israel understood living in Egypt all those years. 'Pesh' means to 'spread wings over' like an eagle spreading her wings over her young to protect them. If this meaning is applicable, then the Lord not only crossed over into a threshold covenant in the homes where the blood was applied, but also wrapped His 'wings' over the home in protection.[5] Consider what Yeshua said:

Matthew 23:37-39 *O Jerusalem, Jerusalem, thou that killest the prophets, and stonest them which are sent unto thee, how often would I have gathered thy children together, even as a hen gathereth her chickens under her wings, and ye would not! Behold, your house is left unto you desolate. For I say unto you, Ye shall not see me henceforth, till ye shall say, Blessed is he that cometh in the name of the Lord.* (KJV)

A couple of days before Yeshua's crucifixion at Passover, he makes this rather remarkable comment of Himself wanting to be like a mother hen to Jerusalem by protecting its inhabitants with His wings. But because Jerusalem would not accept this crossover threshold covenant, she would become desolate. She would not see Yeshua any more for these were His last public words in the Temple before His arrest.

The Hebrew's sacrifice with blood on the threshold of their homes was also recognized as a rite of marriage between God and Israel as the very Threshold Covenant itself had its origin in the rite of primitive marriage as earlier mentioned:

Jeremiah 31:32 *Not according to the covenant that I made with their fathers in the day that I took them by the hand to bring them out of the land of Egypt; which my covenant they brake, although I was an husband unto them, saith the LORD:* (KJV)

That first Passover night in Egypt God took to Himself in covenant union [betrothal] 'the children of Israel,' and became a husband to her. The covenant was made 'in the day' that God took them by the hand to bring them out of Egypt. From that time forward if Israel recognized or gave credence to another god, the prophets called her a whore, adulterer, or fornicator.

Ezekiel 16:4-14 *And as for thy nativity, in the day thou wast born thy navel was not cut, neither wast thou washed in water to supple thee; thou wast not salted at all, nor swaddled at all. None eye pitied thee, to do any of these unto thee, to have compassion upon thee; but thou wast cast out in the open field, to the lothing of thy person, in the day that thou wast born. And <u>when I passed by thee</u>, and saw thee polluted in thine own blood, I said unto thee when thou wast <u>in thy blood, Live</u>; yea, I said unto thee when thou wast <u>in thy blood, Live</u>. I have caused thee to multiply as the bud of the field, and thou hast increased and waxen great, and thou art come to excellent ornaments: thy breasts are fashioned, and thine hair is grown, whereas thou wast naked and bare. Now <u>when I passed by thee</u>, and looked upon thee, behold, <u>thy time was the time of love; and I spread my skirt over thee</u>, and covered thy nakedness: yea, I sware unto thee, and entered into a covenant with thee, saith the Lord GOD, and thou becamest mine. Then washed I thee with water; yea, I throughly washed away thy blood from thee, and I anointed thee with oil. I* *clothed thee also with broidered work, and shod thee with badgers' skin, and I girded thee about with fine linen, and I covered thee with silk. I decked thee also with ornaments, and I put bracelets upon thy hands, and a chain on thy neck. And I put a jewel on thy forehead, and earrings in thine ears, and a beautiful crown upon thine head. Thus wast thou decked with gold and silver; and thy raiment was of fine linen, and silk, and broidered work; thou didst eat fine flour, and honey, and oil: and thou wast exceeding beautiful, and thou didst prosper into a kingdom. And thy renown went forth among the heathen for thy beauty: for it was perfect through my comeliness, which I had put upon thee, saith the Lord GOD. (KJV)*

Ruth 3:9 *And he [Boaz] said, Who art thou? And she answered, I am Ruth thine handmaid: spread therefore thy skirt over thine handmaid; for thou art a near kinsman. (KJV)*

Exodus 6:7 *And I will take you to me for a people, and I will be to you a God: and ye shall know that I am the LORD your God, which bringeth you out from under the burdens of the Egyptians. (KJV)*

The rabbis explained that Ezekiel 16 alluded to how God lavished His Bride. The spreading of a skirt over the handmaid and using the phrase 'I will take you unto Me' in Hebrew are equivalents of marriage.[6] Oil was representative of the Levitical priesthood chosen out of her. The broidered work was reminiscent of the curtains in the Tabernacle as well as the badger's skin [tachash in Hebrew]. Therefore, very clearly, the Passover in Egypt was a threshold covenant of betrothal between God and Israel.

The Home Altar

The Passover lamb sacrificed on Nisan 13 in Egypt is often interpreted as not being a korban [sacrifice]. In the Temple God demanded two things from the animal sacrifices; the animal's blood applied to the Altar and certain innards such as the kidneys, part of the liver, diaphragm, and fat all called emurin, to be burnt on the Altar.

There was no Altar in Egypt so how could the Passover there be described as a sacrifice. We know that later in Temple times that the Passover was definitely a sacrifice. However, upon further analysis it appears that the Egyptian Passover was a korban [sacrifice].

Exodus 12:5 *Your lamb shall be without blemish, a male of the first year: ye shall take it out from the sheep, or from the goats:* (KJV)

Exodus 12:10 *And ye shall let nothing of it remain until the morning; and that which remaineth of it until the morning ye shall burn with fire.* (KJV)

Leviticus 7:15 *And the flesh of the sacrifice of his peace offerings for thanksgiving shall be eaten the same day that it is offered; he shall not leave any of it until the morning.* (KJV)

The specific requirement of an unblemished male sheep of the first year is definitely characteristic of many of the sacrifices in the Temple. The Peace Offerings in the Temple must be eaten before morning just as the requirement of the Passover Offering. Among these and other reasons, the rabbis concluded that the Passover was offered as a Peace Offering.

Whereas in the Temple the blood of the sacrifices was applied to the Altar, the blood was applied to the lintel and doorposts of the Israelite homes in Egypt. From this perspective the doors of these homes in Egypt represented the altar. In Pesachim 96a Rav Yosef states: 'There were three altars there [in Egypt] - the lintel and the two doorposts'.

The home in which the Passover lamb was eaten was an altar of sorts. Then we can say with confidence that the Passover sacrifice in Egypt was a korban [sacrifice]. This understanding of the Israelite homes being as altars also opens the door to further understanding the Passover.

Exodus 12:8 *And they shall eat the flesh [Passover] in that night, roast with fire, and <u>unleavened bread</u>; and with bitter herbs they shall eat it.* (KJV)

Leviticus 2:11 *No meat offering, which ye shall bring unto the LORD, shall be made with leaven: for ye shall burn no leaven, nor any honey, in any offering of the LORD made by fire.* (KJV)

It is a commandment that unleavened bread be eaten with the Passover. Also, the Israelite homes in the second Temple period were to be totally cleansed of leavened products at the Passover in preparation for the seven days of the festival of Unleavened Bread. In their homes on the night of the Egyptian Passover, the Israelites had only unleavened bread. Interestingly, leaven of any kind was forbidden upon the Altar in the Tabernacle/Temple.

Exodus 19:6 *And ye shall be unto me a kingdom of priests, and an holy nation. These are the words which thou shalt speak unto the children of Israel.* (KJV)

Exodus 12:6 *And ye shall keep it up until the fourteenth day of the same month: and the whole assembly of the congregation of Israel shall kill it in the evening.* (KJV)

The Aaronic priesthood was not chosen until Israel had sinned with the Golden Calf at Mt. Sinai. The priesthood that was in practice prior to this in Egypt and before arriving at Mt. Sinai was more of a 'home' priesthood. We are not told the identity of the individual responsible for sacrificing the Passover lamb and applying the blood on the doorposts and lintel. It may have been the Father, or the first-born if old enough who performed this act of priesthood.

It is interesting that the Scripture states that 'the whole assembly of the congregation shall kill' the Passover lamb. Although only one Israelite per home would cut the lamb's throat and apply the blood, the entire nation gets credit for the sacrifice and the application of blood. From this point of view, all Israel was performing the role of priests with the Passover in Egypt in relation to the home as the altar. Even before the Levites descended from Aaron were singled out for priestly duty alone, the nation of Israel was as a kingdom of priests unto the Lord.

The Change in Priesthood

Exodus 4:22-23 *And thou shalt say unto Pharaoh, Thus saith the LORD, Israel is my son, even my firstborn: And I say unto thee, Let my son go, that he may serve me: and if thou refuse to let him go, behold, I will slay thy son, even thy firstborn.* (KJV)

Exodus 12:12 *For I will pass through the land of Egypt this night, and will smite all the firstborn in the land of Egypt, both man and beast [behemah]; and against all the gods of Egypt I will execute judgment: I am the LORD.* (KJV)

Exodus 12:29 *And it came to pass, that at midnight the LORD smote all the firstborn in the land of Egypt, from the firstborn of Pharaoh that sat on his throne unto the firstborn of the captive that was in the dungeon; and all the firstborn of cattle [behemah].* (KJV)

Nehemiah 10:36 *Also the firstborn of our sons, and of our cattle [behemah], as it is written in the law, and the firstlings of our <u>herds</u> and of our <u>flocks,</u> to bring to the house of our God, unto the priests that minister in the house of our God:* (KJV)

Exodus 13:1-2 *And the LORD spake unto Moses, saying, Sanctify unto me all the firstborn, whatsoever openeth the womb among the children of Israel, both of man and of beast: it is mine.* (KJV)

Numbers 18:15-17 *Every thing that openeth the matrix in all flesh, which they bring unto the LORD, whether it be of men or beasts, shall be thine: nevertheless the firstborn of man shalt thou surely redeem, and the firstling of <u>unclean</u> beasts shalt thou redeem. And those that are to be redeemed from a month old shalt thou redeem, according to thine estimation, for the money of five shekels, after the shekel of the sanctuary, which is twenty gerahs. But the firstling of a cow, or the firstling of a sheep, or the firstling of a goat, thou shalt not redeem; they are holy: thou shalt sprinkle their blood upon the altar, and shalt burn their fat for an offering made by fire, for a sweet savour unto the LORD.* (KJV)

Scripture and rabbinic writings declare that not only Pharaoh and all of Egypt's firstborn sons died on Passover, but so did all their firstborn male 'beasts'. The KJV translates 'behemah' with different English words. In some places it is interpreted as 'beasts' and in others 'cattle'. When Nehemiah re-instituted the Temple service in the Second Temple period, the firstborn laws applied to both the 'herds' and the 'flocks'. Scripture declares that even the firstborn 'unclean' animals had to be redeemed.

It is interesting to note that in the midst of the Passover sacrifice in Egypt, God tells Moses to sanctify the firstborn male of man and beast. The Threshold Covenant of the Passover lamb is directly linked to the womb and the firstborn. Later, in the Tabernacle [and Temple], the clean male firstborn animal was sacrificed by a priest and eaten only by priests. The unclean male firstborn animal had to be redeemed by paying money to the priest. The male firstborn human, of course, also had to be redeemed with money to the priest.

It was not all the Israelites that were protected from the Death Angel on the Egyptian Passover; it was only the firstborn males of both man and beast. No harm came to Pharaoh and the Egyptian people, just their firstborn male of both man and beast. The Threshold Covenant of the Passover is therefore linked to the Firstborn.

Exodus 24:4-5 *And Moses wrote all the words of the LORD, and rose up early in the morning, and builded an altar under the hill, and twelve pillars, according to the twelve tribes of Israel. And he sent young men of the children of Israel, which offered burnt offerings, and sacrificed peace offerings of oxen unto the LORD.* (KJV)

Rabbinic tradition states that the 'young men' in Exodus 24 were the firstborn males [of the Seventy Elders] among Israel chosen to offer burnt offerings and peace offerings 'prior' to the time of the Levitical priesthood.[7] The rabbis also very clearly taught that the firstborn held a priestly status.[8] The firstborn priesthood came out of those spared during the Egyptian Passover. They also may have been involved in sacrificing the Passover lambs and/or applying the threshold blood covenant on the doorposts and lintel.

Numbers 3:12-13 *And I, behold, I have taken the Levites from among the children of Israel instead of all the firstborn that openeth the matrix among the children of Israel: therefore the Levites shall be mine; Because all the firstborn are mine; for on the day that I smote all the firstborn in the land of Egypt I hallowed unto me all the firstborn in Israel, both man and beast: mine shall they be: I am the LORD.* (KJV)

Numbers 8:16-18 *For they [the Levites] are wholly given unto me from among the children of Israel; instead of such as open every womb, even instead of the firstborn of all the children of Israel, have I taken them unto me. For all the firstborn of the children of Israel are mine, both man and beast: on the day that I smote every firstborn in the land of Egypt I sanctified them for myself. And I have taken the Levites for all the firstborn of the children of Israel.* (KJV)

The commandment for the redemption of Israel's firstborn is in commemoration of the Exodus linked to Passover.[9] Egypt's firstborn sons were killed, but Israel's firstborn sons lived. From that day forward Israel's firstborn males belonged to God and must be appropriately redeemed.

However, because of the firstborn's role in the sin of the Golden Calf, God chose the Levites in their stead because they had become unfit for priesthood. According to the rabbis the Levites did not participate in the Golden Calf incident so they were granted the priesthood.[10]

Numbers 3:46-48 *And for those that are to be redeemed of the two hundred and threescore and thirteen of the firstborn of the children of Israel, which are more than the Levites; Thou shalt even take five shekels apiece by the poll, after the shekel of the sanctuary shalt thou take them: (the shekel is twenty gerahs:) And thou shalt give the money, wherewith the odd number of them is to be redeemed, unto Aaron and to his sons.* (KJV)

The firstborn were set aside and sanctified to serve God. Although the firstborn had disqualified themselves, they still retained their quality of sanctity as divinely given. This sanctity was transferred to the Levites through redemption and substitution.[11] All the first-born Israelite males were replaced by the Levites. There were two hundred and seventy three more firstborn then Levites that had to be redeemed. Of course, it should be pointed out that these Levites were not all priests. Only the Levite house of Aaron maintained the priesthood. The other Levites worked for the Temple as guards, officers, musicians, etc.

Yeshua, the First-Born of Israel

Zechariah 12:10 *And I will pour upon the house of David, and upon the inhabitants of Jerusalem, the spirit of grace and of supplications: and they shall look upon me whom they have pierced, and they shall mourn for him, as one mourneth for his only son, and shall be in bitterness for him, as one that is in bitterness for his firstborn.* (KJV)

I John 4:9 *In this was manifested the love of God toward us, because that God sent his only begotten Son into the world, that we might live through him.* (KJV)

John 1:14, 18 *And the Word was made flesh, and dwelt among us, (and we beheld his glory, the glory as of the only begotten of the Father,) full of grace and truth...No man hath seen God at any time; the only begotten Son, which is in the bosom of the Father, he hath declared him.* (KJV)

Hebrews 5:6 *As he saith also in another place, Thou art a priest for ever after the order of Melchisedec.* (KJV)

The Scripture is clear that the Messiah IS Israel's 'First-Born' and ONLY 'Son'. He is the only 'Begotten' of the Father. There is no other like Him. In Yeshua's First-Born status, His flesh was crucified and His blood shed. His Passover blood represents the Threshold Covenant and the Marriage Rite. As the priestly status and sanctity of the firstborn was transferred to the Levites in the Wilderness, so to does God desire to transfer the priestly sanctity of His First-Born Messiah to those that will worship Him. Through His resurrection Yeshua gained a High Priest status, not after the Levitical Order of Aaron, but after the Eternal Order of Melchizedek.

1 Peter 2:5, 9 *Ye also, as lively stones, are built up a spiritual house, an holy priesthood, to offer up spiritual sacrifices, acceptable to God by Jesus Christ...But ye are a chosen generation, a royal priesthood, an holy nation, a peculiar people; that ye should shew forth the praises of him who hath called you out of darkness into his marvellous light:* (KJV)

Exodus 19:6 *And ye shall be unto me a kingdom of priests, and an holy nation. These are the words which thou shalt speak unto the children of Israel.* (KJV)

Romans 12:1 *I beseech you therefore, brethren, by the mercies of God, that ye present your bodies a living sacrifice, holy, acceptable unto God, which is your reasonable service.* (KJV)

Believers in Yeshua have not replaced the Levites. The believer's temple is their body built up into a spiritual house. As a royal and holy priesthood believers offer up spiritual sacrifices pleasing to God. Their life, as living sacrifices, puts them into the category of the 'heavenly' priesthood. Peter was quoting from Exodus 19:6 referring to a holy priesthood and a kingdom of priests when discussing the priesthood of the believers. This was not the Aaronic priesthood, but that of the firstborn at Mt. Sinai.

The Aaronic priesthood is not bad nor has it ended [there will be Aaronic priests serving in the Third Temple in the Millennium - see Ezekiel 40-48]. They represent an earthly priesthood, but Yeshua's priesthood is of the eternal order of Melchizedek. While there is no earthly Temple standing, believers can only offer spiritual sacrifices. When the Temple stands, however, the righteous offer not only spiritual sacrifices, but sacrifices under the Mosaic code. The believing Jews in the first century continued to offer sacrifices in the Temple after Yeshua's resurrection [Acts 21:26]. If the Temple stands and one has a flesh and blood body, the Temple sacrifices are valid. When a believer crosses the Threshold of Yeshua's blood and enters into covenant with Him, he has entered the world of the heavenly priesthood.

Yeshua the First-Born [Firstfruits] of the Dead

Revelation 1:5-6 *And from Jesus Christ, who is the faithful witness, and the first begotten of the dead, and the prince of the kings of the earth. Unto him that loved us, and washed us from our sins in his own blood, And hath made us kings and priests unto God and his Father; to him be glory and dominion for ever and ever. Amen.* (KJV)

Romans 8:23, 29, 30 *And not only they, but ourselves also, which have the firstfruits of the Spirit, even we ourselves groan within ourselves, waiting for the adoption, to wit, the redemption of our body. For whom he did foreknow, he also did predestinate to be conformed to the image of his Son, that he might be the firstborn among many brethren. Moreover whom he did predestinate, them he also called: and whom he called, them he also justified: and whom he justified, them he also glorified.* (KJV)

Colossians 1:15, 18 *Who is the image of the invisible God, the first-born of every creature...And he is the head of the body, the church: who is the beginning, the firstborn from the dead; that in all things he might have the preeminence.* (KJV)

Hebrews 12:22-28 *But ye are come unto mount Sion, and unto the city of the living God, the heavenly Jerusalem, and to an innumerable company of angels, To the general assembly and church [Ekklesia] of the firstborn, which are written in heaven, and to God the Judge of all, and to the spirits of just men made perfect, And to Jesus the mediator of the new covenant, and to the blood of sprinkling, that speaketh better things than that of Abel. See that ye refuse not him that speaketh. For if they escaped not who refused him that spake on earth, much more shall not we escape, if we turn away from him* *that speaketh from heaven: Whose voice then shook the earth: but now he hath promised, saying, Yet once more I shake not the earth only, but also heaven. And this word, Yet once more, signifieth the removing of those things that are shaken, as of things that are made, that those things which cannot be shaken may remain. Wherefore we receiving a kingdom which cannot be moved, let us have grace, whereby we may serve God acceptably with reverence and godly fear:* (KJV)

The writer of Hebrews clearly associates the heavenly Jerusalem as 'the city of the living God'. Heavenly [new] Jerusalem is the mystical Mt. Zion. The writer says that when believers in Yeshua come to that upper celestial city they are coming 'to the general assembly and church of the firstborn' and 'to the spirits of just men made perfect'. What does this mean? The general assembly of the firstborn involves resurrected saints because no flesh and blood human can be 'just' and 'perfect' before God on their own merit. The 'Ekklesia,' the Called Out Ones, are meeting together in the General Assembly, which is Mt. Zion or Heavenly [New] Jerusalem. Now let us look at what it means to be part of the Church [Ekklesia] of the Firstborn.

In Colossians we learn that the Son [Messiah] is the 'firstborn of every creature'. Paul elaborates further saying that the Messiah 'is the head of the body, the church [Ekklesia]'. He is the Head of the Church-Ekklesia in that He 'is the beginning'. Yeshua is the beginning because He is 'the firstborn of the dead'. Paul very clearly is referring to Yeshua's resurrection as being the 'firstborn'.

In Romans 8, Paul speaks of the indwelling Spirit in the believers as 'the firstfruits of the Spirit'. The Holy Spirit was sent down from 'Heaven' as a foretaste (firstfruits) of the believer's adoption and redemption when they receive their glorified resurrected body. The 'firstfruits of the Spirit' in the believer leads to the Son [Messiah], who is 'the firstborn among many brethren'. From our previous example we know that Paul is speaking of the 'firstborn' as related to Messiah's resurrected body.

Ephesians 1:12-14 *That we should be to the praise of his glory, who first trusted in Christ. In whom ye also trusted, after that ye heard the word of truth, the gospel of your salvation: in whom also after that ye believed, ye were sealed with that holy Spirit of promise, Which is the earnest of our inheritance until the redemption of the purchased possession, unto the praise of his glory.* (KJV)

Paul elaborates on the 'firstfruits of the Spirit' from Romans 8 in Ephesians 1. The moment that an individual becomes a believer in the God of Israel through His Messiah, they are 'sealed with that Holy Spirit of promise'. This phrase is 'loaded' with the High Holy Days [Rosh Hashana to Yom Kippur, Tishri 1-10] terminology where the individual's fate is 'sealed'.[12]

Paul goes on to say that the 'Holy Spirit of Promise' is 'the earnest of our inheritance until the redemption of the purchased possession'. The Greek word for 'earnest' is 'arrabon'. Arrabon was a technical legal term that meant a down payment in advance of a full purchase of something. The down payment secured a legal claim to what was being purchased.[13]

The Greek word for firstfruits, 'aparche,' is a synonym for 'arrabon' [earnest].[14] Therefore, Paul's use of 'firstfruits of the Spirit' in Romans 8 may be equivalent to his use of 'earnest of the Spirit' in 2 Corinthians 1:21-22.

2 Corinthians 1: 21-22 *Now he which stablisheth us with you in Christ, and hath anointed us, is God; Who hath also sealed us, and given the earnest of the Spirit in our hearts.* (KJV)

Paul also uses this phrase in:

2 Corinthians 5: 4-5 *For we that are in this tabernacle do groan, being burdened: not for that we would be unclothed, but clothed upon, that mortality might be swallowed up of life. Now he that hath wrought us for the selfsame thing is God, who also hath given unto us the earnest of the Spirit.* (KJV)

1 Corinthians 15:20-23 *But now is Christ risen from the dead, and become the firstfruits of them that slept. For since by man came death, by man came also the resurrection of the dead. For as in Adam all die, even so in Christ shall all be made alive. But every man in his own order: Christ the firstfruits; afterward they that are Christ's at his coming.* (KJV)

In 1 Corinthians 15, Paul describes Messiah's resurrection as 'the firstfruits of them that slept'. Yeshua was the first man to enter the Olam Haba (The World To Come) upon His resurrection. Afterwards, 'every man [righteous] in his own order,' will be resurrected at 'His coming'.

Revelation 20:6 *Blessed and holy is he that hath part in the first resurrection: on such the second death hath no power, but they shall be priests of God and of Christ, and shall reign with him a thousand years.* (KJV)

All the righteous will be resurrected in the 'First Resurrection' in their specific order. The first [and only] resurrection is for those who will receive glorified bodies. They reign with Messiah during the Day of the Lord (Millennium) and will be heavenly priests sent out among the nations. The Levitical priests will perform the Temple sacrifices in Jerusalem during the Millennium [Ezekiel 40-48]. After the Millennium is over, there will not be a need for priesthood because only the righteous in resurrected bodies will be living in New Jerusalem. No mediation between God and man will be needed anymore.

Yeshua opened the 'Door' for man to enter God's Kingdom. The earth is God's footstool [Matthew 5:35] and He offered a blood welcoming at this 'Door' for anyone who would 'Crossover' the Threshold into covenant relationship with Him. Yeshua's blood spilled to the earth on the Threshold of God's Kingdom. When we crossover that Heavenly Passover's blood, we enter into God's protection. The Destroyer has no place in us eternally. We are the firstborn adopted sons of God and have been redeemed by the blood of the Passover Lamb. After we make the choice to enter in, Yeshua will carry us over the Threshold into Holy Marriage that we may sit with Him on His Throne as a queen.

The Mezuzah

The Jews recite a prayer called the Shema, which includes the following Scriptures:

Deuteronomy 6:5-9 *And thou shalt love the LORD thy God with all thine heart, and with all thy soul, and with all thy might. And these words, which I command thee this day, shall be in thine heart: And thou shalt teach them diligently unto thy children, and shalt talk of them when thou sittest in thine house, and when thou walkest by the way, and when thou liest down, and when thou risest up. And thou shalt bind them for a sign upon thine hand, and they shall be as frontlets between thine eyes. And thou shalt write them upon the posts (Mezuzah) of thy house, and on thy gates.* (KJV)

Deuteronomy 11:13-21 *And it shall come to pass, if ye shall hearken diligently unto my commandments which I command you this day, to love the LORD your God, and to serve him with all your heart and with all your soul, That I will give you the rain of your land in his due season, the first rain and the latter rain, that thou mayest gather in thy corn, and thy wine, and thine oil. And I will send grass in thy fields for thy cattle, that thou mayest eat and be full. Take heed to yourselves, that your heart be not deceived, and ye turn aside, and serve other gods, and worship them; And then the LORD's wrath be kindled against you, and he shut up the heaven, that there be no rain, and that the land yield not her fruit; and lest ye perish quickly from off the good land which the LORD giveth you. Therefore shall ye lay up these my words in your heart and in your soul, and bind them for a sign upon your hand, that they may be as frontlets between your eyes. And ye shall teach them your children, speaking of them when thou sittest in thine house, and when thou walkest by the way, when thou liest down, and when thou risest up. And thou shalt write them upon the door posts of thine house, and upon thy gates: That your days may be multiplied, and the days of your children, in the land* *which the LORD sware unto your fathers to give them, as the days of heaven upon the earth.* (KJV)

Observant Jews affix a Mezuzah outside the entrance door to their homes. It is a small container placed on the upper-third right-hand doorpost that by tradition they touch with their lightly kissed right hand as they enter the home. The Mezuzah usually has the letter shin שׁ on its front surface, which stands for Shaddai שׁ ד י. It serves as a reminder that the house is a sanctuary of the Almighty, El-Shaddai, which usually translates as 'all-powerful,' or 'omnipotent.'[15] The rabbis stated that 'Shaddai' was also an acronym for 'Shomer Delatot Yisrael,' which means, 'Guardian of the doors of Israel'.[16]

But inside the Mezuzah is a very tiny scroll inscribed with these two passages of Scripture: Deuteronomy 6:5-9 and 11:13-21. In these two sets of verses we have the Hebrew word for 'posts' and 'door posts,' which is Mezuzah מ ז ו ז ה. The Mezuzah is nailed to the doorpost and it becomes one with the doorpost. The words of Deuteronomy are literally written on Israel's doorposts.

Notice that in the Scripture segments of Deuteronomy 6 and 11 in the Mezuzah are also connected to what is called Tefillin or Phylacteries. They are to be a sign upon your hand and frontlets between your eyes. The hand Tefillin is worn on the left hand opposite the heart. It is symbolic of dedicating one's heart to God. The head Tefillin are worn next to the brain dedicating one's soul and intellect to God.

The Tefillin for the hand consists of a single box. The one for the head, however, is made up of four boxes pressed tightly together. Each box of the Tefillin must be inscribed with the Hebrew letter shin שׁ. The Tefillin must be bound with leather straps and tied with a knot in the shape of the Hebrew letter Dalet ד. The hand Tefillin must be tied with a knot shaped like a Yud י. Therefore, the Tefillin contain the three Hebrew letters, Shin, Dalet and Yud, as a part of their basic structure. These spell out God's name Shadai שׁ ד י, the same name that appears on the Mezuzah...[17]

Exodus 13:8-9 *And thou shalt shew thy son in that day, saying, This is done because of that which the LORD did unto me when I came* *forth out of Egypt. And it shall be for a sign unto thee upon thine hand, and for a memorial between thine eyes, that the LORD's law may be in thy mouth: for with a strong hand hath the LORD brought thee out of Egypt.* (KJV)

Exodus 13:15-16 *And it came to pass, when Pharaoh would hardly let us go, that the LORD slew all the firstborn in the land of Egypt, both the firstborn of man, and the firstborn of beast: therefore I sacrifice to the LORD all that openeth the matrix, being males; but all the firstborn of my children I redeem. And it shall be for a token upon thine hand, and for frontlets between thine eyes: for by strength of hand the LORD brought us forth out of Egypt.* (Kev)

In Exodus 13 there is a clear connection between the Passover and the Tefillin (Phylacteries). Four sets of Scripture were contained in the Tefillin: Deuteronomy 6:5-9; 11:13-21 and Exodus 13:1-10; 11-16.[18] If the Tefillin are commandments connected to the Exodus at Passover, it stands to reason that the Mezuzah also is connected to the Exodus and Passover. Also because the Mezuzah was located on the doorpost, it was a reminder of the Threshold Crossing-over covenant of Passover.

BIBLIOGRAPHY

1. The Threshold Covenant. H. Clay Trumbull. Impact Christian Book, Inc., Kirkwood, Missouri, 2000. Page 3.
2. Ibid. Page 23.
3. Ibid. Page 189.
4. Gesenius Hebrew-Chaldee Lexicon to the Old Testament. H.W.F. Gesenius. Baker Books, Grand Rapids, Michigan, 1979. Page 683.
5. Christ in the Passover. Ceil and Moishe Rosen. Moody Press, Chicago, 1978. Page 22.
6. The Artscroll Tanach Series - Ezekiel. Rabbi Moshe Eisemann. Mesorah Publications, Ltd., Brooklyn, New York. 1977. Pages249-253.

7. The JPS Torah Commentary - Exodus. Nahum M. Sarna. The Jewish Publication Society, Philadelphia, New York, Jerusalem, 1991. Pages 151-152.

8. The JPS Torah Commentary - Numbers. Jacob Milgrom. The Jewish Publication Society, Philadelphia, New York, Jerusalem, 1990. Page 18.

9. Yalkut Me'am Lo'ez - The Torah Anthology Exodus Volume 2, Book 5 in the series. Translated by Rabbi Aryeh Kaplan. Moznaim Publishing Corporation, New York, Jerusalem, 1979. Page 130.

10. Yalkut Me'am Lo'ez - The Torah Anthology Numbers Volume 1, Book 13 in the series. Translated by Dr. Tzvi Faier. Moznaim Publishing Corporation, New York, Jerusalem, 1990. Page 50.

11. Yalkut Me'am Lo'ez - The Torah Anthology Numbers Volume 1, Book 13 in the series. Translated by Dr. Tzvi Faier. Moznaim Publishing Corporation, New York, Jerusalem, 1990. Pages 56-58.

12. The Artscroll Mesorah Series - Rosh hashana. Rabbi Nosson Scherman, Rabbi Hersh Goldwurm, Rabbi Avie Gold. Mesorah Publications, Ltd., Brooklyn, New York, 1983. Page 75.

13. Word Meanings in the New Testament. Ralph Earle. Baker Book House, Grand Rapids, Michigan, 1974. Page 293.

14. The Complete WordStudy New Testament. Spiros Zodhiates, Th.D. World Bible Publishers, Iowa Falls, Iowa, 1992. Page 887.

15. The Mezuzah Prophecy. Prophecy In the News - October 1997. J. R. Church. Oklahoma City, Oklahoma.

16. Yalkut Me'am Lo'ez - The Torah Anthology Deuteronomy Volume 3, Book 17 in the series. Translated by m. and S. Sprecher. Moznaim Publishing Corporation, New York, Jerusalem, 1992. Page 102.

17. The Aryeh Kaplan Anthology II. Mesorah Publications, Ltd., Brooklyn, New York, 1974. Pages 237-243

18.	The JPS Torah Commentary - Deuteronomy. Jeffrey H. Tigay. The Jewish Publication Society, Philadelphia, New York, Jerusalem, 1996. Page 441.

10

THE TWO MESSIAHS OF ANCIENT JUDAISM

Luke 3:15-16 *And as the people were in expectation, and all men mused in their hearts of John, whether he were the Christ, or not; John answered, saying unto them all, I indeed baptize you with water; but one mightier than I cometh, the latchet of whose shoes I am not worthy to unloose: he shall baptize you with the Holy Ghost and with fire:* (KJV)

Within Judaism of the first century of this Common Era, Messianic fervor reached its zenith as the people expected the Messiah to come based upon the prophetic visions of Daniel. The rabbis by this time had dissected the Tanach [Old Testament] and commented on all verses alluding to the Messiah. The study of the Messiah is a very complex issue, but for our purposes in this book we will focus on what we will call 'The Dual Role of Messiah'.

The sages concluded that the Scripture demonstrated that Messiah would be killed. However, they also found from Scripture that Messiah was to be the Redeemer who would bring in a thousand-year Messianic Kingdom. These two views were irreconcilable so they devised a scheme of splitting the personage of Messiah into two. One of them was called Messiah ben Joseph or Ephraim who would be slain. The other, Messiah ben David, was believed to come after him and would lead Israel to the ultimate victory during the Messianic era of bliss.

This division of the roles of Messiah resolved the conflict of the Scriptures foretelling a slain Messiah. The Sages saw a prefiguring of Messiah in Moses' life. As Moses died before Israel entered into the Promised Land, so would the Messiah die before achieving the final redemption. Here the rabbis had a solution. The Messiah had to bring complete redemption to be the True One prophesied of in Scripture. The solution was to assign the redemption to a second and final Messiah, whereas a first Messiah as Moses would die first.[1]

The Messiah as Conquering King can be seen from such verses as Zechariah 14, Psalm 2, Isaiah 63-66, and Jeremiah 23. On the other hand verses such as Isaiah 40-53, 61, Psalm 22, and Daniel 9 describe the Messianic figure as suffering and even dying.[2] The major focus of the people and the rabbinic writings was on the Messiah ben David character.

Matthew 11:2-3 *Now when John had heard in the prison the works of Christ, he sent two of his disciples, And said unto him, Art thou he that should come, or do we look for another?* (KJV)

Luke 7:18-21 *And the disciples of John shewed him of all these things. And John calling unto him two of his disciples sent them to Jesus, saying, Art thou he that should come? or look we for another? When the men were come unto him, they said, John Baptist hath sent us unto thee, saying, Art thou he that should come? or look we for another? And in that same hour he cured many of their infirmities and plagues, and of evil spirits; and unto many that were blind he gave sight.* (KJV)

From a Christian perspective it appears that John's memory has failed him, or he is starting to have doubts of whether Yeshua is the Messiah? This is unlikely if John was the prophesied Elijah-like forerunner to Messiah's First Coming. It becomes clear that John has learned of the two Messiah theory and wants to know from the first Messiah if there will be another one after Him. Rather then giving John a straight yes or no answer, Yeshua replies in the following verses:

Matthew 11:4-6 *Jesus answered and said unto them, Go and shew John again those things which ye do hear and see: The blind receive* *their sight, and the lame walk, the lepers are cleansed, and the deaf hear, the dead are raised up, and the poor have the gospel preached to them. And blessed is he, whosoever shall not be offended in me.* (KJV)

Luke 7:22-23 *Then Jesus answering said unto them, Go your way, and tell John what things ye have seen and heard; how that the blind see, the lame walk, the lepers are cleansed, the deaf hear, the dead are raised, to the poor the gospel is preached. And blessed is he, whosoever shall not be offended in me.* (KJV)

Yeshua's reply is coded with the two-messiah teaching of the rabbis. In the Tanach, particularly in Isaiah, these miracles are attested to the coming Messiah. Yeshua is informing John that the rabbinical teaching of two different Messiahs was wrong and only One Messiah would fulfill both roles of the Suffering Servant and Conquering King. As a matter of fact, the list of signs that Yeshua told John is a combination of what both Messiah's were to accomplish as taught by the rabbis.[3]

Yeshua was demonstrating that He would fulfill all the Messianic prophecies. Rather than two Messiahs coming in two different roles, there would only be One Messiah who would suffer and die as Messiah ben Joseph, who in turn would be resurrected by the Father, and would return at a future time as Messiah ben David to bring about the final redemption.

Psalm 90:4 *For a thousand years in thy sight are but as yesterday when it is past, and as a watch in the night.* (KJV)

2 Peter 3:8 *But, beloved, be not ignorant of this one thing, that one day is with the Lord as a thousand years, and a thousand years as one day.* (KJV)

In ancient Judaism it was a generally accepted fact by the rabbi's that one thousand years of man on earth was to be compared to one day with the Lord. This was an allusion to the Genesis Creation story: For six days God created or labored and on the seventh day

He rested. Therefore, it was taught that man would toil on the earth for six days (6,000 years) and eventually finds his rest on the seventh day (the last 1,000 years). The last one thousand years was to be man's Sabbath where he would rest in the Messianic Kingdom.

It is of interest that many rabbis taught that the Messiah would come after four thousand years from creation. We know that the Jews were looking for the Messiah in the first century based upon the timing of Daniel's prophecies. Even though modern Rabbinic Judaism denies the two comings of the Messiah, the learned ones anciently taught it. He was to be expected at the four thousand year and the six thousand year marks.[4]

Judaism once taught that the Last Redeemer [Messiah] would be like the First Redeemer [Moses]. Moses made his appearance in Egypt, but then disappeared to the desert for forty years, fearing Pharaoh would have him executed for killing an Egyptian.[5] But Moses would appear to Israel again and bring them out of Egypt. Likewise, the Messiah would appear to Israel and then disappear, only to reappear.[6]

Yeshua came the first time to fulfill the role of Messiah ben Joseph. Yeshua will return a second time in the role of Messiah ben David. His First Coming centers on the Spring Festivals of Passover, Unleavened Bread, Firstfruits of the Barley Harvest, and Shavuot. These are the Festivals that more relate to the role of Messiah ben Joseph. The Messiah's second coming will be centered upon the themes of the Fall Festivals of Rosh Hashana, Yom Kippur and Succot [Tabernacles].

In the next chapter we will be looking at Yeshua's second coming within the 'marriage' context. His first coming was to bring betrothal, but His second coming will be to bring nesuin or full marriage, which will be highlighted with the believers receiving glorified resurrected bodies. These aspects of His second coming are tied to the Conquering King, Messiah ben David. In the remainder of this chapter we will study with more depth the subject of the Suffering Servant, Messiah ben Joseph.

The Suffering Tzaddik/Messiah ben Joseph

In Christianity Yeshua is viewed, as a 'human' sacrifice substituting for what each man and woman deserves, to be put to death for their sins. The blood of the animal sacrifices could only atone by covering sins. What was needed, Christian's say, was a like sacrifice (human for human). In this case Yeshua was without sin and was the only human qualified for the job.

It is true that the New Testament uses phraseology that appears to relate Yeshua's death as a sacrifice. But He was not a sacrifice in the sense of a human sacrifice. God forbids human sacrifices. Yeshua would be disqualified as the Messiah if He represented a human sacrifice. What we are going to learn is that His suffering was a sacrifice, based not upon human terms, but on the divine that also resided in Him. Yeshua, therefore, was not a human sacrifice, but a Heavenly sacrifice, which is far different from the interpretation of Christianity.

Ancient Judaism taught the motif that suffering and/or death of the righteous could atone for the sins of Israel. Ezekiel and Job are given as examples of this teaching. The idea of the sinners seeing the righteous suffer, for what they themselves were guilty of, and then repenting was the purpose. It was considered God's mercy to chastise the righteous in a given generation for the sins of Israel, instead of judging the entire nation. When God sees the suffering of His righteous who does not deserve it, He does not press the issue against the sinners. The rabbis understood that when punishment was administered to the righteous that God's justice for punishment on the entire community was satisfied. It was the merit of the righteous that saved the entire community. The righteous one who suffered was thought of as sinless, but was considered to be a part of the whole community in their sins against God. The righteous who were not sinners became sin to be judged by God for the entire nation.[7]

This author believes that more than any other reason, Yeshua provided atonement for Israel and all mankind as the ultimate Suffering Servant (Messiah) and Tzaddik (Righteous One). It is true that without Yeshua's blood being applied to the Heavenly Tabernacle there would be no eternal atonement, but it is also true that He suffered death as 'The Tzaddik' for the judgment of the sins of the people. This is why one reads of the importance of both Yeshua's death and resurrection (the blood being applied on the Heavenly Altar) in the New Testament.

Luke 23:13-14 *And Pilate, when he had called together the chief priests and the rulers and the people, Said unto them, Ye have brought this man [Yeshua] unto me, as one that perverteth the people: and, behold, I, having examined him before you, have found no fault in this man touching those things whereof ye accuse him: No, nor yet Herod: for I sent you to him; and, lo, nothing worthy of death is done unto him.* (KJV)

The New Testament establishes the fact that the Roman Procurator, Pontius Pilate and King Herod could find no fault in Yeshua that warranted His death. It was the Sadducean chief priests and the rulers who were condemning Yeshua to death. Although, some Pharisees did oppose Yeshua, the majority of them probably would never have required His death. The Sadducees did not believe in resurrection [or life after death] and were definitely challenged by Yeshua's message. Their political power was being threatened. They had every reason to see that Yeshua was killed.

Isaiah 53:10-11 *Yet it pleased the LORD to bruise him; he hath put him to grief: when thou shalt make his soul an offering for sin, he shall see his seed, he shall prolong his days, and the pleasure of the LORD shall prosper in his hand. He shall see of the travail of his soul, and shall be satisfied: by his knowledge shall my righteous servant justify many; for he shall bear their iniquities.* (KJV)

Christian theologians cite Isaiah 53 as referring to Yeshua's crucifixion. With this knowledge of the Suffering Tzaddik, it is very clear to what the prophet is speaking. Yeshua was the Suffering Tzaddik similar to Ezekiel. Yeshua as the Righteous One, suffered to 'bear the iniquities' to 'justify many'. The Targum Yonatan says of the Suffering Servant in Isaiah 42:1, 'Behold, My Servant, the Messiah, whom I bring near...'

John 11:47-53 *Then gathered the chief priests and the Pharisees a council, and said, What do we? for this man doeth many miracles. If we let him thus alone, all men will believe on him: and the Romans shall come and take away both our place and nation. And one of them, named Caiaphas, being the high priest that same year, said unto them, Ye know nothing at all, Nor consider that it is expedient for us, that one man should die for the people, and that the whole nation perish not. And this spake he not of himself: but being high priest that year, he prophesied that Jesus should die for that nation; And not for that nation only, but that also he should gather together in one the children of God that were scattered abroad. Then from that day forth they took counsel together for to put him to death.* (KJV)

Many Christian theologians have no answer as to why the Sadducean High Priest prophesied about Yeshua's death. He, the Sadducean chief priests, and those consenting Pharisees, agreed to put Yeshua to death as a Righteous Tzaddik. It is true that they were afraid to lose their political clout, but they were more worried about Yeshua's message of the Kingdom of God attracting many Jewish followers, and hence causing a rebellion against the Romans. They knew that the Roman Caesar would wipe out Judea as a people and a nation if such occurred. Caiaphas understood that Judaism taught about the Suffering Tzaddik and that Yeshua must be put to death in order for the nation to be saved and the Jews scattered abroad in other nations to eventually return to the land of Israel. Even though their thinking was 'twisted,' God had ultimately planned this outcome and put the Suffering Tzaddik into Israel's history to atone for their sins as a people and a nation.

Notice that the chief priests, Pharisees, and the High Priest Caiaphas recognized that Yeshua must fulfill the role of the Suffering Tzaddik. They did not see Him as the Messiah, but realized that He was a righteous one (tzaddik). This is very significant in sorting out theological aspects of His death and resurrection. The author believes that we as fleshly human beings cannot fully grasp Who Yeshua was and is in His totality, but God has given us pictures and symbols to help us identify His actions.

Zechariah 12:12-14 *And the land shall mourn, every family apart; the family of the house of David apart, and their wives apart; the family of the house of Nathan apart, and their wives apart; The family of the house of Levi apart, and their wives apart; the family of Shimei apart, and their wives apart; All the families that remain, every family apart, and their wives apart.* (KJV)

Rabbi Dosa explained that the future mourning in the Land of Israel will be do to the slaying of the Messiah from the house of Joseph who precedes the Messiah of the house of David.[8] Another source in speaking of the Messiah called Ephraim (the son of Joseph), said that the sins of Israel will be upon Him as a yoke of iron and will cause His tongue to cleave to the roof of His mouth. The Suffering Messiah will accept this burden upon Himself with joy and gladness that not a single person from Israel should perish.[9]

It is not difficult to understand why the Suffering Servant Messiah is called Messiah ben Joseph. Although Joseph was an innocent righteous man, he suffered greatly. In the beginning he was backstabbed by his brothers and sold into slavery. Judas also betrayed Yeshua for a slave's price. After Joseph's rise to power in Egypt, his brothers fully embraced him. When all of the family of Israel [Jacob] came into Egypt, Joseph saved them from the famine. In the future Yeshua will be accepted by all Israel as the Messiah.

Pharaoh named Joseph Zaphnath-paaneah, which has a dual meaning (Genesis 41:43-45). In Hebrew it means 'revealer of secrets,' which may allude to him revealing his true identity to his brothers. Yeshua will be revealed to Israel one day also. In the Egyptian language, the name means 'Savior of the World'. Anyone who believes in Yeshua will be saved.

Daniel 7:13 *I saw in the night visions, and, behold, one like the Son of man came with the <u>clouds </u>of heaven, and came to the Ancient of days, and they brought him near before him.* (KJV)

Zechariah 9:9 *Rejoice greatly, O daughter of Zion; shout, O daughter of Jerusalem: behold, thy King cometh unto thee: he is*

*just, and having salvation; <u>lowly</u>, and riding upon an ass, and upon
a colt the foal of an ass.* (KJV)

A discussion in the Talmud clearly demonstrates that the ancient
rabbis saw the two comings of the Messiah. He would come on a
donkey if Israel was unworthy, and again to a worthy Israel on the
clouds of Heaven.[10] These two appearances were pointed from the
prophecies of Zechariah 9:9 and Daniel 7:13.

This Talmudic interpretation appears to be reinforced by the
construction of the two Hebrew words that described the two
comings of Messiah. The Hebrew word for 'lowly' in Zechariah
9 is 'ani' י נ ע and denotes the first coming. Daniel 7 is written
in Aramaic and the word used for 'clouds' in verse 13 is 'anani'
י נ נ ע, which denotes the second coming. The only difference is
the extra nun נ in 'clouds'. 'Ani' with one nun represents the first
coming, and 'anani' with two nuns represents Messiah's second
coming. The rabbis even called the Messiah by the name 'Son of
the Clouds'.[11]

Zechariah 12:10 *And I will pour upon the house of David, and upon
the inhabitants of Jerusalem, the spirit of grace and of supplications: and <u>they shall look upon me whom they have pierced</u>, and they
shall mourn for him, as one mourneth for his only son, and shall be
in bitterness for him, as one that is in bitterness for his firstborn.*
(KJV)

We have already mentioned that the rabbis connected the
mourning in Zechariah 12 to be for the slain Messiah ben Joseph.
This makes even more sense when we look at verse 10 stating their
mourning was connected to looking upon the one they had pierced.
Yeshua was pierced on His execution stake. Again, contrary to what
some teach today, there is a clear history of translating Zechariah
12:10 accordingly as 'the one pierced' (or 'thrust through'), as well
as interpreting this as referring to the Messiah.

Let's focus upon the phrase 'they shall look upon me whom they
have pierced' in Hebrew: ו ט י ב ה ו (They shall) י ל א (Look
upon Me) ת א (Aleph-Tav) ו ר ר ק ד ר ש א (Whom they have

pierced). In other words it should read: 'They shall look upon Me, Aleph-Tav (ת א), Whom they have pierced'.

Revelation 1:7-8 (KJV) *Behold, <u>he cometh with clouds;</u> and every eye shall see him, and they also which <u>pierced</u> him: and all kindreds of the earth shall wail (mourn) because of him. Even so, Amen. <u>I am Alpha (Aleph) and Omega (Tav),</u> the beginning and the ending, saith the Lord, which is, and which was, and which is to come, the Almighty.* (KJV)

We know that this interpretation of Zechariah 12:10 is correct because of Revelation 1:7-8. John writes a Midrash on Zechariah relating the Pierced One to the Messiah, whom is called the Alpha and Omega. Alpha is the first letter of the Greek alphabet, whereas Omega is the last. Aleph is the first letter of the Hebrew alphabet, whereas Tav is the last. This Greek rendering, Alpha-Omega, therefore, is a reference to the Messiah Yeshua, the 'Aleph-Tav,' the 'first and the last,' and the 'beginning and the end'.

Notice that Messiah is recognized as Messiah ben Joseph [the pierced one] when He comes in the clouds because 'all kindreds of the earth shall wail because of Him'. Whereas only some had recognized Him at His first appearance, everyone will recognize Him at His second coming as Messiah ben David.

A concept in ancient Judaism was that the Righteous Tzaddik [Messiah] must first be 'humbled' in order to later be 'exalted'. At that time He would also raise up his brethren with Him. This is known as 'the descent of the Tzaddik,' or 'the descent for the sake of ascent'.[12] The concept of the Tzaddik lowering Himself is shown in the New Testament:

Philippians 2:5-11 *Let this mind be in you, which was also in Christ Jesus: Who, being in the form of God, thought it not robbery to be equal with God: But made himself of no reputation, and took upon him the form of a servant, and was made in the likeness of men: And being found in fashion as a man, he humbled himself, and became obedient unto death, even the death of the cross. Wherefore God also hath highly exalted him, and given him a name which is above* *every name: That at the name of Jesus every knee should bow, of things in heaven, and things in earth, and things under the earth; And that every tongue should confess that Jesus Christ is Lord, to the glory of God the Father.* (KJV)

Ephesians 4:9-10 (*Now that he ascended, what is it but that he also descended first into the lower parts of the earth? He that descended is the same also that ascended up far above all heavens, that he might fill all things.*) (KJV)

The term 'halikhah' is used to describe the Tzaddik that descends from His grade to another in order to rebuke and instruct others, which lead them to repent.[13] Joseph foreshadowed the concept of the Tzaddik Messiah lowering Himself in order to be raised again. Consider also the following verses:

2 Corinthians 8:9 *For ye know the grace of our Lord Jesus Christ, that, though he was rich, yet for your sakes he became poor, that ye through his poverty might be rich.* (KJV)

2 Corinthians 5:21 *For he hath made him to be sin for us, who knew no sin; that we might be made the righteousness of God in him.* (KJV)

In Jewish mystical thought the Righteous Tzaddik Messiah was thought to be wholly pure. However, on a specific occasion [the Suffering Messiah] He might have impurity in Him to join the ranks of the impure, so that He can elevate them to a state of purity.[14]

The idea of a single Tzaddik atoning for his entire generation is found in Jewish mystical literature. Rabbi Moshe Chaim Luzzatto approaches the subject by stating that there can even be a 'more highly perfected Tzaddik,' who can atone for his generation as well as for all the generations of men.[15]

Isaiah 52:10 *The LORD hath made bare his holy arm [Zeroah] in the eyes of all the nations; and all the ends of the earth shall see the salvation of our God.* (KJV)

Isaiah 53:5 *But he was wounded for our transgressions, he was bruised for our iniquities: the chastisement of our peace was upon him; and with his stripes we are healed.* (KJV)

The mystical Jewish work called the Zohar speaks of one righteous man [Tzaddik] being smitten by God with disease and suffering for the healing of all. Sinful man is compared to an afflicted body from which blood is drawn from the smitten righteous arm [Zeroah, taken from Isaiah 52:10, a term representing the Messiah] to bring healing to the entire body. The same text then comments on Isaiah 53:5 as to one righteous man being afflicted to bring healing and 'atonement' to their generation.[16]

Hebrews 9:7, 14-15 *But into the second went the high priest alone once every year [Yom Kippur], not without blood, which he offered for himself, and for the errors of the people...How much more shall the blood of Christ, who through the eternal Spirit offered himself without spot to God, purge your conscience from dead works to serve the living God? And for this cause he is the mediator of the new testament, that by means of death, for the redemption of the transgressions that were under the first testament, they which are called might receive the promise of eternal inheritance.* (KJV)

The writer of Hebrews shows that Yeshua's sacrifice fulfilled the purpose of the Yom Kippur sacrifices, but also contrasts Yeshua's sacrifice on a higher level, dimension, and order. One of the purposes that God ordained the Temple sacrifices was for atonement, so what makes Yeshua's sacrifice superior? The blood 'drawn' from the Righteous Tzaddik [Messiah], Who is the Mediator of the New Covenant, provided an 'everlasting and permanent' atonement for those who believe and follow His Way.

Exodus 25:9, 40 *According to all that I shew thee, after the pattern of the tabernacle, and the pattern of all the instruments thereof, even so shall ye make it...And look that thou make them after their pattern, which was shewed thee in the mount.* (KJV)

Hebrews 8:4-5 *For if he were on earth, he should not be a priest, seeing that there are priests that offer gifts according to the law: Who serve unto the example and shadow of heavenly things, as Moses was admonished of God when he was about to make the tabernacle: for, See, saith he, that thou make all things according to the pattern shewed to thee in the mount.* (KJV)

If Yeshua's blood atonement is Eternal, then it should have pre-existed Creation. This may seem confusing, but this is exactly what the Scripture teaches. Everything regarding the Tabernacle/Temple service including all the instruments/furnishings and the priesthood were but examples and shadows of a heavenly/eternal reality that Moses was allowed to glimpse. God instructed Moses to make everything after the 'pattern' he was shown on Mt. Sinai. The Aaronic priesthood and the Temple were more like copies of the original. The original Heavenly 'Tabernacle' is the real substance.

Jewish sources name seven things already created or existed before the foundation of the world. They include the Messiah and his Name, the Torah, Repentance, the Garden of Eden, Gehinnom, the Throne of Glory, and the Temple. The general belief among the sages was that the Messiah was part of the Creator's plan at the inception of the Universe and in His mind before the world was created.[17] Consider the following verses that relate the Messiah Yeshua and His Kingdom being prepared before the foundation of the world.

Revelation 13:8 *And all that dwell upon the earth shall worship him, whose names are not written in the book of life of <u>the Lamb slain from the foundation of the world</u>.* (KJV)

1 Peter 1:18-20 *Forasmuch as ye know that ye were not redeemed with corruptible things, as silver and gold, from your vain conversation received by tradition from your fathers; But with the precious blood of Christ, as of <u>a lamb</u> without blemish and without spot: Who verily <u>was foreordained before the foundation of the world</u>, but was manifest in these last times for you,* (KJV)

Matthew 25:34 *Then shall the King say unto them on his right hand, Come, ye blessed of my Father, inherit the <u>kingdom prepared for you from the foundation of the world</u>:* (KJV)

John 17:24 *Father, I will that they also, whom thou hast given me, be with me where I am; that they may behold my glory, which thou hast given me: for <u>thou lovedst me before the foundation of the world</u>.* (KJV)

Yeshua, the Guilt-Trespass [Asham] Offering

Leviticus 17:5, 11 *To the end that the children of Israel may bring their sacrifices, which they offer in the open field, even that they may bring them unto the LORD, unto the door of the tabernacle of the congregation, unto the priest, and offer them for peace offerings unto the LORD...For the life of the flesh is in the blood: and I have given it to you upon the altar to make an atonement for your souls: for it is the blood that maketh an atonement for the soul.* (KJV)

Clearly Paul established that Yeshua is our Pesach [Passover] Sacrifice [1 Corinthians 5:7]. However, Yeshua being symbolic of the Passover Lamb was slain for our redemption and not for the expiation of sins. The Passover sacrifice was a Peace Offering [Shelamim][18], which means it absolutely has nothing to do with forgiveness of sins. A peace offering provides atonement by substituting a life [soul] for a life. The atonement is in the blood since the life of the flesh is in the blood.

Leviticus 16:15 *Then shall he kill the goat of the sin offering, that is for the people, and bring his blood within the vail, and do with that blood as he did with the blood of the bullock [for the High priest], and sprinkle it upon the mercy seat, and before the mercy seat:* (KJV)

Hebrews 13:11-12 *For the bodies of those beasts, whose blood is brought into the sanctuary by the high priest for sin, are burned* *without the camp. Wherefore Jesus also, that he might sanctify the people with his own blood, suffered without the gate.* (KJV)

Also, the writer of Hebrews very clearly shows Yeshua's sacrifice to symbolically represent the expiation of sins with the Musaf Sin Offerings [Chataat] of Yom Kippur. A bull and a goat were sacrificed as Sin Offerings and their blood was brought into the Holy of Holies just as Yeshua's blood was placed in the Heavenly Holy of Holies. But the carcasses of the bull and goat were intertwined together [the priests did not eat these sacrifices] and carried by priests through the Damascus Gate north of the Altar to be burned. 'Without the camp' is a Hebraism standing for outside the walls of the city and in this case it means Jerusalem. Yeshua being crucified 'without the camp' means He was executed outside the Damascus Gate in the first century.

Outside of the High Priest's Sin Offering of the bull, all other Sin Offerings had to be a 'goat' according to Torah law.[19] If Yeshua is called the 'Lamb of God' who expiates the sins of the people in the New Testament, we have to rectify this with the Torah. The 'Lamb of God' cannot symbolize the Passover Peace Offering or the Yom Kippur bull/goat Sin Offering.

John 1:29, 36 *The next day John seeth Jesus coming unto him, and saith, Behold the Lamb [amnos] of God, which taketh away the sin of the world...And looking upon Jesus as he walked, he saith, Behold the Lamb [amnos] of God!* (KJV)

Upon encountering Yeshua for the first time John the Immerser declared, 'Behold the Lamb of God, which taketh away the sin of the world'. If John was referring to Yeshua as the Passover Lamb, then he had erred according to the Scriptures. What did John mean by this expression? In order to discover the truth we must understand his statement within the context of John 1.

John 1:23 *He said, I am the voice of one crying in the wilderness, Make straight the way of the Lord, as said the prophet Esaias.* (KJV)

The Priests, Levites, and Pharisees asked John the Immerser if he was Elijah, or the Prophet, or the Messiah. His answer was in the negative. He was fulfilling the office of Elijah but was not literally Elijah. Of course, John speaks of the one who comes after him who is the Messiah. He quotes Isaiah 40:3 and tells them that he is 'the voice of one crying in the wilderness, Make straight the way of the Lord'.

Isaiah 40 opens up a series of chapters that talk about a Suffering Servant. In this context what did John's statement to the Messiah, 'Behold the Lamb of God, which taketh away the sin of the world' really mean? Once again, the Torah offers no ceremonial rite where a lamb could atone for the sins of the people [the entire world]. So John the Immerser either totally missed it, or there is something in the translation that is missed.

The latest research suggests that the original Gospels were written in Hebrew, not Aramaic, and definitely not Greek. The early 'church fathers' such as Papias, Irenaeus, Origen, and Eusebius all attributed the Gospel of Matthew being originally written in Hebrew. Several Post-Nicene fathers including Epiphanius and Jerome mention the same.[20] The commentaries on the Scriptures called Targumim were written and read in Aramaic in the synagogues in the first century.[21] The common Hebrew language of the first century had adopted certain loan words from both the Aramaic and Greek languages into normal conversation. This makes sense in light of portions of certain writings, such as Daniel, were written in the Chaldean or Aramaic language.

In a French work by Oscar Cullmann, we read: 'The works of C.F. Burney and J. Jeremias have shown that the Aramaic phrase א ה ל א ד א י ל מ which means both 'Lamb of God' and 'Servant of God', very probably lies behind the Greek expression 'amnos ho theos' [Lamb of God]. Since the expression 'Lamb of God' is not commonly used in the Old Testament as a designation for the paschal lamb, it is probable that the author of John thought primarily of the ebed Yahweh [Servant of God]'.[22]

So instead of John the Immerser saying 'Behold the Lamb of God, which taketh away the sin of the world,' more than likely he stated, 'Behold the Servant of God, which taketh away the sin of the world'. With this insight we now have the tool to understand the context of John's message from Isaiah 40:3 '...the voice of one crying in the wilderness, Make straight the way of the Lord'.

Isaiah 42:1, 6, 7 *Behold my servant, whom I uphold; mine elect, in whom my soul delighteth; I have put my spirit upon him: he shall bring forth judgment to the Gentiles. I the LORD have called thee in righteousness, and will hold thine hand, and will keep thee, and give thee for a covenant of the people, for a light of the Gentiles; To open the blind eyes, to bring out the prisoners from the prison, and them that sit in darkness out of the prison house.* (KJV)

Isaiah 42 begins 'Behold, My Servant [Hebrew - Ebed]'. This is the 'Servant of God' that John was referring to in the person of Yeshua. Isaiah said that God's Spirit would be upon this Servant [Ebed] and He would make a covenant with Israel and be a Light to the Gentiles. When this Servant [Ebed] came, the blind would see, the prisoners would be set free and those residing in darkness should see light.

Isaiah 61:1-2 *The Spirit of the Lord GOD is upon me; because the LORD hath anointed me to preach good tidings unto the meek; he hath sent me to bind up the brokenhearted, to proclaim liberty to the captives, and the opening of the prison to them that are bound; To proclaim the acceptable year of the LORD, and the day of vengeance of our God; to comfort all that mourn;* (KJV)

In Luke 4 Yeshua was reading the Haftarah of Isaiah 61 on Sabbath in the Synagogue at Nazareth. He referred to the 'Spirit of the Lord' being upon Him, which was in reference to His role as the Servant (Ebed). He had come 'to preach deliverance to the captives' and the 'recovering of sight to the blind'. Once again these are signs associated with the coming of the Servant (Ebed) in Isaiah. Notice that Yeshua said, 'This day is this scripture fulfilled in your ears'. Yeshua is directly telling the people that He is Isaiah's Servant (Ebed).

Isaiah 52:13 *Behold, my servant shall deal prudently, he shall be exalted and extolled, and be very high.* (KJV)

We once again have the phrase, 'Behold, My Servant (Ebed)' in Isaiah 52:13. Modern Judaism in response to Christianity teaches that Isaiah 52 has nothing to do with the Messiah and applies only to Israel. Is that really the truth, however? What did the ancient rabbis say? The section of Isaiah 52:13 through 53:12 has been interpreted in Messianic terms by a wide variety of Jewish commentators over a long period of time. The Aramaic Targum read in the synagogues in the late Second Temple period states of Isaiah 52:13: 'Behold, My Servant the Messiah shall prosper'.[23]

The Greek word for 'Lamb' in John's phrase, 'Behold the <u>Lamb</u> of God, which taketh away the sin of the world,' is 'amnos'. As already stated the Lamb in this instance was probably better translated as the 'Servant'. But since the translators interpreted John's Aramaic loan word as 'lamb' instead of 'servant,' they chose the Greek word 'amnos'. The next time 'amnos' is used in the New Testament; Philip encounters the Ethiopian eunuch (Acts 8), who happened to be reading from Isaiah 53, the Suffering Servant prophecy.

Acts 8:32 *The place of the scripture which he read was this, He was led as a sheep to the slaughter; and like a lamb [amnos] dumb before his shearer, so opened he not his mouth:* (KJV)

Isaiah 53:7 *He was oppressed, and he was afflicted, yet he opened not his mouth: he is brought as a <u>lamb</u> to the slaughter, and as a sheep before her shearers is dumb, so he openeth not his mouth.* (KJV)

The only other time 'amnos' is used in the New Testament is in 1 Peter:

1 Peter 1:18-19 *Forasmuch as ye know that ye were not redeemed with corruptible things, as silver and gold, from your vain conversation received by tradition from your fathers; But with the precious blood of Christ, as of a lamb [amnos] <u>without blemish and without spot</u>:*

In both of these instances of the use of 'amnos' it appears that there was no Aramaic loan word involved for 'servant'. Peter's use of 'without blemish and without spot' indicates a 'lamb' was intended. Peter's message is about the 'blood' of the Lamb and its redeeming power. So here in 1 Peter we have the indication of Yeshua symbolically being a sacrificed lamb, which must be rectified with the Torah. This in conjunction with Yeshua being called the 'Lamb' [Greek word is 'arnion'] throughout the book of Revelation also needs to be understood.

This leads us into the concept of Yeshua being an Asham [Guilt or Trespass Offering]. The Asham was the only other expiatory sacrifice in addition to the Sin Offering [Chataat]. A major difference between the two is that when restitution could be accomplished an Asham was offered. The rabbis believed that the Asham offering kept the 'soul' of the offerer from the danger of sin. The Asham was considered the 'higher' sacrifice of the two, because sins requiring an Asham were on the borderline of being outright intentional. The Asham was brought to clear the conscience of the offerer. Josephus says of the Asham sacrifice: 'But if anyone sin, and is conscience of it himself, but hath nobody that can prove it upon him, he offers a ram...'[24] Therefore, because God knows every hidden sin, the Asham relieves a guilty conscious before God.

Leviticus 7:7 *As the sin offering [Chataat] is, so is the trespass offering [Asham]: there is one law for them: the priest that maketh atonement therewith shall have it.* (KJV)

Whereas the Sin Offering was always a goat [a bull for the high priest on Yom Kippur], the Asham [Guilt Offering] is demanded from the Torah to always be a ram, which is a male sheep from its fourteenth month until its second birthday.[25] Outside of this difference the laws regarding the Asham and Chataat were identical in the way they were sacrificed and burned, etc.

Isaiah 53:10 *Yet it pleased the LORD to bruise him; he hath put him to grief: when thou shalt make his soul an offering [asham] for sin,* *he shall see his seed, he shall prolong his days, and the pleasure of the LORD shall prosper in his hand.* (KJV)

R. Mosheh Kohen ibn Crispin said in the 14th century regarding Isaiah 53:10, 'If his soul makes itself into a trespass-offering, implying that his soul will treat itself as guilty, and so receive punishment for our trespasses and transgressions'.[26] If Yeshua as the Suffering Messiah ben Joseph was an Asham [Guilt-Trespass] Offering for sin, we will need to rectify Him being called the 'Lamb slain from the foundation of the world,' when only a ram could be offered as an Asham in the Scripture. Before we do that we will develop the motif of Yeshua, the Asham.

We know that a communal [national] Sin Offering [Chataat] was available at the Yom Kippur ceremony for atonement, but there is a rabbinical dispute about whether a communal Trespass Offering [Asham] was available. There is no such ceremony in the Scripture. There are no special Guilt Offerings commanded for Sabbaths and Festivals. All the Communal Sacrifices consisted of Peace Offerings [Shelamim - Shavuot], Burnt Offerings [Olah - Festivals, etc.], Grain Offerings [Mincha - Firstfruits, Shavuot], or Sin Offerings [Chataat - Yom Kippur]. The Asham was considered an individual offering for the soul regarding their sin.

The Talmud in Temurah 14a states that there is no such Communal Asham. From a Temple ceremony standpoint, the author would agree with this assessment. However, Isaiah 53 explicitly tells us that the Suffering Servant Messiah will be an Asham [Guilt Offering] for sin.

Did the sages of old believe that Isaiah 53 was referring to a Communal Asham Offering? Any rabbi who believed that the Torah and Prophets were the direct Word of God would have known that this Suffering Servant was to be a Guilt Offering from the Hebrew text. The author's guess is that they knew but didn't fully understand it. Also, what is coming out in Rabbinical Judaism today is not exactly the same thinking of the wise sages of old. In response to the early believers in Yeshua, Isaiah 53 has been reinterpreted from the interpretations of the ancient rabbis that lived before Him.

Leviticus 7:1-2 *Likewise this is the law of the trespass offering [Asham]: <u>it is most holy</u>. In the place where they kill the burnt offering shall <u>they</u> kill the trespass offering [Asham]: and the blood thereof shall he sprinkle round about upon the altar.* (KJV)

Rashi interpreted the plural 'they' in Leviticus 7:2 taught that these laws applied to an Asham that was to be offered on behalf of the entire nation. However, Rabbinic Judaism says that in the older editions of Rashi's work, this comment is not found and none of the classic commentaries on Rashi even discuss this statement. Therefore, it has been concluded that this was an erroneous addition added in later versions.[27] If this is true the question remains then, who added it? Who would have had access to Rashi's work? Why not look at the other possibility of who deleted it out of his work and why? This author believes that there is no communal Asham Temple ceremony in Scripture because it was reserved for the work of the Messiah as the Suffering Servant/Lamb of God, slain from the foundation of the world.

Genesis 26:10 *And Abimelech said, What is this thou [Isaac] hast done unto us? one of the people might lightly have lien with thy wife, and thou shouldest have brought guiltiness [Hebrew Asham] upon us.* (KJV)

The only pre-Tabernacle usage of the word Asham in Scripture is in the story of Isaac, Rebecca, and Abimelech. Isaac presented his wife as his sister causing Abimelech to desire her for his wife. Before Abimelech could act upon his desires, he discovered that she was Isaac's wife. Abimelech chided Isaac and accused him that he almost 'brought an Asham' upon him and his people. Alshich understood that if this sin had occurred, then Isaac would have had the responsibility to bring an Asham on all the Philistine's behalf.[28] The principle that is demonstrated here is Communal Culpability.[29]

1 Corinthians 5:7 *Purge out therefore the old leaven, that ye may be a new lump, as ye are unleavened. For even Christ our passover is sacrificed for us:* (KJV)

The Asham is a 'Most Holy' sacrifice [Leviticus 7:1]. What does this mean? The Chataat [Sin Offering] and the Olah [Burnt Offering] had the same designation. A 'Most Holy' designation implies a higher degree of sanctity.[30] The Asham had to be eaten within the Temple precincts by the priests. The Shelamim [Peace Offerings] were of a lesser sanctity called kedashim kalim and could be eaten outside the Temple such as the Passover lambs. This is another proof that Yeshua, the Lamb of God, cannot be referring to Him as the Passover lamb [Peace Offering]. Isaiah says He is the Suffering Messiah who is an Asham, a 'Most Holy' sacrifice. This in no way takes away what the Apostle Paul said in referring to Yeshua as our Passover [he doesn't say lamb]. Yeshua fulfills the Eternal/Heavenly Peace Offering purposes of redemption, but Peace Offerings did not atone for sins.

1 Peter 1:19-23 *But with the precious blood of Christ, as of a lamb without blemish and without spot: Who verily was foreordained before the foundation of the world, but was manifest in these last times for you, Who by him do believe in God, that raised him up from the dead, and gave him glory; that your faith and hope might be in God. Seeing ye have purified your* <u>souls</u> *in obeying the truth through the Spirit unto unfeigned love of the brethren, see that ye love one another with a pure heart fervently: Being born again, not of corruptible seed, but of incorruptible, by the word of God, which liveth and abideth for ever.* (KJV)

We return back to the issue that a personal Asham must be a ram, not a lamb. How can Yeshua, the Suffering Servant Messiah, be the Communal Guilt Offering, and also be the Lamb of God who takes away the sins of the world? Peter uses the Greek 'amnos' for Yeshua being the slain 'Lamb'. He was slain 'before the foundation of the world' to 'purify...[our] souls'. This indicates that Yeshua the Lamb was sacrificed to remove our 'guilt,' hence the relationship to an Asham. The incorruptible Word of God also directly relates this Heavenly Asham to being 'born-again' of the spirit.

Being 'born-again' is being birthed into the Kingdom through Yeshua's sacrifice. Believers' sins have been forgiven and their slate is clean and free of guilt. It is not an earthly kingdom that believers are birthed into, but a spiritual one. One day the spiritual kingdom will physically reside in the Messianic Kingdom here on earth, but this makes the Lamb's sacrifice as an Asham, not earthly, but heavenly.

The rabbis commented that Ezekiel suffered [Ezekiel 4] as a righteous Tzaddik for the sins of the people. God was satisfied when His justice to punish the entire community was meted out on the righteous. Ezekiel atoned his people because the pain he suffered mitigated the 'Communal Guilt'.[31]

Hebrews 10:2-10 *For then would they not have ceased to be offered? because that the worshippers once purged should have had no more conscience of sins [the need for a Communal Asham]. But in those sacrifices there is a remembrance again made of sins every year [Communal Sin Offering of Yom Kippur]. For it is not possible that the blood of bulls and of goats [Yom Kippur Sin Offerings] should take away sins. Wherefore when he cometh into the world, he saith, Sacrifice [Hebrew - Zabach refers to Peace Offerings] and offering [Hebrew - Minchah, Grain Offering] thou wouldest not, but a body hast thou prepared me [Suffering Servant Tzaddik - Asham]: In burnt offerings [Hebrew - Olah] and sacrifices for sin [Hebrew - Chataat] thou hast had no pleasure. Then said I, Lo [Hebrew - hinneh], I come (in the volume of the book it is written of me,) to do thy will, O God [Psalm 40:6-8]. Above when he said, Sacrifice [Shelamim] and offering [Mincha] and burnt offerings [Olah] and offering for sin [Chataat] thou wouldest not, neither hadst pleasure therein; which are offered by the law; Then said he, Lo [Hinneh], I come to do thy will, O God. He taketh away the first [Communal Sin Offering for Atonement], that he may establish the second [The Communal Asham Offering of the Lamb for Atonement]. By the which will we are sanctified through the offering [The Communal Asham Offering of the Lamb] of the body [Suffering Servant Tzaddik] of Jesus Christ once for all.* (KJV)

Leviticus 23:19 *Then ye shall sacrifice [Asah] one kid of the goats for a sin offering [Chataat], and two lambs of the first year for a sacrifice [Zebach] of peace offerings [Shelamim].* (KJV)

In Hebrews 10, which quotes from Psalm 40, it is clear that the writer is contrasting the Burnt Offering and Sin Offerings of Yom Kippur to that of a superior Offering that can take-away sins of man once and for all. Psalm 40 contrasts all of the sacrifices except one: The Asham [Guilt/Trespass Offering]. The Hebrew word 'Zebach' is used regarding Peace Offerings and 'Minchah' is used as Grain Offerings.[32]

The Hebrew word for 'Lo' in the phrase 'Lo, I come,' is 'Hinneh'. It is the same word used for 'Behold,' in 'Behold My Servant [the Messiah]' in Isaiah 52:13. Once again the writer of Hebrews is explicitly saying that the Suffering Servant [Ebed] is the missing Communal Asham-Guilt Offering that expiates sins once and for all time.

Isaiah 53:4 *Surely he hath borne our griefs, and carried our sorrows: yet we did esteem him stricken, smitten of God, and afflicted.* (KJV)

Searching through the rabbinic literature, we discover that some rabbis associated the Suffering Servant Messiah of Isaiah 53 as the Leper or Beggar Messiah.[33] This is the Pure Righteous Tzaddik who descended to take upon Himself the impurity of man to elevate them to a state of total purity. The Hebrew words in Isaiah 53:4, stricken (nagua) and smitten (mukkay) are interpreted as referring to a leprous condition. Yeshua was stricken and smitten by the Roman floggings and the crucifixion. The Suffering Servant Messiah was rejected and despised comparably to how lepers were rejected and despised. It was Yeshua's struggle to die and bring atonement for sins. This ordeal is spelled out in Isaiah 53 and more graphically in Psalm 22.

Isaiah 53:5 *But he was wounded for our transgressions, he was bruised for our iniquities: the chastisement of our peace was upon him; and with his stripes we are healed [rapha].* (KJV)

Leviticus 14:3 *And the priest shall go forth out of the camp; and the priest shall look, and, behold, if the plague of leprosy be healed [rapha] in the leper;* (KJV)

Leviticus 13:46 *All the days wherein the plague shall be in him he shall be defiled; he is unclean: he shall dwell alone; without the camp shall his habitation be.* (KJV)

Hebrews 13:12-13 *Wherefore Jesus also, that he might sanctify the people with his own blood, suffered without the gate. Let us go forth therefore unto him without the camp, bearing his reproach.* (KJV)

This brings us to the cleansing of the leper in Leviticus 14. First of all, the leper while unclean had to dwell 'without the camp'. This reminds us of Yeshua being the Yom Kippur Sin Offering [Chataat]. Hebrews 13 tells us to symbolically go to Yeshua 'without the camp' where He sanctifies us with His own blood. This puts us in the Leper state where 'healing' [rapha] comes by His stripes that dripped with blood.

Leviticus 14:10-18 *And on the eighth day he shall take two he lambs without blemish, and one ewe lamb of the first year without blemish, and three tenth deals of fine flour for a meat offering [mincha], mingled with oil, and one log of oil. And the priest that maketh him clean shall present the man that is to be made clean, and those things, before the LORD, at the door of the tabernacle of the congregation: And the priest shall take one he lamb, and offer him for a trespass offering [asham], and the log of oil, and wave them for a wave offering [tenufah] before the LORD: And he shall slay the lamb in the place where he shall kill the sin offering and the burnt offering, in the holy place: for as the sin offering is the priest's, so is the trespass offering [asham]: it is most holy: And the priest shall take some of the blood of the trespass offering [asham], and the priest shall put it upon the tip of the right ear of him that is to be cleansed, and upon the thumb of his right hand, and upon the great toe of his right foot: And the priest shall take some of the log of oil, and pour it into the palm of his own left hand: And the priest* *shall dip his right finger in the oil that is in his left hand, and shall sprinkle of the oil with his finger seven times before the LORD: And of the rest of the oil that is in his hand shall the priest put upon the tip of the right ear of him that is to be cleansed, and upon the thumb of his right hand, and upon the great toe of his right foot, upon the blood of the trespass offering [asham]: And the remnant of the oil that is in the priest's hand he shall pour upon the head of him that is to be cleansed: and the priest shall make an atonement for him before the LORD.* (KJV)

Before the Chataat [Sin Offering] and the Olah [Burnt Offering] were offered to complete the cleansing of the Leper, an Asham [Guilt Offering] must be offered. However, this Asham for the cleansing [purifying, sanctifying] of the Leper is unlike any other Asham Offering. A Leper's Asham must be a he-lamb, not a he-ram as specified for all other Asham offerings by individuals. The he-lamb must be under a year old, whereas a ram is in its second year. Could the Asham of the Leper be representative of the Messiah, the Lamb slain from the foundation of the world? [When one took a Nazarite vow and inadvertently broke it before the time, he had to also bring a he-lamb instead of a he-goat for an Asham].

A normal Asham offering does not have a Mincha [Grain Offering] with it. A normal Asham also does not have a wine libation such as in the leper's case. No other Asham Offering was waved before the Lord as the lepers'. A log of oil was waved with the live lamb before the Lord. The Shelamim [Peace Offerings], Bikkurim [Firstfruits of the Barley], and the Wheat Loaves of Shavuot were the only offerings waved before the Lord normally.

Normally one priest collects the blood of a sacrifice to sprinkle at the altar. For the Leper's Asham offering, two priests are required. One priest receives the blood of the Asham lamb in a certain vessel and applies it to the Brazen Altar. The other priest receives blood afterwards from the Asham lamb in his right hand, pours it in his left hand, and then takes his right index finger dipping it into the blood to apply it to the Leper.[34]

The priest places the blood of the Asham on the leper's right ear, right thumb, and right toe. No blood of any sacrifice ever touches the body of the one who offers the sacrifices. Only after the blood has been sprinkled on the Altar is it then placed upon the leper. It was forbidden that blood from any burnt, sin, or any other offering be applied on a human being [except for the installation ceremony for priests].[35]

The sacrificial system was tailored for the poor by allowing them to substitute cheaper animals for a particular sacrifice. The poor could also substitute birds for animals in the system. The leper's Asham offering of a lamb was the exception; it could not be substituted.[36] Yeshua's Asham blood must be spiritually applied to the leper [sinner] for cleansing. There is no other sacrifice that can substitute for the blood of God's Asham Lamb.

The priest then pours some of the oil that was waved into the left hand of another Kohen. He dips his right index finger seven times and sprinkles it before the Lord in the direction of the Holy of Holies.[37] Obviously there is some connection here to the blood of the Yom Kippur Sin Offerings [Chataat] that were sprinkled seven times before the mercy seat in Leviticus 16.

The oil is then applied to the leper in the same areas (right ear, right thumb, and right toe) that the blood was previously applied. The oil must go over the blood. Oil is usually symbolic of anointing or the Holy Spirit. The blood has to be applied first, and then the Anointing [Holy Spirit] only comes upon the blood where it is applied. The priest then takes the remainder of the oil and smears it on the Leper's head.

There are striking similarities between the Asham offered by the leper and the Peace Offering associated with the consecration of Aaron's and his sons as priests. Yeshua's priesthood is of the Heavenly Order of Melchizedek and is a higher order than the earthly order of Aaron. We need to keep this in mind as we look at the comparisons of believers in Yeshua as spiritual lepers who are transformed by the Suffering Servant Leper Messiah. Believers are called into a holy priesthood that Peter likened unto the 'firstborn' priesthood in the wilderness before the Levitical priesthood was ordained. In Exodus 29 and Leviticus 8 the 'ram of consecration' was waved before the Lord and its blood applied to the right ears, right thumbs, and right toes of the priests. They were also sprinkled with oil.

Spiritually we are all lepers in need of purification. We must go outside the camp to find Yeshua, the Leper Messiah, Who takes away our sins. He is our Heavenly/Eternal Asham Offering. The Holy Spirit only comes and testifies to where His blood is applied. Through the Spirit Yeshua transforms lepers into a spiritual priesthood dedicated in offering spiritual sacrifices to Him. Believers in Yeshua live with His Promise to make us both kings and priests unto God in the resurrection. The ancient kings were ordinated by oil being poured over their heads.

BIBLIOGRAPHY

1. The Messiah Texts. Raphael Patai. Wayne State University Press, Detroit, Michigan, 1979. Pages 166-167.
2. Rosh HaShanah and the Messianic Kingdom to Come. Joseph Good. Hatikva Ministries, Port Arthur, Texas, 1989. Page 2.
3. The Book of Isaiah - Volume 2. Rabbi Redak; Shorasim (a Rabbinic Commentary); Rabbi A.J. Rosenberg. Judaica Press, New York, 1982. Page 544.
4. Everyman's Talmud. Abraham Cohen. Schocken Books, New York, 1949. Page 356.
5. Ruth Rabbah 5:6
6. Messiah Conspiracy: The End of History. Philip N. Moore. The Conspiracy, Incorporated, Atlanta, Georgia, 1996. Page 63.
7. Jewish Encyclopedia. Internet Edition.
8. Talmud. Succah 52a.
9. Midrash Pesiqta Rabbah 36
10. Talmud. Sanhedrin 98a.
11. Talmud. Sanhedrin 96b.
12. On the Mystical Shape of the Godhead: Basic Concepts in the Kabbalah. Gershom Scholem. Schocken Books, New York, 1991, Pages 138-139.

13. Along the Path: Studies in Kabbalistic Myth, Symbolism, and Hermeneutics. Elliot R. Wolfson. State University of New York Press, Albany, 1995. Page 97.

14. IBID. Page 98.

15. Derech Hashem (The Way of God). Rabbi Moshe Chaim Luzzatto, Translated and annotated by Aryeh Kaplan. Feldheim Publishers, Jerusalem, 1997. Page 122.

16. Soncino Zohar, Bemidbar, Section 3, Page 218a.

17. Everyman's Talmud. Abraham Cohen. Schocken Books, New York, 1949. Page 347.

18. Talmud. Pesachim 64a.

19. The Artscroll Tanach Series - Vayikra (Leviticus) - Volume III(a). Rabbis Nosson Scherman and Hersh Goldwurm. Mesorah Publications, Ltd., Brooklyn, New York, 1989. Pages 328-329.

20. Understanding the Difficult Words of Jesus. David Bivin & Roy Blizzard, Jr - Center for Judaic-Christian Studies. Destiny Image Publishers, Shippensburg, Pennsylvania, 1983. Pages 23-26.

21. Rosh Hashana and the Messianic Kingdom to Come. Joseph Good. Hatikva Ministries, Port Arthur, Texas, 1989. Page 2.

22. The Christology of the New Testament. Oscar Cullmann. Westminster . Page 71.

23. The Messiah: An Aramaic Interpretation; the Messianic Exegesis of the Targum. Samson H. Levey. Hebrew Union College, Cincinnati, 1974, Page 63.

24. The Works of Josephus. The Antiquities of the Jews - Book 3 Chapter 9 part 3. William Whiston. Hendrickson Publishers. Peabody, Massachusetts, 1987. Page 95.

25. The Artscroll Tanach Series - Vayikra (Leviticus) - Volume III(a). Rabbis Nosson Scherman and Hersh Goldwurm. Mesorah Publications, Ltd., Brooklyn, New York, 1989. Pages 328-328.

26. R. Mosheh Kohen ibn Crispin (14th c.) Driver and Neubauer, Page 112.

27. The Artscroll Tanach Series - Vayikra (Leviticus) - Volume III (a). Rabbis Nosson Scherman and Hersh Goldwurm.

Mesorah Publications, Ltd., Brooklyn, New York, 1989. Page 109.

28. The Artscroll Tanach Series - Bereishis (Genesis) - Volume I (a). Rabbi Meir Zlotowitz. Mesorah Publications, Ltd., Brooklyn, New York, 1986. Pages 1088-1089.

29. The JPS Torah Commentary - Genesis. Nahum M. Sarna. The Jewish Publication Society, Philadelphia, New York, Jerusalem, 1989. Pages 184-185.

30. Yalkut Me'am Lo'ez - The Torah Anthology - Leviticus volume 1 - Volume 11 in series. Translated by Rabbi Aryeh Kaplan. Moznaim Publishing Corporation, New York, Jerusalem, 1898. Pages 138-139.

31. The Artscroll Tanach Series - Yechezkel (Ezekiel). Rabbi Moshe Eisemann. Mesorah Publications, Ltd., Brooklyn, New York, 1977. Appendix III - Suffering of the Zaddik.

32. The Artscroll Tanach Series - Tehillim (Psalms) - Volume I. Rabbi Avrohom Chaim Feuer. Mesorah Publications, Ltd., Brooklyn, New York, 1977. Page 503.

33. The Messiah Texts. Raphael Patai. Wayne State University Press, Detroit, Michigan, 1979. Page 105.

34. The Artscroll Tanach Series - Vayikra (Leviticus) - Volume III (a). Rabbis Nosson Scherman and Hersh Goldwurm. Mesorah Publications, Ltd., Brooklyn, New York, 1989. Page 226.

35. The JPS Torah Commentary - Leviticus. Baruch A. Levine. The Jewish Publication Society, Philadelphia, New York, Jerusalem, 1989. Page 87.

36. IBID. Page 88.

37. The Artscroll Tanach Series - Vayikra (Leviticus) - Volume III (a). Rabbis Nosson Scherman and Hersh Goldwurm. Mesorah Publications, Ltd., Brooklyn, New York, 1989. Page 226

11

THE FULL-MARRIAGE FALL FESTIVALS

Rosh Chodesh - New Moon and Marriage

Numbers 10:10 *Also in the day of your gladness, and in your solemn days, and in the beginnings of your months, ye shall blow with the trumpets over your burnt offerings, and over the sacrifices of your peace offerings; that they may be to you for a memorial before your God: I am the LORD your God.* (KJV)

Ezekiel 46:3 *Likewise the people of the land shall worship at the door of this gate before the LORD in the <u>sabbaths</u> and in the <u>new moons</u>.* (KJV)

2 Chronicles 2:4 *Behold, I build an house to the name of the LORD my God, to dedicate it to him, and to burn before him sweet incense, and for the continual shewbread, and for the burnt offerings morning and evening, on the sabbaths, and on the <u>new moons</u>, and on the solemn feasts of the LORD our God. <u>This is an ordinance for ever to Israel</u>.* (KJV)

Colossians 2:16-17 *Let no man therefore judge you in meat, or in drink, or in respect of an holyday, or of the new moon, or of the sabbath days: Which are a shadow of things to come; but the body is of Christ.* (KJV)

Rosh Chodesh, the festival of the New Moon, is not listed with the seven festivals and Sabbaths in Leviticus 23. However, in Solomon's Temple Rosh Chodesh had a higher status and sanctity than the Sabbath.[1] Throughout the Scripture the New Moons were equated with the Sabbaths.

If the Sabbath is a macrocosm of God's plan, then the New Moon festival is of the grandest scale in symbolism of God's great plan. As a matter of fact, as we will see, the Sabbath (Sign-Owot) and the moedim (seasons/festivals/rehearsals) all point to this grandest theme of God's plan represented in New Moon ceremony [in relationship to the Sun].

In ancient Israel the New Moon occurred at the first visible crescent. The Israelites would have been observing the 'waning moon' and notice it getting smaller and smaller in the morning sky. When the morning moon disappeared, or as the rabbi's understood as being 'concealed,' they would have waited for its reappearance 1.5-3.5 days later in the evening sky. After its observation by Two Witnesses and the notification of the Sanhedrin, the news was relayed throughout Israel and the Diaspora by beacons or fires on the mountaintops, starting with the Mount of Olives in Jerusalem.[2] The spread of these fires proceeded to the northeast in the direction of the Babylonian city of Pumbedita. The shofar [ram's horn] was sounded and Rosh Chodesh began!

The New Moon festival had a stigma associated with it that 'no man knew the day and hour' it would come, which was the idiomatic phrase Yeshua used in Matthew 24:36 in referring to His second coming. Clearly Yeshua was saying that His coming would coincide with Rosh Chodesh. We will come back to this momentarily.

After the Two Witnesses verified the New Moon to the Sanhedrin, Rosh Chodesh would be declared. We are not sure if a blessing for the New Moon was well established at the end of the Second Temple period or not. By the third century, however, the sanctification of the New Moon was definitely being practiced. In the synagogue today the service is known as Kiddush Levanah. Included in the liturgy is Psalm 148:

Psalm 148:1-6 *Praise ye the LORD. Praise ye the LORD from the heavens: praise him in the heights. Praise ye him, all his angels: praise ye him, all his hosts. Praise ye him, sun and moon: praise him, all ye stars of light. Praise him, ye heavens of heavens, and ye waters that be above the heavens. Let them praise the name of the LORD: for he commanded, and they were created. He hath also stablished them for ever and ever: he hath made a decree which shall not pass.* (KJV)

Why would the New Moon be sanctified with a prayer that also mentioned the Sun? In Hebraic thought the Sun is in relationship with the Moon. The Sun was viewed as a picture of the Messiah (see Malachi 4:2), who in turn was a picture of the celestial Bridegroom. The Moon, therefore, symbolically represented Israel or the bride. This is why the festival of Rosh Chodesh has over time become the only festival [moedim] that is solely dedicated to women. The Bridegroom [Messiah] sanctifies the New Moon [Bride]. The monthly cycle of the moon became symbolic of a woman's monthly cycle.[3]

The sages also explained to us that the sanctification of the New Moon should be recited with joy and celebration that should parallel that of a wedding. The festival of Rosh Chodesh is symbolic of the Betrothal (Erusin). In Jewish literature Rosh Chodesh has a nickname associated with it as the festival of the Born-Again.[4] Every month the Moon is 'born-again' at Rosh Chodesh. The new thin crescent is known in Hebrew as Molad ד ל ו מ, a word connoting birth.[5] In a traditional synagogue the following portion of a prayer is said as part of the Kiddush Levanah service:

'...To the moon He [God] said that it should renew itself, which will be a crown of splendor for those borne [by Him] from the womb, those who are destined to renew themselves like it, and to glorify their Molder for the name of His glorious kingdom. Blessed are You, HASHEM, Who renews the months'.[6]

In the commentary to this prayer the rabbis said that 'to renew themselves like it,' referred to the renewal of Israel and ultimately the resurrection from the dead.[7] The symbolism of the New Moon was to remind Israel that God desires them to find Him again with fresh Light. Israel, having let periods of darkness and obscurity run their course, will once again reflect the Light of God and be reborn.

The Midrash Rabbah Exodus 15:26 infers from the verse, 'This month [new moon] shall be for you' (Exodus 12:2), that the royalty of Israel will resemble the cycle of the moon. Initially, it will only endure for thirty generations just as the lunar month has [nearly] thirty days. The light of Jewish royalty began its ascent in the time of the patriarch Abraham. David [whose Hebrew name has a numerical value of 14] was the 14th generation from Abraham and he resembled nearly the full moon.

Matthew 1:17 *So all the generations from Abraham to David are fourteen generations...* (KJV)

When Solomon, the 15th generation, became king, the royal House of David reached its zenith like the full moon. The Scripture tells us that the kings of the earth sought out the presence of Solomon for his wisdom and riches (1 Kings 10:23-24). From that point on, the House of David began to wane until it was lost from view completely with the destruction of the First Temple, during the reign of King Zedekiah, thirty generations after Abraham. At that time the royalty of David disappeared into the darkness of exile, like the vanished moon. Nebuchadnezzar blinded Zedekiah [2 Kings 25:7], symbolizing the total disappearance of the moon's light. Every month, therefore, when the new moon is sanctified, the proclamation of David [Messiah], King of Israel, lives on and endures.

Matthew 1:11 *And Josias [Josiah] begat Jechonias [Jehoiachin] and his brethren, about the time they were carried away to Babylon:* (KJV)

Matthew 1:17 *...from David until the carrying away into Babylon are fourteen generations* (KJV)

Jehoiachin was not the final king of Judah. Under his rule however, the Babylonian captivity had already begun, and many Jews were taken captive [there were actually three waves of Jews taken into Babylonian captivity]. The Jews that remained in Judah still had a king until Zechariah totally rebelled against Nebuchadnezzar, who came and took them all away into captivity when he destroyed the First Temple. This can account for the Midrash attesting to thirty generations ending with the last king of Judah, but according to Matthew it was twenty-eight generations from Abraham (14 + 14) when the first wave of Babylonian captivity began.

Matthew 1:17 *...and from the carrying away into Babylon unto Christ are fourteen generations.* (KJV)

Matthew could be midrashically speaking that after the Davidic reign went into captivity that the David [Messiah] appears fourteen generations later, right before the full moon symbolism. This means that the Messiah ben Joseph [the Suffering Messiah] symbolizes David's reign. Messiah ben David [the Conquering Messiah] represents the 15th and final generation, the Messianic Kingdom, symbolized by Solomon's reign when the kingdom reached its zenith. This Kingdom will never end and will remain a 'full moon' forever.

Song of Solomon 2:8 *The voice of my beloved! behold, he cometh leaping upon the mountains, skipping upon the hills.* (KJV)

Also in the synagogue service for the sanctification of the New Moon [Kiddush Levanah], Song of Solomon 2:8 was recited. This verse allegorically states that the Bridegroom will come back for His betrothed bride like 'leaping upon the mountains, skipping upon the hills'. This is linked to the concept of lighting the fires on the hilltops at Rosh Chodesh. The second coming of Messiah for His betrothed bride will occur on a Rosh Chodesh (New Moon).

Ephesians 4:23-24 *And be renewed in the spirit of your mind; And that ye put on the new man, which after God is created in righteousness and true holiness.* (KJV)

Every month the Moon is 'born-again' or renewed. When a believer in Messiah becomes born-again as betrothed to Him, they still have to live in their three-dimensional physical flesh and blood bodies. In this state, the believer must be renewed 'in the spirit' of their minds. This means that the believer in Yeshua must be continually 'filled' with the Ruwach haKodesh [Holy Spirit] on a regular basis. It is the 'fuel' that empowers believers to live in holiness and righteousness in their physical bodies. A believer cannot live on a one-time Shavuot-Pentecostal experience; this is only the beginning of a process of continually being renewed. It is impossible to live in holiness and righteousness without the continual renewal of the Ruwach haKodesh.

Rosh Hashana - Rosh Chodesh

If Yeshua fulfilled the four spring festivals (Moedim) of Passover, Unleavened Bread, Firstfruits, and Pentecost at His first coming to betroth His bride in physical flesh and blood bodies, then we should expect that His second coming for the Nesuin marriage and resurrection of the righteous should occur exactly with the fall festivals of Rosh Hashana, Yom Kippur, and Succot (Tabernacles). We have learned that the Scripture hints at the Messiah's coming for His betrothed bride to take her to the second stage of marriage (Nesuin) on a future Rosh Chodesh (New Moon). The only festival (Moedim) to occur on Rosh Chodesh is the festival of Rosh Hashana.

Leviticus 23:23-25 *And the LORD spake unto Moses, saying, Speak unto the children of Israel, saying, In the seventh month, in the first day of the month [ROSH HASHANA], shall ye have a sabbath, a memorial [ZIKKARON] of blowing of trumpets [TEURAH], an holy convocation. Ye shall do no servile work therein: but ye shall offer an offering made by fire unto the LORD.* (KJV)

Numbers 29:1 *And in the seventh month, on the first day of the month [ROSH HASHANA], ye shall have an holy convocation; ye shall do no servile work: it is a day of blowing the trumpets [YOM TEURAH] unto you.* (KJV)

The Hebrew phrase 'zikkaron teurah,' can be literally translated as 'a remembrance blast.' Every Moedim [Appointed Rehearsal] was given a Biblical name such as Passover, Day of Atonement, and Sabbath, etc. Tishri 1 [the first day of the seventh month] has no Biblical name; it is simply just a day of 'memorial blasts,' which the rabbis understood were to be made with the shofarim [ram's horns]. This is how Tishri 1 gained its common name, the feast of Shofarim [Trumpets]. Tishri 1 was also known as Rosh Hashana, or the 'Head of the Year,' because it began the Jewish civil year. The Scripture never really spells out why this festival is observed. This is why the rabbis mentioned Rosh Hashana was a most mysterious festival.

Some Biblical and Rabbinical Names for Rosh Hashana:

HaMelek	The King [Corononation]
Yom haKeseh	Day of Enthronement/Wedding
Yom Teurah	Day of the Awakening Blast/Shout-Resurrection
Yom haDin	Day of Judgement
Yom haZikkaron	Day of Remembrance-Book of Life
Day of the Lord	Last Millennium/7,000-Year Plan of God/Sabbath

Of course, the very fact that Rosh Hashana falls on Rosh Chodesh (New Moon) automatically places this Moedim (Festival) into the marriage symbolism. The moon in relationship to the sun is symbolic of the bride and bridegroom. The second stage of marriage (Nesuin) is represented in the New Moon of Rosh Hashana and betrothal is represented in the spring Moedim (Festivals) at Messiah's first coming.

Psalms 81:3 *Blow the shofar at the new moon, at the covered [KESEH] time for our feastday.* (KJV)

An ancient name for Rosh Hashana is Yom haKeseh, which means Day of Hiding or Concealment. It is based upon Psalm 81:3 where the New Moon of the feast day of Rosh Hashana (the only feast day that falls on a New Moon is Rosh Hashana) is called 'keseh' or 'covering'.[8] In modern Hebrew 'keseh' means chair, but anciently it meant a throne covered by a chuppah (wedding canopy). So here we see that 'keseh' represents the New Moon of Rosh Hashana when the wedding of a king takes place.

The moon is covered at Rosh Hashana. On a very specific Rosh Hashana in the future, the moon [the bride] will become hidden in relationship to the Sun [the bridegroom]. The 'Molad' is when the moon is directly between the earth and the sun and is therefore invisible.[9] This is directly related to the second stage of marriage when the bride will be hidden under the 'heavenly' chuppah spiritually consummating the marriage with the bridegroom.

Matthew 23:39 *For I say unto you, Ye shall not see me henceforth, till ye shall say, Blessed is he that cometh in the name of the Lord.* (KJV)

Psalm 118:26 *Blessed be he that cometh in the name of the LORD: we have blessed you out of the house of the LORD.* (KJV)

As Yeshua made His final exit from the Temple the announcement was made that He would not return henceforth and Israel will not see Him again until that day when she proclaims ב שׁ ם י ה ו ה ב ר ו ך ה ב א, Baruch Haba b'Shem Adonai! (Blessed is He who comes in the Name of the LORD). Yeshua alludes to His triumphal entry at the time of His second coming. The words, 'Blessed is He Who Comes' is a formula from the Jewish wedding custom, spoken when the groom enters the chuppah (marriage canopy) to be wed to His bride at the second stage of marriage (Nesuin).[10] When the bride and groom meet under the chuppah for the Nesuin-marriage, Psalm 118 is read. The message was clear! Judah would not see Yeshua publicly again until the Nesuin marriage when Israel as a whole had repented and entered the Kingdom of God.

Matthew 24:36 *But of that day and hour knoweth no man, no, not the angels of heaven, but my Father only.* (KJV)

Matthew24:42 *Watch therefore: for ye know not what hour your Lord doth come.* (KJV)

Matthew 24:44 *Therefore be ye also ready: for in such an hour as ye think not the Son of man cometh.* (KJV)

Matthew 24:50 *The lord of that servant shall come in a day when he looketh not for him, and in an hour that he is not aware of* (KJV)

Matthew 25:13 *Watch therefore, for ye know neither the day nor the hour wherein the Son of man cometh.* (KJV)

Immediately after Yeshua speaks His last public words about His next triumphant appearance at his second coming [the Nesuin marriage], He takes His disciples up to the Mount of Olives and teaches on the destruction of Jerusalem and the Temple in their days. Because of His rejection, the Jews would face birth pangs [a rabbinic term for judgment]. Yeshua was also addressing His return and the end of the world as He spoke. These birth pangs were also prophetic of the seven years of Birth Pangs that will precede His literal return.[11]

Yeshua tells a number of parables which the theme of 'watching' and being 'ready' for His return is highlighted. He opens up with 'But of that day and hour knoweth no man, no, not the angels of heaven, but my Father only'. Although His statement is directly related to the festival of Rosh Hashana, the second stage of marriage (Nesuin) is in view from the context of what He had just earlier stated publicly. Israel would not see Him again until the second stage of marriage when she truly would 'welcome' Him.

Yeshua ends this theme of watching and being ready for His coming in Matthew 25 with the Parable of the Ten Virgins. Clearly, this shows Yeshua's intentional marriage (Nesuin) symbolism. The five wise virgins went into the wedding chamber with the groom to consummate the marriage. The oil in their lamps is symbolic of the Torah/Word/Holy Spirit. They had 'rehearsed' or had made themselves ready through the spring festivals [Moedim] of betrothal concluding with the receiving of the Holy Spirit through Shavuot (Pentecost). Yeshua very clearly states that the Second Stage of marriage occurs on a New Moon [Rosh Chodesh] (No man knows the day or hour) and more specifically Rosh Hashana.

Psalm 45:14 *She shall be brought unto the king in raiment of needlework: the virgins her companions that follow her shall be brought unto thee.* (KJV)

The Parable of the Ten Virgins is built around a midrash of Psalm 45, which is always recited on Rosh Hashana. The 'virgins' represent the betrothed bride who has rehearsed through God's Moedim [festivals] and have prepared and made themselves ready for the Bridegroom's return to take them to the second stage of marriage [nesuin]. Alshich and Hirsch explain Psalm 45, known as 'a song of endearment,' as a wedding song celebrating the marriage of a bride and groom.[12] Radak and Ibn Ezra believed that Psalm 45 was dedicated to the Messiah and that 'she' in verse 14 above is referring to her being brought to an embroidered wedding canopy in the presence of the king.[13] Interestingly, Rashi comments that the maidens are the gentiles who in the future will be the companions who will follow in the path of Israel.[14]

Roland De Vaux writes that Psalm 45 can be viewed as a wedding hymn composed for a king of Israel. Therefore, Psalm 45 was composed for a royal wedding.[15] It could be that this Psalm was used for both the enthronement of the king and his wedding.

We know that the Passover Seder that Yeshua had with His disciples was symbolic of many things. The unleavened bread became associated to Yeshua's broken body and the cup of wine symbolized His shed blood. What if Yeshua's blessing over the cup of wine was also symbolic of the cup drank by the groom and bride at their betrothal (erusin) marriage? When Yeshua said the Ha Gafen prayer: 'Baruch Atah Adonai, Eloheynu Melech Ha Olam Boray P'ri Ha Gafen' [Blessed are You, O Lord, our God, King of the universe, who creates the fruit of the vine], it was the exact same blessing that was said when the couple drank the cup of wine.

John 14:1-3 (KJV) *Let not your heart be troubled: ye believe in God, believe also in me. In my Father's house are many mansions: if it were not so, I would have told you. I go to prepare a place for you. And if I go and prepare a place for you, I will come again, and receive you unto myself; that where I am, there ye may be also.*

When we come to John 14 we are still at the Passover Seder with Yeshua speaking these words to His disciples. When Yeshua said, 'I go to prepare a place for you. And if I go and prepare a place for you, I will come again, and receive you unto myself,' it is clearly a picture of the Jewish Betrothal marriage ceremony. Yeshua stated that He would return for His Bride, which is exactly what the husband would say to his betrothed bride upon leaving her father's house. During the wait, which was an unknown time, except to the fathers' of the couple, the bridegroom would prepare a place for his bride with his father's help while the bride made preparations to be ready for his return. The bride was expected to have faith that her groom would come back for her. She was to 'watch' and be 'ready'. Of course ten days before Shavuot in Acts 2, Yeshua ascended into the Heavens to His Father's house. He is symbolically constructing the wedding chamber and when the Father gives Him the consent to go, He will return for His betrothed bride and take her to the Nesuin Marriage in 'Heaven'.

At the second stage of marriage (nesuin) the Sheva Berakhot (The Seven Blessings) are recited over a second cup of wine. The first of the seven blessings is again the same Ha Gafen prayer that Yeshua prayed with His disciples at the Passover. These seven blessings pertain to the chuppah and symbolically represent the bride and Bridegroom [Messiah] entering the 'Heavenly' chuppah. The Seven Blessings complete the wedding ceremony.[16] Anciently this is when the bride and groom enter the chaddar [wedding chamber] to consummate the marriage.

Yeshua very clearly stated that His second coming was associated with the festival of Rosh Hashana, the Rosh Chodesh (New Moon) of the month of Tishri. The major themes associated in Jewish literature to Rosh Hashana are the coronation of God [Messiah] as King, the resurrection of the righteous at the last shofar, being sealed in the Book of Life, and the wedding (second stage of marriage) of Messiah to His bride (who rules with Him as His Queen).

More Aspects to Rosh Chodesh Rosh Hashana

Because of the unknown aspect of the exact beginning of the festival of Rosh Hashana, the rabbi's called it the most 'mysterious' of all the Moedim [festivals]. Rosh Hashana being the Day of Concealment of the Moon/Bride also added to the mystique of the festival. Indeed, Rosh Hashana's understanding was shrouded in mystery.

Numbers 29:1 *And in the seventh month, on the first day of the month [ROSH HASHANA], ye shall have an holy convocation [MIKRA KODESH - HOLY REHEARSAL]; ye shall do no servile work: it is a day of blowing the trumpets [YOM TEURAH] unto you.* (KJV)

The festival of Rosh Hashana is explicitly declared to be a 'Holy (Wedding) Rehearsal' in Scripture. The Biblical name for Rosh Hashana is 'Yom Teurah'. Yom Teurah literally translates as 'Day of the Awakening Blast' or 'Day of the Awakening Shout'. According to the Talmud the trumpet used for this purpose is the ram's horn (shofar).[17] Christianity often calls Rosh Hashana (Yom Teurah), the feast of Trumpets, which in reality is the feast of ram's horns [shofarim].

Ephesians 5:14 *Wherefore he saith, Awake thou that sleepest, and arise from the dead, and Christ shall give thee light.* (KJV)

The concept of 'Awakening Blast' or 'Awakening Shout' is understood to be the 'Voice of God that sounds like a Shofar' and awakes the dead or slumbering. Rambam interpreted that it was a commandment to HEAR THE SHOFAR blown, not so much to blow the shofar (Shut ha-Rambam 142). One custom for this day is to avoid sleeping, especially during evening and morning hours. Take note that words such as AWAKE and ARISE are YOM TERUAH (ROSH HASHANA) liturgical code words and could be referring to Rosh Chodesh [New Moon] of Rosh Hashana.

Rambam gives his interpretation of the shofar in Hilchos Teshuvah
3:4

> *Although the sounding of the shofar on Rosh Hashanah is
> a Divine decree, nevertheless, we can discern a purpose
> in doing so. It is as if it tells us: Sleepers, arise from your
> slumber, and those who are dozing, wake from you lethargy.
> Review your actions, repent of your sins, and remember the
> Creator! Those who forget the truth with the passing of time
> and who waste their years pursuing vanity and folly that is
> purposeless and cannot save you - look into your souls and
> improve your ways and your deeds. Let all abandon the ways
> of evil and thoughts that offer no benefit.*[18]

Psalm 121:1-8 *I will lift up mine eyes unto the hills, from whence
cometh my help. My help cometh from the LORD, which made
heaven and earth. He will not suffer thy foot to be moved: he that
keepeth thee will not slumber. Behold, he that keepeth Israel shall
neither slumber nor sleep. The LORD is thy keeper: the LORD is thy
shade upon thy right hand. The sun shall not smite thee by day, nor
the moon by night. The LORD shall preserve thee from all evil: he
shall preserve thy soul. The LORD shall preserve thy going out and
thy coming in from this time forth, and even for evermore.* (KJV)

This same contrast of Awake/Sleep is recited in the Kiddush
Levanah [Blessing of the Moon] service. Psalm 121 is recited as
part of the liturgy.[19] It is then very appropriate that Rosh Hashana
occurs at Rosh Chodesh.

Leviticus 25:8-10 *And thou shalt number seven sabbaths of years
unto thee, seven times seven years; and the space of the seven
sabbaths of years shall be unto thee forty and nine years. Then shalt
thou cause the trumpet of the jubile to sound on the tenth day of the
seventh month, in the day of atonement shall ye make the trumpet
sound throughout all your land. And ye shall hallow the fiftieth year,
and proclaim liberty throughout all the land unto all the inhabitants
thereof: it shall be a jubile unto you; and ye shall return every man*

unto his possession, and ye shall return every man unto his family. (KJV)

The shofar blown at Rosh Hashana had a very specific meaning as explained by the rabbis. First of all, there are three shofarim [rams' horns] of importance in Jewish liturgy. The shofar blown on Yom Kippur [Tishri 10] was separate from the other two. It was called the Shofar HaGadol (The Great Trumpet) to announce the Year of Jubilee every fiftieth year.

The rite of shofar blowing became associated with Rosh Hashana because of the historical account of the shofar sounding at the giving of the Torah at Mt. Sinai. Yom Teruah presented one with the opportunity to set one's spiritual life in order through the liberation of transgression and sin in their life.[20]

Genesis 22:13 *And Abraham lifted up his eyes, and looked, and behold behind [Acherit - In the Future] him a ram caught in a thicket by his horns: and Abraham went and took the ram, and offered him up for a burnt offering in the stead of his son.* (KJV)

Hebrews 11:18-19 *Of whom it was said, That in Isaac shall thy seed be called: Accounting that God was able to raise him up, even from the dead; from whence also he received him in a figure.* (KJV)

The other two shofarim are related to each other through the Akeida [Genesis 22] where God tells Abraham to sacrifice his only son Isaac at Mount Moriah, the future site of the Temple. Abraham obeyed and would have done it except for an angel impeding him. Abraham believed that even if Isaac were sacrificed that God could raise him from the dead. The Akeida story, therefore, symbolically represents resurrection. The rabbis declared that it was as if Isaac was really sacrificed and God raised him from the dead.

As the angel stopped him, Abraham saw a ram caught in the thicket. Abraham sacrificed the ram instead of Isaac. The two horns of this special ram placed in the thicket by God have deep mystical meaning in rabbinic writings. When Abraham looked 'behind' him to see the ram, it was a symbolic reference to the 'future'. The word 'behind' is 'acherit' and literally translates as 'in the future'.

Exodus 19:16 *And it came to pass on the third day in the morning, that there were thunders and lightnings, and a thick cloud upon the mount, and the voice of the trumpet [SHOFAR] exceeding loud; so that all the people that was in the camp trembled.* (KJV)

Rabbi Bechaye postulates that God created a new ram from the ram's ashes.[21] Mystically speaking its left horn [shofar], the smaller of the two, was blown at Mt. Sinai as stated in Exodus 19:16. The ram's larger right horn will be blown with the coming of the Messiah.[22] The LEFT HORN, called the FIRST SHOFAR was mystically blown by God on SHAVUOT [PENTECOST] at Mt. Sinai in the wilderness when Israel received the Torah. God sounded like a 'voice of the shofar'. The rabbi's concluded from the Scriptures that Israel was fully betrothed to God at Mt. Sinai. Therefore, the First Shofar, left horn of the ram, was symbolic of betrothal marriage.

The other horn, the right shofar of the ram caught in the thicket, was called the LAST SHOFAR.[23] There were only two horns on the ram. This Last Shofar was the shofar mystically blown on Rosh Hashana. The Last Shofar is mystically symbolic of the second stage of marriage (Nesuin/Resurrection).

From the Midrash Rabbah, we read:

"At the end of all generations Israel will fall into the clutches of sin and be the victims of persecution; yet eventually they will be redeemed by the ram's horn, as it says, 'And the Lord God will blow the horn'".[24]

"The Holy One, blessed be He, said to Abraham; 'In a similar manner are your children destined to be caught by iniquities and entangled in troubles, but they will ultimately be redeemed through the horns of the ram.' Hence it is written, 'The Lord God will blow the horn'".[25]

Sa'adyah Gaon, a 9th century rabbi, codified a list of ten reasons why the shofar was anciently blown on Rosh Hashana:[26]

1. Rosh Hashana marks the anniversary of Adam's Creation
   Shofar blown in acceptance of God's dominion and sovereignty

2. Rosh Hashana marks the first day of the Ten Days of Awe concluding at Yom Kippur
   Shofar blown as a warning to repent now or face a worse fate

3. Rosh Hashana is a reminder of the Revelation at Mt. Sinai
   Shofar blown to once again accept that covenant of Torah

4. Rosh Hashana reminds us of the words of the prophets
   Shofar blown as a reminder to hear and do God's Word

5. Rosh Hashana reminds us of the destruction pf the Temple
   Shofar blown as a reminder to pray for the rebuilding of the Temple

6. Rosh Hashana reminds us of the ram of the Akeida
   Shofar blown as a reminder of Isaac's 'spiritual' sacrifice

7. Rosh Hashana reminds us to fear the Lord
   Shofar blown so that we will tremble with humility

8. Rosh Hashana reminds us of the Great Day of the Lord Judgment.
   Shofar blown to remind us about the Birth Pangs of the Messiah

9. Rosh Hashana reminds us of the Great Ingathering of the exiles
   Shofar blown to remind us of the Great Shofar blown at the Jubilee/Yom Kippur every fiftieth year

10. Rosh Hashana reminds us of the resurrection of the dead
    Shofar blown to remind us of God's Last Shofar to raise the dead

Isaiah 18:3 *All ye inhabitants of the world, and <u>dwellers on [IN] the earth, see ye, when he lifteth up an ensign [Nissi] on the mountains;</u> and when <u>he bloweth a trumpet [SHOFAR], hear ye.</u>* (KJV)

Sa'adyah Gaon based his tenth reason that the shofar blast of Rosh Hashana heralds the resurrection of the dead upon Isaiah 18:3. The sages of old understood this verse as alluding to the resurrection of the righteous. The 'inhabitants of the world' are the righteous living. The 'dwellers in the earth' represent the righteous dead. The Hebrew literally says 'in' the earth.[27] The 'ensign' lifted upon the mountains could be a veiled reference to Rosh Chodesh [New Moon] ceremony of the lighting of fires. Isaiah commands the living righteous and dead to HEAR the Shofar. A dead person can only hear a shofar through resurrection at the Awakening Blast or Shout. Isaiah 18:3 is the backdrop verse to Paul's resurrection verses in 1 Corinthians and 1 Thessalonians. Paul was writing a Midrash on this verse.

1Thessalonians 4:16-17 *For the Lord himself shall descend from heaven with a shout [Teurah], with the voice of the archangel, and with the trump of God: and the dead in Christ shall rise first: Then we which are alive and remain shall be caught up together with them in the clouds, to meet the Lord in the air: and so shall we ever be with the Lord.* (KJV)

1 Corinthians 15:51-52 *Behold, I shew you a mystery; We shall not all sleep, but we shall all be changed, In a moment, in the twinkling of an eye, at the last trump [Last Shofar]: for the trumpet shall* *sound, and the dead shall be raised incorruptible, and we shall be changed.* (KJV)

The Lord will descend from heaven with an Awakening Shout [Teurah - Rosh Hashana] and an Awakening Blast of the Last Shofar at Rosh Hashana. The dead in Messiah will arise, and then the righteous living will join them in resurrection. The shofar is announcing the Bridegroom coming back for His betrothed bride. Paul says, 'I show you a Mystery'. Rosh Hashana is the most mysterious of all the festival (wedding) rehearsals because it was on a Rosh Chodesh and in ancient times its day and hour could not be predetermined.

Exodus 12:11, 39, 40, 42 *And thus shall ye eat it; with your loins girded, your shoes on your feet, and your staff in your hand; and ye shall eat it in haste: it is the LORD's passover...And they baked unleavened cakes of the dough which they brought forth out of Egypt, for it was not leavened; because they were thrust out of Egypt, and could not tarry, neither had they prepared for themselves any victual...And it came to pass at the end of the four hundred and thirty years, even the selfsame day it came to pass, that all the hosts of the LORD went out from the land of Egypt.* (KJV)

The resurrection will come in a moment, in the twinkling of an eye. In Hebraic literature the phrase K'heref Ayin, 'In the blink [twinkling] of an eye' is very common. The redemption of Israel in Egypt was said to have occurred in a 'twinkling of an eye' (k'heref ayin). Rashi said that God did not detain them even for the twinkling of an eye (k'heref ayin). The phrase 'Yeshuat Hashem k'heref ayin,' which means the 'redemption of God comes in the twinkling of an eye,' is also very common.

God's betrothal of Israel happened in the twinkling of an eye. When a believer becomes born-again in Messiah by His blood through the Ruwach haKodesh [Holy Spirit], they are betrothed to God in a twinkling of an eye. Likewise, at the second redemption when they are resurrected to the secong stage of marriage (Nesuin), it will occur in the twinkling of an eye.

Isaiah 13:2-3 *Lift ye up a <u>banner [Nes]</u> upon the high mountain, exalt the <u>voice [Teurah]</u> unto them, shake the hand, that they may go into <u>the gates of the nobles</u>. I have commanded <u>my sanctified ones, I have also called my mighty ones for mine anger,</u> even them that rejoice in my highness.* (KJV)

Isaiah 11:10 *And in that day there shall be a root of Jesse, which shall stand for an ensign (Nes) of the people; to it shall the Gentiles seek: and his rest shall be glorious.* (KJV)

Isaiah 18:3 *All ye inhabitants of the world, and dwellers on the earth, see ye, when he lifteth up an ensign (Nes) on the mountains; and when he bloweth a trumpet [shofar], hear ye.* (KJV)

Isaiah 13:2 states 'Lift ye up a banner upon the high mountain'. The Hebrew word for 'banner' is 'Nes'. The same Hebrew word is also translated 'ensign' in Isaiah 11:10 and 18:3. By Scriptural definition we can say with absolute certainty that the 'banner' lifted up in Isaiah 13:2 and 18:3 is the Messiah. Isaiah 11:10 defines the 'Nes' as the 'Root of Jesse'. The 'Root of Jesse' is defined as the Branch [Tzemach] a few verses earlier and also by the prophet Jeremiah:

Isaiah 11:1 *And there shall come forth a rod out of the stem of Jesse, and a Branch shall grow out of his roots:* (KJV)

Jeremiah 23:5 *Behold, the days come, saith the LORD, that I will raise unto David a righteous Branch, and a King shall reign and prosper, and shall execute judgment and justice in the earth.* (KJV)

In Isaiah 13:2-3 we read, 'exalt the voice unto them'. This is the 'Teurah - Awakening Shout or Blast' at Rosh Hashana. It is the 'shout' and the 'voice' of the archangel in 1 Thessalonians 4:16-17 that describes the resurrection of the righteous at Rosh Hashana.

Continuing in Isaiah 13, we read, 'Shake the hand, that they may go into the gates of the nobles'. The 'gates' being opened are a definite Hebrew reference to the festival of Rosh Hashana. Heavenly 'Gates' or 'Doors' being opened are part of the liturgy of Rosh

Hashana.[28] These 'nobles' represent the leaders (or the believers in Yeshua the Messiah) at the resurrection on Rosh Hashana. Not all Israel goes up to be with the Messiah on this eschatological Rosh Hashana.

Isaiah 13:3 continues, 'I have commanded my sanctified ones, I have also called my mighty ones for mine anger, even them that rejoice in my highness'. God has commanded (called) His sanctified (mighty) ones 'for mine anger'. 'For mine anger' is mistranslated from the Hebrew. It should be interpreted as 'to my nose'. In reality God will call the righteous up 'to His nose'. What does this mean? The righteous will be resurrected on Rosh Hashana and they will rise before God's 'nose' as a sweet-smelling savor.

The Shofar and the Silver Trumpets

Numbers 10:1-4, 9-10 (KJV) *And the LORD spake unto Moses, saying, Make thee two trumpets of silver [Hebrew Chatsotserot]; of a whole piece shalt thou make them: that thou mayest use them for the calling of the assembly, and for the journeying of the camps. And when they shall blow [Hebrew - taka] with them, all the assembly shall assemble themselves to thee at the door [gate] of the tabernacle of the congregation. And if they blow [Hebrew - taka] but with one trumpet, then the princes, which are heads of the thousands of Israel, shall gather themselves unto thee...And if ye go to war in your land against the enemy that oppresseth you, then ye shall blow an alarm [Hebrew ruwa] with the trumpets [Hebrew Chatsotserot]; and ye shall be remembered before the LORD your God, and ye shall be saved from your enemies. Also in the day of your gladness, and in your solemn days [Hebrew - Moedim], and in the beginnings of your months [Hebrew - Rosh Chodesh], ye shall blow [Hebrew - taka] with the trumpets [Hebrew Chatsotserot] over your burnt offerings, and over the sacrifices of your peace offerings; that they may be to you for a memorial before your God: I am the LORD your God.* (KJV)

Moses was instructed to make two silver trumpets for the calling up of the people in the camp. These were not shofarim (rams' horns).

When both silver trumpets were blasted, the entire congregation was to assemble before the Lord. When only one silver trumpet was blasted only the princes (nobles) were to assemble. The priests also blew these silver trumpets on the Sabbaths, Festivals, and New Moons. The Hebrew word 'taka' is the root for the standard 'tekiah' blast, which is a longer blast than a teurah. This contradicts the command for the festival of Yom Teurah [Rosh Hashana], which the Scripture explicitly commands a teurah, or shorter blast.[29]

On every Sabbath and Festival gathering, including the Rosh Chodesh (New Moon), three trumpets were blasted from the Temple area for all of Israel to hear. The priest blowing the shofar was flanked on both his sides with the priests blowing the silver trumpets. On all these occasions, except Rosh Hashana, the two silver trumpets were featured over the shofar. On Rosh Hashana, the shofar was the center of the celebration with the silver trumpets playing a lesser role. In this instance the blast of the shofar outlasts that of the silver trumpets so the congregation can obey God's command 'to hear' the shofar.

The silver trumpets are called 'Chatsotserot' and the ram's horns 'shofarim.' There are a couple of Hebrew terms here that need explaining. As just mentioned only priests could blow these silver trumpets. Numbers 10:9 explains that the priests are to blow, Hebrew 'ruwa', the Chatsotserot [silver trumpets] when going out to battle the enemy in war. This is related to the High Priest anointed for war, which we will discuss in further detail in the next chapter.

Numbers 31:6 *And Moses sent them to the war, a thousand of every tribe, them and Phinehas the son of Eleazar the priest, to the war, with the holy instruments, and the trumpets [Chatsotserot] to blow [Teurah] in his hand.* (KJV)

In this instance, Phinehas the High Priest anointed for war was instructed to give teurah [shorter blasts] on the silver trumpets. Not only were the silver trumpets used in battle, but also for the coronation of the Judean kings as well as when David brought the Ark of the Covenant to Jerusalem. Nowhere, in Scripture is a priest commanded to blow the shofar in going to battle.

Joel 2:1 *Blow ye the trumpet [shofar] in Zion, and sound an alarm [ruwa] in my holy mountain: let all the inhabitants of the land tremble: for the day of the LORD cometh, for it is nigh at hand;* (KJV)

Zephaniah 1:14-16 *The great day of the LORD is near, it is near, and hasteth greatly, even the voice of the day of the LORD: the mighty man shall cry there bitterly. That day is a day of wrath, a day of trouble and distress, a day of wasteness and desolation, a day of darkness and gloominess, a day of clouds and thick darkness, A day of the trumpet [shofar] and alarm [teurah] against the fenced cities, and against the high towers.* (KJV)

However, Scriptures refer to the eschatological Day of the Lord [the last one thousand years], as a day of the shofar blast. It is an alarm to the inhabitants of the world that God will war against them who refuse to accept His mercy and repent. Specifically the first seven years, the Birth Pangs of the Messiah, of the Day of the Lord are being addressed. The only conclusion we can make from Scripture is that these shofar references to the Day of the Lord are tied to Yom Teurah, the festival of Rosh Hashanah. The sages understood that the 'Day of the Lord' judgment would commence at Rosh Hashana.

Rosh Chodesh - Rosh Hashana - The Day of the Lord

Jewish tradition believes that Adam was created on Rosh Hashana, which is the head of the civil year.[30] Because of this, the rabbis understood that after six thousand years on a Rosh Hashana, the Day of the Lord [Messianic Kingdom] would begin as foreshadowed by the six days of creation and God's day of rest [see also Psalm 90:4 & 2 Peter 3:8].[31] The great one thousand year Sabbath is the Day of the Lord, and it begins at Rosh Hashana at the blowing of the Shofar.[32] The first seven years of the Day of the Lord are known as the Birth Pangs of the Messiah [Tribulation Period], when Israel is birthed into Messiah. The resurrection of the righteous at Rosh Hashana after six thousand years marks the beginning of the

Day of the Lord when the resurrections will occur in their order [1 Corinthians 15:23].

Psalm 27:5 *For in the time of trouble he shall hide me in his pavilion: in the secret of his tabernacle shall he hide me; he shall set me up upon a rock.* (KJV)

Jeremiah 30:7 *Alas! for that day is great, so that none is like it: it is even the time of Jacob's trouble; but he shall be saved out of it.* (KJV)

Psalm 27 is read on Rosh Hashana and indicates that Jacob's trouble [the seven years of Birth Pangs - Jeremiah 30:7] will not affect the righteous living before it starts. The rabbis deduced that the seven years of Birth Pangs were an allusion to the extra seven years Jacob had worked for Laban in order to marry his daughter Rachel [see Genesis 29]. The righteous will be hidden 'in His pavilion' and 'His tabernacle'. The Hebrew for 'hide' should be translated as 'conceal' as in the new moon being concealed on Rosh Hashana. This word is only used of storing something very precious as in a spiritual treasure.[33] With Psalm 27 the 'spirit' of the Ten Days of Awe are ushered in.[34]

Psalm 47:1-9 *O clap your hands, all ye people; shout unto God with the voice of triumph. For the LORD most high is terrible; he is a great King over all the earth. He shall subdue the people under us, and the nations under our feet. He shall choose our inheritance for us, the excellency of Jacob whom he loved. Selah. God is gone up with a shout [Teurah], the LORD with the sound of a trumpet [Shofar]. Sing praises to God, sing praises: sing praises unto our King, sing praises. For God is the King of all the earth: sing ye praises with understanding. God reigneth over the heathen: God sitteth upon the throne of his holiness. The princes of the people are gathered together, even the people of the God of Abraham: for the shields of the earth belong unto God: he is greatly exalted.* (KJV)

In another example from Rosh Hashana liturgy, Psalm 47 is recited seven different times before the shofar is blown.[35] This is because it is an ancient coronation song for the kings of Judah.[36] There are two distinct Jewish elements of Rosh Hashana described in this Psalm: kingship and resurrection. This ties together the purpose of the shofar with the announcement of the King's arrival. The Resurrection/Wedding and Coronation of Messiah all occur on the same eschatological Rosh Hashana. The King Messiah's rule of one thousand years begins on Rosh Hashana, which then is the beginning of the Sabbath - Day of the Lord.

The seventh day Sabbath is like a bride to believers teaching them lessons about the marriage of Messiah to His bride.[37] The seventh day Sabbath becomes, in a sense, a wedding rehearsal that is connected to the feast of Shofarim [Rosh Hashana]. In the religious calendar Rosh Hashana begins the seventh new moon [or month] from Nisan [the beginning of the religious calendar].[38] Tishri 1, Rosh Hashana, is the Sabbatical Month, which initiates the Sabbath [Day of the Lord] Millennium with the wedding of the bride and Bridegroom. Rosh Hashana also prophetically initiates the fulfillment of all the fall festivals, which are all in the Sabbatical month of Tishri.

The Month of Elul - Preparation for the Ten Days of Awe

Jewish tradition states that man is judged on the same day of the anniversary of his creation (Adam's creation). The offspring of Adam could also find forgiveness from God by repenting during the Ten Days of Penitence.[39] Prophetically, the Birth Pangs introduce this time of judgment. The annual observance of Rosh Hashana allows one to take spiritual inventory by judging themselves before God through repentance instead of God bringing His judgment on their continued sin.

As stated already, Rosh Chodesh Rosh Hashana occurs at the beginning of the seventh month of the Hebrew religious calendar. There were six New Moons starting with the month of Nisan before Rosh Hashana. Each of these prior six new moons was similar to a mini-Yom Teurah, a day of blowing the shofarim. The seventh New

Moon on Tishri 1 was the climax of these series of new moons. One writer mentions that only short blasts of the shofar were performed on all Rosh Chodesh ceremonies, except on Rosh Hashana when long alarm blasts were sounded.[40]

The season of Teshuvah [Repentance] actually began a full month before Rosh Hashana. At the New Moon of Elul began forty days of Teshuvah that lasted until Yom Kippur on Tishri 10.[41] The entire month of Elul [always thirty days] was in preparation for the final Ten Days of Repentance. To serious Jews, the month of Elul was a time of a crash spiritual regimen preparing for Rosh Hashana. They understood that they were going on trial before God and had become very conscientious about it. The month of Elul became a time of forgiving and reconciling with enemies. It was also a time of personal introspection to correct flaws and vows never to return to them. Although one was repenting in fear and trembling, the trial was considered to be before a merciful Judge.[42]

The Jewish sages instituted that the shofar should be blown on Rosh Chodesh Elul and afterward every day of the month just after the daily Shacherit [morning] service. It was not blown, however, on the last day of Elul, the day before Tishri 1, so that the shofar blast of Rosh Hashana would stand out and not be confused with those blasts during Elul.[43] Also, this was done to confuse Satan, keeping him ignorant of the approach of Rosh Hashana where he brings charges against man. Satan may have thought that the Day of Judgment had already passed.[44]

The purpose of these shofar blasts during Elul was to prepare the person for the Ten Days of Penitence beginning with Rosh Hashana. One rabbi likened the thirty-day period of opportune repentance before the great judgment day of Rosh Hashana, to thirty days of grace that a Court might grant a debtor to pay his debts before having to go to Court and face the creditors.[45] In this writer's opinion, the month of Elul is the opportunity for believers to get themselves prepared for the royal eschatological wedding. In this case, the shofar blasted at Rosh Hashana, is one of a groom announcing his coming to fetch his betrothed bride away from her father's house.

But the shofar at Rosh Hashana was also blasted to warn people to repent because the time of judgment had come. Every man's life was heading for trial and the Heavenly Court was now in session. The Judge of the Whole Earth was presiding. If an individual is found guilty, the death sentence may be handed down.[46] Many Jews live out this aspect of repentance and judgment associated with Rosh Hashana and the Ten Days of Awe in reality every year. What was rehearsed every year was symbolic of the prophetic eschatological final judgment related to the Days of Awe.

Ezekiel 33:1-7 *Again the word of the LORD came unto me, saying, Son of man, speak to the children of thy people, and say unto them, When I bring the sword upon a land, if the people of the land take a man of their coasts, and set him for their watchman: If when he seeth the sword come upon the land, he blow the trumpet [shofar], and warn the people; Then whosoever heareth the sound of the trumpet [shofar], and taketh not warning; if the sword come, and take him away, his blood shall be upon his own head. He heard the sound of the trumpet [shofar], and took not warning; his blood shall be upon him. But he that taketh warning shall deliver his soul. But if the watchman see the sword come, and blow not the trumpet, and the people be not warned; if the sword come, and take any person from among them, he is taken away in his iniquity; but his blood will I require at the watchman's hand. So thou, O son of man, I have set thee a watchman unto the house of Israel; therefore thou shalt hear the word at my mouth, and warn them from me.* (KJV)

In many Jewish synagogues Psalm 27 and Ezekiel 33:1-7 are recited during the month of Elul in preparation for judgment on Rosh Hashana. Ezekiel's prophecy is about a watchman warning the people about the sword that is about to come upon the land in judgment. The watchman warns them by blasting the shofar, which is the call to repent and turn to God. A Midrash mentions that the shofar blown in Ezekiel 33 is the shofar related to Yom Teurah [Rosh Hashana].[47]

Yom HaDin - The Day of Judgment

Psalm 118:19-20 *Open to me the gates of righteousness: I will go into them, and I will praise the LORD: This gate of the LORD, into which the righteous shall enter.* (KJV)

Isaiah 26:2 *Open ye the gates, that the righteous nation which keepeth the truth may enter in.* (KJV)

Another name for Rosh Hashanah is Yom HaDin, the Day of Judgment. It was understood that on this day, God would sit in court and all men would pass before Him to be judged. Three great books will be opened as each man is weighed in the balance and placed into one of three categories (Talmud, Rosh HaShanah 16b). It has been taught that the school of Shammai says that there will be three classes on the Final Day of Judgment, one of the wholly righteous, one of the wholly wicked, and one of the intermediates. The wholly righteous are at once inscribed and sealed for life in the world to come; the wholly wicked are at once inscribed and sealed for perdition (Talmud, Rosh HaShanah 16b-17a).

1 Peter 4:5-8 *Who shall give account to him that is ready to judge [Rosh Hashana] the quick and the dead. For for this cause was the gospel preached also to them that are dead, that they might be judged [Rosh Hashana] according to men in the flesh, but live according to God in the spirit. But the end of all things is at hand: be ye therefore sober [Rosh Hashana], and watch [Rosh Hashana] unto prayer. And above all things have fervent charity among yourselves: for charity [Love in action] shall cover the multitude of sins.* (KJV)

It was the custom in Israel for all the country folk to come to the city for Rosh Hashana to pray in the multitude of the people.[48] Those who may have had a more difficult time in preparing for the Days of Awe may find repentance with the multitude of the people. Peter uses Rosh Hashana phraseology when describing how love for God can cover a multitude of sins. There are times that the unity of the people in repentance draws those who haven't prepared for the judgment into repentance.

In the traditional morning service [Musaf] of Rosh Hashana this aspect of Divine Judgment is seen through a hymnal prayer entitled 'Unetanneh Tokef,' which means, 'Now let us recite the majesty of this day.' In this prayer God is seen sitting as the exalted King on His Throne in Judgment. The Great Heavenly Book will be opened with every soul listed. The shofar is sounded amidst a still small voice. The angels fear and tremble as they say in unison: 'Behold, the Day of Judgment is here, when the hosts on high shall be visited with judgment'. All mankind will pass before the Judge like sheep before the Shepherd. They will all pass under His staff for inspection and He will affix their verdict.[49]

The righteouses are separated and will be with God. The wicked will face the wrath of God during the Days of Awe (Yamim Nora'im), known in Hebrew as the Chevlai shel Mashiach [Birth Pangs of the Messiah], and will never repent. The average person has until Yom Kippur when his fate is sealed forever. In other words, the average person will have until the end of the seven years of Birth Pangs [tribulation] to repent and turn to God. The average person on Rosh Hashanah is judged by God and is neither written in the Book of Life nor the Book of the Wicked. Their fate is yet to be decided. The average person and the wicked have to go through the 'Awesome Days,' the tribulation, until they reach Yom Kippur (the end of the tribulation when their fate is sealed forever). One can never get out of the book of the wicked once they are written in it (Revelation 17:8). These are people who never, ever, will accept the Messiah Yeshua.

Romans 14:10 *But why dost thou judge thy brother? or why dost thou set at nought thy brother? for we shall all stand before the judgment seat of Christ.* (KJV)

2 Corinthians 5:10 *For we must all appear before the judgment seat of Christ; that every one may receive the things done in his body, according to that he hath done, whether it be good or bad.* (KJV)

1 Corinthians 3:9-15 *For we are labourers together with God: ye are God's husbandry, ye are God's building. According to the grace of God which is given unto me, as a wise masterbuilder, I have laid the foundation, and another buildeth thereon. But let every man take heed how he buildeth thereupon. For other foundation can no man lay than that is laid, which is Jesus Christ. Now if any man build upon this foundation gold, silver, precious stones, wood, hay, stubble; Every man's work shall be made manifest: for the day shall declare it, because it shall be revealed by fire; and the fire shall try every man's work of what sort it is. If any man's work abide which he hath built thereupon, he shall receive a reward. If any man's work shall be burned, he shall suffer loss: but he himself shall be saved; yet so as by fire.* (KJV)

On Rosh Hashana, all people are judged individually like sheep [the righteous] passing single file before their owner [Talmud - Rosh Hashana 16a]. On this day, God will open the Book of Life and hold a trial. This is known as the Bema judgment. God will judge the works of the believers in Messiah, but not their salvation. This is a judgment of the believers only. All people in this judgment will be saved. This is not a judgment of one's salvation, but a judgment of their rewards based upon their works.

Zephaniah 2:1-3 *Gather yourselves together, yea, gather together, O nation not desired; Before the decree bring forth, before the day pass as the chaff, before the fierce anger of the LORD come upon you, before the day of the LORD's anger come upon you. Seek ye the LORD, all ye meek of the earth, which have wrought his judgment; seek righteousness, seek meekness: it may be ye shall be hid in the day of the LORD's anger.* (KJV)

In Zephaniah the fierce anger of the Lord will be released in His judgment during the Day of the Lord. This is clearly related to Rosh Hashana. Notice that the meek, who are the righteous, will be 'hidden' during the Lord's anger. This is another picture of the righteous being 'concealed' on Rosh Hashana.

The customary greeting for Rosh Hashanah is 'Le-shanah tovah tikateivu' (May you be inscribed in the book of life for a good year) and on Yom Kippur, 'Chatimah tovah' (May you have a good sealing of your destiny in the book of life).[50] Tradition states that on Rosh Hashanah God opens the heavenly books and judges the people according to their works, writing in them who will die and what kind of life the living will enjoy during the coming year.[51] The Ten Days of Penitence (Rosh Hashanah through Yom Kippur) are thought of as offering an opportunity for introspection, repentance, and preparation for the Day of Atonement, that will influence God to change these fates for the better. On Yom Kippur these fates are fixed or sealed. Jews view the Ten Days of Penitence as a process of 'continuous' judgment culminating in individuals' fates' being sealed at Yom Kippur.[52]

Nehemiah 8:1, 2, 13 *And all the people gathered themselves together as one man into the street that was before the water gate; and they spake unto Ezra the scribe to bring the book of the law of Moses, which the LORD had commanded to Israel. And Ezra the priest brought the law before the congregation both of men and women, and all that could hear with understanding, upon the first day of the seventh month...And on the second day were gathered together the chief of the fathers of all the people, the priests, and the Levites, unto Ezra the scribe, even to understand the words of the law.* (KJV)

On Tishri 1 (Rosh Hashana) Ezra and Nehemiah led those Jews who returned from Babylonian captivity into Teshuvah [repentance]. It is interesting that the people gathered 'as one man' on Rosh Hashana. This reminds us that Israel was like one man with one heart before Mt. Sinai when they received the Torah of Moses. The receiving of the Torah was at Pentecost [Shavuot], which represent Israel's full betrothal to God. Here in Nehemiah the people are in one accord again receiving the Torah of Moses, but at Rosh Hashana, the eschatological day of the resurrection and full marriage [Nesuin].

Anciently Rosh Hashana was held for two days, Tishri 1 & 2 as seen in Nehemiah 8. Creating a two-day Rosh Hashanah was also intended to strengthen observance of each day, but in the rabbinic view, the two days are regarded as a yoma arikhta, one long day.[53] Tishri 1 & 2 are Rosh Hashana and Tishri 10 is Yom Kippur. Eschatologically Tishri 3-9, the Seven Days of Awe in between, represent the 'Seven Years' of the Birth Pangs of the Messiah [Tribulation]. Messiah is coronated as King on Rosh Hashana and returns to earth at Yom Kippur to set up His Kingdom.

Rosh Hashana is called a 'minor' Yom haDin [Day of Judgment] by the rabbis, where as Yom Kippur is called the 'major' Yom haDin. Ultimately all fates of those in-between sinners will be sealed on Yom Kippur. Since Rosh Hashana is also a Rosh Chodesh, the New Moon sacrifices were also offered in the Temple. The New Moon ceremony required a goat as a sin offering [Numbers 29:5]. Yom Kippur also required a goat as a sin offering [Numbers 29:11]. This is one of the connections between Rosh Hashana and Yom Kippur being linked together as Yom haDin [Day of Judgment].

1 Thessalonians 5:1-10 *But of the times and the seasons, brethren, ye have no need that I write unto you. For yourselves know perfectly that the day of the Lord so cometh as a thief in the night. For when they shall say, Peace and safety; then sudden destruction cometh upon them, as travail upon a woman with child; and they shall not escape. But ye, brethren, are not in darkness, that that day should overtake you as a thief. Ye are all the children of light, and the children of the day: we are not of the night, nor of darkness. Therefore let us not sleep, as do others; but let us watch and be sober. For they that sleep sleep in the night; and they that be drunken are drunken in the night. But let us, who are of the day, be sober, putting on the breastplate of faith and love; and for an helmet, the hope of salvation. For God hath not appointed us to wrath, but to obtain salvation by our Lord Jesus Christ, Who died for us, that, whether we wake or sleep, we should live together with him.* (KJV)

The word 'seasons' in Greek is 'kairoon' [Strongs' # 2540) meaning 'times at which certain foreordained events take place'. Paul is saying to the Thessalonians that they have already been taught about the festivals [Moedim and Holy Rehearsals]. They already knew that the 'Day of the Lord' [term for the last Millennium] that begins after six thousand years on Rosh Hashana was to come as a 'thief in the night'. This is strict second stage Nesuin marriage symbolism. When the bridegroom came for his betrothed bride, he was to symbolically kidnap her and steal her from her father. A 'thief in the night' is symbolic of this taking of the bride.

The Birth Pangs of the Messiah begin the Day of the Lord 'as travail upon a woman with child'. This is the Seven-Year Tribulation. Paul reverses the symbolism by stating that the betrothed bride does not abide in darkness, and the Day of Lord will not come as a thief to her. In other words, the betrothed bride will be prepared for her bridegroom, the Messiah. The betrothed bride is to 'Watch' and be 'Sober,' definite words linked to the New Moon of Rosh Hashana.

Isaiah 59:10-17 *We grope for the wall like the blind, and we grope as if we had no eyes: we stumble at noonday as in the night; we are in desolate places as dead men. We roar all like bears, and mourn sore like doves: we look for judgment, but there is none; for salvation, but it is far off from us. For our transgressions are multiplied before thee, and our sins testify against us: for our transgressions are with us; and as for our iniquities, we know them; In transgressing and lying against the LORD, and departing away from our God, speaking oppression and revolt, conceiving and uttering from the heart words of falsehood. And judgment is turned away backward, and justice standeth afar off: for truth is fallen in the street, and equity cannot enter. Yea, truth faileth; and he that departeth from evil maketh himself a prey: and the LORD saw it, and it displeased him that there was no judgment. And he saw that there was no man, and wondered that there was no intercessor: therefore his arm brought salvation unto him; and his righteousness, it sustained him. For he put on righteousness as a breastplate, and an helmet of salvation upon his head; and he put on the garments of vengeance for clothing, and was clad with zeal as a cloke.* (KJV)

Notice Paul's statement to the Thessalonians who are sober: 'putting on the breastplate of faith and love; and for an helmet, the hope of salvation'. 'God hath not appointed us to wrath, but to obtain salvation by our Lord Jesus Christ'. Paul's backdrop comes from Isaiah 59, which was probably an ancient Haftarah reading in the Temple Services for Rosh Chodesh Rosh Hashana.

Yom HaZikkaron - Day of Remembrance

Leviticus 23:24-25 *Speak unto the children of Israel, saying, In the seventh month, in the first day of the month [Rosh Hashana], shall ye have a sabbath, a memorial [zikkaron] of blowing of trumpets [Teurah], an holy convocation. Ye shall do no servile work therein: but ye shall offer an offering made by fire unto the LORD.* (KJV)

Earlier in this chapter Leviticus 23 was referenced for Rosh Hashana being a 'zikkaron teurah,' a day of 'remembrance shouts, or blasts.' It is highly probable that in the Second Temple era there were three blessings associated with the Rosh Hashana Musaf Service [additional sacrifices for the holiday as laid out in Scripture]. Later, after the Temple was destroyed, the liturgies from the Musaf service were transferred to the synagogue liturgy. The blessings are called Malkhuyot (Kingship), Zikhronot (Remembrance), and Shofrot (Shofar). These represent the themes of the morning (Shacherit) service of Rosh Hashana.[54] The Mishnah states, 'No less than ten kingship verses, ten remembrance verses and ten shofar verses must be recited...' (M. Rosh Hashana 4.6)

Malachi 3:16 *Then they that feared the LORD spake often one to another: and the LORD hearkened, and heard it, and a book of remembrance was written before him for them that feared the LORD, and that thought upon his name.* (KJV)

Hebrews 6:10 *For God is not unrighteous to forget your work and labour of love, which ye have shewed toward his name, in that ye have ministered to the saints, and do minister.* (KJV)

At the end of six thousand years of the Olam Hazeh [This Present Age], God will remember all the righteous dead and living for their work of labor in their lifetimes. They will be resurrected before the

Throne of God to attend the coronation and wedding of the Messiah. They will receive their reward and function in the Kingdom.

The Remembrance section of the Rosh Hashana service expresses the concept that God remembers the past of every living creature that comes before Him. God will judge more than their actual deeds. In the Zikkaron prayers, He also judges their thoughts and plans. The Remembrance section concludes with a prayer that God remember the Akeidah of Isaac. On the second day of Rosh Hashana, Tishri 2, Genesis 22 (The Akeidah) is the Torah reading for the day.[55]

Romans 12:1 *I beseech you therefore, brethren, by the mercies of God, that ye present your bodies a living sacrifice, holy, acceptable unto God, which is your reasonable service.* (KJV)

As we have studied in a previous chapter, God sees Isaac as a living sacrifice. In ancient rabbinic thought it was as if Isaac was actually sacrificed because of the substituted ram. As Isaac, believers in Yeshua are called to be living sacrifices.

Leviticus 26:42 *Then will I remember my covenant with Jacob, and also my covenant with Isaac, and also my covenant with Abraham will I remember; and I will remember the land.* (KJV)

In Leviticus 26:42 the term 'remember' is used of the covenant with Abraham and Jacob, but not with Isaac. 'Remember' is the concept of bringing something from the past into present thought, but it is only a memory. Isaac's ashes are always before God through the ram as a 'living reminder' of his covenant with God. As Isaac was prepared to sacrifice himself to sanctify God's Name, so we should offer our lives as living sacrifices. Sacrificing one's life for God's purpose means more than just physical death. It also means that while remaining alive unto God that we sacrifice our personal desires and preferences for His Will. When we 'remember' the Akeidah, we are reminded of our priority to identify with the Will of the King because we are His subjects.[56]

The ram of the Akeidah is symbolic of Messiah Yeshua who became the ultimate Heavenly Living Sacrifice. The right horn of the ram, the last shofar, is mystically blasted at Rosh Hashana for all those righteous who have followed in Isaac's, and therefore, Yeshua's footsteps as living sacrifices in their time. God will 'remember' the labors of all the righteous on Rosh Hashana and they will be rewarded on the merit of Yeshua (the Greater Isaac), who was dead, but is alive [Revelation 1:18].

Therefore, it is easy to conclude that the shofar blast associated with Rosh Hashana had a dual function. The shofar blast called the people to repentance at the start of the Days of Awe. At the same time the shofar blast was an assurance that the repentant would find favor with God. God will remember the righteous, those who are repentant, and acquit them on the Day of Judgment.

The Coronation of King Messiah

<u>2 Kings 11:1-3</u> *And when Athaliah the mother of Ahaziah saw that her son was dead, she arose and destroyed all the seed royal. But Jehosheba, the daughter of king Joram, sister of Ahaziah, took Joash the son of Ahaziah, and stole him from among the king's sons which were slain; and they hid him, even him and his nurse, in the <u>bedchamber</u> from Athaliah, so that he was not slain. And he was with her hid in <u>the house of the LORD six years</u>. And Athaliah did reign over the land.* (KJV)

The seed of David, and therefore the Messiah, was left for extinction when Ahaziah, king of Judah was dead. His mother, Athaliah, who was of the seed of the northern kingdom of Israel [2 Kings 8:26, 1 Kings 16:28], had all the royal seed of Judah killed. She set herself up as ruler of Judah. Unknown to her was that Jehosheba, the brother of Ahaziah [who was dead] was able to save Joash before he would have been slain. Jehosheba had a different mother than Athaliah. Jehosheba cared for Joash for six years in the 'bedchamber,' which the rabbis understood to be either the cells surrounding the Holy of Holies or the attic rooms over it.[57] This makes sense since Jehosheba was the wife of the High Priest Jehoiada [2 Chronicles 22:11]. The High Priest, of course, had direct access to the area around [or above] the Holy of Holies.

2 Kings 11:9-21 *And the captains over the hundreds did according to all things that Jehoiada the priest commanded: and they took every man his men that were to come in on the sabbath, with them that should go out on the sabbath, and came to Jehoiada the priest. And to the captains over hundreds did the priest give king David's spears and shields, that were in the temple of the LORD. And the guard stood, every man with his weapons in his hand, round about the king [Joash], from the right corner of the temple to the left corner of the temple, along by the altar and the temple. And he brought forth the king's son, and put the crown upon him, and gave him the testimony [edut]; and they made him king, and anointed [mashiach] him; and they clapped their hands, and said, God save the king. And when Athaliah heard the noise of the guard and of the people, she came to the people into the temple of the LORD. And when she looked, behold, the king stood by a pillar, as the manner was, and the princes and the trumpeters [Chatsotserot] by the king, and all the people of the land rejoiced, and blew with trumpets [Chatsotserot]: and Athaliah rent her clothes, and cried, Treason, Treason. But Jehoiada the priest commanded the captains of the hundreds, the officers of the host, and said unto them, Have her forth without the ranges: and him that followeth her kill with the sword. For the priest had said, Let her not be slain in the house of the LORD. And they laid hands on her; and she went by the way by the which the horses came into the king's house: and there was she slain. And Jehoiada made a covenant between the LORD and the king and the people, that they should be the LORD's people; between the king also and the people. And all the people of the land went into the house of Baal, and brake it down; his altars and his images brake they in pieces thoroughly, and slew Mattan the priest of Baal before the altars. And the priest appointed officers over the house of the LORD. And he took the rulers over hundreds, and the captains, and the guard, and all the people of the land; and they brought down the king from the house of the LORD, and came by the way of the gate of the guard to the king's house. And he sat on the throne of the kings. And all the people of the land rejoiced, and the city was in quiet: and they slew Athaliah with the sword beside the king's house. Seven years old was Jehoash when he began to reign.* (KJV)

The six years that Joash was hidden can be viewed to be symbolic of six thousand years of 'This Present Age' [Olam Hazeh]. In the seventh year Joash was proclaimed king, which is symbolic of the Messiah Yeshua being coronated as King for the last Millennium. Also, Joash was coronated as king of Judah on the seventh day Sabbath emphasizing this symbolism.

Although there is no mention of the shofar being blown at Joash's coronation, other Scriptures allude to them being blown at a king's coronation [1 Kings 1:32-48]. In the account of Joash's coronation, however, the silver trumpets are recorded as blown. There are several more interesting details that appear in Joash's coronation that shed light on Messiah's coronation as the King of kings.

2 Kings 11:4 *And the seventh year Jehoiada sent and fetched the rulers over hundreds, with the captains and the guard, and brought them to him into the house of the LORD, and made a covenant with them, and took an oath of them in the house of the LORD, and shewed them the king's son. (KJV)*

2 Chronicles 23:1-3 *And in the seventh year Jehoiada strengthened himself, and took the captains of hundreds, Azariah the son of Jeroham, and Ishmael the son of Jehohanan, and Azariah the son of Obed, and Maaseiah the son of Adaiah, and Elishaphat the son of Zichri, into covenant with him. And they went about in Judah, and gathered the Levites out of all the cities of Judah, and the chief of the fathers of Israel, and they came to Jerusalem. And all the congregation made a covenant with the king in the house of God. And he said unto them, Behold, the king's son shall reign, as the LORD hath said of the sons of David. (KJV)*

Isaiah 13:2 *Lift ye up a banner [Messiah] upon the high mountain, exalt the voice [Teurah] unto them, shake the hand, that they may go into the gates of the nobles. (KJV)*

It was not all of Judah who was at the coronation of Joash. The High Priest gathered the 'rulers over hundreds,' and 'the captains and the guard'. The Levites and the chief of the fathers of Israel were gathered from the cities of Judah to Jerusalem's Temple for the coronation of Joash. Earlier we discussed how Isaiah 13 was a reference to the resurrection at Rosh Hashana and that the nobles [not all Israel] are summoned to the heavenly coronation of Messiah Yeshua.

Psalm 27:5 *For in the time of trouble [Birth Pangs] he shall hide me [Concealment - Rosh Hashana] in his pavilion: in the secret of his tabernacle shall he hide me; he shall set me up upon a rock.* (KJV)

Joash represented the 'resurrection' of the Davidic dynasty, which was thought to have become extinct. The High Priest, Jehoiada, is perceived as the savior of the Davidic dynasty. Of course, Jehoiada is also a picture of Yeshua HaMashiach, the Heavenly High Priest, who through Himself saved the Davidic dynasty. The Seder Olam 18 comments about Joash being hidden in the Holy of Holies through the prophetic knowledge of King David when he wrote Psalm 27 especially verse five above. Of course, we have mentioned already that Psalm 27 is read on Rosh Hashana. The Seder Olam comments on the phrase, 'he shall set me upon a rock'. Jehoiada was viewed as the 'rock' in which Israel's future Messiah could rest firmly upon.[58]

2 Samuel 1:10 *So I [the Amalekite] stood upon him [King Saul], and slew him, because I was sure that he could not live after that he was fallen: and I took the crown that was upon his head, and the bracelet that was on his arm, and have brought them hither unto my lord.* (KJV)

These leaders placed the crown upon Joash and gave him 'the testimony'. The Hebrew word for 'testimony' is 'edut,' which probably had something to do with the insignia of the king that represented his authority. Some have taken the 'bracelet' on King Saul's arm to be the form of the edut. Edut is synonymous with 'berit,' which means, 'covenant'.[59] A more standard interpretation is that the edut is the Torah scroll the king had hung upon his arm and he was required to have with him at all times.[60]

Psalm 2:6-8 *Yet have I set my king upon my holy hill of Zion. I will declare the decree: the LORD hath said unto me, Thou art my Son; this day have I begotten thee. Ask of me, and I shall give thee the heathen for thine inheritance, and the uttermost parts of the earth for thy possession.* (KJV)

The rabbis taught that Psalm 2 described Messianic times, but also was a literal reading of the time of David, and especially immediately following his coronation.[61] Many scholars view Psalm 2 as an ancient enthronement Psalm of the kings of Judah. God establishes His king in Zion and a 'decree' is declared. The 'decree' is the edut.[62] The receiving of the edut-decree makes the king the adopted son of God and in this Messianic Psalm promises Him dominion over all nations. The kings of Judah of the line of David were understood to be the 'adopted' sons of God.[63]

Next, king Joash was anointed. The Hebrew word for anointed is 'mashiach,' which is the same word for 'Messiah'. The anointed High Priests and Kings of ancient Judah were called 'mashiach'. The prophets were also called 'mashiach'. Yeshua, the 'Mashiach' fulfills all these roles of prophet, priest, and king. The anointing of the king represented his change in status to that of reigning monarch. The anointing of the king was also viewed as his sanctification [being set apart] and appointment.

Matthew 3:16-17 *And Jesus, when he was baptized, went up straightway out of the water: and, lo, the heavens were opened unto him, and he saw the Spirit of God descending like a dove, and lighting upon him: And lo a voice from heaven, saying, This is my beloved Son, in whom I am well pleased.* (KJV)

Matthew 17:5 *While he yet spake, behold, a bright cloud overshadowed them: and behold a voice out of the cloud, which said, This is my beloved Son, in whom I am well pleased; hear ye him.* (KJV)

Both at Yeshua's Immersion and Transfiguration a voice from heaven said, 'This is My Beloved Son'. Understood in its Hebraic context, the Father was stating to those who witnessed His Voice, that Yeshua was the Anointed One, the Mashiach [Messiah].

Next with the coronation of Joash the people present clapped their hands and said, 'God save the king'. This is the acclamation of the king. We have already seen this in Psalm 47, which is a coronation Psalm recited seven times at Rosh Hashana:

Psalm 47:1-2, 5-9 *O clap your hands, all ye people; shout unto God with the voice of triumph. For the LORD most high is terrible; he is a great King over all the earth...God is gone up with a shout [teurah], the LORD with the sound of a trumpet [shofar]. Sing praises to God, sing praises: sing praises unto our King, sing praises. For God is the King of all the earth: sing ye praises with understanding. God reigneth over the heathen: God sitteth upon the throne of his holiness. The princes of the people are gathered together, even the people of the God of Abraham: for the shields of the earth belong unto God: he is greatly exalted.* (KJV)

Those summoned at the resurrection of Rosh Hashana will give acclamation to the King as He has His coronation in 'Heaven'. In verses 6-7, the resurrected righteous will sing praises to the King [mentioned five times]. In verse 8 God sits on His Throne and reigns over the heathen meaning that many Gentile believers will be resurrected. These Gentiles are called 'the princes of the people... the people of the God of Abraham'. The Artscroll commentary on Tehillim [Psalms] translates 47:9, 'the nobles of the nations gathered, the nation of the God of Abraham'.

The rabbis identified these as the great nobles of the Gentile nations who follow in the footsteps of Abraham. The name Abraham is a contraction of the Hebrew phrase, 'Father of a multitude of nations'. Those Gentile nobles who follow in the way of Abraham are considered his descendants.[64] Those who believe and follow after Messiah Yeshua are Abraham' seed (Galatians 3:7).

1 Kings 1:47 *And moreover the king's servants came to bless our lord king David, saying, God make the name of Solomon better than* *thy name, and make his throne greater than thy throne. And the king bowed himself upon the bed.* (KJV)

As we have just seen, after the coronation the king is enthroned by sitting on his throne as Joash did in 2 Kings 11:19. It was at this point that the king began his rule as king on the 'Throne of the Lord'. Then, finally, after the king's ascension to the Throne, the highest officials of the kingdom come before him and do homage. These officials show forth their allegiance to the king and receive commissioning from him as to their roles in the kingdom.

In Pirqe Mashiah BhM 3:73-74 we learn of a rabbinic teaching of the resurrection occurring in proximity to the coronation of the Messiah. In this passage the Messiah is named Ephraim, which in rabbinic literature is just another name for Messiah ben Joseph, the suffering servant of Israel. Messiah ben Joseph in all accounts dies. But here He is being crowned as King Messiah. The implication is that God has resurrected Ephraim. From here the text continues with the resurrected Messiah bringing the Glad Tidings [Gospel] of resurrection to the righteous patriarchs of renown. Then at the very end of this text a parable is given that relates the resurrection with a wedding.[65]

In the book entitled <u>Entering the High Holy Days</u>, the author has a section detailing the prayers of the morning Shacherit service for Rosh Hashana, which he labels as 'A Coronation Ceremony'.[66] The theme of this service is the 'Kingship' of God. The first word spoken by the leader of the service is 'HaMelech,' which means 'The King.' The word 'melech' is the single word that stands out the entire service as it is repeatedly spoken.

If God is King, then why is this coronation service repeated every year at Rosh Hashana? It is a rehearsal for the coronation of the Messiah. The sages had always understood Rosh Hashana to be the day that the world [Adam] was created. After exactly six thousand years, the Messianic Kingdom was to begin on the 'Day of Coronation'.[67]

<u>**Luke 19:37-38**</u> *And when he [Yeshua] was come nigh, even now at the descent of the mount of Olives, the whole multitude of the*

disciples began to rejoice and praise God with a loud voice for all the mighty works that they had seen; Saying, Blessed be the <u>King</u> that cometh in the name of the Lord: peace in heaven, and glory in the highest. (KJV)

As Yeshua rode a donkey into Jerusalem, those that believed in Him as the fulfillment of the promised Messiah of Scripture broke out in praise to God. They said, 'Blessed be the King that cometh in the name of the Lord'. But in order for the Messiah to be King He must first have a coronation. Yeshua lived His life as 'The Prophet,' resurrected as 'The High Priest,' and will become 'The King' at His coronation.

<u>Daniel 7:9-10, 13-14</u> *I beheld till the thrones were cast down, and the Ancient of days did sit, whose garment was white as snow, and the hair of his head like the pure wool: <u>his throne</u> was like the fiery flame, and his wheels as burning fire. A fiery stream issued and came forth from before him: thousand thousands ministered unto him, and ten thousand times ten thousand stood before him: <u>the judgment was set, and the books were opened</u>...I saw in the night visions, and, behold, one like <u>the Son of man</u> came with the clouds of heaven, and came to the Ancient of days, and they brought him near before him. And <u>there was given him dominion, and glory, and a kingdom, that all people, nations, and languages, should serve him: his dominion is an everlasting dominion</u>, which shall not pass away, and his kingdom that which shall not be destroyed.* (KJV)

In Daniel 7 we clearly see a picture of the Day of Judgment [Yom haDin] and the fact that the 'books were opened' strongly suggests it is Rosh Hashana symbolism. One of the Hebraic titles for the Messiah is the Son of Man. The Son of Man receives His Kingdom at this stage. The Coronation and Kingdom are received in Heaven, not on earth. In fact, the first seven years of His Kingdom are in Heaven while the Birth Pangs of the Messiah are occurring on earth. After the seven years of Birth Pangs, King Messiah will establish His Heavenly Kingdom on earth. It needs to be understood that

Messiah's Kingdom is everlasting and will never end. Every earthly kingdom has come and faded into the past.

2 Samuel 2:3-4, 11 *And his men that were with him did David bring up, every man with his household: and they dwelt in the cities of Hebron. And the men of Judah came, and there they anointed David king over the house of Judah...And the time that David was king in Hebron over the house of Judah was seven years and six months.* (KJV)

2 Kings 2:11 *And the days that David reigned over Israel were forty years: seven years reigned he in Hebron, and thirty and three years reigned he in Jerusalem.* (KJV)

2 Samuel 5:1-5 *Then came all the tribes of Israel to David unto Hebron, and spake, saying, Behold, we are thy bone and thy flesh. Also in time past, when Saul was king over us, thou wast he that leddest out and broughtest in Israel: and the LORD said to thee, Thou shalt feed my people Israel, and thou shalt be a captain over Israel. So all the elders of Israel came to the king to Hebron; and king David made a league with them in Hebron before the LORD: and they anointed David king over Israel. David was thirty years old when he began to reign, and he reigned forty years. In Hebron he reigned over Judah seven years and six months: and in Jerusalem he reigned thirty and three years over all Israel and Judah.* (KJV)

    The Scripture tells us that David reigned forty years as King. In actuality it tells us he reigned for exactly forty years and six months. We are told that David first reigned as king of Judah only from Hebron for exactly seven and a half years. But 2 Kings 2:11 rounds it down to seven years. What does this mean symbolically?

    Some ancient Jewish thought ascribed the location of Hebron near Paradise and Hebron became one of several synonyms for Heaven or Paradise.[68] It was believed that the resurrection would start with Abraham who was buried in Hebron. In other words, David was king over Judah from Hebron [Paradise] his first seven years. Afterward, he reigned over Judah and all Israel from earthly

Jerusalem. Yeshua, Who is the Son of David, will be seated upon the throne as King in Heaven [spiritual Hebron]. He will rule 'Judah' for seven years [while the seven years of Birth Pangs are occurring on earth]. After seven years in 'Heaven,' the anointed King Messiah will come to earthly Jerusalem. From there the Messianic Kingdom will expand to include not only Judah, but also Israel. Israel and Judah will become one in the Messianic Kingdom under Messiah's reign.

Revelation 4:1-2 *After this I looked, and, behold, a door was opened in heaven [Yom haDin - Rosh Hashana]: and the first voice [Tuerah] which I heard was as it were of a trumpet [Shofar] talking with me; which said, Come up hither, and I will shew thee things which must be hereafter. And immediately I was in the spirit [Resurrection]: and, behold, a throne [Coronation] was set in heaven, and one sat on the throne.* (KJV)

John was given a glimpse of the Coronation of Messiah on the New Moon of Rosh Hashana after six thousand years in Revelation 4 & 5. The 'door opened in heaven' can only represent Rosh Hashana in Hebraic thought. The Voice is symbolic of the Day of the Awakening Shout, and the Trumpet [Shofar] is symbolic of the Day of the Awakening Blast. There is also resurrection symbolism tied to John being in the 'spirit'. There was a 'throne' set in heaven, which gives us the setting for the Coronation of the Messiah.

Revelation 4 & 5 represent Yeshua's coronation at Rosh Hashana. The Yom haDin judgment of the believers associated with Rosh Hashana is described in Revelation 2 & 3 with the seven churches. We will study them in the next chapter of this book. Revelation 6 through 19 represents the seven years of Birth Pangs on the earth. The end of Revelation 19 describes the return of Messiah and the resurrected believers after seven years in the 'Heavenly' Chadar [Wedding Chamber]. The Beast and False Prophet are cast alive into the Lake of Fire. Revelation 20 describes the remainder of the final Millennium ruled by Messiah and then the Final Judgment of all those who did not turn to God. Revelation 20 & 21 describe the new heaven and earth apart from any sin and all those present in glorified bodies for eternity.

Revelation 4:8 *And the four beasts had each of them six wings about him; and they were full of eyes within: and they rest not day and night, saying, Holy, holy, holy [Kedushah], Lord God Almighty, which was, and is, and is to come.* (KJV)

Isaiah 6:1-5 *In the year that king Uzziah died I saw also the Lord sitting upon a throne, high and lifted up, and his train filled the temple. Above it stood the seraphims: each one had six wings; with twain he covered his face, and with twain he covered his feet, and with twain he did fly. And one cried unto another, and said, Holy, holy, holy, is the LORD of hosts: the whole earth is full of his glory. And the posts of the door [Rosh Hashana] moved at the voice of him that cried, and the house was filled with smoke. Then said I, Woe is me! for I am undone; because I am a man of unclean lips, and I dwell in the midst of a people of unclean lips: for mine eyes have seen the King, the LORD of hosts.* (KJV)

The Four Beasts in Heaven say the Kedushah Prayer [or Sanctification of God's Name], which is based upon Isaiah 6. Isaiah saw the Lord as King, putting this in a Rosh Hashana context. The four beasts in Revelation appear to be related with the seraphim. In Isaiah's account 'the posts of the door moved' at the seraphim's voice. This is equivalent to the door being opened and the Teurah shout of Rosh Hashana.

The Kedushah prayer in conjunction with 'Kedushat ha-Yom (Sanctification of the Day),' are of particular importance on Rosh Hashana.[69] The several paragraphs of the Kedushah are clearly 'kingship' prayers. They speak of Israel's return to the Land and the kingship of David and Messiah. The prayers include the righteous rejoicing over the removal of the wicked when God reigns from Jerusalem. These prayers are also recited on Yom Kippur, but they were originally written for Rosh Hashana.[70]

Isaiah 5:16 *But the LORD of hosts shall be exalted in judgment, and God that is holy shall be sanctified in righteousness.* (KJV)

The final verse of the Kedushah is Isaiah 5:16. The concept of judgment is linked to the Holiness of God. Judgment is a primary theme of Rosh Hashana.

The Kedushat ha-Yom Prayer is composed of three sections. The first division refers to Rosh Hashana as Yom Teurah, or the day of the sounding of the shofar. The second section asks God to remember Israel by sending the Messiah and the rebuilding of the Temple. Rosh Hashana is referred to as Yom ha-Zikkaron, the Day of Remembrance. Although this prayer is recited on all the festivals, there is strong support that it was originally written for Rosh Hashana. The last part of this second section of 'Sanctification of the Day' reads:

> Remember us, O Lord our God, on this day [Rosh Hashana] for good.
> Visit us on this day [Rosh Hashana] for blessing.
> Save us upon this day [Rosh Hashana] for life.
> Have mercy, pity and show grace unto us according to Your word of salvation.[71]

The final section of Kedushat ha-Yom is only recited on Rosh Hashana. The motif is God's kingship over the entire world and universe. This prayer ends with, 'King of the entire world who sanctifies Israel and the Day of Remembrance'. This phrase appears in every Rosh Hashana service and is a hallmark of the liturgy.[72]

Revelation 5:1, 5 *And I saw in the right hand of him that sat on the throne a book written within and on the backside, sealed with seven seals... And one of the elders saith unto me, Weep not: behold, the Lion of the tribe of Juda, the Root of David, hath prevailed to open the book, and to loose the seven seals thereof.* (KJV)

In Revelation 4, the Ancient of Days [Father] was seated on the throne very similarly to Daniel 7. Revelation 5 represents the

'Heavenly' coronation of the Messiah. The scroll sealed with seven seals represents the edut, the insignia and authority of Yeshua as King. The Lion of the tribe of Judah and the Root of David are symbolic of Messiah. Later in Revelation 5 the Lion is described as a Lamb. When Joash received the edut his crown was already placed upon his head.

Revelation 5:8-9 *And when he had taken the book, the four beasts and four and twenty elders fell down before the Lamb, having every one of them harps, and golden vials full of odours, which are the prayers of saints. And they sung a new song, saying, Thou art worthy to take the book, and to open the seals thereof: for thou wast slain, and hast redeemed us to God by thy blood out of every kindred, and tongue, and people, and nation;* (KJV)

When the Lamb-Messiah takes the scroll [edut], the four beasts and twenty-four Elders fell down in homage before Him. They all had 'harps' and 'sung a new song'. The implication is that the Lamb already has his crown on his head. Revelation 14:14 describes the Son of Man with a golden crown on his head.

Psalm 96:1 *O sing unto the LORD a new song: sing unto the LORD, all the earth.* (KJV)

Psalm 98:1 *O sing unto the LORD a new song; for he hath done marvellous things: his right hand [Messianic term], and his holy arm [Messianic term], hath gotten him the victory.* (KJV)

Zechariah 14:9 *And the LORD shall be king over all the earth: in that day [Day of the Lord] shall there be one LORD, and his name one.* (KJV)

When we study the Biblical understanding of the harps and the new song, it leads us back to the Messiah and His Kingdom. The Sages viewed the 'New Song' as referring to the time of the Messianic Kingdom.[73] In others words the 'New Song' relates directly to the Sabbath of God (The Day of the Lord/Millennium).

The 'new song' can only be sung after the Messiah has become King over all the earth. When does this happen? It happens on Rosh Hashana after the six thousand years of the Olam Hazeh [This Present Age] has been fulfilled. Notice that Revelation 4 & 5 represents the coronation of Yeshua HaMashiach as King. It is then that we hear about the four beasts and twenty-four elders singing a 'new song' before the throne.

Psalm 98:4-6 *Make a joyful noise unto the LORD, <u>all the earth</u>: make a loud noise, and rejoice, and sing praise. Sing unto the LORD with the harp; with the harp, and the voice of a psalm. With trumpets (shofarot) and sound of cornet make a joyful noise before <u>the LORD, the King</u>.* (KJV)

In Psalm 98:4-6 we have another reference to 'all the earth' and 'the Lord, the King'. Once again we have this reference of 'singing' to the Lord related to the Messiah being crowned King. Yeshua is crowned King on Rosh Hashana at His coronation in Heaven with the sounding of the shofarot [rams' horns].

Psalm 92:1 *A Psalm or Song for the sabbath day . It is a good thing to give thanks unto the LORD, and to sing praises unto thy name, O most High:* (KJV)

God specifically designated Psalm 92 as a 'Song for the Sabbath Day'. In most English translations of the Hebrew Scriptures this phrase is not placed as Scripture. This is an error in the translations. However, many English versions such as the KJV do place the title 'Song for the Sabbath Day' before the Psalm. The Jews understand that verse one begins with 'A Song for the Sabbath Day'. It is in the Hebrew and was placed there by Divine Design. Therefore we can have no doubt that God intended that Psalm 92 be a 'Song for the Sabbath Day'.

The singing of Psalm 92 on the Sabbath predates the first century and was observed during the time of Yeshua. In Temple times Psalm 92 was sung by the Levites as part of their Sabbath prayers. The Mishnah (Tamid 7:4) clearly states that Psalm 92 refers to the 'Day of Everlasting Sabbath' of the Messianic Kingdom and not the weekly Sabbath.[74] The message of this Psalm is highly relevant to the seventh millennium.

The days of the week are symbolic of successive stages in God's Will developing on earth. The final stage, the seventh day Sabbath is Kingship. It is during the final millennium that God's glory becomes fully manifest on the earth. This final millennium is symbolic of the Sabbath. The ultimate harmony of creation with God is expressed through 'song'. Song is Kingship. David, the sweet singer of Israel, sung as to express his royal mission for making known the harmony of God's work.[75]

It is fitting that Psalm 92 was dedicated to the Tribe of Judah.[76] In the Messianic era the 'Lion of the Tribe of Judah, the Root of David/Messiah' (Revelation 5:5) will reign as King of the earth from Jerusalem to bring peace to the world.

Psalm 92:2-4 *To show forth thy lovingkindness in the morning, and thy faithfulness every night, Upon an instrument ten strings (Hebrew - Assor ע ש ו ר), and upon the psaltery (Hebrew - Neival נ ב ל); upon the harp (Hebrew - Kinor כ נ ו ר) with a solemn sound. For thou, LORD, hast made me glad through thy work: I will triumph in the works of thy hands.* (KJV)

Psalm 33:2-3 *Praise the LORD with harp (Hebrew - Kinor): sing unto him with the psaltery and an instrument of ten strings (Hebrew - Neival Assor). Sing unto him a new song; play skilfully with a loud noise.* (KJV)

Psalm 92:3 speaks of three different Hebrew instruments that anciently accompanied singing praises to the Lord. They are the 'Assor, Neival, and the Kinor,' which are all types of harps. These instruments to the Sages had prophetic implications. The Assor was a ten-stringed instrument that produced ten different tones. The Kinor used in the Temple had seven strings, but the rabbis taught that it would have eight strings during the Messianic Kingdom. Then in the Olam Haba [World To Come], when it is completely Sabbath, the sages said it would have ten strings.[77]

In Psalm 33:2, we find that the Assor and the Neival is a single instrument. It is also in this psalm that we read about the 'New Song,' which is found seven times in the Old Testament. It is believed that all ten notes exist now but that the finite human body can only perceive eight of them (the octive). In the Olam Haba, the state of the resurrected, the righteous will be able to enjoy the ten note musical scale.

In Revelation 5 we are told of twenty-four Elders that are before the Lamb (the Messiah) who have harps. We know that the harp here is the ten-stringed Kinor of the future because they 'sung a new song'. The entire chapter is easily seen to be taking place in 'Heaven'. The Messianic Kingdom, the seventh millennium has begun. But the righteous who are resurrected to Messiah's coronation in 'Heaven' will also be in the Olam Haba [World To Come] and able to sing the new song unto the Lord.

Revelation 5:10 *And hast made us unto our God kings and priests: and we shall reign on the earth.* (KJV)

The resurrected believers will be as 'kings and priests' in the service of the Lord. In the Talmud [Gittin 52a] the Rabbis are called 'Kings'. They were nobility without scepters and armies, only having the authority of God's Word. These resurrected believers in Revelation 5 are the nobles who will receive their assignment and responsibility in King Messiah's Kingdom.

The Ten Days of Awe [Penitence]

Now we will turn our attention toward the Days of Awe leading to Yom Kippur. These ten Days of Penitence from Rosh Hashana to Yom Kippur have existed as a coherent unit since the third century B.C.E.[78] 'The Ten Days of Awe,' or literally 'The Awesome Days' (Yamim Noraim) are also known as 'Aseret Yemai Teshuvah,' the 'Ten Days of Repentance.' These days are even known as 'bein keseh L'asor,' which means 'between concealments' of Rosh Hashanah and Yom Kippur. These names serve to remind us that we are suspended between two days of judgement: Rosh Hashanah, when our verdict is inscribed, and Yom HaKippurim (Yom Kippur) when our judgement is sealed.

Usually the fate of those 'in-between' sinners are said to be in suspension until the judgment of Yom Kippur. A literal reading of the Talmud's phrase 'remain suspended' can be interpreted as 'hang and stand'. These in-between are actually sentenced to death on Rosh Hashana. Since they are not completely wicked, their sentence is postponed until Yom Kippur. If they repent during the Ten Days of Awe they will be found worthy.[79]

Rosh Hashana consists of two days, Tishri 1 & 2, and Yom Kippur is Tishri 10. Although all ten days from Tishri 1 through Tishri 10 are known as the Awesome Days, there are exactly seven days (Tishri 3-9), between Rosh Hashana and Yom Kippur. During these seven days the shofar is blasted as it was during the month of Elul leading up to Rosh Hashana. Also, Psalm 27 is recited every day.[80]

Hosea 14:1-9 O *Israel, return [Hebrew - Shuvah] unto the LORD thy God; for thou hast fallen by thine iniquity. Take with you words, and turn to the LORD: say unto him, Take away all iniquity, and receive us graciously: so will we render the calves of our lips. Asshur shall not save us; we will not ride upon horses: neither will we say any more to the work of our hands, Ye are our gods: for in thee the fatherless findeth mercy. I will heal their backsliding, I will love them freely: for mine anger is turned away from him. I will be as the dew unto Israel: he shall grow as the lily, and cast forth his roots as Lebanon. His branches shall spread, and his beauty shall be as the olive tree, and his smell as Lebanon. They that dwell under his shadow shall return; they shall revive as the corn, and grow as the vine: the scent thereof shall be as the wine of Lebanon. Ephraim shall say, What have I to do any more with idols? I have heard him, and observed him: I am like a green fir tree. From me is thy fruit found. Who is wise, and he shall understand these things? prudent, and he shall know them? for the ways of the LORD are right, and the just shall walk in them: but the transgressors shall fall therein.* (KJV)

The weekly Sabbath that occurs between Rosh Hashana [Tishri 1 & 2] and Yom Kippur [Tishri 10] during the Days of Awe [Tishri

3-9] is called Shabbat Shuvah, the Sabbath of Return. Always on this day the Haftarah reading is Hosea 14:1-9 [14:2-10 in a Hebrew Tanach]. In later Jewish literature, this Sabbath was called Shabbat Teshuvah, the Sabbath of Repentance.

Micah 7:18-20 *Who is a God like unto thee, that pardoneth iniquity, and passeth by the transgression of the remnant of his heritage? he retaineth not his anger for ever, because he delighteth in mercy. He will turn again, he will have compassion upon us; he will subdue our iniquities; and thou wilt cast all their sins into the depths of the sea. Thou wilt perform the truth to Jacob, and the mercy to Abraham, which thou hast sworn unto our fathers from the days of old.* (KJV)

Joel 2:15-27 *Blow the trumpet [shofar] in Zion, sanctify a fast, call a solemn assembly: Gather the people, sanctify the congregation, assemble the elders, gather the children, and those that suck the breasts: let the bridegroom go forth of his chamber, and the bride out of her closet. Let the priests, the ministers of the LORD, weep between the porch and the altar, and let them say, Spare thy people, O LORD, and give not thine heritage to reproach, that the heathen should rule over them: wherefore should they say among the people, Where is their God? Then will the LORD be jealous for his land, and pity his people. Yea, the LORD will answer and say unto his people, Behold, I will send you corn, and wine, and oil, and ye shall be satisfied therewith: and I will no more make you a reproach among the heathen: But I will remove far off from you the northern army, and will drive him into a land barren and desolate, with his face toward the east sea, and his hinder part toward the utmost sea, and his stink shall come up, and his ill savour shall come up, because he hath done great things.   Fear not, O land; be glad and rejoice: for the LORD will do great things. Be not afraid, ye beasts of the field: for the pastures of the wilderness do spring, for the tree beareth her fruit, the fig tree and the vine do yield their strength. Be glad then, ye children of Zion, and rejoice in the LORD your God: for he hath given you the former rain moderately, and he will cause to come down for you the rain, the former rain, and the latter rain in the first month. And the floors shall be full of wheat, and the fats shall* *overflow with wine and oil. And I will restore to you the years that the locust hath eaten, the cankerworm, and the caterpiller, and the palmerworm, my great army which I sent among you. And ye shall eat in plenty, and be satisfied, and praise the name of the LORD your God, that hath dealt wondrously with you: and my people shall never be ashamed. And ye shall know that I am in the midst of Israel, and that I am the LORD your God, and none else: and my people shall never be ashamed.* (KJV)

Usually the Haftarah consists of one reading, but the rabbis of old added Micah 7:18-20 and Joel 2:15-17 to the readings. The message of these three readings on Shabbat Shuvah is repent and prepare for the shofar connected to Yom Kippur, the fast day sanctified by God. We will have more to say regarding Joel's portion when we look at the liturgy associated with Yom Kippur.[81]

Isaiah 55:6 *Seek ye the LORD while he may be found, call ye upon him while he is near*: (KJV)

The Talmud and many other rabbis connected Isaiah 55:6 with the Ten Days of Pentinence between Rosh Hashana and Yom Kippur.[82] It was during this time that the repentant could find God. God was seen as being nearer to His creation during this period.

Yom Kippur

Leviticus 23:26-32 *And the LORD spake unto Moses, saying, Also on the tenth day of this seventh month there shall be a day of atonement: it shall be an holy convocation unto you; and ye shall afflict your souls, and offer an offering made by fire unto the LORD. And ye shall do no work in that same day: for it is a day of atonement, to make an atonement for you before the LORD your God. For whatsoever soul it be that shall not be afflicted in that same day, he shall be cut off from among his people. And whatsoever soul it be that doeth any work in that same day, the same soul will I destroy from among his people. Ye shall do no manner of work: it shall be a statute for ever throughout your generations in all your dwellings. It shall be* *unto you a sabbath of rest, and ye shall afflict your souls: in the ninth day of the month at even, from even unto even, shall ye celebrate your sabbath.* (KJV)

We have already discussed the annual rehearsal of the judgement at Rosh Hashana when the righteous are sealed for life and the totally wicked are inscribed for death. But the in-between sinners are allotted Ten Days until Yom Kippur to repent in order that their verdict will be changed to 'life' instead of death. Yom Kippur is the day that all verdicts are 'sealed' for the coming year.

Numbers 28:11-15 *And in the beginnings of your months [Rosh Chodesh] ye shall offer a burnt offering unto the LORD; two young bullocks, and one ram, seven lambs of the first year without spot; And three tenth deals of flour for a meat offering, mingled with oil, for one bullock; and two tenth deals of flour for a meat offering, mingled with oil, for one ram; And a several tenth deal of flour mingled with oil for a meat offering unto one lamb; for a burnt offering of a sweet savour, a sacrifice made by fire unto the LORD. And their drink offerings shall be half an hin of wine unto a bullock, and the third part of an hin unto a ram, and a fourth part of an hin unto a lamb: this is the burnt offering of every month throughout the months of the year. And one kid of the goats for a sin offering unto the LORD shall be offered, beside the continual burnt offering, and his drink offering.* (KJV)

Numbers 29:1-6 *And in the seventh month, on the first day of the month [Rosh Hashana], ye shall have an holy convocation; ye shall do no servile work: it is a day of blowing the trumpets unto you. And ye shall offer a burnt offering for a sweet savour unto the LORD; one young bullock, one ram, and seven lambs of the first year without blemish: And their meat offering shall be of flour mingled with oil, three tenth deals for a bullock, and two tenth deals for a ram, And one tenth deal for one lamb, throughout the seven lambs: And one kid of the goats for a sin offering, to make an atonement for you: Beside the burnt offering of the month, and his meat offering, and the daily burnt offering, and his meat offering, and their drink offer-*

ings, according unto their manner, for a sweet savour, a sacrifice made by fire unto the LORD. (KJV)

Numbers 29:7-11 *And ye shall have on the tenth day of this seventh month [Yom Kippur] an holy convocation; and ye shall afflict your souls: ye shall not do any work therein: But ye shall offer a burnt offering unto the LORD for a sweet savour; one young bullock, one ram, and seven lambs of the first year; they shall be unto you without blemish: And their meat offering shall be of flour mingled with oil, three tenth deals to a bullock, and two tenth deals to one ram, A several tenth deal for one lamb, throughout the seven lambs: One kid of the goats for a sin offering; beside the sin offering of atonement, and the continual burnt offering, and the meat offering of it, and their drink offerings.* (KJV)

There is a 'sacrificial' connection that links the Ten Days of Awe together beginning with Rosh Hashana and ending with Yom Kippur. The Scripture declares that for all New Moon ceremonies and the major festivals that a goat must be sacrificed as a sin offering in the Temple. As we would expect Numbers 29 details that on Rosh Hashana [New Moon] a sin offering goat was to be sacrificed. Therefore, a sin offering goat was offered at the commencement of the Days of Awe on Rosh Hashana and at the end on Yom Kippur for atonement.

The Rosh Chodesh Musaf prayer service states that the New Moon is 'z'man kapara,' a 'time of atonement'.[83] The New Moon ceremonies appear to be rehearsals for a wedding, and specifically the wedding associated with Rosh Chodesh Rosh Hashana. Rosh Chodesh is also known as Yom Kippur Katan, a miniature Day of Atonement.[84] This later custom involved fasting the day before the New Moon and praying penitential prayers resembling Yom Kippur liturgy in preparation for receiving the new moon.

Prophetically, we have established that the righteous will be resurrected and inscribed in the Book of Life on Rosh Hashana after six thousand years from Adam's creation. Rosh Hashana is the first two days of the Ten Awesome Days and Yom Kippur is the last. There are exactly seven days in-between which are prophetically symbolic of the seven years of Birth Pangs on the earth while the Bride and Groom reside in the 'heavenly' Chadar (wedding chamber). Therefore, prophetically, Yom Kippur represents the end of the Birth Pangs and the coming of the Messiah to set up His Kingdom on earth.

Joel 2:15-18 *Blow the trumpet [SHOFAR (HAGADOL)] in Zion, sanctify a fast [YOM KIPPUR], call a solemn assembly: Gather the people, sanctify the congregation, assemble the elders, gather the children, and those that suck the breasts: let the bridegroom [MESSIAH] go forth of his chamber [CHADAR] , and the bride out of her closet [CHUPPAH-CANOPY]. Let the priests, the ministers of the LORD, weep between the porch and the altar, and let them say, Spare thy people, O LORD, and give not thine heritage to reproach, that the heathen should rule over them: wherefore should they say among the people, Where is their God? Then will the LORD be jealous for his land, and pity his people.* (KJV)

The bride and groom will go to the wedding chamber, or 'Chadar' in Hebrew, where the marriage will be consummated. They will stay in that wedding chamber for seven days, or a week. At the end of the seven days, the bride and groom will come out from the wedding chamber. This can be seen in Joel 2:16 after the Shofar HaGadol, the Great Shofar is blown on Yom Kippur. The word 'week' in Hebrew is 'shavuah.' It means a 'seven'. It can mean seven days or seven years. In context, shavuah here represents seven years in the Chadar (wedding chamber) in Heaven while there are seven years of the Birth Pangs of the Messiah on the earth.

We had discussed that the entire month of Elul preceding Rosh Hashana plus the Ten Days of Awe equaled a forty-day period of Teshuvah (Repentance). What started on Elul 1 ends on Tishri 10, Yom Kippur. Jewish Midrashim state that Moses was up on Mt. Sinai another time during the season of Teshuvah. Moses descended the last time on Yom Kippur having found favor from the God for Israel.[85] As Moses 'second coming' was traditionally on Yom Kippur, Jews believe that Messiah is coming on Yom Kippur. For believers, this would represent Yeshua's second coming.

Earlier in this chapter we learned that all verdicts regarding the in-between sinners not entirely inscribed in the Book of Life or Book of Death at Rosh Hashana, will be sealed on Yom Kippur, the final of the two days of Judgment [Yom haDin]. Those who repent during the Days of Awe will be inscribed in the Book of Life and those who do not will be inscribed in the Book of Death on Yom Kippur. Nachmanides said, 'Rosh Hashanah is a day of judgment with mercy and Yom Kippur is a day of mercy with judgment'.[86]

If a Jew only attends the synagogue once in a year, more than likely it is the evening service of Yom Kippur popularly known as Kol Nidre. This is the only evening service that Jews wear their tallits. It is a time of forgiveness and unity among the people. There is a declaration at the outset of the service granting permission to pray with transgressors. The barriers between the righteous and sinners are annulled.[87]

Kol Nidre is chanted to a melody that brings one's emotions to the forefront as they approach God on the most solemn day of the year. The participant first offers contriteness and then seeks the forgiveness and mercy of God. Finally, he confesses a belief that God will pardon him and inscribe him in the Book of Life.[88]

In all there are five services on Yom Kippur. They are in order from evening to daytime, and to evening again: Ma'ariv, Shacherit, Musaf, Minchah, and Ne'ilah. There are two sections of prayers similar in each of these services called Selihot [Forgiveness] and Vidui [Confession].

Elsewhere we mentioned that on Rosh Hashana the 'Gates/Doors' of Heaven are opened, but on Yom Kippur they are symbolically closed. During the course of the Yom Kippur services, references to the Gates being opened are found in the liturgy. In one place they are referred to as the 'Gates of Mercy,' which appear to be a reference to the Eastern Gate of the Temple with the same name. It was a tradition that the Messiah would enter Jerusalem through this Gate.[89]

The last service of Yom Kippur, called Ne'ilah, means 'closing/locking'. The authorities are agreed that Ne'ilah is in reference to 'Ne'ilat she'arim,' meaning 'the closing of the gates'. Most commentators refer to the closing of the 'heavenly' gates instead of the gates of the Temple.[90] However, the Temple gates are symbolic of the Heavenly Gates. From Rosh Hashana to Yom Kippur the liturgy describes the pleas of the people to 'inscribe us in the Book of Life'. At Yom Kippur during the Ne'ilah prayers the focus has changed to 'Seal us in the Book of Life'. The 'Heavenly' Gates being closed represents the verdicts of the in-between sinners as becoming 'sealed'.

Leviticus 25:8-13 *And thou shalt number seven sabbaths of years unto thee, seven times seven years; and the space of the seven sabbaths of years shall be unto thee forty and nine years. Then shalt thou cause the trumpet [shofar] of the jubile [teurah] to sound on the tenth day of the seventh month, in the day of atonement shall ye make the trumpet [shofar] sound throughout all your land. And ye shall hallow the fiftieth year, and proclaim liberty throughout all the land unto all the inhabitants thereof: it shall be a jubile [Yovel] unto you; and ye shall return every man unto his possession, and ye shall return every man unto his family. A jubile [Yovel] shall that fiftieth year be unto you: ye shall not sow, neither reap that which groweth of itself in it, nor gather the grapes in it of thy vine undressed. For it is the jubile; it shall be holy unto you: ye shall eat the increase thereof out of the field. In the year of this jubile ye shall return every man unto his possession.* (KJV)

At the conclusion of Yom Kippur a shofar is blasted as a memorial of the Jubilee.[91] This is known as the Great Shofar or Shofar haGadol. Jewish tradition states when Moses went up Mt. Sinai again on the New Moon of Elul to receive the second tablets of stones, a shofar was blown. When he came down with them forty days later on Tishri 10, Yom Kippur, another shofar was blown.[92]

After the shofar is blasted at the end of Yom Kippur, it is the custom for those outside Israel to say, 'Next year in Jerusalem!' One custom is to repeat it three times to remember the exile in Egypt, Babylon, and Rome. Also, at the end of the Passover Seder, 'Next year in Jerusalem,' is exclaimed. These are the only two times during the year this is stated in the Jewish liturgy. The Talmud alludes to this commenting that Israel was first redeemed in Nisan [Passover] and will also be redeemed in Tishri [Yom Kippur] (Talmud - Rosh Hashana 11a).[93]

On another level the shofar blast at Yom Kippur is connected to the shofar blast of Rosh Hashana. The shofar of Rosh Hashana announces that the 'Heavenly' gates are open and the blast at Yom Kippur announces that the gates are closed. The Hebrew word for 'jubilee' in Leviticus 25:9 is the same 'teurah,' that is used Scripturally of Rosh Hashana (Yom Teurah), the Day of the Awakening Blast or Shout. But in verses 11-13 the Hebrew word for 'jubilee' is 'Yovel,' which means 'ram' or 'ram's horn (shofar)'.

The concept of Yovel (Jubilee) is the proclamation of liberty throughout the land. All slaves become free and all people return to their clans and possessions. When the Messiah returns on Yom Kippur, He will proclaim the Yovel. Interestingly, the background of the Jubilee Year is tied to a new King beginning to reign from his throne. Remember that Yeshua is crowned 'King' in 'Heaven' with the presence of the nobles. We saw references to the 'Heavenly' Throne in Revelation 4 & 5. But after seven years in the wedding chamber [while the seven years of Birth Pangs are occurring on earth], Messiah and His Bride [the nobles] return to earth and He establishes His reign over all Israel on the 'throne' of Jerusalem. The Messiah will come to Jerusalem as King on Yom Kippur and set up His Kingdom. He will proclaim a 'Release' or 'Liberty' to His People. The shofar will be blown and all Israel can rightfully return to the Land.[94]

Ezekiel 43:4 *And the glory of the LORD came into the house by the way of the gate whose prospect is toward the east.* (KJV)

In his vision Ezekiel saw 'the glory of the Lord' come into the Third and final Temple in Jerusalem through the Eastern Gate. 'The Glory of the Lord' is an allusion to the Messiah. East of the Temple is the well-known Mount of Olives.

Zechariah 14:4-9 *And his feet shall stand in that day upon the mount of Olives, which is before Jerusalem on the east, and the mount of Olives shall cleave in the midst thereof toward the east and* *toward the west, and there shall be a very great valley; and half of the mountain shall remove toward the north, and half of it toward the south. And ye shall flee to the valley of the mountains; for the valley of the mountains shall reach unto Azal: yea, ye shall flee, like as ye fled from before the earthquake in the days of Uzziah king of Judah: and the LORD my God shall come, and all the saints with thee. And it shall come to pass in that day [Day of the Lord], that the light shall not be clear, nor dark: But it shall be one day which shall be known to the LORD, not day, nor night: but it shall come to pass, that at evening time it shall be light. And it shall be in that day, that living waters shall go out from Jerusalem; half of them toward the former sea, and half of them toward the hinder sea: in summer and in winter shall it be. And the LORD shall be king over all the earth: in that day shall there be one LORD, and his name one.* (KJV)

Judaism understands Zechariah's prophecy as alluding to the Messiah who will come to Jerusalem via the Mount of Olives to bring the final redemption of the Kingdom.[95] Notice that after the Messiah splits the mountain that the people will recognize that God is King over all the earth. The Talmud in Rosh Hashana 2.4 calls the Mount of Olives 'Har HaMashiach,' which means 'The Mountain of Messiah/Anointed One'.

Acts 1:6-12 *When they therefore were come together, they asked of him, saying, Lord, wilt thou at this time restore again the kingdom to Israel? And he said unto them, It is not for you to know the times or the seasons, which the Father hath put in his own power. But ye shall receive power, after that the Holy Ghost is come upon you: and ye shall be witnesses unto me both in Jerusalem, and in all Judaea, and in Samaria, and unto the uttermost part of the earth. And when he had spoken these things, while they beheld, he was taken up; and a cloud received him out of their sight. And while they looked sted-fastly toward heaven as he went up, behold, two men stood by them in white apparel; Which also said, Ye men of Galilee, why stand ye gazing up into heaven? this same Jesus, which is taken up from you into heaven, shall so come in like manner as ye have seen him go into* *heaven. Then returned they unto Jerusalem from <u>the mount called</u> <u>Olivet</u>, which is from Jerusalem a sabbath day's journey.* (KJV)

Yeshua had gathered His disciples one last time upon the Mount of Olives when they asked Him if He would now restore the kingdom of Israel. Yeshua told them that it was not for them to currently know the 'times and seasons,' a definite reference to 'appointed times' and 'festivals'. Yeshua ascended from them into 'Heaven' from the Mount of Olives. Two angelic witnesses appeared and told the disciples that Yeshua would return in like manner. In other words, Yeshua will set up His Kingdom by returning to this same spot on the Mount of Olives, splitting it in two at the appointed 'time and season' of Yom Kippur fulfilling Zechariah 14.

Isaiah 26:1, 2, 17-21 *In that day [Day of the Lord] shall this song be sung in the land of Judah; We have a strong city; salvation will God appoint for walls and bulwarks. Open ye the gates [Rosh Hashana], that the righteous nation which keepeth the truth may enter in...Like as a woman with child, that draweth near the time of her delivery, is in pain, and crieth out in her pangs [Birth Pangs of Messiah]; so have we been in thy sight, O LORD. We have been with child, we have been in pain, we have as it were brought forth wind; we have not wrought any deliverance in the earth; neither have the inhabitants of the world fallen. Thy dead men shall live, together with my dead body shall they arise [Last Shofar - Rosh Hashana]. Awake [Rosh Hashana] and sing, ye that dwell in dust: for thy dew is as the dew of herbs, and the earth shall cast out the dead. Come, my people, enter thou into thy chambers [Chadar - Wedding Chamber], and shut thy doors about thee: hide thyself [in the Heavenly Chadar] as it were for a little moment, until the indignation [Birth Pangs] be overpast. For, behold, the LORD cometh out of his place to punish the inhabitants of the earth for their iniquity: the earth also shall disclose her blood, and shall no more cover her slain.* (KJV)

Isaiah 27:1, 12, 13 *In that day [Day of the Lord] the LORD with his sore and great and strong sword shall punish leviathan [Name for False Messiah] the piercing serpent, even leviathan that crooked* *serpent; and he shall slay the dragon [term for Satan] that is in the sea...And it shall come to pass in that day [Day of the Lord], that the LORD shall beat off from the channel of the river unto the stream of Egypt, and ye shall be gathered one by one, O ye children of Israel. And it shall come to pass in that day [Day of the Lord], that the great [Gadol] trumpet [Shofar] shall be blown, and they shall come which were ready to perish in the land of Assyria, and the outcasts in the land of Egypt, and shall worship the LORD in the holy mount at Jerusalem. (KJV)*

The prophet Isaiah gave a synopsis of the eschatological seven-year period in chapters 26 and 27. Isaiah 26:1 starts with 'in that day,' a clear reference to the future Day of the Lord. Clearly it is in reference to the first seven years of the Day of the Lord (The Birth Pangs of the Messiah) by saying, 'Like as a woman with child, that draweth near the time of her delivery, is in pain, and crieth out in her pangs'. But right before this statement Isaiah states, 'Open ye the gates,' which is a clear reference to the festival of Rosh Hashana. Isaiah is cryptically discussing the resurrection as occurring on Rosh Hashana and even says later, 'Thy dead men shall live, together with my dead body shall they arise. Awake and sing, ye that dwell in dust: for thy dew is as the dew of herbs, and the earth shall cast out the dead'. 'Awake' is another term associated with Rosh Hashana and is used here in Hebrew Parallelism with 'dew' referring to the resurrection of the righteous as occurring on Rosh Hashana at the outset of the Birth Pangs of the Messiah.

Then at the end of chapter 26, the prophet says, 'Come, my people, enter thou into thy chambers, and shut thy doors about thee: hide thyself as it were for a little moment, until the indignation be overpast'. The resurrected saints on Rosh Hashana enter into God's wedding chamber (Chadar) in 'Heaven' to be hidden from the 'indignation' [The seven year Birth Pangs of the Messiah] on the earth.

Isaiah 27 starts again with 'in that day' 'the LORD with his sore and great and strong sword shall punish leviathan the piercing serpent, even leviathan that crooked serpent; and he shall slay the dragon that is in the sea...' Isaiah goes immediately to the very end of the Birth Pangs of the Messiah where God defeats Leviathan

[False Messiah] and the dragon [Satan]. Isaiah confirms this Yom Kippur appointment by stating, 'in that day, that the great trumpet shall be blown, and they shall come which were ready to perish in the land of Assyria, and the outcasts in the land of Egypt, and shall worship the LORD in the holy mount at Jerusalem'. The Great Trumpet (Shofar haGadol) is only blown at Yom Kippur (Tishri 10). Then all the people who remain alive will be gathered to Jerusalem and the righteous will worship God at the Temple in Jerusalem.

Matthew 24:30-31 *And then shall appear the sign of the Son of man in heaven: and then shall all the tribes of the earth mourn, and they shall see the Son of man coming in the clouds of heaven with power and great glory. And he shall send his angels with a <u>great</u> sound of a <u>trumpet</u>, and they shall gather together his elect from the four winds, from one end of heaven to the other.* (KJV)

Notice in Matthew 24 that after 'they shall see the Son of man coming in the clouds of heaven with power and great glory,' He will 'send his angels with a great sound of a trumpet, and they shall gather together his elect from the four winds, from one end of heaven to the other'. This is the Great Trumpet (Shofar haGadol) of Yom Kippur blasted on Tishri 10 when the Messiah comes to the Mount of Olives. Yeshua will send out His angels to gather together all His elect (believers).

Matthew 25:31-46 *When the Son of man shall come in his glory, and all the holy angels with him, <u>then shall he sit upon the throne of his glory</u>: And before him shall be gathered all nations: and he shall separate them one from another, as a shepherd divideth his sheep from the goats: And he shall set the sheep on his right hand, but the goats on the left. Then shall the <u>King</u> say unto them on his right hand, Come, ye blessed of my Father, <u>inherit the kingdom prepared for you from the foundation of the world</u>: For I was an hungred, and ye gave me meat: I was thirsty, and ye gave me drink: I was a stranger, and ye took me in: Naked, and ye clothed me: I was sick, and ye visited me: I was in prison, and ye came unto me. Then shall the righteous answer him, saying, Lord, when saw we thee an hungred, and fed* *thee? or thirsty, and gave thee drink? When saw we thee a stranger, and took thee in? or naked, and clothed thee? Or when saw we thee sick, or in prison, and came unto thee? And the King shall answer and say unto them, Verily I say unto you, Inasmuch as ye have done it unto one of the least of these my brethren, ye have done it unto me. Then shall he say also unto them on the left hand, Depart from me, ye cursed, into everlasting fire, prepared for the devil and his angels: For I was an hungred, and ye gave me no meat: I was thirsty, and ye gave me no drink: I was a stranger, and ye took me not in: naked, and ye clothed me not: sick, and in prison, and ye visited me not. Then shall they also answer him, saying, Lord, when saw we thee an hungred, or athirst, or a stranger, or naked, or sick, or in prison, and did not minister unto thee? Then shall he answer them, saying, Verily I say unto you, Inasmuch as ye did it not to one of the least of these, ye did it not to me. And these shall go away into everlasting punishment: but the righteous into life eternal. (KJV)*

After Yeshua returns to Jerusalem on Yom Kippur (Tishri 10) and His angels have gathered the nations to Him, He will judge them. The 'sheep' (righteous) are gathered to His right unto eternal life, while the 'goats' (wicked) will be gathered to His left into everlasting punishment. Notice that the Son of Man [Messiah] is coming in His Glory to sit upon His Throne. In this parable Yeshua compares Himself to the coming King at Yom Kippur, Yom haDin, the Day of Judgment. In Hebraic mystical thought the left side of God is associated with judgment and His right side is associated with mercy.[96]

It also appears that the nations will be judged based upon how they dealt with Israel. Yeshua said to His sheep, 'Inasmuch as ye have done it unto one of the least of these my brethren, ye have done it unto me'. Yeshua compares the nations that did not support Israel to goats: 'Inasmuch as ye did it not to one of the least of these, ye did it not to me'.

Ezekiel 20:35-38 *And I will bring you into the wilderness of the people, and there will I plead with you face to face (Yom Kippur – Yom haDin). Like as I pleaded with your fathers in the wilderness of the land of Egypt, so will I plead with you, saith the Lord GOD.*

And I will cause you to pass under the rod (Rosh Hashana – Yom haDin), and I will bring you into the bond of the covenant: And I will purge out from among you the rebels, and them that transgress against me: I will bring them forth out of the country where they sojourn, and they shall not enter into the land of Israel: and ye shall know that I am the LORD. (KJV)

Notice that Ezekiel 20:35 states that God 'will bring you [Israel] into the wilderness of the people, and there will I plead with you 'face to face,' which is a well-established phrase associated with Yom Kippur in rabbinic literature.[97] The people passing under the rod of the shepherd is symbolism related to Rosh Hashana, which as we have seen has a strong connection with Yom Kippur. God will purge out the wicked from the righteous on the Day of Judgement.

Isaiah 1:18-25 *Come now, and let us reason together, saith the LORD: though your sins be as scarlet, they shall be as white as snow; though they be red like crimson, they shall be as wool. If ye be willing and obedient, ye shall eat the good of the land: But if ye refuse and rebel, ye shall be devoured with the sword: for the mouth of the LORD hath spoken it. How is the faithful city become an harlot! it was full of judgment; righteousness lodged in it; but now murderers. Thy silver is become dross, thy wine mixed with water: Thy princes are rebellious, and companions of thieves: every one loveth gifts, and followeth after rewards: they judge not the father-less, neither doth the cause of the widow come unto them. Therefore saith the Lord, the LORD of hosts, the mighty One of Israel, Ah, I will ease me of mine adversaries, and avenge me of mine enemies: And I will turn my hand upon thee, and purely purge away thy dross, and take away all thy sin:* (KJV)

Isaiah 1 is definitely a Yom haDin (Day of Judgment) passage and the phrase 'though your sins be as scarlet, they shall be as white as snow; though they be red like crimson, they shall be as wool,' clearly identifies it as Yom Kippur. This is a form of writing called Hebrew parallelism. 'Though your sins be as scarlet' is exactly the same as 'though they be red like crimson'. It is just a different way of saying the same thing in a parallel fashion. Then 'they shall be as white as snow' is the same as 'they shall be as wool'. The Talmud [Shabbat 86a] relates this verse in Isaiah to the Yom Kippur ceremony in Leviticus 16 and the 'Azazel' goat.

There can be no doubt that Isaiah's setting is Yom Kippur, Israel's Day of Judgment and Redemption. The Assyrians under Sennacherib have already attacked and the fortress of Jerusalem is all that remains. Judah under king Hezekiah is ready to fall to the Assyrians. God is saying to Judah, 'repent,' and He will deliver them out of the situation.

Leviticus 16:7-10,14,15,20-22,29 *And he shall take the two goats, and present them before the LORD at the door of the tabernacle of the congregation. And Aaron shall cast lots upon the two goats; one lot for the LORD, and the other lot for the scapegoat. And Aaron shall bring the goat upon which the LORD's lot fell, and offer him for a sin offering. But the goat, on which the lot fell to be the scapegoat, shall be presented alive before the LORD, to make an atonement with him, and to let him go for a scapegoat into the wilderness... And he shall take of the blood of the bullock, and sprinkle it with his finger upon the mercy seat eastward; and before the mercy seat shall he sprinkle of the blood with his finger seven times. Then shall he kill the goat of the sin offering, that is for the people, and bring his blood within the vail, and do with that blood as he did with the blood of the bullock, and sprinkle it upon the mercy seat, and before the mercy seat...And when he hath made an end of reconciling the holy place, and the tabernacle of the congregation, and the altar, he shall bring the live goat: And Aaron shall lay both his hands upon the head of the live goat, and confess over him all the iniquities of the children of Israel, and all their transgressions in all their sins, putting them upon the head of the goat, and shall send him away by the hand of a fit man into the wilderness: And the goat shall bear upon him all their iniquities unto a land not inhabited: and he shall let go the goat in the wilderness...And this shall be a statute for ever unto you: that in the seventh month (Tishri), on the tenth day (Yom Kippur) of the month...(KJV)*

During the Second Temple period the High Priest would stand before the Nicanor Gate where two identical goats stood near an urn called Kalphi, a box with two golden lots, one written with 'la Azazel' (to Azazel), and the other 'la Adonai' (to Adonai). The High Priest stood between the two goats and drew the lots simultaneously with both hands. The Kalphi is raised so that he cannot see the two lots inside. The High Priest would then put one of the lots on the head of one goat, and the other on the head of the other goat. The goat with the lot that says 'la Adonai' will be the sin offering for the High Priest. The goat with the lot that says 'la Azazel' will be taken out to the wilderness where it is killed.[98] Azazel is linked to a 'demon' that dwells in the Judean wilderness.

The High Priest proclaims the goat 'to Adonai' and the people would respond and say, 'Blessed is the Name of His Glorious Kingdom forever and ever'. Then the High Priest tied a scarlet (red, crimson) woolen band on the horns of the goat marked 'la Azazel'. This goat was then turned to face the Eastern Gate and would be led into the wilderness to be killed.

After performing other Yom Kippur services in the Holy of Holies, the High Priest went back to the Nicanor Gate, where the goat designated 'la Azazel' had remained the entire time. He then pressed down on the goat with his bloodstained hands covering the goat's head. He then confessed on behalf of the entire nation of Israel, 'O Lord, they have committed iniquity, they have transgressed, they have sinned, your people the house of Israel. Oh, then Lord, cover over, I entreat you upon their iniquities, their transgressions, and their sins which they have wickedly committed, transgressed and sinned before You your people the house of Israel, as it is written in the Torah of your servant Moses for on that Day (Day of the Lord) shall it be covered over for you to make you clean from all of your sins before the Lord you shall be cleansed'. The High Priest would finish this prayer by saying, 'You shall be cleaned'.

The High Priest would then send the goat along with the priests assigned to leading it through Solomon's Porch, through the Eastern Gate to the fierce desert wilderness. They went over the bridge straight to the Mount of Olives, to the south, over the Kidron Valley. The goat and its escort of priests and some of the most prominent men of Jerusalem traveled together on a twelve-mile journey to a high ridge named Mount Tzok (or Mount Azazel).[99]

From the beginning of the procession to Mount Tzok there were ten different 'stations' or succot (booths) on the way. At each one the escort was formally offered food and drink, but refused because it was Yom Kippur (Day of Fasting). On approaching the tenth and final succah, the prominent men of Jerusalem halted, and only the priests assigned for the final 'leg' made the treacherous ascent up Mount Tzok to push the goat backwards off the cliff.

Before pushing the goat off the cliff, the priests divided the band of scarlet (red-crimson) wool, and tied half of it to an established rock they called 'Chudo,' and the other half between the goat's horns. As the goat fell from the cliff it would be ripped to shreds from colliding with the sharp rocks before it hit the bottom. It is recorded in the Talmud that a great miracle occurred. As the goat was cast to its death, the scarlet (red-crimson) colored wool tied to the Rock Chudo turned white. When it turned white, the priests signaled to the men of prominence at the tenth succah, that the goat was dead. They, in turn, passed the signal by kerchiefs and flags from succah to succah until the news reached the Temple.

Crowds stood over the Temple Gate where a now white thread was suspended (remember the same scarlet thread was placed on the Nicanor Gate where the High Priest chose lots over the two goats). The young people anxiously waited on the hillsides for the good news and on its arrival they celebrated by dancing, singing, and rejoicing. Until the news came nothing could happen in the Temple. When the news arrived the High Priest would continue with the Yom Kippur Services.[100]

Israel's national sins were to be transferred to the Azazel goat and their sins would go into the desert-wilderness with the goat. Why kill the goat? 'For the wages of sin is death' (Romans 6:23). Since this ceremony was done every year when the Temple stood, it demonstrated that a price had to be paid for sin. This Azazel ceremony on Yom Kippur has a prophetic side. Since Israel will be redeemed (their sin's forgiven) on a future Yom Kippur, the author believes that the ceremony here is descriptive of what befalls the False Messiah.

Zechariah 14:4-5, 8 *And his feet shall stand in that day upon the mount of Olives, which is before Jerusalem on the east, and the mount of Olives shall cleave in the midst thereof toward the east and toward the west, and there shall be a very great valley; and half of the mountain shall remove toward the north, and half of it toward the south. And ye shall flee to the valley of the mountains; for <u>the valley of the mountains shall reach unto Azal</u>: yea, ye shall flee, like as ye fled from before the earthquake in the days of Uzziah king of Judah: and <u>the LORD my God shall come, and all the saints with thee</u>...And it shall be in that day, that living waters shall go out from Jerusalem; half of them toward the former sea, and half of them toward the hinder sea: in summer and in winter shall it be.* (KJV)

The prophecy of Zechariah's splitting of the Mount of Olives when the Messiah and the saints physically return to Jerusalem was always understood as occurring on a future Yom Kippur when the Kingdom will be established on earth. The Mount of Olives is east of the location of the two ancient Temples. At that time the mountain will split into two with half of it removing to the north and the other half removing to the south. This means that a great rift (valley) forms in between running east and west. We are told that the valley reaches unto 'Azal'. There is no historical documentation to where 'Azal' was located. This author personally believes that Azal is directly related to the area termed Azazel and is connected to the 'la Azazel' goat of Yom Kippur in Leviticus 16. Azal appears to be just as mysterious as 'la Azazel'. The la Azazel goat was pushed backwards off a cliff on the Rock Chudo down into the Dead Sea area. [This was a little distance southeast of Jericho, about two miles west of the northern tip of the Dead Sea today, and twelve miles east of Jerusalem]. This could represent the judgment of the False Messiah.

After this judgment Zechariah tells us that this created valley will have living waters that spring up out of Jerusalem and will flow to the 'former' [kadmonee - east] sea and the other half to the 'hinder' [acharon - west] sea. The west sea is the Mediterranean Sea, whereas the east sea, is of course, the Dead Sea.

Ezekiel 47:1, 8, 10 *...waters issued out from under the threshold of the house eastward...These waters issue out toward the east country, and go down into the desert, and go into the sea [Dead Sea]...the fishers shall stand upon it from Engedi ... (KJV)*

Ezekiel gives us the same account of the waters flowing into the Dead Sea. Engedi is currently just off the western shore of the Dead Sea. So wherever Azal was located, it was in the same vicinity where the Azazel goat was pushed off the cliff.

Joel 3:2-3,14,18 *I will also gather all nations, and will bring them down into the valley of Jehoshaphat, and will plead with them there for my people and for my heritage Israel, whom they have scattered among the nations, and parted my land. And they have cast lots for my people...Multitudes, multitudes in the valley of decision: for the day of the LORD is near in the valley of decision...a fountain shall come forth of the house of the LORD, and shall water the valley of Shittim. (KJV)*

Joel calls this great valley, The Valley of Jehoshaphat. There is no known valley to have ever existed by that name. Jehoshaphat means 'God will Judge'. God is saying that He will bring the wicked nations into the valley of 'God will Judge'. This is the created valley by the dividing of the Mount of Olives on Yom Kippur. Notice that Joel says that the nations 'have cast lots for My People'. This could be a veiled reference to the casting of lots on Yom Kippur in Leviticus 16 for the la Adonai and la Azazel goats. Also, a fountain came forth from the Temple [House of the Lord] and flowed to the valley of Shittim, which is known to lie just east of the Jordan River in the Dead Sea vicinity.

In the Mishnah Tractate 'Parah Adumah' [Red Heifer] the Mount of Olives is called Har Mashiach, 'the mountain of Messiah'. The Mishnah also states that there have been a total of nine red cows burned in the history of Judaism. It was taught that the tenth heifer would be burned in the time of the Messiah. Thus, the Red Heifer is a harbinger of the coming of the Messiah.

In ancient times, a pure native-born red heifer would be led through the Eastern Gate of the Temple on an arched bridge leading over the Kidron Valley, to the Place of Burning located just below the northern summit of the Mount of Olives. This spot was on a direct line from the entrance to the Temple through the Eastern Gate. The red heifer would be bound and pushed into a pile of wood prepared for this ritual sacrifice. The priest would then sacrifice the cow with his right hand, and catch some of its blood in a container held in his left hand. The priest then dipped his finger in the blood and sprinkled it seven times toward the Most Holy Place that was supposed to have been in full view through the Eastern Gate. [This ritual of sprinkling is very similar to what the High Priest did with the bull and goat's blood in the Holy of Holies on Yom Kippur]. Originally, one standing on the Mount of Olives could look over the Eastern Gate (also called Shushan or HaKohan gate) into the huge area (presently north of the Dome of the Rock) and see all the gates (at different levels) in a perfect line. The Eastern wall was lower than the other sides so that the priest who sacrificed and burned the red heifer on the Mount of Olives could look directly through the gateway of the Sanctuary when he sprinkled the blood. [Mishnah, Middot 2:4]

Ezekiel 47:1 *...waters issued out from under the threshold of the house eastward: for the forefront of the house stood toward the east, and the waters came down from under from the right side of the house, <u>at the south side of the altar</u>.* (KJV)

It is quite possible that the Messiah Yeshua will go to the exact spot where the red heifer was sacrificed on the Mount of Olives. From there the mountain will split into two and the valley will go east to the Dead Sea area, and west down the center of the Mount of Olives. This may be some of the mystery that has surrounded the Red Heifer.

Revelation 19:20-21 *And the beast [False Messiah] was taken, and with him the false prophet that wrought miracles before him, with which he deceived them that had received the mark of the beast, and* *them that worshipped his image. These both were cast alive into a lake of fire burning with brimstone.* (KJV)

Returning back to the Azazel goat, we learn of its connection to the demonic realm and False Messiah. Israel's sins were transferred to the goat of Azazel for judgment so that they would never be brought up again. Ultimately this speaks of Satan being judged into the Lake of Fire as previewed first by the False Messiah [and False Prophet] being cast alive into it. When man's sins are atoned for through Yeshua's eternal blood, these sins will return to their source, Satan [or the Azazel], and will ultimately bring him destruction.

Leviticus 17:7 *And they shall no more offer their <u>sacrifices unto devils</u> [seirim - normally translated as 'kid' or 'he-goat'.], after whom they have gone a whoring. This shall be a statute for ever unto them throughout their generations.* (KJV)

Azazel is a name for a wilderness demon, known as the 'seirim,' goat-demons. This is mentioned in Leviticus 17:7 where the Israelites once worshiped them. Notice that Leviticus 17 immediately follows the Yom Kippur ceremony in chapter 16. Ibn Ezra appears to take note of this mysterious link to the Azazel goat. The Yom Kippur ceremony actually forced the iniquities of the people back upon Azazel where evil returns to its point of origin. Another way of looking at this is that God will pit Satan against himself to ultimately defeat him.[101]

There are several ancient sources, which describe the activity of the Dead Sea in Biblical times. It has been described as a land of fires from the seepage of bitumen and other gaseous fumes. Many report of volcanic activity in the Dead Sea at or around the first century. This activity was not continuous, but irregular. Eyewitnesses in the first century called the Dead Sea a 'lake of fire and smoke'.[102] The last real record of any smoke and fire coming off the Dead Sea was around mid-1800 C.E.

1 Enoch, Book II, Chapter 53, Verses 1,2 '*My eyes saw there a deep valley with a wide mouth. And all those who dwell upon the* *earth, the sea, and the islands shall bring to it gifts, presents, and tributes; yet this deep valley shall not become full. They shall fulfill the criminal deeds of their hands and eat all the produce of crime which the sinners toil for. Sinners shall be destroyed from before the face of the Lord of the Spirits – they shall perish eternally, standing before the face of his earth...'*[103]

One of the most popular Jewish writings in the first century era, 1 Enoch, Book 2, reveals a vision of a 'deep valley with a wide mouth' that will never become full. This is where the 'sinners shall be destroyed...[and] perish eternally'. Yeshua was probably alluding to this valley when He said in Matthew 7:13, "Enter ye in at the strait gate: for wide is the gate, and broad is the way, that leadeth to destruction, and many there be which go in thereat (KJV)". The prophet Isaiah says, "Therefore hell (Sheol) hath enlarged herself, and opened her mouth without measure: and their glory, and their multitude, and their pomp, and he that rejoiceth, shall descend into it (Isaiah 5:14 KJV)".

1 Enoch, Book II, Chapter 54, Verses 1-6 *Then I looked and turned to another face of the earth and saw there a valley, deep and burning with fire. And they were bringing kings and potentates and were throwing them into this deep valley. And my eyes saw there their chains while they were making them into iron fetters of immense weight. And I asked the angel of peace, who was going with me, saying, 'For whom are these imprisonment chains being prepared?' And he said unto me, 'These are being prepared for the armies of Azazel, in order that they may take them and cast them into the abyss of complete condemnation, and as the Lord of the Spirits has commanded it, they shall cover their jaws with rocky stones. Then Michael, Raphael, Gabriel, and Phanuel themselves shall seize them on that great day of judgment and cast them into the furnace (of fire) that is burning that day, so that the Lord of the Spirits may take vengeance on them on account of their oppressive deeds which (they performed) as messengers of Satan, leading astray those who dwell upon the earth.*[104]

In the next chapter of Enoch we learn that the deep valley burning with fire is prepared for the 'armies of Azazel'. Clearly, we have established that Azazel represents the False Messiah. His armies will be prepared in chains and cast into the valley as judgment from the Lord. Azazel, the False Messiah, is a picture of the Azazel goat on Yom Kippur that is cast off the cliff into permanent punishment in the Dead Sea (Lake of Fire) symbolism. He and the False Prophet will be awaiting the arrival of Satan and all the sinners about a thousand years later when the Day of the Lord has ended at the Great Judgment of the Lord.

1 Enoch, Book 2, Chapter 55, Verse 4 *Kings, potentates, dwellers upon the earth: You would have to see my Elect One, how he sits in the throne of glory and judges Azazel and all his company, and his army, in the name of the Lord of the Spirits!*[105]

Enoch refers to the Messiah as 'Lord of the Spirits' and 'Elect One'. He 'sits in the throne of glory' which suggest He has been crowned King. The Lord of the Spirits will judge Azazel and his armies in this great valley.

Succot

Leviticus 23:33-43 *And the LORD spake unto Moses, saying, Speak unto the children of Israel, saying, The fifteenth day of this seventh month shall be the feast of tabernacles for seven days unto the LORD. On the first day shall be an holy convocation: ye shall do no servile work therein. Seven days ye shall offer an offering made by fire unto the LORD: on the eighth day shall be an holy convocation unto you; and ye shall offer an offering made by fire unto the LORD: it is a solemn assembly; and ye shall do no servile work therein. These are the feasts of the LORD, which ye shall proclaim to be holy convocations, to offer an offering made by fire unto the LORD, a burnt offering, and a meat offering, a sacrifice, and drink offerings, every thing upon his day: Beside the sabbaths of the LORD, and beside your gifts, and beside all your vows, and beside all your freewill offerings, which ye give unto the LORD. Also in the fifteenth* *day of the seventh month, when ye have gathered in the fruit of the land, ye shall keep a feast unto the LORD seven days: on the first day shall be a sabbath, and on the eighth day shall be a sabbath. And ye shall take you on the first day the boughs of goodly trees, branches of palm trees, and the boughs of thick trees, and willows of the brook; and ye shall rejoice before the LORD your God seven days. And ye shall keep it a feast unto the LORD seven days in the year. It shall be a statute for ever in your generations: ye shall celebrate it in the seventh month. Ye shall dwell in booths seven days; all that are Israelites born shall dwell in booths: That your generations may know that I made the children of Israel to dwell in booths, when I brought them out of the land of Egypt: I am the LORD your God.* (KJV)

In our eschatological picture of the fall festivals, Succot is the time of the marriage supper of the Lamb [Messiah/Bridegroom]. At the end of the week (seven-year tribulation, or birth pangs of the Messiah), the marriage supper will take place. The marriage supper will not take place in Heaven. After the marriage in 'Heaven,' the bride and Groom will return to earth. The marriage supper will occur on earth and only the invited guests of the Father of the Groom will be present at this banquet meal. This can be seen in Revelation 19:7-14.

Revelation 19:7-14 *Let us be glad and rejoice, and give honour to him: for the marriage of the Lamb is come, and his wife hath made herself ready. And to her was granted that she should be arrayed in fine linen, clean and white: for the fine linen is the righteousness of saints. And he saith unto me, Write, Blessed are they which are called unto the marriage supper of the Lamb. And he saith unto me, These are the true sayings of God. And I fell at his feet to worship him. And he said unto me, See thou do it not: I am thy fellowservant, and of thy brethren that have the testimony of Jesus: worship God: for the testimony of Jesus is the spirit of prophecy. And I saw heaven opened, and behold a white horse; and he that sat upon him was called Faithful and True, and in righteousness he doth judge and make war. His eyes were as a flame of fire, and on his head were* *many crowns; and he had a name written, that no man knew, but he himself. And he was clothed with a vesture dipped in blood: and his name is called The Word of God. And the armies which were in heaven followed him upon white horses, clothed in fine linen, white and clean.* (KJV)

Yeshua also spoke of the marriage supper and the banquet in Luke 12:35-38 and Matthew 8:11.

Luke 12:35-38 *Let your loins be girded about, and your lights burning; And ye yourselves like unto men that wait for their lord, when he will return from the wedding; that when he cometh and knocketh, they may open unto him immediately. Blessed are those servants, whom the lord when he cometh shall find watching: verily I say unto you, that he shall gird himself, and make them to sit down to meat, and will come forth and serve them. And if he shall come in the second watch, or come in the third watch, and find them so, blessed are those servants.* (KJV)

Matthew 8:11 *And I say unto you, That many shall come from the east and west, and shall sit down with Abraham, and Isaac, and Jacob, in the kingdom of heaven.* (KJV)

During the seven days of Succot, the people were instructed by God to live in a temporary shelter called a succah. This is to remind Israel of their forefathers dwelling in booths in the wilderness. In the evening they would have a meal in the succah dedicated to mystical guests. When they eat, they are to set a plate for a different exalted guest each night, a total of seven exalted guests over the seven days. The exalted guests are the same as those who are recognized during the seven weeks of sabbaths between the Firstfruits of the Barley Harvest and Shavuot: Abraham, Isaac, Jacob, Joseph, Moses, Aaron, and David. This ceremony is called Ushpizin.[106] Matthew 8:11 is directly alluding to this mystical supper during the festival of Succot when Yeshua says, 'sit down with Abraham, and Isaac, and Jacob, in the kingdom of God'. To sit down in the Kingdom can only mean the eschatological banquet for the Righteous.

Isaiah 30:26 *Moreover <u>the light of the moon shall be as the light of the sun</u>, and the light of the sun shall be sevenfold, as the light of seven days, <u>in the day</u> that the LORD bindeth up the breach of his people, and healeth the stroke of their wound.* (KJV)

The Moon (Betrothed Bride) has no light of her own. The Light of the Moon (Bride) is the Messiah. She reflects His Light. The Moon (Bride) reflects the most of the Sun's (Messiah) Light on the Full Moon, the 15th of the month. This is a picture of the Bride being fully married in the second stage of marriage with the Messiah. At this time the Bride will receive resurrected bodies and her light shall be as the light of the Sun (Messiah). At that time the Bride will enter complete intimacy with her bridegroom, the Messiah.

Genesis 1:3-5 *And God said, Let there be light [or]: and there was light [or]. And God saw the light [or], that it was good: and God divided the light [or] from the darkness. And God called the light [or] Day, and the darkness he called Night. And the evening and the morning were the first day.* (KJV)

1 Thessalonians 5:4-5 *But ye, brethren, are not in darkness, that that day should overtake you as a thief. Ye are all the children of light, and the children of the day: we are not of the night, nor of darkness.* (KJV)

Genesis 1:16 *And God made two great lights [meorah]; the greater light [meorah] to rule the day, and the lesser light [meorah] to rule the night: he made the stars also.* (KJV)

Obviously the 'Light' generated on Day One of Creation is mystical, and not 'light' as we know it, because the sun wasn't created until the Fourth Day. Rabbinic commentary details this Light of Day One as referring to the Messiah and the righteous; it was called Primeval Light.[107] Some rabbis believed that the sun was only one-seventh the illumination of the Primeval Light of Messiah and that the righteous in the World To Come [Olam Haba] will enjoy the more illuminating Light of Messiah.[108] Isaiah spoke of a day when the sun would be sevenfold.

The Primeval Light is not the same as the 'light' associated with the sun and moon. The Hebrew words are 'or' and 'meorah' respectively. 'Or' can be taken to mean physical light or metaphorical/spiritual light, but 'meorah' is a luminous body giving off light. Obviously, the light associated with the sun and moon is only a 'shadow' of the essence of the real 'Light ' of Messiah.

The nature of the Primeval Light of Messiah can be viewed through physical light. Light represents truth. The nature of truth is revealed through light's non-hidden nature. Darkness represents wickedness, concealment, secretive, and hiding. A little light dispels much darkness, for darkness has no power over light. Nothing is hidden when everything is illuminated. This is the picture of truth and light brings truth to bear. On a spiritual level, the Primeval Light of Messiah is the all-revealing Truth of God where nothing such as sin can be hidden from Him.

John 8:12 *Then spake Jesus again unto them, saying, I am the light of the world: he that followeth me shall not walk in darkness, but shall have the light of life.* (KJV)

Another name for Succot is 'The Festival of Lights'. During the Festival of Succot four great lampstands were lit at night in the Courtyard of the Women and could be seen many miles away from Jerusalem.[109] It was probably to these lampstands that Yeshua referred Himself as the 'Light of the World' at the end of the festival of Succot in John 8:12.

The Passover Seder is held at the season of the full moon of the month of Nisan. This is a picture of the beginning of the betrothal process of a believer leading to Pentecost and the receiving of the Ruwach haKodesh [Holy Spirit - The Promise of the Father]. We are to partake of the Passover in remembrance of Yeshua freeing us from the bondage of sin and the ownership of haSatan [Satan].

The ancient sages spoke of two redemptions. The first redemption with Moses as the mediator occurred with the exodus from Egypt. The second and final redemption is to occur with Messiah as

Mediator resulting in the establishment of the Messianic Kingdom. The first redemption coincides with the Passover on the full moon. The second redemption coincides with the season of the full moon of Tishri, which occurs during the festival of Succot.

Luke 22:15-20 *And he said unto them, With desire I have desired to eat this passover with you before I suffer: For I say unto you, I will not any more eat thereof, until it be fulfilled in the kingdom of God. And he took the cup, and gave thanks, and said, Take this, and divide it among yourselves: For I say unto you, I will not drink of the fruit of the vine, until the kingdom of God shall come. And he took bread, and gave thanks, and brake it, and gave unto them, saying, This is my body which is given for you: this do in remembrance of me. Likewise also the cup after supper, saying, This cup is the new testament in my blood, which is shed for you.* (KJV)

At Yeshua's last Passover He said, "I will not any more eat thereof, until it be fulfilled in the kingdom of God". He also said, "I will not drink of the fruit of the vine, until the kingdom of God shall come". What did He mean? He will not eat the Passover again until it finds its fulfillment in the Kingdom of God. When will the Passover be fulfilled in the Kingdom of God? The final redemption will be the Great Passover.

A Jewish poet named Yosef bar Yaakov (probably 12th Century) expressed this concept in the liturgical poem Pesach of the Last Days. This poem can be found in its entirety in The Complete Artscroll Machzor for Pesach. The first two stanzas are included here to illustrate the message:

Pesach, the Faithful sang a song to Him,
'And the LORD saved on that day'.
The Pesach of Egypt.

Pesach, a Heavenly Voice will be heard from the Heights
Announcing, 'Israel is saved in the LORD, and eternal
salvation'.
The Pesach of the Last Days

*Pesach, the Redeemed crossed over [the Reed Sea] with a
    lifted hand
'and Israel saw the Hand'.
The Pesach of Egypt.*

*Pesach, the Exalted One in the strength of His Glory,
My Lord will add another Salvation by His hand.
The Pesach of the Last Days.*

The Great Eschatological Messianic Banquet in the Kingdom of
God is none other than the final eschatological Pesach Seder of the
second and final redemption. Based upon Revelation 19 Christianity
calls it 'The Wedding Supper of the Lamb,' which is associated with
the Festival of Succot. There is a definite link between the Passover
Seder and the Feast of Succot. These are the only Festivals of God
appointed at the Full Moon and they are exactly six months apart.

The wedding feast was called 'hillula,' which means the feast
of 'Joyful Song'. Notice that those called to the Marriage Supper
of the Lamb are to be 'glad' and 'rejoice'. It is then very interesting
when one realizes that another ancient name given to the Festival of
Succot was the 'Festival of Our Joy'.[110]

The Wedding Supper was associated with all seven days of
Succot. So where Yeshua's Passover Seder left off, it is continued
on Succot at Tishri 15, connected by the full moon, and lasts for
the duration of the Millennium. Because Succot is the festival that
symbolizes the Great Wedding Banquet of God, the righteous resurrected believers have a permanent blissful sitting with Messiah at
this feast. Those righteous that survive of the nations from the Birth
Pangs of the Messiah will be invited as guests during the remainder
of the Day of the Lord. This is a very important point to comprehend, that both resurrected saints and human flesh and blood beings
will dwell in the Messianic Kingdom together for the duration of
the thousand years. The resurrected, although participating in the
Kingdom, are actually already in the Olam Haba [World To Come].
Eventually all the righteous will be resurrected into the Olam Haba
after the entire seven thousand years are accomplished.

Zechariah 14:16-19 *And it shall come to pass, that every one that is left of all the nations which came against Jerusalem shall even go up from year to year to worship the King, the LORD of hosts, and to keep the feast of tabernacles. And it shall be, that whoso will not come up of all the families of the earth unto Jerusalem to worship the King, the LORD of hosts, even upon them shall be no rain. And if the family of Egypt go not up, and come not, that have no rain; there shall be the plague, wherewith the LORD will smite the heathen that come not up to keep the feast of tabernacles. This shall be the punishment of Egypt, and the punishment of all nations that come not up to keep the feast of tabernacles.* (KJV)

Zechariah 14 declares Messiah's Coming to the Mount of Olives on Yom Kippur. Immediately afterward the prophet mentions, "every one that is left of all the nations which came against Jerusalem shall even go up from year to year to worship the King, the LORD of hosts, and to keep the feast of tabernacles". The seventy oxen that were sacrificed in the Temple during the seven days of Succot were directly linked to atonement for the Gentile nations.[111]

Revelation 19:7-9,17-21 *Let us be glad and rejoice, and give honour to him: for the marriage of the Lamb is come, and his wife hath made herself ready. And to her was granted that she should be arrayed in fine linen, clean and white: for the fine linen is the righteousness of saints. And he saith unto me, Write, Blessed are they which are called unto the marriage supper of the Lamb. And he saith unto me, These are the true sayings of God...And I saw an angel standing in the sun; and he cried with a loud voice, saying to all the fowls that fly in the midst of heaven, Come and gather yourselves together unto the supper of the great God; That ye may eat the flesh of kings, and the flesh of captains, and the flesh of mighty men, and the flesh of horses, and of them that sit on them, and the flesh of all men, both free and bond, both small and great. And I saw the beast, and the kings of the earth, and their armies, gathered together to make war against him that sat on the horse, and against his army. And the beast [False Messiah] was taken, and with him the false prophet that wrought miracles before him, with which he deceived them that* *had received the mark of the beast, and them that worshipped his image. These both were cast alive into a lake of fire burning with brimstone. And the remnant were slain with the sword of him that sat upon the horse, which sword proceeded out of his mouth: and all the fowls were filled with their flesh.* (KJV)

Zephaniah 1:7-8 *Hold thy peace at the presence of the Lord GOD: for the day of the LORD is at hand: for the LORD hath prepared a sacrifice, he hath bid his guests. And it shall come to pass in the day of the LORD's sacrifice, that I will punish the princes, and the king's children, and all such as are clothed with strange apparel.* (KJV)

The 'feast of Leviathan' is a particular ceremony held at the time of the festival of Succot.[112] When the False Messiah (Leviathan) is defeated by Messiah ben David, the feast of Leviathan will be held. The fowls of the air are summoned 'unto the supper of the great God'. Notice the connection between the feast of Leviathan and the 'marriage supper of the Lamb'. Out of all the major feasts, the banquet at Succot was considered the largest. Succot speaks of the Millennium after the Messiah has returned and established His Kingdom on earth.

Revelation 13:1,4 *And I stood upon the sand of the sea, and saw <u>a beast [False Messiah] rise up out of the sea, having seven heads</u> and ten horns...And they worshipped the dragon which gave power unto the beast [False Messiah]...*(KJV)

Revelation 12:3,9 *And there appeared another wonder in heaven; and behold <u>a great red dragon [Satan], having seven heads</u> and ten horns...And the great dragon was cast out, that old serpent, called the Devil, and Satan...*(KJV)

Psalm 74:13 *Thou didst divide the sea by thy strength: thou brakest the heads of the dragons (Tanninim) in the waters.* (KJV)

Isaiah 27:1 *In that day [Day of the Lord] the LORD with his sore and great and strong sword shall <u>punish leviathan the piercing</u>*

serpent (Nachash), even leviathan that crooked serpent (Nachash);
and he shall slay the dragon (Tannin) that is in the sea. (KJV)

Very clearly throughout Scripture Leviathan is connected to the Dragon/Serpent and can be easily deduced as representing the seven-headed beast [False Messiah] in Revelation. Leviathan was known throughout ancient Mesopotamia as a seven-headed sea monster.[113] It is the Nachash/Tannin (representations of Satan) that give the Beast (Leviathan) his power.

According to ancient mystical rabbinic thinking, Leviathan's importance is directed into Messianic times and the World To Come when mankind achieves its creative purpose. The ancient rabbinical teaching of Leviathan is clearly to be taken only in an allegorical/spiritual fashion. The only time that Jews specifically speak of Leviathan is in their prayers while dwelling in their succah at Succot.

The picture being painted is the defeat of the False Messiah where his followers are consumed by birds of prey when Messiah comes to Jerusalem. The Leviathan (False Messiah) is not literally eaten by the righteous, but their feasting upon Leviathan is symbolic of their victory over him and all evil. The feast of Leviathan is directly related to the wedding feast of the Lamb and is directly connected to Succot.

Romans 14:17 *For the kingdom of God is not meat and drink; but righteousness, and peace, and joy in the Holy Ghost.* (KJV)

The Messianic Kingdom and the World To Come are not really about eating and drinking, although it appears that believer's resurrected glorified bodies can eat physical food as Yeshua did after His resurrection (Luke 24:36-43). 'Eating and drinking' is a metaphor used to describe the 'Heavenly' bliss of the righteous. The feast of Leviathan (Wedding Banquet) represents the righteous taking in the 'spiritual' and growing from its nourishment on an eternal level.

Deuteronomy 29:5-6 *And I have led you forty years in the wilderness: your clothes are not waxen old upon you, and thy shoe is not waxen old upon thy foot. Ye have not eaten bread, neither have ye* *drunk wine or strong drink: that ye might know that I am the LORD your God. (KJV)*

The festival of Succot commemorates when Israel was in the wilderness. What Israel encountered was a foretaste for the righteous during the Millennium (Day of the Lord). Israel had the 'cloud by day' and 'fire by night' (Exodus 13:22). They had the heavenly manna (symbol of wedding supper/Leviathan) to nourish them. They received supernatural water from a rock (Exodus 17:6). Their clothes and shoes did not wear in forty years, which is a symbol of resurrection (Deuteronomy 29:5). On a physical level, this represents in type and shadow, the provisions for the righteous in the Day of the Lord.

Job 41:1-4,6,34 *Canst thou draw out leviathan with an hook? or his tongue with a cord which thou lettest down? Canst thou put an hook into his nose? or bore his jaw through with a thorn? Will he make many supplications unto thee? will he speak soft words unto thee? Will he make a covenant with thee? wilt thou take him for a servant for ever?...Shall the companions make a banquet of him? shall they part him among the merchants?...He beholdeth all high things: he is a king over all the children of pride [Rahab].* (KJV)

Since we have established that 'Leviathan' is a code name for the 'False Messiah,' we can approach certain Scriptures prophetically as referring to him. In Job 41 notice the implications of a 'Banquet-Feast' being made from Leviathan. Leviathan (False Messiah) is the 'king over all the children of pride'. 'Rahab' itself can mean 'prideful'.

Symbolically, the festival of Succot teaches that the eschatological [Passover] banquet prepared for the righteous will be made from the feast of Leviathan, symbolic of his defeat by the Messiah. Obviously, the future Seder will be spiritual in nature, as the righteous will dwell in resurrected bodies. The fact that the False Messiah and Satan have been officially defeated appears to be the satisfaction and bliss of the banquet in which the righteous will maintain a spiritual ecstasy with the Messiah.

A most-famous Jewish liturgical poem read at the festival of Shavuot (Pentecost) is called 'Akdamut'. Rabbi Meir Yitzhak composed it during the 11th century. A portion of Akdamut is as follows:

> The sport with the Leviathan
> And the ox of the lofty mountains –
> When they will interlock with one another and engage in
>   combat,
> With his horns the Behemoth will gore with strength,
> The fish will leap to meet him, with power.
> Their creator will approach them with His mighty sword.
> A banquet for the righteous will He prepare, and a feast.
> They will sit around tables of precious stones and gems,
> Before them will be flowing rivers of balsam.
> They will delight and drink their fill
> From overflowing goblets
> Of sweet wine that since Creation was preserved [114]

Akdamut speaks of the feast of Leviathan as we have previously discussed. But here we learn of a Jewish mystical understanding of an epic battle between Leviathan and Behemoth (the other large creature in the book of Job), prior to Messiah's return and the banquet (wedding) supper. What is this battle? We know that the Leviathan is a picture of the False Messiah. So who is Behemoth representing prophetically at the end of the Birth Pangs of the Messiah prior to the Lord's return? The author believes that the Behemoth is a mystical teaching that represents the 'Kings of the East,' who will cross the Euphrates and march toward Jerusalem to battle the Leviathan (False Messiah) only to join with him against the coming Messiah (Revelation 16:12-16).

Another theme of Succot liturgy is the 'Clouds of Glory'. The succah was compared to the great clouds of glory that encompassed Israel in the wilderness.[115] The sages taught that the 'Clouds of Glory' symbolically represented the righteous dead forefathers including Abraham, Isaac, and Jacob who were in the midst of the righteous living who still possessed physical bodies such as Moses, Aaron,

Joshua, and Caleb. This is a picture of the Millennium where the resurrected saints with glorified bodies will dwell among the living with physical bodies.

Deuteronomy 1:32-33 *...the LORD your God, Who went in the way before you, to search you out a place to pitch your tents in, in fire by night, to shew you by what way ye should go, and in a cloud by day.* (KJV)

Surrounded by the 'Clouds of Glory,' Israel lived supernaturally for their forty years in the wilderness. Although God judged the first generation of them for not entering into the Promised Land, the ones who remained and were born later were completely nourished supernaturally by God. Truly, being under the 'Clouds of Glory' was a picture of the future Sabbath Rest (Millennium) of God. The rabbis shared that the 'Clouds of Glory' transported all Israel like a chariot through the wilderness and in that environment the clothes and shoes of the young children grew along with them as they aged.[116]

The Midrash Tanchuma actually states that there were seven clouds in the wilderness flanking Israel on all four directions, above and below, and the seventh which led them as a cloud by day and a fire by night. The six surrounding clouds were compared to the six days of the week, whereas the seventh leading cloud was compared to the Sabbath, a time of resting in God.[117] The Zohar relates that the 'Clouds of Glory' formed a supernatural succah around Israel in the wilderness, called 'the Shelter of Faith'.[118]

By dwelling in a succah during the festival of Succot believers can reach back to the past with our spiritual forefathers and remember the shelter of faith in the wilderness. As we 'remember' we place ourselves under the divine environment of God that through faith one day we will dwell with Him when it is completely Sabbath. In that day we will be one with the clouds of glory and forever dwell in God's supernatural environment.

Hebrews 11:1-3 *Now faith is the substance of things hoped for, the evidence of things not seen. For by it the elders obtained a good report. Through faith we understand that the worlds were framed* *by the word of God, so that things which are seen were not made of things which do appear.* (KJV)

Now we can understand the background of Hebrews 11 & 12. A person without faith is limited to what tangible evidence shows him. The writer of Hebrews states that true 'faith is the substance of things hoped for, the evidence of things not seen'. The sages believed that 'faith' was the integrating of the experiences of the patriarchs, prophets, and teachers into our own experiences.[119] They are dead in Messiah but yet still alive in the living believers. The writer of Hebrews mentions several of the saints that preceded the first century as examples of the 'Shelter of Faith'.

Hebrews 11:4	*By faith Abel ...*
Hebrews 11:5	*By faith Enoch...*
Hebrews 11:7	*By faith Noah...*
Hebrews 11:8	*By faith Abraham...*
Hebrews 11:11	*Through faith...Sara*
Hebrews 11:20	*By faith Isaac...*
Hebrews 11:21	*By faith Jacob...*
Hebrews 11:22	*By faith Joseph...*
Hebrews 11:23	*By faith Moses...*
Hebrews 11:31	*By faith the harlot Rahab...*
Hebrews 11:32	*And what shall I more say? for the time would fail me to tell of Gedeon, and of Barak, and of Samson, and of Jephthae; of David also, and Samuel, and of the prophets:*

Hebrews 11:39 *And these all, having obtained a good report through faith...*(KJV)

Hebrews 12:1 *Wherefore seeing we also are compassed about with so great a cloud of witnesses...*(KJV)

The clincher comes in Hebrews 12:1, which calls all these people of faith a great 'Cloud of Witnesses'. The righteous dead are symbolically represented in Jewish thought as the 'Clouds of Glory', which provided the 'Shelter of Faith' for the righteous living. The 'Clouds of Glory' (the resurrected righteous saints) who accompany the Messiah when He returns to Earth appear to be directly linked to the 'Sign' of His Coming.

Matthew 24:30 *And then shall appear the sign of the Son of man in heaven: and then shall all the tribes of the earth mourn, and they shall see the Son of man coming in <u>the clouds of heaven</u> with power and great glory.* (KJV)

Revelation 1:7 *Behold, he cometh with <u>clouds</u>; and every eye shall see him, and they also which pierced him: and all kindreds of the earth shall wail because of him. Even so, Amen.* (KJV)

In the New Testament Yeshua talked about 'The Sign' of the Son of Man's appearance in heaven. The Gospel of Matthew relates the Sign to: 'then shall all the tribes of the earth mourn, and they shall see the Son of man coming in the clouds of heaven with power and great glory'. We find a similar reference in Revelation 1:7.

Daniel 7:13 *I saw in the night visions, and, behold, one like the Son of man came with <u>the clouds of heaven</u>, and came to the Ancient of days, and they brought him near before him.* (KJV)

Zechariah 12:10 *And I will pour upon the house of David, and upon the inhabitants of Jerusalem, the spirit of grace and of supplications: and <u>they shall look upon me</u> whom they have pierced, and <u>they shall mourn for him</u>, as one mourneth for his only son, and shall be in bitterness for him, as one that is in bitterness for his firstborn.* (KJV)

The 'Sign' in Matthew, therefore, is taken from Daniel 7:13 and Zechariah 12:10. 'Every eye' (both Jew and Gentile) will see the 'Sign' of the Son of Man coming from Heaven. In these verses there is a 'veiled' reference to Yeshua coming with the 'Clouds'. Could the 'Clouds' also be part of the Sign?

Jude 1:14-15 *And Enoch also, the seventh from Adam, prophesied of these, saying, Behold, <u>the Lord cometh with ten thousands of his saints, To execute judgment upon all</u>, and to convince all that are ungodly among them of all their ungodly deeds which they have ungodly committed, and of all their hard speeches which ungodly sinners have spoken against him. (KJV)*

<u>1 Enoch [Book 1] Chapter 1 verse 9</u> *Behold he will arrive with ten million of the holy ones to execute judgment upon all.*[120]

It is not difficult to make the connection with these resurrected saints and the 'Clouds of Glory'. Jude mentions that the Messiah will come 'with ten thousands of his saints,' which is a quote from the Apocrypha Book of Enoch. In the other Scriptures the Messiah is coming with the 'Clouds of Heaven'. The 'Clouds' therefore, symbolically represent the resurrected righteous saints who return to earth with Him. This most assuredly will be a great Sign of the Coming of the Messiah.

The entire seven days of Succot can also be viewed as a preview of the seven thousand years of man on earth before the World To Come [Olam Haba] is completely revealed. The seventh and last day of Succot has a special name called Hoshanna Rabbah. It was known as the Great Day of the Feast. Hoshanna Rabbah is symbolic of the seventh millennium and the transition into the Olam Haba.

As we have already studied in this chapter every human is judged at the eschatological Rosh Hashana after six thousand years have been concluded. The righteous saints are sealed in the Book of Life and the entirely wicked are sealed in the Book of Death. This includes both living and dead. Those who are alive and are in-between [sinners] are judged to be in the Book of Death, but have until Yom Kippur to repent so that their verdicts can be changed to be included in the Book of Life. Eschatologically, after the seven years of the Birth Pangs all sinners will either be sealed in the Book of Life or the Book of Death. On Yom Kippur all verdicts are sealed, but interestingly the rabbis of old taught that it was on Hoshanna Rabbah, the seventh day of Succot, that these verdicts or sentences were actually carried out.[121] In other words, eschatologically speaking, the decreed punishment for the wicked will be carried out at the end of the seventh Millennium.

Revelation 20:7-9 *And when the thousand years are expired, Satan shall be loosed out of his prison, And shall go out to deceive the nations which are in the four quarters of the earth, Gog and Magog, to gather them together to battle: the number of whom is as the sand of the sea. And they went up on the breadth of the earth, and compassed the camp of the saints about, and the beloved city: and fire came down from God out of heaven, and devoured them.* (KJV)

The Scripture is very clear that after the Millennium (Day of the Lord) is 'expired,' 'Satan shall be loosed out of his prison [Bottomless Pit]'. What is God's purpose in this? Obviously, Satan cannot affect the resurrected righteous. The physical flesh and blood humans born during the Millennium will be his targets to deceive. They had never been given the true choice to serve God or Satan. Even though mankind would have been under the peaceful reign of the Messiah Yeshua for a thousand years, these people reveal the decadence of human nature that needs repentance and a Savior.

Satan will 'deceive the nations which are in the four quarters of the earth' and 'to gather them together to battle'. Notice the number of people who turn easily toward Satan's deception: 'the number of whom is as the sand of the sea'. Since people will live as long as they did just after the Garden of Eden, there will be billions of living flesh and blood humans. With Messiah reigning as King, the world will be populated and operating more efficiently then at any time in the earth's history. But sin and lack of repentance will still be the issues facing man even during the Millennium.

The armies of Satan will encompass 'the camp of the saints about, and the beloved city [Jerusalem]'. Since Messiah will reign from Jerusalem, it would appear that these armies would come up against Him. But who are these saints? Earlier in Revelation 20 the 'First Resurrection' was mentioned whereby making these 'saints' the resurrected ones. This doesn't mean that the righteous flesh and blood living saints will not be there also. However, just like before the Flood in Noah's day, and also the coming of the Messiah at the end of the Birth Pangs, so will the majority of flesh and blood living human beings deny God at the end of the Day of the Lord. 'Fire came down from God out of heaven, and devoured them'. This is all we are told, so the war is probably over before it even started.

Revelation 20:10-15 *And the devil that deceived them was cast into the lake of fire and brimstone, where the beast and the false prophet are, and shall be tormented day and night for ever and ever. And I saw a great white throne, and him that sat on it, from whose face the earth and the heaven fled away; and there was found no place for them. And I saw the dead, small and great, stand before God; and the* <u>books</u> *were opened: and another book was opened, which is the* <u>book of life</u>: *and the dead were judged out of those things which were written in the* <u>books</u>, *according to their works. And the sea gave up the dead which were in it; and death and hell delivered up the dead which were in them: and they were judged every man according to their works. And death and hell were cast into the lake of fire. This is the second death. And whosoever was not found written in the book of life was cast into the lake of fire.* (KJV)

Satan (Devil) will be cast into the Lake of Fire and Brimstone. Then comes the 'Great White Throne' judgment of all the wicked throughout all of man's history. This is when the sealed verdicts from Yom Kippur are carried out for all the ages. It is highly probable that this Great White Throne Judgment will be carried out at the end of Hoshana Rabbah (Tishri 21); the seventh day of the Festival of Succot, just after the seven thousand year plan of God is accomplished.

All the unrepentant wicked sinners throughout all the ages will be raised before the Throne of God to account for their works and deeds. Every single one of them will not be listed in the Book of Life and will be cast into the Lake of Fire. This is the second death, which is an eternal death. All those who don't take part in the First Resurrection are appointed to the second death. The Scripture doesn't indicate what happens to the believing flesh and blood humans at the end of the Day of the Lord, but surely they will be translated before these wicked are cast into the Lake of Fire. It is quite possible there will be another sequence of Rosh Hashana through Yom Kippur that concludes the seventh Millennium just as it started.

Shemini Atzeret

<u>Leviticus 23:36</u> *Seven days ye shall offer an offering made by fire unto the LORD: on the eighth day shall be an holy convocation unto you; and ye shall offer an offering made by fire unto the LORD: it is a solemn assembly; and ye shall do no servile work therein...Also in the fifteenth day of the seventh month, when ye have gathered in the fruit of the land, ye shall keep a feast unto the LORD seven days: on the first day shall be a sabbath, and on the eighth day shall be a sabbath.* (KJV)

The day after Hoshanna Rabbah (Tishri 21), the last of the seven days of Succot, is Shemini Atzeret, the Eighth Day (Tishri 22). Just as Shavuot [Pentecost] is the atzeret [conclusion] of Passover, so is Shemini Atzeret the conclusion of the fall festivals starting at Rosh Hashana. Shemini Atzeret is attached to the festival of Succot, but is still considered a separate holiday. It is also a High Sabbath as the first and seventh day's of Unleavened Bread, Shavuot, Rosh Hashana, Yom Kippur, and the first day of Succot.

<u>Isaiah 60:19-22</u> *The sun shall be no more thy light by day; neither for brightness shall the moon give light unto thee: but the LORD shall be unto thee an everlasting light, and thy God thy glory. Thy sun shall no more go down; neither shall thy moon withdraw itself: for the LORD shall be thine everlasting light, and the days of thy mourning shall be ended. Thy people also shall be all righteous: they shall inherit the land for ever, the branch of my planting, the work of my hands, that I may be glorified. A little one shall become a thousand, and a small one a strong nation: I the LORD will hasten it in his time.* (KJV)

<u>Revelation 21:22-27</u> *And I saw no temple therein: for the Lord God Almighty and the Lamb are the temple of it. And the city had no need of the sun, neither of the moon, to shine in it: for the glory of God*

did lighten it, and the Lamb is the light thereof. And the nations of them which are saved shall walk in the light of it: and the kings of the earth do bring their glory and honour into it. And the gates of it shall not be shut at all by day: for there shall be no night there. And they shall bring the glory and honour of the nations into it. And there shall in no wise enter into it any thing that defileth, neither whatsoever worketh abomination, or maketh a lie: but they which are written in the Lamb's book of life. (KJV)

In Isaiah 60, the prophet prophesies directly from the Day of the Lord (Millennium) to the Olam Haba (The World To Come). This is after the Day of the Lord and the seven thousand year plan of God is completed. It appears that the sun and moon will still exist, but they will not be the source of light for the day and night respectively because 'the LORD shall be unto thee an everlasting light'. This relates back to the Primeval Light of Messiah on the first day of Creation. 'The days of thy mourning shall be ended' and 'Thy people also shall be all righteous'. All dwellers in the Olam Haba will have partaken of the 'First Resurrection,' and no sorrow, mourning, or even sin will exist in the Olam Haba.

Revelation 21:1-2 *And I saw a new heaven and a new earth: for the first heaven and the first earth were passed away; and there was no more sea. And I John saw the holy city, new Jerusalem, coming down from God out of heaven, prepared as a* <u>*bride*</u> *adorned for her husband.* (KJV)

If Hoshanna Rabbah, the seventh day of Succot, represents the last millennium and the end of seven thousand years, then Shemini Atzeret, the Eighth Day connected to Succot, represents Eternity or the Olam Haba. Shemini Atzeret became associated with new beginnings and the Olam Haba (The World To Come). In Revelation 21 John sees 'a new heaven and a new earth'. The topography of this world will definitely be different for 'there was no more sea'. John sees a 'holy city, new Jerusalem, coming down from God out of heaven, prepared as a bride adorned for her husband'.

This is exactly what the sages had to say about the symbolism associated with Shemini Atzeret. The rabbis concluded that Shemini Atzeret transcended the seven days of creation ending with Shabbat. Shemini Atzeret is symbolic of the Sabbath/World To Come that will always be Sabbath. Arizal referring to Shemini Atzeret said, 'God will then rejoice over us as a bridegroom with his beloved bride'.[122]

Revelation 21:4 *And God shall wipe away all tears from their eyes; and there shall be no more death, neither sorrow, nor crying, neither shall there be any more pain: for the former things are passed away.* (KJV)

The rabbis understood the symbolism of the 'Eighth Day' as alluding to the future when all wickedness has been removed from the earth. Israel and God are said to be in total unity at that time and there are no more physical limitations. Shemini Atzeret is viewed as a separate festival and is the 'crowning glory' of the three pilgrimage festivals.[123] New Jerusalem has come down from heaven and all the righteous are resurrected and dwell there in perfect harmony with God and the Lamb.

So what exactly is 'new Jerusalem, coming down from God out of heaven?' Did the concept of New Jerusalem originate with John's vision? Or did the Jews have a definite concept of New Jerusalem? As a matter of fact they did!

Psalm 122:1-3 *A Song of degrees of David. I was glad when they said unto me, Let us go into the house of the LORD. Our feet shall stand within thy gates, O Jerusalem. Jerusalem is builded as a city that is compact together:* (KJV)

In Judaism there is the concept of a 'Lower/Earthly Jerusalem' ה ט מ ל ש ס י ל ש ו ר י and an 'Upper/Heavenly Jerusalem ה ל ע מ ל ש ס י ל ש ו ר י. Jerusalem was viewed in a dualistic nature. When David designed Jerusalem he modeled it after the 'Upper Jerusalem,' which is the ideal of a perfected utopian city.[124] In its perfection Upper Jerusalem will come down and hover completely over earthly Jerusalem like a city that is compacted together.

Gan Edan [Garden of Eden] was viewed as this kind of utopia. However, because of sin, God lifted the 'Heavenly' Garden [Jerusalem] away from the earthly. What ascended in the past will descend back in the future Olam Haba. The Tanach [Old Testament] clearly teaches that Moses modeled the Tabernacle from the 'Heavenly' pattern. A 'Heavenly' Temple is a synonym for Gan Edan. Therefore, John's vision of New Jerusalem coming down from 'Heaven' is consistent with the Hebraic thought of a 'Heavenly' Temple and Garden of Eden.

BIBLIOGRAPHY

1. The Biblical and Historical Background of Jewish Customs and Ceremonies. Abraham P. Bloch. KTAV Publishing House, Inc., New York, 1980. Page 295.
2. Encyclopedia Judaica CD-ROM Edition. New Moon. Judaica Multimedia, Jerusalem, 1997.
3. Seasons of Our Joy - A Modern Guide to the Jewish Holidays. Arthur Waskow. Beacon Press, Boston, Massachusetts, 1982. Page 229.
4. Messiah: Understanding His Life and Teachings in Hebraic Context - Volume 1. Avi ben Mordecai. A Millennium 7000 Communications Int'l Publication, 1997. Page 152.
5. Gesenius' Hebrew-Chaldee Lexicon to the Old Testament. H.W.F. Gesenius. Baker Books, Grand Rapids, Michigan, 1979. Page 456.
6. The Complete Artscroll Siddur. Rabbi Nosson Scherman. Mesorah Publications, Ltd., Brooklyn, New York, 1985. Page 649.
7. IBID. Page 649.
8. Talmud - Sanhedrin 11b
9. Encyclopedia Judaica CD-ROM Edition. Calendar. Judaica Multimedia, Jerusalem, 1997.

10. Made in Heaven: A Jewish Wedding Guide . Rabbi Aryeh Kaplan. Moznaim Publishing Corporation, New York, Jerusalem, 1983. Page 156.
11. Talmud - Sandedrin 97a.
12. The Artscroll Tanach Series - Tehillim - Volume 1. Rabbi Avrohom Chaim Feuer. Mesorah Publications, Ltd., Brooklyn, New York, 1977. Page 559.
13. IBID. Page 560 & 573.
14. IBID. Page 573.
15. Ancient Israel - Its Life and Institutions, Roland De Vaux. William B. Eerdmans Publishng Company, Grand Rapids, Michigan, 1961. Pages 109 & 119.
16. Made in Heaven: A Jewish Wedding Guide . Rabbi Aryeh Kaplan. Moznaim Publishing Corporation, New York, Jerusalem, 1983. Pages 186-205.
17. Talmud - Rosh HaShanah 16a.
18. The Book of Our Heritage: The Jewish Year and its Days of Significance - Volume 1. Eliyahu Kitov. Feldheim Publishers, New York, Jerusalem, 1968. Page 17.
19. The Complete Artscroll Siddur. Rabbi Nosson Scherman. Mesorah Publications, Ltd., Brooklyn, New York, 1985. Page 651.
20. The Biblical and Historical Background of the Jewish Holy Days. Abraham P. Bloch. KTAV Publishing House, Inc., New York, 1978. Page 21.
21. Tz'enah Ur'enah - The Weekly Midrash. Translated by Miriam Stark Zakon. Mesorah Publications, Ltd., Brooklyn, New York, 1983. Page 383.
22. IBID. Pages 383-384.
23. Festivals of the Jewish Year. Theodor Gaster.
The High Holy Days. Herman Kieval. The Burning Bush Press, New York, 1959. Page 120.
24. Midrash Rabbah Genesis 56.9. Volume 1 (Zechariah 9:14). Page 498.
25. Ibid. Genesis 29:10. Page 376

26. The Book of Our Heritage: The Jewish Year and its Days of Significance - Volume 1. Eliyahu Kitov. Feldheim Publishers, New York, Jerusalem, 1968. Pages17 - 19.
27. IBID. Page 19.
28. The Artscroll Mesorah Series - Rosh Hashana - Its Significance, Laws, and Prayers. Rabbis Nosson Scherman and Meir Zlotowitz. Mesorah Publications Ltd., 1983. Page 75.
29. The JPS Torah Commenatary - Numbers. Jacob Milgrom. The Jewish Publication Society, Philadelphia, New York, 1990. Page 75.
30. The Artscroll Mesorah Series - Rosh Hashana - Its Significance, Laws, and Prayers. Rabbis Nosson Scherman and Meir Zlotowitz. Mesorah Publications Ltd., 1983. Page 16.
31. The Encyclopedia of the Jewish Religion - Millennium. R.J. Zwi Werblowsky and Geoffrey Wigoder. Adama Books, 1986. Page 263.
32. Daily Prayer Book. Joseph Hertz. Bloch Publishing Company, New York, 1975. Page 415.
33. The Artscroll Tanach Series - Tehillim - Volume 1. Rabbi Avrohom Chaim Feuer. Mesorah Publications, Ltd., Brooklyn, New York, 1977. Page 332.
34. IBID. Page 327.
35. Encyclopedia Judaica CD-ROM Edition. Shofar. Judaica Multimedia, Jerusalem, 1997.
36. Ancient Israel - Its Life and Institutions, Roland De Vaux. William B. Eerdmans Publishng Company, Grand Rapids, Michigan, 1961. Page 504.
37. The Artscroll Mesorah Series - Shabbos [The Sabbath] - Its Essence and Significance. Rabbis Nosson Scherman and Meir Zlotowitz. Mesorah Publications Ltd., 1991. Page 89.
38. Seasons of Our Joy - A Modern Guide to the Jewish Holidays. Arthur Waskow. Beacon Press, Boston, Massachusetts, 1982. Page 1.
39. Tanchuma, Vayero 22:13.
40. Guide to Jewish Holy Days. Hayyim Schauss. New York, 1961. Page 117.

41. The Artscroll Mesorah Series - Rosh Hashana - Its Significance, Laws, and Prayers. Rabbis Nosson Scherman and Meir Zlotowitz. Mesorah Publications Ltd., 1983. Page 79.

42. The Jewish Way. Living the Holidays. Rabbi Irving Greenberg. New York, 1988. Pages 188-189.

43. Entering the High Holy Days: A Complete Guide to the History, Prayers, and Themes. Reuven Hammer. The Jewish Publication Society, Philadelphia, Jerusalem, 1998. Page 38.

44. Days of Awe: A Treasury of Jewish Wisdom for Reflection, Repentance, and Renewal on the High Holy Days. S.Y. Agnon. Schocken Books, New York, 1948. Pages 45-46.

45. IBID. Page 24.

46. The Jewish Way. Living the Holidays. Rabbi Irving Greenberg. New York, 1988. Pages 186, 195.

47. The High Holy Days. Herman Kieval. The Burning Bush Press, New York, 1959. Page 98.

48. Days of Awe: A Treasury of Jewish Wisdom for Reflection, Repentance, and Renewal on the High Holy Days. S.Y. Agnon. Schocken Books, New York, 1948. Page 49.

49. New Year: Its History, Customs and Superstitions. Theodor Gaster. New York, 1955, Page 122.

50. Rosh Hashana and the Messianic Kingdom to Come. Joseph Good. Hatikva Ministries, Port Arthur, Texas, 1989. Pages 96-97.

51. The Book of Our Heritage: The Jewish Year and its Days of Significance - Volume 1. Eliyahu Kitov. Feldheim Publishers, New York, Jerusalem, 1968. Pages 9-10.

52. The Biblical and Historical Background of Jewish Customs and Ceremonies. Abraham P. Bloch. KTAV Publishing House, Inc., New York, 1980. Page 156.

53. The Book of Our Heritage: The Jewish Year and its Days of Significance - Volume 1. Eliyahu Kitov. Feldheim Publishers, New York, Jerusalem, 1968. Page 7.

54. Entering the High Holy Days: A Complete Guide to the History, Prayers, and Themes. Reuven Hammer. The Jewish Publication Society, Philadelphia, Jerusalem, 1998. Pages 76-77.

55. The Artscroll Mesorah Series - Rosh Hashana - Its Significance, Laws, and Prayers. Rabbis Nosson Scherman and Meir Zlotowitz. Mesorah Publications Ltd., 1983. Pages 30-31.

56. IBID. Pages 31-35.

57. Artscroll Tanach Series - Divrei hayamim II - 2 Chronicles. Rabbi Moshe Eisemann. Mesorah Publications, Ltd., Brooklyn, New York, 1992. Page 164.

58. IBID. Page 165.

59. JPS Torah Commentary - Exodus. Nahum M. Sarna. The Jewish Publication Society, Philadelphia, New York, Jerusalem, 1991. Page 92.

60. Artscroll Tanach Series - Divrei hayamim II - 2 Chronicles. Rabbi Moshe Eisemann. Mesorah Publications, Ltd., Brooklyn, New York, 1992. Pages 170-171.

61. Artscroll Tanach Series - Tehillim - Psalms - Volume 1. Rabbi Avroham Chaim Feuer . Mesorah Publications, Ltd., Brooklyn, New York, 1977. Page 65.

62. Ancient Israel: Its Life and Institutions. Roland De Vaux. William B. Eerdmans Publishing Company, Grand Rapids, Michigan, 1961. Page 109.

63. Encyclopedia Judaica - Adoption. CD-Rom Edition. Keter Publishing House Ltd., Judaica Multimedia Ltd., Jerusalem, 1997.

64. Artscroll Tanach Series - Tehillim - Psalms - Volume 1. Rabbi Avroham Chaim Feuer . Mesorah Publications, Ltd., Brooklyn, New York, 1977. Page 595-597.

65. Rosh Hashana and the Messianic Kingdom to Come. Joseph Good. Hatikva Ministries, Port Arthur, Texas, 1989. Pages 128-129.

66. Entering the High Holy Days: A Complete Guide to the History, Prayers, and Themes. Reuven Hammer. The Jewish Publication Society, Philadelphia, Jerusalem, 1998. Page 57.

67. The High Holy Days. Herman Kieval. The Burning Bush Press, New York, 1959. Pages 42-43.

68. Jewish Encyclopedia - Book of Adam. Internet Edition.

69. Entering the High Holy Days: A Complete Guide to the History, Prayers, and Themes. Reuven Hammer. The Jewish Publication Society, Philadelphia, Jerusalem, 1998. Page 54.
70. IBID. Page 207.
71. IBID. Page 55-56.
72. IBID. Page 56.
73. Artscroll Tanach Series - Tehillim - Psalms - Volume 2. Rabbi Avroham Chaim Feuer . Mesorah Publications, Ltd., Brooklyn, New York, 1977. Page 1186.
74. The Artscroll Mesorah Series - Shabbos [The Sabbath] - Its Essence and Significance. Rabbis Nosson Scherman and Meir Zlotowitz. Mesorah Publications Ltd., 1991. Page 55.
75. The Artscroll Mesorah Series - Shabbos [The Sabbath] - Its Essence and Significance. Rabbis Nosson Scherman and Meir Zlotowitz. Mesorah Publications Ltd., 1991. Page27.
76. Artscroll Tanach Series - Tehillim - Psalms - Volume 2. Rabbi Avroham Chaim Feuer . Mesorah Publications, Ltd., Brooklyn, New York, 1977. Page 1147.
77. IBID. Page 1148.
78. Entering the High Holy Days: A Complete Guide to the History, Prayers, and Themes. Reuven Hammer. The Jewish Publication Society, Philadelphia, Jerusalem, 1998. Page 97.
79. The Artscroll Mesorah Series - Rosh Hashana - Its Significance, Laws, and Prayers. Rabbis Nosson Scherman and Meir Zlotowitz. Mesorah Publications Ltd., 1983. Page 45.
80. Entering the High Holy Days: A Complete Guide to the History, Prayers, and Themes. Reuven Hammer. The Jewish Publication Society, Philadelphia, Jerusalem, 1998. Page 101.
81. IBID. Page 102.
82. Days of Awe: A Treasury of Jewish Wisdom for Reflection, Repentance, and Renewal on the High Holy Days. S.Y. Agnon. Schocken Books, New York, 1948. Page 109.
83. The Complete Artscroll Siddur. Rabbi Nosson Scherman. Mesorah Publications, Ltd., Brooklyn, New York, 1985. Pages 690-691.

84. Seasons of Our Joy - A Modern Guide to the Jewish Holidays. Arthur Waskow. Beacon Press, Boston, Massachusetts, 1982. Page 228.

85. The Artscroll Mesorah Series - Yom Kippur - Its Significance, Laws, and Prayers. Rabbis Nosson Scherman and Meir Zlotowitz. Mesorah Publications Ltd., 1989. Pages 52-53.

86. The Rosh Hashanah Anthology. Philip Goodman. The Jewish Publication Society, Philadelphia, Jerusalem, 1992. Page 40.

87. Entering the High Holy Days: A Complete Guide to the History, Prayers, and Themes. Reuven Hammer. The Jewish Publication Society, Philadelphia, Jerusalem, 1998. Page 110.

88. IBID. Page 117.

89. IBID. Page 146.

90. IBID. Page 167.

91. Days of Awe: A Treasury of Jewish Wisdom for Reflection, Repentance, and Renewal on the High Holy Days. S.Y. Agnon. Schocken Books, New York, 1948. Page 270.

92. IBID. Page 271.

93. IBID. Page 272.

94. Encyclopedia Judaica CD-ROM Edition. Sabbatical Year and Jubilee. Judaica Multimedia, Jerusalem, 1997.

95. IBID. Temple.

96. Messiah - Understanding His Identity and Teachings Through the Soul of the Torah - Volume 3. Avi ben Mordecai. Millennium 7000 Communications, 2001. Page 250.

97. Seasons of Our Joy - A Modern Guide to the Jewish Holidays. Arthur Waskow. Beacon Press, Boston, Massachusetts, 1982. Page 27.

98. The Pictorial Avodah Series - The Yom Kippur Avodah. Menachem Moshe Oppen. C.I.S. Publishers. New York, London, Jerusalem, 1995. Pages 32, 62-65.

99. Yalkut Me'am Lo'ez - The Torah Anthology - Leviticus I - Book 11 in the series. Translated by Rabbi Aryeh Kaplan. Mozaim Publishing Corporation, New York, Jerusalem, 1989. Pages 361-378.

100. Talmud. Yoma 66b-68b.

101. The JPS Torah Commenatary - Leviticus. Baruch A. Levine. The Jewish Publication Society, Philadelphia, New York, 1989. Pages 251-253.

102. The Works of Josephus. Translated by William Whiston. Hendrickson Publishers, Peabody, Massachusetts, 1987. Page 687.

103. The Old Testament Pseudepigrapha - Apocalyptic Literature & Testaments - Volume 1. Edited by James H. Charlesworth. Doubleday, New York, 1983. Page 37.

104. IBID. Page 38.

105. IBID. Page 38.

106. Seasons of Our Joy - A Modern Guide to the Jewish Holidays. Arthur Waskow. Beacon Press, Boston, Massachusetts, 1982. Pages 56-57.

107. The Artscroll Tanach Series - Bereishis (Genesis) - Volume 1(a). Rabbi Meir Zlotowitz, Mesorah Publications, Ltd., Brooklyn, New York, 1986. Page 42.

108. The Wisdom In the Hebrew Alphabet. Rabbi Michael L. Munk. Mesorah Publications, Ltd., Brooklyn, New York, 1983. Page 174.

109. The Fall Feasts of Israel. Mitch and Zhava Glaser. Moody Press, Chicago, 1987. Page 182.

110. The Artscroll Mesorah Series - Succos - Its Significance, Laws, and Prayers. Rabbis Nosson Scherman and Meir Zlotowitz. Mesorah Publications, Ltd., Brooklyn, New York, 1982. Page 24.

111. IBID. Page 47.

112. IBID. Pages 34-38.

113. Dictionary of Deities and Demons. Karel van der Toorn, Bob Becking, and Pieter W. Van der Horst. E. J. Brill, Leiden, New York, Koln, 1995. Pages 956-963.

114. The Complete Artscroll Machzor - Shavuos. Rabbi Avie Gold. Mesorah Publications, Ltd., Brooklyn, New York, 1991. Pages 293-295.

115.   The Sukkot/Simhat Torah Anthology. Philip Goodman. The Jeewish Publication Society, Philadelphia, New York, Jerusalem, 1988. Pages 77-78.

116.   Yalkut Me'am Lo'ez - The Torah Anthology -Deuteronomy IV - Book 18 in the series. Translated by Rabbi Eliyahu Touger. Mozaim Publishing Corporation, New York, Jerusalem, 1991. Page 189.

117.   The Artscroll Mesorah Series - Succos - Its Significance, Laws, and Prayers. Rabbis Nosson Scherman and Meir Zlotowitz. Mesorah Publications, Ltd., Brooklyn, New York, 1982. Page 17.

118.   IBID. Page 23.

119.   IBID. Page 24.

120.   The Old Testament Pseudepigrapha - Apocalyptic Literature & Testaments - Volume 1. Edited by James H. Charlesworth. Doubleday, New York, 1983. Pages 13-14.

121.   The Artscroll Mesorah Series - Succos - Its Significance, Laws, and Prayers. Rabbis Nosson Scherman and Meir Zlotowitz. Mesorah Publications, Ltd., Brooklyn, New York, 1982. Page 70.

122.   The Artscroll Mesorah Series - Shemini Atzeret/Simchas Torah - Its Significance, Laws, and Prayers. Rabbis Nosson Scherman and Meir Zlotowitz. Mesorah Publications, Ltd., Brooklyn, New York, 1996. Page 51.

123.   IBID. Pages 41-42, 50-51, 55.

124.   Artscroll Tanach Series - Tehillim - Psalms - Volume 2. Rabbi Avroham Chaim Feuer . Mesorah Publications, Ltd., Brooklyn, New York, 1977. Pages 1517-1518.

12

THE MESSAGE TO
THE 7 ASSEMBLIES

To 'overcome' by definition is to be victorious and to prevail. Believers in Messiah are to 'overcome' the world, evil, and all adversaries to God's Kingdom. Becoming a child of faith in God automatically identifies one as an 'overcomer' with our spiritual forefathers. First, let's look at Jacob!

Genesis 32:28 *And he said, Thy name shall be called no more Jacob, but <u>Israel</u>: for as a prince hast thou power with God and with men, and hast <u>prevailed</u>.* (KJV)

Jacob refused to let the angel of the Lord loose until He blessed him. Jacob's name was changed to Israel because he had prevailed or overcome. Through some manipulation Jacob had gained his twin-brother Esau's birthright through Isaac. Esau wanted to kill him, so Jacob left Canaan for Padan-Aram where he lodged at Laban's house for about twenty years. After leaving Laban's house, Jacob came back to Canaan only to have another showdown with Esau. This blessing where the angel of the Lord revealed to Jacob that God intended to change his name to Israel, was to establish that the blessing from his father Isaac, was being recognized by God and Jacob had prevailed or overcome.

The term 'Israel' has no etymological meaning. 'El' represents 'God,' therefore 'Isra-EL' has something to do with Him. The rabbis deduced the meaning of 'Israel' from the text in which it was first used. In other words, since Jacob has 'prevailed' his name will be 'Prevailer of God'. Therefore, the term 'Israel' is connected to 'victory' and could be understood as an 'Overcomer' or 'Champion' for God.[1]

Jews who follow after God and His Commandments are 'Overcomers' of God. Gentiles who follow after God are grafted into 'Israel' and are also 'Overcomers' of God. As Jacob had to fight 'spiritually,' so is it necessary for believers to 'wrestle' with the 'angel of the LORD for His blessings.

Revelation 12:11 *And they overcame him by the blood of the Lamb, and by the word of their testimony; and they loved not their lives unto the death.* (KJV)

An 'Overcomer' is one who is victorious by the blood of the Lamb. Our victory with God over the enemy can only come through the blood of the Lamb. Those who are 'washed' in His blood will ultimately comprise 'Israel,' the 'Overcomers' of God.

Revelation 1:10-20 *I was in the Spirit on the Lord's day, and heard behind me a great voice, as of a trumpet [Shofar], Saying, I am Alpha and Omega, the first and the last: and, What thou seest, write in a book, and send it unto the seven churches which are in Asia; unto Ephesus, and unto Smyrna, and unto Pergamos, and unto Thyatira, and unto Sardis, and unto Philadelphia, and unto Laodicea. And <u>I turned to see the voice that spake with me.</u> And being turned, I saw seven golden candlesticks; And in the midst of the seven candlesticks one like unto the Son of man, clothed with a garment down to the foot, and girt about the paps with a golden girdle. His head and his hairs were white like wool, as white as snow; and his eyes were as a flame of fire; And his feet like unto fine brass, as if they burned in a furnace; and his voice as the sound of many waters. And he had in his right hand seven stars: and out of his mouth went a sharp twoedged sword: and his countenance was as the sun shineth in his strength. And when I saw him, I fell at his feet as dead. And he laid his right hand upon me, saying unto me, Fear not; I am the first and the last: I am he that liveth, and was dead; and, behold, I am alive for evermore, Amen; and have the keys of hell and of death. Write* *the things which thou hast seen, and the things which are, and the things which shall be hereafter; The mystery of the seven stars which thou sawest in my right hand, and the seven golden candlesticks. The seven stars are the angels of the seven churches: and the seven candlesticks which thou sawest are the seven churches.* (KJV)

John encounters a heavenly vision, which causes him to be 'in the spirit' on 'the Lord's Day'. Christianity has corrupted the meaning of the Lord's Day in the book of Revelation to represent Sunday worship. John wrote the book of Revelation between 90-100 CE and we know that Sunday worship did not start within the church until later in the second century. In ancient Judaism 'the Lord's Day' could only mean one of two things. First it represented the seventh day Sabbath, and secondly it represented the seventh millennium known in Scripture as 'the Day of the Lord'.[2] John was given a vision of the Day of the Lord that commences with seven years of the Birth Pangs of the Messiah [Tribulation Period] and concludes with the Messiah ruling as king for one thousand years.

John 'hears' a 'great voice' behind him that sounds like a trumpet [shofar/ram's horn]. In this book we have shown how the shofar is linked to the Day of the Lord commencing at Rosh Hashana after six thousand years have been completed. The fact that John hears this Awakening Shout or Blast [Teurah] 'behind him' gives strong allusions to the Akeidah of Genesis 22 where 'behind' Abram was a ram caught in the thicket. Of course, we have detailed the mysticism of the two horns of that ram as alluding to the shofar that was blown at Mount Sinai [Pentecost] and to the 'last' shofar blown at Rosh Hashana. Throughout the first three chapters of the book of Revelation we see this connection with Shavuot [Pentecost] and Rosh Hashana.

The shofar-like voice that John heard was the Son of Man/ Yeshua. He declared to John that He was the Aleph [Alpha] and Tav [Omega]. John was instructed by Yeshua to write what he is about to see to the seven churches in Asia Minor. There can be no doubt that Revelation is written to these seven literal churches in John's day. These seven churches are also prophetic to the Day of the Lord and the Birth Pangs of the Messiah. The entire context of Revelation is prophetic about the 'Lord's Day'. What follows in Revelation 4-19 are the seven years of Birth Pangs followed by the remainder of the final Millennium. Finally we get a picture of the Olam Haba, New Jerusalem coming down from Heaven.

John then turns 'to see' the voice behind him. Seeing God's voice has definite allusions back to Pentecost at Mt. Sinai and Acts 2:

Exodus 19:16 *And it came to pass on the third day in the morning, that there were thunders [Hebrew kol - voices] and lightnings, and a thick cloud upon the mount, and the voice of the trumpet [Hebrew shofar] exceeding loud; so that all the people that was in the camp trembled.* (KJV)

Exodus 20:18-19 *And all the people saw the thunderings [Hebrew kol - voices], and the lightnings [Hebrew lapid - flames], and the noise [Hebrew kol - voice] of the trumpet [Hebrew shofar], and the mountain smoking: and when the people saw it, they removed, and stood afar off. And they said unto Moses, Speak thou with us, and we will hear: but let not God speak with us, lest we die.* (KJV)

Hebrews 12:18-23 *For ye are not come unto the mount [Sinai] that might be touched, and that burned with fire, nor unto blackness, and darkness, and tempest, And the sound of a trumpet [shofar], and the voice of words [plural]; which voice they that heard intreated that the word should not be spoken to them any more: (For they could not endure that which was commanded, And if so much as a beast touch the mountain, it shall be stoned, or thrust through with a dart: And so terrible was the sight, that Moses said, I exceedingly fear and quake:) But ye are come unto mount Sion, and unto the city of the living God, the heavenly Jerusalem, and to an innumerable company of angels, To the general assembly and church of the first-born, <u>which are written in heaven,</u> and to God the Judge of all, and to the spirits of just men made perfect,* (KJV)

Acts 2:1-4 *And when the day of Pentecost was fully come, they were all with one accord in one place. And suddenly there came a sound from heaven as of a rushing mighty wind, and it filled all* *the house where they were sitting. And there appeared unto them cloven tongues like as of fire, and it sat upon each of them. And they were all filled with the Holy Ghost, and began to speak with other tongues, as the Spirit gave them utterance.* (KJV)

Moses was given an open vision of the Heavenly Tabernacle on Mt. Sinai. He was instructed by God to make the earthly Tabernacle after the one he saw. The Tabernacle/Temple on earth was only a shadow and replica of the true heavenly Tabernacle:

Exodus 25:9 *According to all that I shew thee, after the pattern of the tabernacle, and the pattern of all the instruments thereof, even so shall ye make it.* (KJV)

Exodus 25:40 *And look that thou make them after their pattern, which was shewed thee in the mount.* (KJV)

Hebrews 8:5 *Who serve unto the example and shadow of heavenly things, as Moses was admonished of God when he was about to make the tabernacle: for, See, saith he, that thou make all things according to the pattern shewed to thee in the mount.* (KJV)

When John turns to 'see' the voice behind him he sees seven 'golden candlesticks'. In Revelation 1:20 John is told explicitly that these seven golden candlesticks are the seven churches [assemblies] he was told to write to in Revelation 2 & 3. In John's time they were 'lampstands' because candles had yet to be invented.[3]

In the literal understanding we see a golden Menorah with seven lights and Yeshua appears in the midst on the seven lights aligning Himself with the middle lamp. This would make sense according to the Hebraic understanding that the middle lamp of the Menorah was called the Shamash, or Servant Lamp.[4] It was to be lit at all times and the flame from it was used to relight the other six lamps. The Shamash was known as 'The Light' of the world. It was called 'Ner Elohim,' the Light of God.[5]

Some rabbinical commentaries identified the Servant Lamp of the Menorah with that of the work of Messiah. For example, Genesis

1:1 consists of seven Hebrew words, which the rabbis mentioned paralleled the seven branches of the Menorah.[6] The fourth Hebrew word of Genesis 1:1, the middle Servant Lamp, is 'et' ת א. This is the Aleph-Tav, or the first and last letter of the Hebrew alphabet, equivalent to Yeshua calling Himself the Alpha and Omega [the first and last letters of the Greek alphabet] in Revelation 1:8,11 and 21:6; 22:13. 'In the beginning' Yeshua was in the 'middle' of the 'Creation'.

The Menorah itself was one of the instruments that Moses was instructed to make according to the pattern he saw in the Heavenly Tabernacle:

Numbers 8:4 *And this work of the candlestick [Hebrew menorah - 7 branched lampstand] was of beaten gold, unto the shaft thereof, unto the flowers thereof, was beaten work: according unto the pattern which the LORD had shewed Moses, so he made the candlestick [Hebrew menorah].* (KJV)

Hebrews 9:2 *For there was a tabernacle made; the first, wherein was the candlestick [singular - one menorah], and the table, and the shewbread; which is called the sanctuary.* (KJV)

This author believes that God wants us to see a larger dimensional picture. In Hebrews 9:2, when the writer was clearly speaking of the one singular candlestick in the Holy Place of the Temple, he was clearly speaking of the seven-branched Menorah. The word for candlestick here in Hebrews is the same Greek word used in Revelation, but only in the singular. When John sees Yeshua in the midst of seven golden candlesticks [plural] in Revelation, He was actually in the midst of seven golden Menorahs each having seven lights. Therefore, Yeshua is the fiftieth Light, Who is 'The Shamash' (Servant Light), that is in the midst of the forty-nine lights from the seven Menorahs.

What is the significance of these fifty Lights? They are directly related to the festival of Pentecost [Shavuot]. Shavuot is the fiftieth day of the Firstfruits count after the counting of the omer. It was on Shavuot [Pentecost] that Israel appeared before God at Mt. Sinai to receive the Torah. At Mt. Sinai the Israelites 'saw' the 'thunderings and lightnings,' which literally translates from the Hebrew as 'voices and flames'. In addition they heard the noise or 'voice' of the shofar.

At Pentecost in Acts 2 we see a similar occurrence. There was a sound or voice from heaven as a rushing mighty wind, or possibly a shofar. Cloven tongues or voices appeared like fire and the believers were all filled with the Holy Spirit. Therefore, the connections to the festival of Shavuot include the sound of a shofar-like voice, flames, the Holy Spirit and, of course, the number fifty.

A believer in Yeshua can now experience the 'Firstfruits' Pentecost as given in Acts 2. This is linked to the betrothal of the believer as they await the second stage of marriage, which of course, is the resurrection. One could say, then, that we are still living in the Pentecostal era. However, the Scriptures teach us that Yeshua's second coming will be centered around the Day of the Lord [Lord's Day] and specifically the fall festivals of Rosh Hashana, Yom Kippur, and Tabernacles. The first three chapters in the book of Revelation prophetically detail the transition from the Pentecostal Firstfruits era unto the Day of the Lord in which the resurrections will occur and believers will be fully 'married' to the Lord.

John sees Yeshua, the Ner Elohim [the Light of God] in the midst of the seven golden menorahs. He is the Light, the fiftieth Light, symbolic of Pentecost. The description of Yeshua by John is incredible: 'clothed with a garment down to the foot, and girt about the paps with a golden girdle'. Ancient Aramaic translations of Revelation, which are closer to the original Semitic language than Greek, identify these pieces of clothing as an 'Ephod' and a 'Breastplate'.[7] In other words, John is very clearly seeing Yeshua as the heavenly High Priest of the 'Heavenly' Tabernacle.

Hebrews 5:6 *As he saith also in another place, Thou art a priest for ever after the order of Melchisedec.* (KJV)

The book of Hebrews makes it very clear that Yeshua, Who is at the right hand of the Father, is the Heavenly High Priest after the Order of Melchizedek. Yeshua will continue to be the High Priest throughout the Day of Lord as long as there are human beings still capable of choosing to follow God over Satan. But the transition from the Pentecostal era unto the Day of the Lord is really the transition of Yeshua, the High Priest, unto Yeshua the King. The Messianic Kingdom is only in the hearts of the believers currently. This is what the Pentecostal Firstfruits is all about. The Messianic Kingdom on earth is not yet realized. Not only will Yeshua be King in the believer's heart [as now is the case], but He will also be King of a literal Kingdom, which is the purpose of the Day of the Lord. John is being shown this transition and Yeshua, the Lamb of God, is coronated as King in Revelation 4 & 5.

Revelation 1:5-6 *And from Jesus Christ, who is the faithful witness, and the first begotten of the dead, and the prince of the kings of the earth. Unto him that loved us, and washed us from our sins in his own blood, And hath made us kings <u>and</u> [not in the original text] priests unto God and his Father; to him be glory and dominion for ever and ever. Amen.* (KJV)

Yeshua is clearly the believers' High Priest who washes [bathes] them in His blood. The KJV says He has 'made us kings and priests unto God'. However, 'and' is not in the original text and it should be read that He has made us 'kings-priests unto God,' which actually translates better as a 'kingdom of priests'.[8] Consider the following Scriptures:

Exodus 19:6 *And ye shall be unto me a kingdom of priests, and an holy nation. These are the words which thou shalt speak unto the children of Israel.* (KJV)

1 Peter 2:4-5, 7-10 *To whom coming, as unto a living stone, disallowed indeed of men, but chosen of God, and precious, Ye also, as lively stones, are built up a spiritual house, an holy priesthood, to offer up spiritual sacrifices, acceptable to God by Jesus Christ... Unto you therefore which believe he is precious: but unto them which be disobedient, the stone which the builders disallowed, the same is made the head of the corner, And a stone of stumbling, and a rock of offence, even to them which stumble at the word, being disobedient:*

whereunto also they were appointed. But ye are a chosen generation, a royal priesthood, an holy nation, a peculiar people; that ye should shew forth the praises of him who hath called you out of darkness into his marvellous light: Which in time past were not a people, but are now the people of God: which had not obtained mercy, but now have obtained mercy. (KJV)

At the base of Mount Sinai God instructed Moses to tell Israel that they were to be a 'kingdom of priests'. This was to occur through the covenant at Shavuot [Pentecost]. Peter picks up on these verses in Exodus 19 and calls believers in Yeshua a 'holy priesthood,' and a 'royal priesthood', which hints at a kingdom of priests. God, and therefore Peter, was not making reference to the Levitical priesthood, for they were selected only after the Golden Calf incident. So who was the kingdom of priests that the Scripture was alluding to?

It is interesting to note that in the midst of the Passover sacrifice in Egypt, God tells Moses to sanctify the firstborn male of man and beast. The covenant of the Passover is directly linked to the womb and the firstborn male. Later, in the Tabernacle [and Temple], the clean male firstborn animal was sacrificed by a priest and eaten only by priests. The unclean male firstborn animal had to be redeemed by paying money to the priest. The male firstborn human, of course, had to be redeemed with money to the priest.

It wasn't all the Israelites that were protected from the Death Angel on the Egyptian Passover; it was only the firstborn male of man and beast. No harm came to Pharaoh and the Egyptian people, just their firstborn male of man and beast. Why is the covenant of the Passover linked to the Firstborn? Because the firstborn males of the Israelites were the first priests, who belonged to God after the Egyptian Passover. We discussed this at length in the chapter entitled *The Threshold Covenant*.

The priesthood of believers today has absolutely no links to the Levitical priesthood. Because we are only in the Firstfruits-Pentecostal era, the priesthood of believers is spiritual in the hearts of the believers. The resurrected believers will literally become a kingdom of priests ruling and reigning with Messiah during the Day of the Lord. It is all based upon the firstborn principle. John writes in Revelation 1:5 that Yeshua is the 'first begotten of the dead,' in other words he was the first to experience resurrection. We read in Hebrews 12:23 that believers are called 'to the general assembly and church of the firstborn, which are written in heaven'. Believers experience the spiritual Firstfruits [Pentecostal] priestly kingdom in their hearts, but at the resurrection they will become a literal kingdom of priests in Messiah's Kingdom, who is the High Priest and King.

Revelation 1:14 *His head and his hairs were white like wool, as white as snow; and his eyes were as a flame of fire;* (KJV)

Daniel 7:9 *I beheld till the thrones were cast down, and the Ancient of days did sit, whose garment was white as snow, and the hair of his head like the pure wool: his throne was like the fiery flame, and his wheels as burning fire.* (KJV)

1 Enoch [Book Two] Chapter 46:1 *There I beheld the Ancient of days, whose head was like white wool, and with him another, whose countenance resembled that of a man.*[9]

John sees the Heavenly High Priest's [Son of Man] head [hair] as 'white like wool'. The book of Enoch associates a head of white wool with the Ancient of Days, who has the Son of man standing with him. Daniel also spoke of God in this fashion. Jewish Midrashim view the phrase 'head of wool' as a sign of superiority and judgeship.[10]

Revelation 19:12-15 *His eyes were as a flame of fire, and on his head were many crowns; and he had a name written, that no man knew, but he himself. And he was clothed with a vesture dipped in blood: and his name is called The Word of God. And the armies which were in heaven followed him upon white horses, clothed in fine linen, white and clean. And out of his mouth goeth a sharp sword, that with it he should smite the nations: and he shall rule them with a rod of iron: and he treadeth the winepress of the fierceness and wrath of Almighty God.* (KJV)

John next makes reference to the Son of Man's eyes appearing as 'a flame of fire' in Revelation 1:14. Clearly this is another symbolism of judgment. Revelation 19 details the same Son of Man coming as King to judge the nations and 'His eyes were as a flame of fire'.

Revelation 1:15 *And his feet like unto fine brass, as if they burned in a furnace; and his voice as the sound of many waters.* (KJV)

Then John sees His feet as 'fine brass' as if they were burned or polished in a furnace. Brass is another symbol of judgment. In the Tabernacle/Temple the Brazen/Copper Altar was where the sacrifices were burned. Instead of God's judgment coming upon man, the sacrificed animal appeased God.

John states that the Son of Man's 'Voice' was as 'the sound of many waters'. This directly relates not only to Shavuot [Pentecost], but also Succot [Tabernacles]. Shavuot is the 'Atzeret' [conclusion] of the spring festival betrothal process, whereas Succot [especially Shemini Atzeret/ The Eighth Day] is the conclusion of the fall festivals and full marriage. The Zohar relates how the sacrifices of seventy bulls for the nations during Succot are symbolically represented by 'brass'.[11]

Revelation 1:16 *And he had in his right hand seven stars: and out of his mouth went a sharp twoedged sword: and his countenance was as the sun shineth in his strength.* (KJV)

Finally, John sees seven stars in the Son of Man's right hand. These explicitly relate to the 'angels' to the seven churches as stated in Revelation 1:20. We will be discussing these 'angels' shortly. John sees a 'sharp two-edged sword' coming out of His mouth. This is another picture of judgment as we just saw in Revelation 19 where the sword is used to smite the nations.

Deuteronomy 8:3 *And he humbled thee, and suffered thee to hunger, and fed thee with manna, which thou knewest not, neither did thy fathers know; that he might make thee know that man doth not live* *by bread only, but by <u>every word that proceedeth out of the mouth of the LORD</u> doth man live.* (KJV)

Hebrews 4:11-13 *Let us labour therefore to enter into that rest, lest any man fall after the same example of unbelief. For the word of God is quick, and powerful, and sharper than any twoedged sword, piercing even to the dividing asunder of soul and spirit, and of the joints and marrow, and is a discerner of the thoughts and intents of the heart. Neither is there any creature that is not manifest in his sight: but all things are naked and opened unto the eyes of him with whom we have to do.* (KJV)

What is the sharp two-edged sword coming out of the Son of Man's mouth? The symbolism is clearly representative of the 'Word' of God. The sword is an allusion to the 'Torah'. Those who refuse to 'hear' the Torah will be judged unto condemnation. All judgment, good or bad, comes from the Torah, the Word of God.

1 Peter 4:17-19 *For the time is come that judgment must begin at the house of God: and if it first begin at us, what shall the end be of them that obey not the gospel of God? And if the righteous scarcely be saved, where shall the ungodly and the sinner appear? Wherefore let them that suffer according to the will of God commit the keeping of their souls to him in well doing, as unto a faithful Creator.* (KJV)

The picture that John sees is Yeshua, the Heavenly High Priest, coming in judgment. To who is He bringing judgment? The sinners will be judged during the Birth Pangs of the Messiah, but Yeshua is only the High Priest to those that accepted His mediation between them and the Father. Yeshua is not the High Priest to sinners who have rejected Him. Therefore, it is safe to conclude that Yeshua in this symbolism is coming to judge the 'Ekklesia' [Congregation], those assemblies who call upon His Name as Lord. In Revelation 19 He returns to earth as King and will judge the nations appropriately. He will be the King-Priest throughout the Millennium because flesh and blood humans will still need a mediator before God.

Deuteronomy 20:1-3 *When thou goest out to battle against thine enemies, and seest horses, and chariots, and a people more than thou, be not afraid of them: for the LORD thy God is with thee, which brought thee up out of the land of Egypt. And it shall be, when ye are come nigh unto the battle, that <u>the priest shall approach and speak unto the people</u>, And shall say unto them, Hear, O Israel, ye approach this day unto battle against your enemies: let not your hearts faint, fear not, and do not tremble, neither be ye terrified because of them;* (KJV)

In the Torah there was a 'second' High Priest who was anointed for war. Although the Scriptures give very little detail to the role of this priest, other Jewish sources mention this priest's purpose and function. The High Priest Anointed for war did not participate in the Tabernacle/Temple ritual. His position was to ready the men of Israel for battle against the enemy. His responsibility was not only to make sure the warriors were physically fit, but also spiritually minded to fight for the Torah.

Numbers 31:6-8 *And Moses sent them to the war, a thousand of every tribe, them and Phinehas the son of Eleazar the priest, to the war, with the holy instruments, and the trumpets to blow in his hand. And they warred against the Midianites, as the LORD commanded Moses; and they slew all the males. And they slew the kings of Midian, beside the rest of them that were slain; namely, Evi, and Rekem, and Zur, and Hur, and Reba, five kings of Midian: Balaam also the son of Beor they slew with the sword.* (KJV)

According to rabbinical tradition the first High Priest Anointed for War was Phineas, the grandson of Aaron.[12] In the Midrash there is a character called the 'War Messiah,' which links the Priest Anointed for War to the Suffering Messiah ben Joseph.[13] Yeshua will judge the 'Congregation' first at the outset of the Day of the Lord prior to the seven-years of Birth Pangs. He will then war against the nations at the end of the Birth Pangs. When He returns to earth to set up His Kingdom, He will be Messiah ben David. Note the following

Scriptures that show the picture of the 'War Messiah' bringing vengeance with blood:

Isaiah 59:17 *For he put on righteousness as a breastplate, and an helmet of salvation upon his head; and <u>he put on the garments of vengeance for clothing</u>, and was clad with zeal as a cloke.* (KJV)

Isaiah 63:3-4 *I have trodden the winepress alone; and of the people there was none with me: for I will tread them in mine anger, and trample them in my fury; and their blood shall be sprinkled upon my garments, and I will stain all my raiment. For the day of vengeance is in mine heart, and the year of my redeemed is come.* (KJV)

Revelation 14:19 *And the angel thrust in his sickle into the earth, and gathered the vine of the earth, and cast it into the great winepress of the wrath of God.* (KJV)

Revelation 19:15 *And out of his mouth goeth a sharp sword, that with it he should smite the nations: and he shall rule them with a rod of iron: and he treadeth the winepress of the fierceness and wrath of Almighty God.* (KJV)

Before discussing the details of the Son of Man's messages to the seven churches in Revelation 2 and 3, we will attempt to show the significance of John seeing 'His voice as the sound of many waters' (Revelation 1:15). We begin with the following verses:

Revelation 1:4 *John to the seven churches which are in Asia: Grace be unto you, and peace, from him which is, and which was, and which is to come; and from the seven Spirits which are before his throne;* (KJV)

Revelation 4:5 *And out of the throne proceeded lightnings and thunderings and voices: and there were seven lamps of fire burning before the throne, which are the seven Spirits of God.* (KJV)

Revelation 5:6 *And I beheld, and, lo, in the midst of the throne and of the four beasts, and in the midst of the elders, stood a Lamb as it had been slain, having seven horns and seven eyes, which are the seven Spirits of God sent forth into all the earth.* (KJV)

Revelation 1:14 *His head and his hairs were white like wool, as white as snow; and his eyes were as a flame of fire;* (KJV)

Putting these Scriptures together we view the Son of Man, the Messiah, with eyes 'as a flame of fire'. Yeshua, the Lamb of God, has 'seven eyes, which are the seven Spirits of God'. The seven lamps of fire [one Menorah] burning 'before the throne' are the 'seven Spirits of God'. The mention of 'lightnings, thunders, voices and fire,' is a direct allusion to Pentecost at Mount Sinai as we have studied throughout this book.

The 'number' of voices is said to be seven, taken from the seven voices mentioned in Psalms 29:3-9:

Psalm 29:1-9 *Give unto the LORD, O ye mighty, give unto the LORD glory and strength. Give unto the LORD the glory due unto his name; worship the LORD in the beauty of holiness. The voice of the LORD is upon the waters [Red Sea]: the God of glory thundereth: the LORD is upon many waters. The voice of the LORD is powerful; the voice of the LORD is full of majesty. The voice of the LORD breaketh the cedars; yea, the LORD breaketh the cedars of Lebanon. He maketh them also to skip like a calf; Lebanon and Sirion like a young unicorn. The voice of the LORD divideth the flames of fire. The voice of the LORD shaketh the wilderness; the LORD shaketh the wilderness of Kadesh. The voice of the LORD maketh the hinds to calve, and discovereth the forests: and in his temple doth every one speak of his glory.* (KJV)

1 Chronicles 16:28-29 *Give unto the LORD, ye kindreds of the people, give unto the LORD glory and strength. Give unto the LORD the glory due unto his name: bring an offering, and come before him: worship the LORD in the beauty of holiness.* (KJV)

The Holy of Holies was viewed as a symbol or pattern of God's Throne room based upon the real Heavenly Throne. The Ark of the Covenant itself was symbolically viewed as God's Throne or Chariot. David probably sang Psalm 29 when he transferred the Ark of the Covenant from its temporary abode in the house of Oved Edom to its permanent place in Jerusalem.[14] Psalm 29:1-2 is almost identical to what was sung in 1 Chronicles 16:28-29 when the Ark was brought to Jerusalem.

The seven usages of 'voice of the LORD' in Psalm 29 symbolize the seven forms through which God reveals Himself. The Sabbath Musaf service has seven blessings based upon these 'seven' Voices.[15] In the synagogue, after the Torah scroll is read on the Sabbath, it is escorted back to its holding place, the Ark, while Psalm 29 is recited. According to the Talmud, Psalm 29 was recited by the Levites in the Temple on the first intermediate-day of the Festival of Succot.[16]

We do not want to limit God, but seek to understand the symbolism that the Scripture is presenting us. A Midrash discusses that God's Voice to Israel at Mt. Sinai, when they received the Torah, divided itself into Seven Voices, and then these Seven Voices further divided into the seventy languages of earth.[17]

Daniel 10:13, 20 *But the prince of the kingdom of Persia withstood me one and twenty days: but, lo, Michael, one of the chief princes, came to help me; and I remained there with the kings of Persia... Then said he, Knowest thou wherefore I come unto thee? and now will I return to fight with the prince of Persia: and when I am gone forth, lo, the prince of Grecia shall come.* (KJV)

Although it is impossible for humans to fully grasp the spiritual dimension, the book of Daniel offers some clues. When Daniel was seeking a response from God, a messenger was sent to him during his twenty-one-day fast. The 'Heavenly' messenger was held by the 'prince of the kingdom of Persia,' and needed help from 'Michael, one of the chief princes,' to get through to Daniel. We are also told of another 'prince of Grecia'.

Daniel 10:21 *But I will shew thee that which is noted in the scripture of truth: and there is none that holdeth with me in these things, but Michael your prince.* (KJV)

Daniel 12:1 *And at that time shall Michael stand up, the great prince which standeth for the children of thy people: and there shall be a time of trouble, such as never was since there was a nation even to that same time: and at that time thy people shall be delivered, every one that shall be found written in the book.* (KJV)

Revelation 12:7-9 *And there was war in heaven: Michael and his angels fought against the dragon; and the dragon fought and his angels, And prevailed not; neither was their place found any more in heaven. And the great dragon was cast out, that old serpent, called the Devil, and Satan, which deceiveth the whole world: he was cast out into the earth, and his angels were cast out with him.* (KJV)

Ephesians 2:2 *Wherein in time past ye walked according to the course of this world, according to the prince of the power of the air, the spirit that now worketh in the children of disobedience:* (KJV)

Daniel tells us twice that Michael is Israel's prince and that he fights spiritual battles on her behalf. In the book of Revelation we learn that Michael is the chief of many angels who fight Satan and his angels. Michael defeats Satan, and he and his angels are literally cast into the earth during the Birth Pangs of the Messiah. Theologians have tried to explain that this has already happened, but the context is the Day of the Lord, hence the Birth Pangs, the first seven years. Satan still is the 'prince of the power of the air,' but will literally be cast from the 'heavenlies' into the earth.

The Zohar states that there are celestial chieftains who have charge over regions of the earth. There are seven zones of earth each divided into ten further divisions. Therefore, seventy divisions exist patterning the seventy nations of the earth, each having a chieftain over it.[18]

We have discussed the Voice of God elsewhere in this book being split into seventy languages on Shavuot [Pentecost] at Mt.

Sinai. We also discussed that the seventy bulls sacrificed during the seven days of Succot were for the atonement of these seventy nations. Therefore, we have a constant picture of seventy nations and one Israel.

2 Chronicles 4:7 *And he made ten candlesticks of gold according to their form, and set them in the temple, five on the right hand, and five on the left.* (KJV)

In Solomon's Temple ten golden menorahs were placed into the Holy Place in addition to the Menorah made by Moses for the Tabernacle. Rabbinic authorities say that the Scripture refers to five being placed on the right to Moses' Menorah, and five to the left of it.[19] What an earthly picture of the Heavenly Throne! John sees seven lamps or one menorah of lights before the Throne. In Solomon's Temple the Ark of the Covenant in the Holy of Holies was symbolic of the Throne. Just outside the curtain that separated the Holy of Holies from the Holy Place resided the Menorah made by Moses for the Tabernacle. Then five menorahs were lined up on each side of Moses' Menorah. There were ten additional menorahs in addition to the Tabernacle Menorah in the Holy Place of Solomon's Temple. These ten menorahs, which had seventy total lights, were symbolic of the Light of Messiah given to the seventy nations. Moses' Menorah was symbolic of the Light of Messiah given to Israel and also represented the seven lights [spirits] of God before His Throne.

Exodus 25:31-40 *And thou shalt make a candlestick [Menorah] of pure gold: of beaten work shall the candlestick be made: his shaft, and his branches, his bowls, his knops, and his flowers, shall be of the same. And six branches shall come out of the sides of it; three branches of the candlestick out of the one side, and three branches of the candlestick out of the other side: Three bowls made like unto almonds, with a knop and a flower in one branch; and three bowls made like almonds in the other branch, with a knop and a flower: so in the six branches that come out of the candlestick. And in the candlestick shall be four bowls made like unto almonds, with their knops and their flowers. And there shall be a knop under two* *branches of the same, and a knop under two branches of the same, and a knop under two branches of the same, according to the six branches that proceed out of the candlestick. Their knops and their branches shall be of the same: all it shall be one beaten work of pure gold. And thou shalt make the seven lamps thereof: and they shall light the lamps thereof, that they may give light over against it. And the tongs thereof, and the snuffdishes thereof, shall be of pure gold. Of a talent of pure gold shall he make it, with all these vessels. And look that thou make them after their pattern, which was shewed thee in the mount.* (KJV)

Hebrews 8:5 *Who serve unto the example and shadow of heavenly things, as Moses was admonished of God when he was about to make the tabernacle: for, See, saith he, that thou make all things according to the pattern shewed to thee in the mount.* (KJV)

Flavius Josephus, who was a priest in the Temple [first century], said that all of the decorations upon the Menorah in the Second Temple, which included the bowls, knops, and flowers, amounted to seventy.[20] Exodus 25:40 clearly states that Moses was to design the Menorah after the 'pattern' he was shown by God on Mt. Sinai. The writer of Hebrews says that the design of the Tabernacle served as an 'example' or 'shadow' of 'Heavenly' things. Moses was given a glimpse of the 'Heavenly' Menorah from which he designed the earthly one.

The Seven Churches

Revelation 1:19 *Write the things which thou hast seen, and the things which are, and the things which shall be hereafter; The mystery of the seven stars which thou sawest in my right hand, and the seven golden candlesticks.* (KJV)

From reading the book of Revelation it is fairly obvious that John was given a vision of the Lord's Day, the Day of the Lord, the final Millennium, which commences with the seven-year Birth Pangs of the Messiah [Tribulation Period]. However, there can be no doubt that John was instructed to write letters to the seven churches in Asia for his day. Why these seven churches in Asia?

Revelation 1:9 *I John, who also am your brother, and companion in tribulation, and in the kingdom and patience of Jesus Christ, was in the isle that is called Patmos, for the word of God, and for the testimony of Jesus Christ.* (KJV)

John was imprisoned on the isle of Patmos in the Aegean Sea just off the coast of what we call 'Asia Minor' where these seven churches were located. These seven churches were located in close proximity to each other and the isle of Patmos. These may have been the only churches that John was able to communicate with under his circumstances. Many researchers believe that Revelation was a letter that was first sent to Ephesus, and than it was forwarded to the second, and so on, unto the seventh church at Laodicea.

Revelation 1:1-3 *The Revelation of Jesus Christ, which God gave unto him, to shew unto his servants <u>things which must shortly</u> come to pass; and he sent and signified it by his angel unto his servant John: Who bare record of the word of God, and of the testimony of Jesus Christ, and of all things that he saw. Blessed is he that <u>readeth</u>, and they that <u>hear</u> the words of this prophecy, and <u>keep</u> those things which are written therein: <u>for the time is at hand</u>.* (KJV)

Revelation 22:10-12 *And he saith unto me, Seal not the sayings of the prophecy of this book: <u>for the time is at hand</u>. He that is unjust, let him be unjust still: and he which is filthy, let him be filthy still: and he that is righteous, let him be righteous still: and he that is holy, let him be holy still. And, behold, <u>I come quickly</u>; and my reward is with me, to give every man according as his work shall be.* (KJV)

Some scholars claim that the phrase 'things which must shortly' are not in the original manuscript but were added by the King James translators. Regardless, John uses the same terminology 'for the time is at hand' and 'I come quickly' at the end of Revelation. This is the basic reason that some teach that all of Revelation has already been fulfilled, but they have to allegorize the book to make that happen. The truth is that this prophecy was set to the future Day of the Lord and the Messiah has not yet set up His Kingdom on earth. So when John mentions 'things which must shortly come to pass' in the beginning verse of Revelation, he was prophesying events associated with the Day of the Lord, although there is truth in the individual messages to the seven churches for them in their day.

Isaiah 13:6 *Howl ye; for the day of the LORD is at hand; it shall come as a destruction from the Almighty.* (KJV)

Joel 1:15 *Alas for the day! for the day of the LORD is at hand, and as a destruction from the Almighty shall it come.* (KJV)

Zephaniah 1:7 *Hold thy peace at the presence of the Lord GOD: for the day of the LORD is at hand: for the LORD hath prepared a sacrifice, he hath bid his guests.* (KJV)

Matthew 4:17 *From that time Jesus began to preach, and to say, Repent: for the kingdom of heaven is at hand.* (KJV)

In Hebraic thought the phrase that John used 'for the time is at hand' is a prophetic phrase understood to be alluding to the future Day of the Lord. It may have been that the prophet's visions were so real and intense that in their eyes it was really happening in their day. There is a common expression in Hebrew that translates: 'Here Now, But Not Yet'. In other words, there are types and shadows of culminating prophetic events that occur on a lesser level in earlier generations. It is occurring now, but not in its fullness. Yeshua used this concept when speaking of the Kingdom of God. On some partial first fruits level, with the Kingdom being in the hearts of believers, it is here now. Prophetically, the Kingdom is still to come, being fully realized at the return of Yeshua during the Day of the Lord.

All this said we could not overlook that the messages for these seven churches are for the time of the end, at the outset of the Day of the Lord. Most theologians believe that the seven messages relate to church history in a chronological order from John's day. The author doesn't support this view, but believes that we are given seven types of churches that still have their menorah lit just prior to the beginning of the 'Day of the Lord'. Yeshua is warning these congregations as the War Messiah High Priest about their judgment if they do not repent and change their ways. Many so-called congregations at the time of the end will have already had their menorah removed from God's presence and are not worthy of any mention because the Lord's vengeance will consume them.

Revelation 1:20 *The seven stars are the angels of the seven churches: and the seven candlesticks which thou sawest are the seven churches.* (KJV)

There are seven congregations listed in Revelation 2 and 3: Ephesus, Smyrna, Pergamos, Thyatira, Sardis, Philadelphia, and Laodicea. Each congregation is represented by one seven-branched Menorah. The vision that John saw was the Son of Man having seven stars in His right hand. These seven stars represent the 'angels' to each of these seven assemblies. Most Christian theologians teach that these 'angels' were the 'pastors' to these particular congregations. Once again, this author does not subscribe to this theology.

At the end of each letter to the churches, we have a phrase 'he that overcometh,' or 'him that overcometh'. The author proposes that each individual as well as each congregation is like Jacob, who had to wrestle [spiritually-speaking] with the angel to get a blessing. Jacob's name was changed to Israel because he 'prevailed' or 'overcame' his flesh and circumstances to walk in God's blessings. It would be ludicrous to think that Jacob defeated the angel.

As we will see a couple of these congregations are promised 'a new name written' and 'my new name,' if they overcome for God. What does it mean to overcome? One has to know what they are overcoming to be an overcomer. In each letter to these assemblies there are specific circumstances that Yeshua is instructing the people who call upon His Name to overcome. This will relate prophetically to what the true believers must overcome at the outset of the Day of Lord.

In addition every epistle ends with: 'he that hath an ear, let him hear what the Spirit saith unto the congregations'. Notice that each message is to be taken universally to all 'assemblies,' not just the one addressed congregation. The emphasis on the 'Spirit' brings us right back to Shavuot [Pentecost]. In Hebraic thought to 'hear' the 'Spirit' means to obey the Torah commandments of God as James said true believers not only 'hear' but 'do' [James 1:23-25]. This is symbolic of one of Seven Spirits before the Throne of God, which is speaking to the congregations in the seventy nations. This is the final call to those who call themselves by His Name to be His betrothed bride at the end of six thousand years. The 'Pentecostal' age [fulfillment of the spring festivals with Yeshua's first coming] will give way to the eschatological fulfillment of the fall festivals and 'full' marriage highlighted by resurrection.

Exodus 25:35 *And there shall be a knop under two branches of the same, and a knop under two branches of the same, and a knop under two branches of the same, according to the six branches that proceed out of the candlestick.* (KJV)

In trying to decipher the message of the Son of Man as the War Messiah High Priest to the assemblies, we need to know one more thing about the Biblical Menorah. Six branches protruded from the central shaft of the Menorah, three branches to the left side, and three identical ones to the right side. The two outer branches connected furthest down the central shaft just above a knop, which Rashi calls a decorative apple-shaped orb.[21]

A little further up the central shaft the two middle branches connect just above another knop. Finally, the two innermost branches connect the furthest up the central shaft just above another knop. Therefore, in the Biblical design of the Menorah, we have the outer branches connected together, the middle branches connected together, and the most inner branches connected together. The central shaft goes up in the middle of the six branches.

This is how we will interpret these seven letters to the congregations at the outset of the Day of the Lord [Birth Pangs of Messiah]. The first and seventh epistles are the outer branches of this Menorah design. The second and sixth assemblies are connected as middle branches, and the third and fifth assemblies are connected as the most upper branches. All the branches connect to the central stem, which is the main message to the 'congregations'. This main message will be the central theme on why God's judgment has come to the congregations.

We will study the first assembly of Ephesus alongside the seventh assembly of Laodicea. We will examine the second congregation of Smyrna with the sixth congregation of Philadelphia. Then we will study the third congregation of Pergamos with the fifth congregation of Sardis. Then, finally, we will study the central [the fourth listed in Revelation] assembly of Thyatira.

Revelation 2:1-7 *Unto the angel of <u>the church of Ephesus</u> write; These things saith he that holdeth the seven stars in his right hand, who walketh in the midst of the seven golden candlesticks; I know thy works, and thy labour, and thy patience, and how thou canst not bear them which are evil: and thou hast tried them which say they are apostles, and are not, and hast found them liars: And hast borne, and hast patience, and for my name's sake hast laboured, and hast not fainted. Nevertheless I have somewhat against thee, because thou hast left thy first love. Remember therefore from whence thou art fallen, and repent, and do the first works; or else I will come unto thee quickly, and will remove thy candlestick out of his place, except thou repent. But this thou hast, that thou hatest the deeds of the Nicolaitans, which I also hate. He that hath an ear, let him hear what the Spirit saith unto the <u>churches</u>; To him that overcometh will I give to eat of the tree of life, which is in the midst of the paradise of God.* (KJV)

The seven congregations described in Revelation 2 and 3 are typical of assemblies that exist right at the conclusion of the six thousand years just prior to the beginning of the Day of the Lord [Birth Pangs of the Messiah]. Unfortunately by that time most congregations will have already departed from truth and the light of their menorah has already been extinguished. These congregations listed in Revelation are symbolic of those assemblies that still have a glimmer of hope to repent and not come under the wrath of the War Messiah High Priest.

Ephesus typifies congregations, which are still doing good works in the name of the Lord. They have been patient, stood up against false apostles and the Nicolaitans, but they are 'lacking' according to Yeshua Who is coming to judge them. This is a congregation that once enjoyed a betrothed relationship with Yeshua, but over time has walked away from their marriage covenant, even though continuing to do 'good' works in His Name. 'Leaving their first love' is a Hebraism that means breaking the marriage covenant.

Very clearly Yeshua is against this congregation. The KJV 'softens' this expression by saying, 'I am somewhat against thee,' but the Greek says that Yeshua is against them because they have left their 'first love,' which is no small matter. Over time this betrothed bride had become complacent and drifted away from their marriage covenant with Yeshua. They quit looking for His return for the second stage of marriage. They had become satisfied in doing their good works.

Yeshua tells them to 'remember' from where they had fallen. This is an injunction to return to the betrothal covenant. Their 'first works' is falling in love with their groom. If Ephesus or those congregations in similar circumstances just prior to the Day of Lord refuse to repent and return, Yeshua promises that He will come quickly and bring judgment by removing their candlestick out of its place. In other words, the War Messiah High Priest will forsake these so-called believers in these kinds of congregations. They will enter the Birth Pangs of the Messiah and the outset of the Day of the Lord and will have to fend for themselves.

Revelation 22:1-2 *And he shewed me a pure river of water of life, clear as crystal, proceeding out of the throne of God and of the Lamb. In the midst of the street of it, and on either side of the river, was there the tree of life, which bare twelve manner of fruits, and yielded her fruit every month: and the leaves of the tree were for the healing of the nations.* (KJV)

Revelation 22:14 *Blessed are they that do his commandments, that they may have right to the tree of life, and may enter in through the gates into the city.* (KJV)

Now comes the blessing to those who are overcomers in the assemblies: 'To him that overcometh will I give to eat of the tree of life, which is in the midst of the paradise of God'. The promised blessing to the overcomers who remain loyal to their first love and faithful to their marriage covenant with the Lord is that they will be allowed to eat of the Tree of Life in the midst of Heavenly New Jerusalem. There are twelve different fruits in all for a total healing from sin's effects on humanity. The overcomers are those who keep God's Torah [Commandments] by 'doing' them. Overcomers are doers who have gained access to the Tree of Life, of course, in the resurrection.

Revelation 3:14-22 *And unto the angel of the church of the Laodiceans write; These things saith the Amen, the faithful and true witness, the beginning of the creation of God; I know thy works, that thou art neither cold nor hot: I would thou wert cold or hot. So then because thou art lukewarm, and neither cold nor hot, I will spue thee out of my mouth. Because thou sayest, I am rich, and increased with goods, and have need of nothing; and knowest not that thou art wretched, and miserable, and poor, and blind, and naked: I counsel thee to buy of me gold tried in the fire, that thou mayest be rich; and white raiment, that thou mayest be clothed, and that the shame of thy nakedness do not appear; and anoint thine eyes with eyesalve, that thou mayest see. As many as I love, I rebuke and chasten: be zealous therefore, and repent. Behold, I stand at the door, and knock: if any man hear my voice, and open the door, I will come in to him, and will sup with him, and he with me. To him that overcometh will I grant to sit with me in my throne, even as I also overcame, and am set down with my Father in his throne. He that hath an ear, let him hear what the Spirit saith unto the churches.* (KJV)

As promised we now look at the seventh listed congregation in Revelation at Laodicea, as it would be on the same outer branch as the first congregation at Ephesus. This kind of assembly is neither hot nor cold toward God. What does this mean? The symbolism focuses around drinking. Water needs to be cold in order for one to enjoy it. Who drinks lukewarm or hot water by itself? Other liquids we drink need to be hot to be enjoyed. The symbolism implies that Yeshua desires them to be either hot or cold in this perspective, but since they are lukewarm, He will spew them out of His mouth in rejection and judgment.

Why are the Laodiceans lukewarm toward the things of God? This same condition will exist in a major portion of the assemblies just prior to the Day of the Lord. The people are 'increased with goods, and have need of nothing' and do not know that they are wretched, miserable, and spiritually poor, blind and naked. Yeshua counsels with them to make their riches in heaven by being tried by the fire of the Holy Spirit. He counsels with them to put on the robes of righteousness and to anoint their eyes to see and awake to the spiritual truth of how they are living. Yeshua is giving them one last opportunity to repent and change their ways.

This kind of congregation is one that is identified with 'wealth'. There is no mention of this kind of assembly being obedient to the Word of God. This is the prosperity 'gospel' that Yeshua will reject and spew out of His mouth. The door of Rosh Hashana is closed to this kind of people and they are destined to enter the Birth Pangs of the Messiah. In one last attempt Yeshua stands at the door and waits upon them. If any will repent and turn to the unadulterated Torah and open the door, Yeshua will come into them and sup with them and protect them from the judgment coming upon the world. This also has allusions to the Egyptian Passover Threshold Covenant where God is invited in as a guest through the Blood Covenant of the Passover Lamb [see earlier chapters in this book].

The people involved in this prosperity gospel have never been redeemed the first time. They came to 'church' and 'God' because of the message of gaining wealth. What is the link with the Ephesus assembly being on the outer branch of the menorah design? Ephesus once had a marriage covenant relationship with Yeshua and walked away, and He is calling them back in repentance. The Laodiceans never really knew Yeshua in marriage covenant and He is calling them to take that first step.

Revelation 21:7-8 *He that overcometh shall inherit all things; and I will be his God, and he shall be my son.* (KJV)

And finally the angel of the assembly of the Laodiceans will bless the overcomers with the right to sit with Yeshua at His Throne. Yeshua overcame the world and Satan and has sat down at the right hand of the Father's Throne. The believers that are the overcomers will inherit all things as the Bride and Queen.

Revelation 2:8-11 *And unto the angel of the church in Smyrna write; These things saith the first and the last, which was dead, and is alive; I know thy works, and tribulation, and poverty, (but thou art rich) and I know the blasphemy of them which say they are Jews, and are not, but are the synagogue of Satan. Fear none of those things which thou shalt suffer: behold, the devil shall cast* some *of you into prison, that ye may be tried; and ye shall have tribulation ten days: be thou faithful unto death, and I will give thee a crown of life. He that hath an ear, let him hear what the Spirit saith unto the churches; He that overcometh shall not be hurt of the second death.* (KJV)

Now we turn our attention to the middle branches beginning with the second congregation at Smyrna. The name 'Smyrna' has a Hebraic root from the word 'myrrh,' a balm used to anoint the dead. Note that Yeshua encourages 'some' in this congregation to be 'faithful unto death'.

This author believes that Smyrna is a menorah-type congregation that comes to life [being lit] after the Day of the Lord commences. This assembly appears to have some faithful believers who do the 'works' of God and have had 'tribulation' and 'poverty' due to following Yeshua. Yeshua says that this portion of Smyrna is 'rich'.

However, Yeshua's message as the War Messiah High Priest is against the blasphemous portion of Smyrna. Who are the blasphemous in this congregation? They are those who say they are Jews but really are not. In modern-day terms, these so-called believers embrace the doctrine of 'Replacement Theology' that teaches the 'Gentile' church has replaced Israel. These are Gentile believers in 'Jesus' calling themselves Jews as replacing the biological Jewish race as the chosen people of God. God hates this doctrine, and so should all believers in Yeshua.

Those that embrace and practice Replacement Theology are not told to look for the resurrection while they are alive. They will be given over to Satan for tribulation. The False Messiah and his followers during the Birth Pangs of the Messiah will attempt to replace God and His people: 'which say they are Jews, and are not, but are the synagogue of Satan'.

These of Smyrna are instructed that the devil will imprison some of the believers through tribulation and suffering. The reference to having 'tribulation ten days' is directly alluding to the Ten Days of Awe starting at Rosh Hashana (Tishri 1) and ending with Yom Kippur (Tishri 10). Rosh Hashana commences the Day of the Lord and seven-year Birth Pangs, and was a festival that lasted two days, Tishri 1 & 2. Yom Kippur, Tishri 10, in Hebraic thought is the day in which the Messiah comes to the Mount of Olives in Jerusalem and sets up His Kingdom. After Moses came down Mount Sinai on Pentecost with the Tables of Stone and saw the Golden Calf, he broke them. He would later ascend Mount Sinai again and retrieve another set of engraved stones from God. Hebraic tradition states that Moses 'second coming' down the mountain with these tablets occurred on Yom Kippur; so also will Messiah's coming. The seven in-between days, Tishri 3 through Tishri 9, are symbolic of the seven years of Birth Pangs.

Those that subscribe to Replacement Theology really don't know Yeshua in marriage relationship because this doctrine is obviously against His Word. These so-called believers will enter the Birth Pangs of the Messiah and the only way they will make it into the Kingdom is by repenting of their sin. In doing that they will have to oppose the False Messiah and they will lose their lives.

Revelation 20:4-6 *And I saw thrones, and they sat upon them, and judgment was given unto them: and I saw the souls of them that were beheaded for the witness of Jesus, and for the word of God, and which had not worshipped the beast, neither his image, neither had received his mark upon their foreheads, or in their hands; and they lived and reigned with Christ a thousand years. But the rest of the dead lived not again until the thousand years were finished. This is the first resurrection. Blessed and holy is he that hath part in the first* *resurrection: on such the second death hath no power, but they shall be priests of God and of Christ, and shall reign with him a thousand years.* (KJV)

Revelation 20:11-15 *And I saw a great white throne, and him that sat on it, from whose face the earth and the heaven fled away; and there was found no place for them. And I saw the dead, small and great, stand before God; and the books were opened: and another book was opened, which is the book of life: and the dead were judged out of those things which were written in the books, according to their works. And the sea gave up the dead which were in it; and death and hell delivered up the dead which were in them: and they were judged every man according to their works. And death and hell were cast into the lake of fire. This is the second death. And whosoever was not found written in the book of life was cast into the lake of fire.* (KJV)

Revelation 21:8 *But the fearful, and unbelieving, and the abominable, and murderers, and whoremongers, and sorcerers, and idolaters, and all liars, shall have their part in the lake which burneth with fire and brimstone: which is the second death.* (KJV)

Those believers who have been divinely allotted for this kind of tribulation are called to be 'faithful unto death'. The blessing is that Yeshua will reward them with a 'crown of life'. These are the overcomers that 'shall not be hurt of the second death'. These are those who are blessed 'in the first resurrection'.

Revelation 3:7-13 *And to the angel of the church in Philadelphia write; These things saith he that is holy, he that is true, he that hath the key of David, he that openeth, and no man shutteth; and shutteth, and no man openeth; I know thy works: behold, I have set before thee an open door, and no man can shut it: for thou hast a little strength, and hast kept my word, and hast not denied my name. Behold, I will make them of the synagogue of Satan, which say they are Jews, and are not, but do lie; behold, I will make them to come and worship before thy feet, and to know that I have loved* *thee. Because thou hast kept the word of my patience, I also will keep thee from the hour of temptation, which shall come upon all the world, to try them that dwell upon the earth. Behold, I come quickly: hold that fast which thou hast, that no man take thy crown. Him that overcometh will I make a pillar in the temple of my God, and he shall go no more out: and I will write upon him the name of my God, and the name of the city of my God, which is new Jerusalem, which cometh down out of heaven from my God: and I will write upon him my new name. He that hath an ear, let him hear what the Spirit saith unto the churches.* (KJV)

The assembly in Philadelphia, which means 'brotherly love,' is the only congregation of the seven that the Lord is not coming to bring judgment against. It is on the opposite branch of Smyrna located in the middle of the branches. Obviously, this is the ideal congregation that all fellowship of believers should model themselves after.

Yeshua appears to the believers as holy, true, and having the key of David in which He opens a door before them that no man can shut. The key of David is symbolic of the Messiah being the 'son of David' and in context of the letter to Philadelphia represents the key that opens the door into the Heavenly Temple/New Jerusalem.

Revelation 4:1-2 *After this I looked, and, behold, a door was opened in heaven: and the first voice which I heard was as it were of a trumpet talking with me; which said, Come up hither, and I will shew thee things which must be hereafter. And immediately I was in the spirit: and, behold, a throne was set in heaven, and one sat on the throne.* (KJV)

In Hebraic thought an 'open door' is explicitly tied to the festival of Rosh Hashana, the beginning of the Day of the Lord, and specifically the seven years of Birth Pangs. John's experience in Revelation 4 with a voice of the shofar, being in the spirit, and seeing a throne set in heaven as he goes through 'a door' that was opened, are symbolic of a resurrection occurring at the 'Last Shofar' of Rosh Hashana.

This is the only congregation of the seven that is promised this open door in their current relationship with God through Yeshua.

Revelation 14:12 *Here is the patience of the saints: here are they that keep the commandments of God, and the faith of Jesus.* (KJV)

This kind of congregation at Philadelphia is rewarded for keeping God's Word, which biblically means faithfully 'hearing' and 'doing' the Torah. Yeshua says that the believers in Philadelphia have 'kept the word of my patience' which is clearly defined as keeping the Torah commandments of God through faith in Yeshua.

These believers have not denied God's Name, which means much more than worshiping God through song and witness. They revere and sanctify His Holy name ה ו ה י and the Messiah Yeshua. This kind of congregation cherishes the Word of God and lives according to the Torah that God gave man.

Isaiah 60:9-16 *Surely the isles [nations] shall wait for me, and the ships of Tarshish [Gentiles] first, to bring thy sons from far, their silver and their gold with them, unto the name of the LORD thy God, and to the Holy One of Israel, because he hath glorified thee. And the sons of strangers [Gentiles] shall build up thy walls, and their kings shall minister unto thee: for in my wrath I smote thee, but in my favour have I had mercy on thee. Therefore thy <u>gates</u> shall be open continually; <u>they shall not be shut day nor night</u>; that men may bring unto thee the forces of the Gentiles, and that their kings may be brought. For the nation and kingdom that will not serve thee shall perish; yea, those nations shall be utterly wasted. The glory of Lebanon shall come unto thee, the fir tree, the pine tree, and the box together, to beautify the place of my sanctuary; and I will make the place of my feet glorious. <u>The sons [Gentiles] also of them that afflicted thee shall come bending unto thee</u>; and all <u>they that despised thee shall bow themselves down at the soles of thy feet</u>; and they shall call thee, The city of the LORD, The Zion of the Holy One of Israel. Whereas thou hast been forsaken and hated, so that no man went through thee, I will make thee an eternal excellency, a joy of many generations. Thou shalt also suck the milk of* *the Gentiles, and shalt suck the breast of kings: and thou shalt know that I the LORD am thy Saviour and thy Redeemer, the mighty One of Jacob.* (KJV)

Whereas some of the congregation of Smyrna, on the other end of this middle branch, embraced Replacement Theology, Philadelphia has taken a hard stand against it. Yeshua states those who subscribe to Replacement Theology will be made to come and worship before these believers' feet and will know that Yeshua has loved these brethren of Philadelphia. This is probably referring to the children of the Synagogue of Satan [Replacement Theology] who will live during the Messianic Kingdom.

Yeshua promises to the brethren of Philadelphia that He 'will keep thee from the hour of temptation, which shall come upon the entire world, to try them that dwell upon the earth'. Clearly, this kind of assembly of believers will be removed from the earth prior to the commencement of the Day of the Lord and the Birth Pangs of the Messiah. Yeshua says, 'Behold, I come quickly. Hold that fast which thou hast, that no man take thy crown'.

Revelation 21:2 *And I John saw the holy city, new Jerusalem, coming down from God out of heaven, prepared as a bride adorned for her husband.* (KJV)

Revelation 21:22 *And I saw no temple therein: for the Lord God Almighty and the Lamb are the temple of it.* (KJV)

Revelation 21:25-27 *And the gates of it shall not be shut at all by day: for there shall be no night there. And they shall bring the glory and honour of the nations into it. And there shall in no wise enter into it any thing that defileth, neither whatsoever worketh abomination, or maketh a lie: but they which are written in the Lamb's book of life.* (KJV)

Isaiah 62:2-3 *And the Gentiles shall see thy righteousness, and all kings thy glory: and thou shalt be called by a new name, which the mouth of the LORD shall name. Thou shalt also be a crown of glory* *in the hand of the LORD, and a royal diadem in the hand of thy God.* (KJV)

The angel of the assembly in Philadelphia is sent to bless the overcomers with the promise of being a pillar in the Heavenly Temple (New Jerusalem). Since Yeshua, the Lamb, is the Temple of New Jerusalem, the overcomers representing His Bride are also associated spiritually with the Heavenly Temple.

Revelation 2:12-17 *And to the angel of the church in Pergamos write; These things saith he which hath the sharp sword with two edges; I know thy works, and where thou dwellest, even where Satan's seat is: and thou holdest fast my name, and hast not denied my faith, even in those days wherein Antipas was my faithful martyr, who was slain among you, where Satan dwelleth. But I have a few things against thee, because thou hast there them that hold the doctrine of Balaam, who taught Balac to cast a stumblingblock before the children of Israel, to eat things sacrificed unto idols, and to commit fornication. So hast thou also them that hold the doctrine of the Nicolaitans, which thing I hate. Repent; or else I will come unto thee quickly, and will fight against them with the sword of my mouth. He that hath an ear, let him hear what the Spirit saith unto the churches; To him that overcometh will I give to eat of the hidden manna, and will give him a white stone, and in the stone a new name written, which no man knoweth saving he that receiveth it.* (KJV)

The first inner branch of the Menorah structure of the seven assemblies is Pergamos. The epistle to the angel of the congregation at Pergamos describes Yeshua having a 'sharp sword with two edges'. The sword is said to be 'projecting' from the mouth of the Lord. This is an allusion to the 'giving' of the Torah. Those who did not 'hear' would be condemned. Judgment comes from the Word of God (Torah). Following God's Torah (which includes following Messiah) in faith brings salvation. Disobedience to God's Torah brings condemnation.

Yeshua chastises Pergamos for holding two doctrines that He hates. The first is the doctrine of Balaam, who taught king Balak of Moab, to deceive Israel to go against God in the wilderness [see Numbers 22-24]. Balak hired Balaam to curse Israel, but every time he spoke Israel was blessed. Therefore, Balaam instructed Balak on how to lure Israel into rebellion against their God. Women were sent out to lure the men of Israel into fornication and as a part of these 'sexual' rites they ate a meal consecrated to false gods. God sent a plague upon Israel that killed twenty four thousand before it was stayed through Phineas, the Priest anointed for war, as we mentioned earlier.

Bringing this doctrine forward prior to the Day of the Lord, Yeshua is speaking against those congregations who allow paganism to mix with their worship of God. These are congregations, which are probably more liberal in their allowance of sin within its members and clergy. It could also represent assemblies who don't call homosexuality sin, and may even allow leaders engaged in such practices to remain in authority. Yeshua hates this doctrine, and so should true believers.

The other doctrine of the congregation of Pergamos that Yeshua hated was the doctrine of the Nicolaitanes. Whoever this group comprised, they were somehow related to the doctrine of Balaam by the context. The second century 'church fathers' Ignatius and Irenaeus said that the Nicolaitanes lived immorally.[22] They were probably very liberal also. A Gnostic sect of Nicolaitanes existed in the third century teaching Christians to indulge in fleshly lusts because the spirit man once saved was always saved.[23]

In a modern understanding, the doctrine of the Nicolaitanes is the 'gospel' of Grace, Grace, and Grace. God's grace is over emphasized and His judgment is diminished. These would be 'believers' who speak out against the Law [Torah] and also anything Jewish as legalism and Judaism. This kind of theology leads to the justification of sin because God's grace forgives everything. The Apostle Paul said:

Romans 6:1-2 *What shall we say then? Shall we continue in sin, that grace may abound? God forbid. How shall we, that are dead to sin, live any longer therein?* (KJV)

Yeshua tells the people embracing these doctrines to repent or He will judge them with the sword of His mouth, which is the Word of God. Those who overcome these doctrines will be blessed with a new name written. They will have the opportunity to eat of the hidden manna, which was an ancient promise to those who will one day enter the Kingdom through the Final Redeemer.[24]

Revelation 3:1-6 *And unto the angel of the church in Sardis write; These things saith he that hath the seven Spirits of God, and the seven stars; I know thy works, that thou hast a name that thou livest, and art dead. Be watchful, and strengthen the things which remain, that are ready to die: for I have not found thy works perfect before God. Remember therefore how thou hast received and heard, and hold fast, and repent. If therefore thou shalt not watch, I will come on thee as a thief, and thou shalt not know what hour I will come upon thee. Thou hast a few names even in Sardis which have not defiled their garments; and they shall walk with me in white: for they are worthy. He that overcometh, the same shall be clothed in white raiment; and I will not blot out his name out of the book of life, but I will confess his name before my Father, and before his angels. He that hath an ear, let him hear what the Spirit saith unto the churches.* (KJV)

The final congregation on the inner branch of the Menorah struc-ture is the fifth assembly of Sardis. Yeshua states that He knows their works in which they have established a name for themselves and think they are alive unto God, but inwardly they were spiritu-ally dead. This could be similar to modern-day congregations who claim that the Holy Spirit has come into their midst, but has not. It could represent a group that is prideful in whom they are and raise their voices in prayer and song claiming that the Spirit is present, but when it all comes down to the bottom line, it is just emotions and 'hot' air from their lips. Whereas the assembly at Pergamos was outwardly sinful, Sardis was inwardly sinful. The congregation of Sardis was instructed to be 'watchful' and strengthen what spiritu-ally remains in them before that dies off as well. This is an end-time congregation that appears to be going through the motions of 'church' and 'service' to the Lord, but are inward spiritually dead.

If this assembly-type is to rectify its situation, the people must remember the Torah that was once delivered through the Apostles, hold fast to it, and live in a state of repentance. If they will not 'watch,' Yeshua will come upon them as a thief and they will not know the hour in which He comes. This terminology is directly related to the festival of Rosh Hashana [New Moon] and the beginning of the Day of the Lord commencing with the seven years of Birth Pangs of the Messiah. In other words those people in the congregations with these conditions will not be protected from the Birth Pangs.

Matthew 24:36 *But of that day and hour knoweth no man [New Moon - Rosh Hashana], no, not the angels of heaven, but my Father only.* (KJV)

Matthew 24:42-44 *Watch therefore: for ye know not what hour your Lord doth come. But know this, that if the goodman of the house had known in what watch the thief would come, he would have watched, and would not have suffered his house to be broken up. Therefore be ye also ready: for in such an hour as ye think not the Son of man cometh.* (KJV)

Matthew 25:13 *Watch therefore, for ye know neither the day nor the hour wherein the Son of man cometh.* (KJV)

2 Peter 3:10 *But the day of the Lord will come as a thief in the night; in the which the heavens shall pass away with a great noise, and the elements shall melt with fervent heat, the earth also and the works that are therein shall be burned up.* (KJV)

1 Thessalonians 5:2-6 *For yourselves know perfectly that the day of the Lord so cometh as a thief in the night. For when they shall say, Peace and safety; then sudden destruction cometh upon them, as travail upon a woman with child [Birth pangs]; and they shall not escape. But ye, brethren, are not in darkness, that that day should overtake you as a thief. Ye are all the children of light, and the chil-*

dren of the day: we are not of the night, nor of darkness. Therefore let us not sleep, as do others; but let us watch and be sober. (KJV)

Clearly, for the Lord to come upon those of Sardis as a 'thief' means that they are not watching for His coming and are considered to be in darkness. As we have studied throughly in this book, this terminology represents those who will miss the open 'door' of Rosh Hashana and will enter into the Birth Pangs.

Yet there were still a few worthy overcomers in Sardis, which had not defiled their garments, that Yeshua promised would walk with Him in white raiment. The white garments referred to in the text are not physical raiment, but of the spiritual realm, and associated with the condition of a person's soul. This condition is directly tied to obedience of God's Torah. Those walking with Yeshua in white reflects the importance of being a 'hearer and doer' of Torah as an integral part of their 'faith'. Those who had defiled their garments have lost their destiny to be a kingdom of priests.

Revelation 6:11 *And white robes were given unto every one of them; and it was said unto them, that they should rest yet for a little season, until their fellowservants also and their brethren, that should be killed as they were, should be fulfilled.* (KJV)

Revelation 7:9-10, 13-14 *After this I beheld, and, lo, a great multitude, which no man could number, of all nations, and kindreds, and people, and tongues, stood before the throne, and before the Lamb, clothed with white robes, and palms in their hands; And cried with a loud voice, saying, Salvation to our God which sitteth upon the throne, and unto the Lamb...And one of the elders answered, saying unto me, What are these which are arrayed in white robes? and whence came they? And I said unto him, Sir, thou knowest. And he said to me, These are they which came out of great tribulation, and have washed their robes, and made them white in the blood of the Lamb.* (KJV)

Revelation 16:15 *Behold, I come as a <u>thief</u>. Blessed is he that <u>watcheth</u>, and <u>keepeth his garments</u>, lest he walk naked, and they see his shame.* (KJV)

Revelation 19:8, 14 *And to her was granted that she should be arrayed in fine linen, clean and white: for the fine linen is the righteousness of saints...And the armies which were in heaven followed him upon white horses, clothed in fine linen, white and clean.* (KJV)

Yeshua will not blot the overcomer's names out of the book of life, but will confess their names before the Father and the angels:

Revelation 20:15 *And whosoever was not found written in the book of life was cast into the lake of fire.* (KJV)

Revelation 21:27 *And there shall in no wise enter into it any thing that defileth, neither whatsoever worketh abomination, or maketh a lie: but they which are written in the Lamb's book of life.* (KJV)

Revelation 2:18-29 *And unto the angel of the church in Thyatira write; These things saith the Son of God, who hath his eyes like unto a flame of fire, and his feet are like fine brass; I know thy works, and charity, and service, and faith, and thy patience, and thy works; and the last to be more than the first. Notwithstanding I have a few things against thee, because thou sufferest that woman Jezebel, which calleth herself a prophetess, to teach and to seduce my servants to commit fornication, and to eat things sacrificed unto idols. And I gave her space to repent of her fornication; and she repented not. Behold, I will cast her into a bed, and them that commit adultery with her into great tribulation, except they repent of their deeds. And I will kill her children with death; and <u>all the churches shall know </u>that I am he which searcheth the reins and hearts: and I will give unto every one of you according to your works. But unto you I say, and unto the rest in Thyatira, as many as have not this doctrine, and which have not known the depths of Satan, as they speak; I will put upon you none other burden. But that which ye have already* *hold fast till I come. And he that overcometh, and keepeth my works unto the end, to him will I give power over the nations: And he shall rule them with a rod of iron; as the vessels of a potter shall they be broken to shivers: even as I received of my Father. And I will give him the morning star. He that hath an ear, let him hear what the Spirit saith unto the churches. (KJV)*

Now we come to the fourth assembly in the sequence of the seven, which is the middle branch of our menorah pattern. Thyatira representing the middle congregation means that they are the center of attention to the War Messiah High Priest. Thyatira is a wicked assembly that calls themselves believers. We have seen how in the positive Yeshua represents the Servant [center] lamp of the 'Heavenly' Menorah design. In contrast however, Thyatira represents the center or main reason for the assemblies being judged by Yeshua.

To the congregation at Thyatira Yeshua is revealed ready for judgment: 'who hath his eyes like unto a flame of fire, and his feet are like fine brass'. Just prior to the time of the Day of Lord a major portion of the congregation will embrace a spirit of Jezebel who has seduced God's chosen to commit spiritual fornication. Those that commit spiritual adultery with Jezebel and will not repent will be cast into 'great tribulation,' which is the Birth Pangs of the Messiah. They will be 'killed' with 'death' which is an over emphasizing of a probable brutal judgment from the Lord.

The reference is to Jezebel (1 Kings 16-21 & 2 Kings 9), who was long dead when Yeshua speaks these words through John, yet He speaks in the present tense. This is a continuation of the false teaching of Jezebel, who taught the children of Israel to compromise Torah by mixing of the worship of God with Baal and Asherah. The seduction of Israel and Judah through Baal worship is what led God to judge both nations by removing them from the Promised Land.

Baal and Asherah can be traced back to the prototype of male god/ female god paganism that was birthed from ancient Mesopotamia. The male god symbolically represented the sun, whereas the female god represented the moon. Most Christians might be surprised to learn that originally Easter and Christmas had nothing to do with

'Jesus'. Easter originated from 'Ishtar,' the female goddess of ancient Babylonia, whereas Christmas came from the annual worship of the sun god at around the winter solstice.[25] It is beyond the scope of this book to put forth the documentation about the origins of Easter and Christmas from ancient paganism. Entire books have already been written regarding that subject.

The facts remain that the 'congregations' in the first century celebrated the death and resurrection of Yeshua at the time of the annual Passover, not Easter, which is a man-made feast. Also, there is no evidence biblically or other that suggests the congregation even celebrated an annual birthday of the Lord in the first century. Many Christians today talk about the 'spirit' of Christmas, but one must ask themselves if this is related to the 'Holy Spirit'.

Matthew 7:21 *Not every one that saith unto me, Lord, Lord, shall enter into the kingdom of heaven; but he that doeth the will of my Father which is in heaven.* (KJV)

The congregations that mimic Thyatira in the end-time will resemble an assembly within an assembly. In other words the majority of the congregation will follow after the fornication of Jezebel, worshiping Baal as God and believing they are worshiping 'Jesus'. The word 'Baal' means 'Master,' or 'Lord'. Yeshua said that not everyone calling upon Him 'Lord, Lord' would enter the Kingdom. The ultimate deception, therefore, is for one to worship Baal as God, but believing that they are worshiping the one true God. Putting it more simply, the greatest deception believes in a 'Jesus' who is not the 'Yeshua' of the New Testament.

Yeshua says to the minority in these assemblies: 'and unto the rest in Thyatira, as many as have not this doctrine, and which have not known the depths of Satan, as they [the majority] speak; I will put upon you none other burden'. These are the believers that keep the Torah commandments as best they know by faith in Yeshua and do not mix Baal worship with God. The Scripture doesn't say explicitly, but this author believes that this minority will be spared from entering the Birth Pangs of the Messiah as Yeshua said: 'But that which ye have already hold fast till I come'.

The angel of the congregation at Thyatira is commissioned to bless the overcomers who keep Yeshua's 'works' unto the end. These works include charity, service, faith, and patience. Yeshua will give these overcomers power over the nations. Of course, Messiah as King, has full power over the nations in the Kingdom, but His Bride, the Queen will rule with Him, Who rules with a rod of iron, on His Throne.

Conclusion

The message to the seven assemblies at the outset of the Day of the Lord is grim. Yeshua is calling upon almost the entire so-called 'congregation' at that time to repent, or face judgment from Him and/or the Birth Pangs of the Messiah. The only glimmer of light was Philadelphia and the other small remnants of a congregation within a congregation that are promised great rewards and an open door of resurrection at Rosh Hashana. The War Messiah High Priest has spoken, but will the 'assemblies' respond to His pleas? Will the Bride make herself ready for the Bridegroom? Will she exchange the 'rehearsals' of the world for God's Holy Moedim [Rehearsals]?

BIBLIOGRAPHY

1. Pentateuch & Haftorahs. Dr. J H Hertz. Soncino Press, London, 1960. Page 124.
2. The Jewish Encyclopedia, Sabbath and Sunday. Funk and Wagnalls Company, New York. Internet Edition.
3. The Ultimate Victory: An Exposition of the Book of Revelation. Stanley M. Horton. Gospel Publishing House, Springfield, Missouri, 1991. Page 32.
4. The Mystery of the Menorah...and the Hebrew Alphabet. J.R. Church and Gary Stearman. Prophecy Publications, Oklahoma City, 1993. Page 21.
5. IBID. Page 21.
6. Me'am Lo'ez - The Torah Anthology - Exodus VI - Book 9 in the series. Translated by Rabbi Aryeh Kaplan. Moznaim Publishing Corportation, New York, Jerusalem, 1990. Page 76.

7. Hebraic-Roots Version 'New Testament'. Translated by James S. Trimm. Society for the Advancement of Nazarene Judaism, Hurst, Texas, 2001. Page 536.
8. IBID. Page 535.
9. The Old Testament Pseudepigrapha - Apocalyptic Literature & Testaments - Volume 1. Edited by James H. Charlesworth. Doubleday, New York, 1983. Page 34.
10. Midrash Rabbah - Esther 1:6
11. Soncino Zohar, Shemoth, Section 2, Page 135a.
12. Midrash Rabbah - Leviticus 20:2. Talmud - Mas. Sotah 43a.
13. Midrash Rabbah - The Song of Songs 2:33.
14. The Artscroll Tanach Series - Tehillim - Volume 1. Rabbi Avrohom Chaim Feuer. Mesorah Publications, Ltd., Brooklyn, New York, 1977. Page 347.
15. Talmud - Berachos 29a.
16. Talmud - Sukkah 55a.
17. Midrash Rabbah - Exodus 28:6.
18. Soncino Zohar, Shemoth, Section 2, Page 30b.
19. Artscroll Tanach Series - Divrei hayamim II - 2 Chronicles. Rabbi Moshe Eisemann. Mesorah Publications, Ltd., Brooklyn, New York, 1992. Page 25.
20. The Works of Josephus. Translated by William Whiston. Hendrickson Publishers, Peabody, Massachusetts, 1987. The Antiquities of the Jews - Book 3 - Chapter 6 - Section 7. Page 88.
21. The Third Beis HaMikdash. Rabbi Shalom Dov Steinberg. Mozaim Publications, Jerusalem, 5753 [Hebrew Calender - 1993]. Page 136-138.
22. Revelation Visualized. Gary G. Cohen and Salem Kirban. AMG Publishers, Chattanooga, Tennessee, 1971. Page 55.
23. The Ultimate Victory - An Exposition of the Book of Revelation. Stanley M. Horton. Gospel Publishing House, Springfield, Missouri, 1991. Page 41.
24. Ecclesiastes Rabbah 1:28 quoting Exodus 4:20, Zechariah 9:9, Exodus 16:4, and Psalm 72:16.
25. Too Long In the Sun. Richard M. Rives. Partakers Publications, Charlotte, North Carolina, 1999. Pages 117-135.

CPSIA information can be obtained at www.ICGtesting.com
Printed in the USA
LVOW102357031111

253432LV00001B/10/A